TO
CHRISTINA AND ANNA

Preface

This book is a study of Anglo-Greek relations in the period from 1935 to 1941. It examines British policy towards Greece, and the influence of Greece's 'British connection' on her internal and external affairs. The Metaxas dictatorship, and British attitudes towards it, are discussed in some detail, as are the Battle of Greece and Anglo-Greek co-operation in the war until the fall of Greece. These, and related subjects, are examined in the light of government and private papers recently made available to public scrutiny. Published sources bearing on Anglo-Greek relations in this period were helpful in examining relations in the years 1940–1; they were of little help in dealing with such controversial topics as the Metaxas dictatorship or British attitudes towards it. The book was submitted to London University in 1972 in fulfilment of the requirements for a Ph.D., but since then it has been radically revised to include a consideration of additional sources of information which were not available earlier.

My work has been made possible by the kindness of many. I should like to express, however inadequately, my gratitude to those who helped me most. I am particularly indebted to Professor Donald Watt of the London School of Economics and Political Science, who supervised the doctoral dissertation. I am grateful to him for his encouragement and support. I am also grateful to Dr. John Campbell, Fellow of St. Antony's College, Oxford. His friendship to me has been unfailing, and I owe him a greater debt than I can adequately express. He has read the book, as a thesis and in its revised form, and his many wise comments have improved the final work. On matters of style, also, his efforts have led to many improvements. I should also like to thank Professor Douglas Dakin of Birkbeck College and Professor James Joll of the London School of Economics and Political Science for their advice and encouragement.

I welcome this opportunity to thank Dr. Dimitris Portolos

for his personal friendship and support. I should also like to thank Mr. J. C. Carras, whose generosity made possible part of my stay in London. Dr. Thanos Veremis discussed with me numerous points in the book, and helped me with his comments. I am grateful for his personal friendship and support. I should also like to express my gratitude to Mr. Richard Clogg of King's College, London University, who read the first chapters and made a number of useful comments. Mrs. Eugenia Hatzidakis has helped me a great deal throughout the years of work on this book. I am grateful for her friendship. The editors of Oxford University Press suggested a number of alterations which have led to material improvements. I thank them for their care and courtesy.

My debts go beyond this, to those who gave me information from private papers in their possession. John Simopoulos, Fellow of St. Catherine's College, Oxford, allowed me to consult his father's private papers at St. Antony's College, Oxford, and to quote freely from them. Mrs. Loukia Metaxas helped me to cope with her father's papers, and gave me valuable information. Professor John Waterlow of the London School of Hygiene and Tropical Medicine discussed with me a number of points concerning his father, and particularly the circumstances of his retirement from the Foreign Service. Mrs. Virginia Zannas put at my disposal a number of letters from her husband's papers, and gave me much useful information. Mrs. Nicholas Lorandos discussed with me several points examined in this book. I am grateful to them for their trust and assistance.

I should also like to thank H.E. the President of the Greek Republic Konstantinos Tsatsos, Mr. Panaghiotis Kanellopoulos, Mr. Spyros Markezinis, Mr. Alekos Kanellopoulos, Mr. Georghios Pesmatzoglou, and Colonel Athanasios Korozis, who were kind enough to discuss a number of points with me.

Most of all I am grateful to my wife for typing the manuscript several times, but particularly for her constant encouragement, and her efforts to make me forget how much I was imposing on her patience and good nature.

Finally, I wish to express my gratitude to the Directors of the Public Record Office, the Library of the British Museum, the

Library of the London School of Economics and Political Science, the Library of Chatham House, the Senate House Library, the General State Archives (Athens), the General Staff Archives (Athens), the Gennadion Library and the Vouli Library (Athens). They made available to me a mass of unpublished documents and published sources.

University of Thessaloniki   J. S. K.
January 1977

Contents

Abbreviations

D.B.F.P. *Documents on British Foreign Policy, 1919–1939*, 3rd Series, vols. iv, v, vi.

D.D.I. *I Documenti Diplomatici Italiani*, Ottava serie (1936–1939), vols. xii, xiii, Nova serie (1939–1943), vols. i, ii.

D.G.F.P. *Documents on German Foreign Policy, 1918–1945*, Series C, vols. iv, v, Series D, vols. v, viii, x, xi, xii.

Chronological Table

1922, August: Asia Minor Catastrophe

1923, 24 July: Lausanne Treaty

    18 December: Exile of King George II

1924, 25 March: Proclamation of the Greek Republic

1935, 1 March: Unsuccessful rising of Venizelist officers in the army and navy

    9 June: Elections for the 5th National Assembly

    10 July: Assembly Act to hold plebiscite on the regime by 15 November 1935

    3 October: Italian attack against Ethiopia

    10 October: General Kondylis's *coup d'état*. Assembly Act proclaiming end of the Republic

    3 November: Plebiscite on the regime in favour of the monarchy

    25 November: Return of King George II of the Hellenes

    30 November: Appointment of caretaker government headed by Konstantinos Demertzis

1936, 26 January: General Elections

    19 February: Secret agreement of co-operation between the Liberals and the Communists (Sophoulis–Sklavainas Pact)

    5 March: Ioannis Metaxas appointed Minister for Army Affairs

    14 March: Metaxas appointed Deputy Premier in the second government of Demertzis

    18 March: Death of Eleutherios Venizelos (Paris)

    13 April: Death of Demertzis. Metaxas appointed Premier

    25 April: Metaxas granted vote of confidence by Parliament

    30 April: Parliament Act to adjourn until 30 September. Government empowered to govern by decree with the consent of a forty-member parliamentary committee

    8–10 May: Riots in Salonika

    17 May: Death of Panaghis Tsaldaris

    18 July: Outbreak of the Spanish Civil War

4 August: Decrees suspending Constitution and dissolving Parliament

20 August: Agreement between the Greek Government and the Council of Foreign Bondholders

1937, 19 April: Agreement between the Greek Government and Cable & Wireless Ltd.

24 July: Agreement between the Greek Government and Electric Transport Co.

November–December: King George's visit to England

1938, January–February: Arrests and deportations of politicians

29 July: Canea insurrection

September: Munich Crisis

30 September: Munich Agreement

3 October: Metaxas's proposal for an Anglo-Greek alliance

October–December: King George's private visit to England

1939, 7 April: Italian invasion of Albania

13 April: Anglo-French Guarantee to Greece and Romania

22 May: Pact of Steel

June: Athens Legation (British) taken over by Sir Michael Palairet

1 September: German attack on Poland

September: Greco-Italian *rapprochement*

9 October: Provisional Anglo-Greek War Trade Agreement (Athens)

1940, 22 January: Shipping Agreement between the British Government and the Greek shipowners (London)

26 January: Anglo-Greek War Trade Agreement (London)

10 June: Italy's entry into the war

15 August: Greek cruiser *Elli* torpedoed by Italian submarine

28 October: Italian attack on Greece. Metaxas's appeal to Britain for help

November–December: Greek counter-attack and victories against the Italians

1941, 4, 5 January: Metaxas's second appeal to Britain for help

8 January: Defence Committee (British) decision to help Greece

13–16 January: General Wavell's talks with Metaxas (Athens)

18 January: Metaxas's statement to the British Government that Greece would resist German aggression. British offer to send land forces to Greece turned down. British landings to take place as soon as German troops entered Bulgaria

29 January: Death of Metaxas. Alexandros Koryzis appointed Premier

8 February: Koryzis's note to the British Government reaffirming Metaxas's statement of 18 January

10 February: Defence Committee decision to dispatch land and air forces to Greece

22 February: Anthony Eden and General Dill arrive at Tatoi Palace. Anglo-Greek talks and military agreement

1 March: Entry of German troops into Bulgaria. Bulgarian adherence to the Tripartite Pact

2 March: Eden and Dill return to Athens. Second round of Anglo-Greek talks (2–4 March) and military agreement

25 March: Yugoslavia's adherence to the Tripartite Pact

27 March: Belgrade *coup* and deposition of the pro-Axis Yugoslav Government

6 April: German attack on Greece and Yugoslavia

9 April: The Germans enter Salonika

18 April: Suicide of Premier Koryzis

20 April: General Tsolakoglou opens *pourparlers* with the Germans (Epirus)

21 April: Emmanouil Tsouderos appointed Premier. Capitulation of the Greek forces in Epirus. Greek communication to the British to withdraw their forces from mainland Greece

23 April: King George and Greek Government evacuated to Crete. Final protocol of armistice signed

27 April: The Germans enter Athens

Introduction

In the following assessment of Anglo-Greek relations in the years 1935–41, the intention is to treat these relations essentially from the Greek point of view, and more particularly to examine the influence of the 'British connection' on Greece's internal and external affairs. This limited scope will make it possible to concentrate on certain aspects of these relations which have been the subject of controversy for more than four decades. Present in Anglo-Greek relations was the old sentimental link between the two peoples that lingered on from the days of the Greek War of Independence. This was the capital invested by Byron and other British philhellenes in the sentiments of successive generations of Greeks and Britons, which tended to create a peculiar atmosphere that bred illusions and misunderstandings, especially on the part of the Greeks. Related to this was another aspect of Anglo-Greek relations, namely the fundamentally different approach of the two sides to these relations, particularly to the role Britain was supposed or expected to play in internal Greek affairs. The British treated their relations with Greece in a businesslike manner, irrespective of regimes and governments; and if they did support an illiberal regime in Greece during the period which concerns us in this book, they did so not because they liked the regime as such, but solely because they were convinced that as far as British interests went this regime suited Britain best. The Greeks, on the other hand, often gave the impression that they viewed these relations in terms of principles. Time and again Metaxas was exasperated by the attitude of the British and bitterly complained about it; and so in fact did Metaxas's opponents, and with greater vehemence. Deeply immersed in political strife where even a delicate tip to the scales made all the difference, and always searching for allies or powerful patrons, it was natural that many Greeks saw Britain's involvement in Greece in this light and tried to use British influence for their own ends. The tradition of British intervention in Greek affairs made it difficult for many Greeks to imagine that Britain would not once more play its 'role' in Greece in one way or another; and in fact the attitude of the British Minister in Athens often confirmed this impression.

The second half of the thirties in Greece was a time of profound crisis, deeply affected by developments which reached back to the 'schism' of World War I, when the followers of King Constantine and Venizelos divided the nation over Greece's alignment in the international conflict. The post-war era carried, along with the debris of war, the passions of those troubled years, channelled now in domestic politics. With anti-Venizelism emasculated after the execution of its leadership in 1922 following the disastrous defeat of the Greek army in Asia Minor, and increasingly meaningless as an effective political force, and Venizelism splintered into many parties and factions, the Greek political scene acquired a kaleidoscopic aspect that changed rapidly and often in a most unpredictable and erratic manner. At the same time, the army appeared on the scene as a political factor. During the years of war and national schism a considerable number of officers associated themselves with one of the two camps, while others found it difficult not to do so: it had become a question of winners or losers, and victory or defeat meant rapid promotion, or expulsion from the Services, as the case might be. Organizations within the army, based on competing clientage networks, as well as the political affiliations and aims of many officers, eroded discipline, and rendered the army's command structure ineffective. After the Revolution of 1922, the army became a powerful political force that often made or unmade governments, and carried out *coups* or suppressed them.[1] Appointed by the Government to examine the conduct of officers during the unsuccessful *coup* of March 1933, a high-ranking officer gave the following appreciation: the 'wavering' attitude of most officers was due to the constant intervention of the army in politics in the preceding fifteen years, and the acquiescence of the lawful governments in many unlawful acts, as well as the repeated *coups*, of which some, when successful, created regimes that took on a legitimate appearance.[2]

[1] Thanos Veremis, 'The Greek Army in Politics, 1922–1935' (doctoral dissertation, Trinity College, Oxford, 1974), Chs. II and V in particular.
[2] Gen. A. Mazarakis-Ainian, *Memoirs* (in Greek), Athens, 1948, pp. 363 ff.

Eleutherios Venizelos could still carry the majority of the Greeks with him when he chose; but he was becoming more of a politician and less of a national leader. In the expulsion of King George II in 1923, Venizelos chose to utter Delphic pronouncements whose meaning his lieutenants were unable to divine; and when he was unable, in early 1924, to prevent the establishment of the Republic in a scandalous and abnormal manner, he chose to leave Greece once more in order to escape a confrontation with the radical republican wing of his following in the army. In this instance Venizelos acted as a republican, yet the Republic established was not to his liking. Venizelos was faced with a situation he was unable to control; his lieutenants had grown independent of his tutelage and could not be checked any longer, while the army had become a sorcerer's apprentice. Finally he made Paris his Delphi, where he received the missions of the Greeks seeking the advice of the oracle; Venizelos had become an institution, but at a distance. It was a tragedy for Greece that when at last Venizelos appeared to be in decline, no one emerged in his place to give the country strong leadership under the new republican constitution. General Plastiras was effective mainly on horseback and as a symbol; Alexandros Papanastasiou, the 'rising sun' as General Kondylis referred to him in rare moments of admiration, was limited by the radical principles he espoused; General Metaxas was in the awkward position of having dissociated himself from his past supporters without being able to find new ones; Panaghis Tsaldaris could not convince many that his apparent modesty was not due to a lack of backbone; G. Kafandaris, A. Michalakopoulos, and T. Sophoulis always felt the shadow of Venizelos one way or another; and Admiral Kountouriotis and A. Zaimis were conveniently placed in turn on the seat of the President of the Republic, from which they observed the waning Republic in felicitous and constitutional inactivity. Among them moved more ruthless and cynical men, politico-military *condottieri* of the type of General Kondylis, General Pangalos, and Admiral Hatzikyriakos, to name only the most prominent.

The first four years of the Republic saw many short-lived governments, one dictatorship, and many still-born *coups*. *Coups*, indeed, had become a sort of sport, undertaken without

serious qualms and without grave consequences for the participants either. Some attempts were made to draw the two camps
together, or parts of them, as in the 'Ecumenical' government
of 1926–7 after Pangalos's dictatorship collapsed, but the
co-operation was short-lived. Essentially, it was due to the
inability of both camps to provide stable governments, since
neither could count on a workable majority in Parliament, and
to their unwillingness to leave the reins of power to the opponent.
Political power was proving the sole means of dispensing
favours and patronage, and thus securing the loyalty of electoral
clienteles at different levels. Also, the influence of Venizelos,
in one way or another, was always present—seldom construc-
tively. The Cretan statesman eventually chose to intervene
directly in the Greek political scene, and after a landslide
electoral victory, entered his final period of power. The Greeks
who voted for him in 1928 as a returning messiah, and those
who did not, could not have been more mistaken; the Venizelos
of 1928–32 was not the Venizelos of 1917–20, let alone of
1910–15.

The last government of Venizelos did not see an appreciable
improvement in the conduct of politics, though military intervention was curbed. His social and labour policy was essentially
an impatient effort to come to terms with a situation he seemed
unable and unprepared to understand. The anti-Communist
legislation of 1929 was repressive and out of all proportion to
the actual threat of Communism, and became a dangerous
precedent and a powerful instrument of repression in the hands
of subsequent governments and regimes. Where Venizelos
dismally failed, however, and this was the primary aim of his
return, was in the conciliation of anti-Venizelism and the
recognition of the Republic by the main anti-Venizelist parties.
But he was not the only one responsible for this failure. Tsaldaris
and other anti-Venizelist leaders, lacking a more realistic
policy, had made their non-recognition of the Republic a trade-
mark that gave them some identity. It is not surprising that
Tsaldaris and the Populist Party recognized the Republic when
there was no longer need not to do so: when it became apparent
that Venizelos's hold on Greece was gone, and that his political
career was in decline. Memories were dying hard, moreover,
and the turbulent past ruled the present in a way that was

becoming meaningless. On the one occasion when a reconciliation could have been effected between the two camps—in 1932 and amidst the deepening financial crisis—Venizelos chose to summon up before his opponents the ghosts of the past. On all sides political leaders consciously began to probe old wounds to bring out their old followers and supporters.

The fall of Venizelos ushered in a new period of political instability and military intervention which culminated in the rising of March 1935 and the final collapse of the Republic in the same year. Politics took on a personal character, conducted in an atmosphere of intense hostility; scandals, true or fabricated, were given great prominence by a press that had gone beyond all bounds of decency and good faith. Any means were used to discredit an opponent, and in the case of Venizelos an attempt on his life was made by a group of conspirators who included an outlawed bandit, the Chief of Police, and a number of high-ranking Government officials and security officers. This, and the subsequent judicial scandal, revealed the Government as accomplices in attempted murder, and Greek justice as an empty word.[1] Parliamentary government was discredited, and the Republic irretrievably undermined.

Serious trouble also emanated from another quarter. The world financial crisis of 1929 dealt a serious blow to the finances of the country, but those who fared worst were manual workers in the towns and peasant farmers. Unorganized and with little support from the State, these workers and farmers were at the mercy of market forces, in particular a sharply reduced demand for their labour and produce. The British Minister in Greece drew a grim picture of the country in 1935: the poor crushed by heavy taxation, which the rich evaded by bribery; the budgets unbalanced, if not wholly fictitious; the country 'poor, naked, miserable and ashamed'.[2] Cynical politicians often channelled public wrath away from the glaring shortcomings of the politico-economic system to the foreign investor and the International Financial Commission imposed on Greece in 1898 by the great powers of Europe to ensure the payment of

[1] G. Daphnis, *Greece Between Two Wars* (in Greek), Athens, 1955, vol. ii, pp. 220 ff.

[2] Sir S. Waterlow, 'The Decline and Fall of Greek Democracy, 1933–1936', *Political Quarterly*, vol. 18, Nos. 2 and 3 (1947), p. 99.

the Greek foreign debt—an agency which had kept a firm grip
on the country since that time. In 1935 the Greek foreign debt
reached 44,971,000,000 drachmas, and there was an adverse
balance of payments of 3,345,000,000 dr.[1] National Income in
the same year was 63,750,000,000 dr.[2] These misfortunes were
outside the control of the Government. Rising tariffs, and the
contraction in world trade caused by controlled exchanges and
barter systems, affected countries in a far better position than
Greece. Greece, moreover, had to deal with the problem created
by the closing of certain countries to her emigrants. But the
shaken economy and finances of the country cannot completely
exonerate the later governments of the Republic from their
responsibility for the almost scandalous lack of care for the
poorer sections of the population.

It was during this period of crisis, when all the major parties
had recognized the Republic, that they also did their utmost to
undermine it. Venizelists dealt the final blow by their attempted
coup in 1935. What was essentially an intense struggle for power
and spoils was presented as a struggle to preserve or strengthen
the Republic. Plastiras had earlier organized an unsuccessful
coup in March 1933 to reverse the defeat the Venizelist parties
had suffered at the polls. The loss of power and patronage was
felt to be more significant than the continuity of legitimate
parliamentary government. Venizelos himself had encouraged
military organizations whose ostensible aim was to safeguard
the Republic by illegally seizing power. Parties and factions
ceased to represent the actual political divisions in the country.
The real issues were relegated to the background, and parliamentary government became an empty process, essentially
limited to Parliament itself and the Press. In the aftermath of
the 1935 *coup*, a thorough purge in the armed services of all
Venizelist and republican officers, and the subsequent restoration of the monarchy, brought in a new and decisive factor, the
King, who held the undisputed loyalty of the military. In this
situation it is not surprising that a man like Metaxas, whose
following was very limited but who had the support of the King,

---

[1] Yearly Economic Review, 1935, by the Athens Legation, F.O. 371/20386,
Public Record Office, London.
[2] C. Evelpidis, *Economic and Social History of Greece* (in Greek), Athens, 1950,
p. 109.

could carry out a bloodless *coup* and establish a dictatorship. The political leadership of the two main parties, long divorced from the people and quite discredited, receded impotently into the background.

Before leaving this introductory chapter, a few words about General Ioannis Metaxas and King George II of the Hellenes, the principal actors involved in Greek affairs and Anglo-Greek relations in the period which concerns us in this book, are necessary. Metaxas was a good staff officer, an ambitious and ruthless politician, and dangerously given to dreaming. A Count by inheritance—he was born to a family of impoverished Cephalonian nobles—he always felt proud of his name and family:

> I felt my responsibility as a soldier and, above all, as a noble and a Metaxas. I belong to the aristocracy which had fought for its King and country long before modern Greece was born. Greece emerged as a result of the struggles and the sacrifices of this aristocracy. The Greece which was born in 1821 is not my Fatherland, because as Metaxas I belong to another, much greater Fatherland, which only the King can now represent.[1]

Metaxas's convictions and attachment to the royal family of Greece seem to have been formed during the Greco-Turkish War of 1897, when he served as a junior officer on the Staff of the Crown Prince, later King Constantine, who was in command of the defeated Greek army. The dynasty, not unjustly, was widely criticized for its role in the national disaster of 1897; and the issues of parliamentarianism and the Constitution dominated the political scene in Greece for many years. Metaxas noted at this time: 'Amidst the moral and national debris my soul has been filled with, only one institution remains standing: the King and his dynasty. And my devotion to them became even greater. There was a moment—only a moment—when I hated my country, but never the King. I needed to lean on something, and I leant on this conviction.'[2] And concerning what he called 'notorious parliamentary institutions', he noted in his diary, prophetically: 'A struggle has started between the Crown Prince and Parliamentarianism

---

[1] I. Metaxas, *His Personal Diary* (in Greek), vol. i, edit. Ch. Christidis, Athens, 1960. 5 Jan. 1941.
[2] Ibid., vol. i. Yearly entry for 1898.

. . . Well! I shall do something myself in order to drink some parliamentary blood . . . There will be opportunities for that.'[1] His friendship with the Crown Prince brought its first major reward in the form of a state scholarship to study at the War Academy of Berlin. While in Germany Metaxas developed an admiration for the Germans, and was irresistibly drawn by the 'German Spirit', which, as he wrote later, left 'indelible marks' on him.[2] During this time, and throughout his life, he was influenced by ideas drawn from Goethe's Faust. By the time he returned to Greece three years later, Metaxas had become a good staff officer, and something of a dreamer. But as a politician he was uninspiring. Metaxas was cheated by life in many respects; and, in his turn, he cheated his way through the maze of Greek politics by calculation, intrigue, and the right connections. Very few seemed to take him seriously, until, in quick succession, he worked his way from Minister for Army Affairs to Premier, and finally dictator. Metaxas had caught the eye of King George, and this would prove as great an asset as any electoral success.

King George seemed out of place in Greece, and often confided as much to close friends. According to Sir Robert Vansittart, the King would always prefer a stay at Brown's Hotel in London to his 'rickety eminence' as King of Greece. He returned to Greece with the best intentions to reign as a constitutional monarch, but he lost his nerve and installed a dictatorship instead. Exasperated by Greek politics, he confided to the British Minister in 1936: 'There is only one real solution, and that is that Greece should be taken over by your civil service and run as a British colony. If only it were possible', and the understanding Minister thought that after twelve years of 'civilized life' the King faced his task 'in the spirit of one carrying the white man's burden among tribes of the jungle'.[3] King George had been shown the way out of Greece in 1923, after a brief reign, and it seems that he never forgave the Greeks. During the long years of exile, he led the life of a mildly bitter monarch in exile, contributing to the gossip of the steadily growing community of exiled royalty. He made his residence in London, visited his royal relatives in

[1] Metaxas, op. cit., vol. i, 4 Dec. 1899.   [2] Ibid., 7 Aug. 1905.
[3] Athens Dispatch No. 351, Confidential, 28 Oct. 1936, F.O. 371/20390.

Europe, hunted tigers in India, and developed a taste for British life and habits. During his second reign—there was to be a third (1946–7)—which coincided with Metaxas's dictatorship, King George visited England twice, and kept alive his connections with influential persons there. The opposition in Greece ungraciously dubbed him the 'British High Commissioner' in Greece. The King regarded Greek politicians with distaste, especially when they were Republicans. The King's anglophile sentiments were reflected in his dislike of the French *kepi* worn by the Greek army until he replaced it by a head-dress of British pattern; and along with the *kepi* he took care also to eradicate the 'democratizing' influence that lingered on from the days of the French Military Mission.

I

Greece and Britain, 1935–1936:
The Connection

The Rising of March 1935 and the
Restoration of the Monarchy

On the night of 1 March 1935—a carnival night in Athens—
a number of Venizelist army officers took over certain key
positions in Athens, and naval officers seized the greater part of
the Greek Fleet. The cannon on Lycabetus Hill sounded the
alarm, and the political world of Athens was thrown into
a frenzy of activity and manœuvring, that favourite Athenian
pastime. The rising seemed to be yet another *coup d'état*, so
frequent an event during the troubled Greek Republic. The
rebels declared that they were taking action to prevent a mon-
archical restoration, and tried to persuade public opinion that
the Republic was in danger. Venizelos, a resident in Crete ever
since the attempt on his life in 1933, accepted the leadership
of the revolt. According to the plan of the rebels, the naval
officers were to seize the Fleet, which would immediately sail
towards Salonika and Kavalla, where the army was mainly
Venizelist. At the same time, Crete and the Islands were
expected to rise. After the initial *coup*, and with the periphery
of the country in revolt, the Government was expected to
surrender. If so, a military government would be set up in
Athens; otherwise, a temporary government would be formed in
Salonika, and an expedition would be launched against Athens.
Lack of co-ordination, however, and loss of nerve prevented the
naval officers from going to the North, as was planned. Instead,
the Fleet headed towards Crete, where it soon arrived. Meanwhile, because of a misunderstanding, the Venizelist officers in
the Salonika and Kavalla garrisons failed to rise in time. Thus
the rising failed in its initial and most critical stage.[1]

[1] Daphnis, op. cit., vol. ii, pp. 306 ff.

The Government of Panaghis Tsaldaris reacted with unexpected vigour, and launched what was essentially a counter-revolution against Venizelism. Metaxas was hurriedly brought in to the Government as Minister without Portfolio, while General Kondylis, the Minister for Army Affairs, donned his military uniform, and rushed to the North to put down the rebels. The rebel officers in Athens were isolated, and soon surrendered after brief fighting. The same happened in the North, where the rebellion fizzled out after sporadic skirmishes. The rebels were not actually defeated, because they did not give decisive battle. After this collapse on the mainland, Venizelos was left isolated in Crete, and had no option but to flee from Greece for the last time. The rebel ships of the Fleet were declared pirates by the Government, and, after a nominal bombardment from the air and the sea, surrendered: they had run out of fuel. Venizelos and a few of his followers fled to the Dodecanese, Italian territory at the time, and subsequently to Paris. General Kammenos, the rebel leader in the North, crossed over to Bulgaria, while a number of Venizelist politicians in Athens trickled out of Greece in all directions. The quick collapse of the March rebellion surprised everyone, and the Greek Government most of all. There is little doubt that, with better organization and leadership, the rising could have easily succeeded.

In an attempt to justify the outbreak of the rebellion, Venizelos wrote from Crete to the British Minister in Athens:

The motive for the revolution has been given by the universal conviction of the democracy that the Athens Government is pursuing the dissolution of the democratic regime and the restoration of the expelled dynasty . . .

Consequently, the aim of the revolution is to settle the question of the regime in such a manner as to exclude all anxiety for the democratic governance of the country, and in order that the democratic composition of the armed forces of the nation may be conserved and secured.[1]

This, however, was only part of the truth. Venizelos kept to himself and his closest collaborators other aims, besides that of defending and strengthening the Republic. He expounded these in a letter to General Plastiras a few days before the *coup*.

[1] Letter from Venizelos to Sir Sydney Waterlow, 8 Mar. 1935, F.O. 371/19506.

The first aim of the new order, he wrote, would be to purge the Armed and Security Services of all anti-Venizelist elements, and subsequently to close these Services to any one who was against the new order. The second step would be a revision of the regime and the constitution, the main feature being the election of the President of the Republic by the people directly, not by Parliament as was laid down by the 1927 Republican Constitution.[1] Venizelos also wished to introduce an article which would empower the President to suppress the articles of the Constitution concerning popular liberties in case of an emergency.[2] What all this amounts to is not so much concern for the Republic—Venizelos in any case was never a convinced republican—but rather a veiled aim to establish one-party rule, and if necessary dictatorship. His long and distinguished service to Greece had led Venizelos to consider himself indispensable, and this conviction might have made a dictator of him in all but name.

The March rising was essentially a Greek affair. Foreign states took care to stay out of the struggle, and did not intervene directly, if only because of its short duration. Of the Balkan partners of Greece only Yugoslavia was favourably disposed towards the Greek Government, and heeded its request for fighter aeroplanes. France and Britain turned down similar requests for fighters, as we shall see, and sent only one destroyer each for the 'protection' of their nationals and property in case of emergency. Italy, the only power that might have been interested in the return of Venizelos to power, since he was an opponent of the Balkan Entente, refused to allow Plastiras to cross over to Greece from Italian territory, while the Bari Radio Station refused to broadcast the manifesto of the rebels.[3] But anti-Italian feeling in Greece ran high during the rising, although there is no evidence that Italy was privy to the affair, as was claimed at the time.[4] Allegations that Italy condoned the rising arose out of the absence of any criticism of Venizelos in the Italian press, the dispatch of Italian warships to the Dodecanese instead of Phaliron Bay,

[1] Daphnis, op. cit., vol. ii, p. 350.   [2] Ibid., pp. 143 ff.
[3] Daphnis, op. cit., vol. ii, p. 353; P. Argyropoulos, *Memoirs* (in Greek), vol. i, Athens, 1970, p. 492.
[4] Foreign Office Correspondence and Minutes in F.O. 371/19506.

and finally Venizelos's flight to the Dodecanese. It cannot be denied, of course, that Italy would have welcomed his return to power. But this pro-Venizelist attitude on the part of Italy did not entirely justify the anti-Italian feeling stirred up in Greece at the time.

The British Government saw the rising as a struggle between 'ins and outs', and tried to keep clear of it, or rather to sit on the fence until one of the contestants appeared to be winning. Sir Sydney Waterlow, the British Minister in Athens, informed the Foreign Office soon after the outbreak of the revolt that he had reason to believe that he might be approached by the Greek Government with a suggestion for mediation between the two sides. He therefore asked for authority to do so. The Foreign Office considered this proposal, and found the idea agreeable. Mediation, it was felt, would save lives and property; moreover, the British Government would earn the 'gratitude' of the victorious party, which the British could then 'exploit' in their relations with Greece.[1] However, despite the tempting advantage, the Foreign Office finally shelved it, and instructed the Minister to refuse mediation 'in the present confused situation'. Instead, it was decided that H.M.S. *Royal Sovereign* should sail immediately to Phaliron Bay.[2]

The Greek Government, however, approached the British Government about a more urgent matter: on 4 March the British were asked to facilitate the supply of five bombers and/or five reconnaissance aeroplanes, together with five fighters. The Air Ministry was very reluctant to agree, since the supply of aircraft to the Greek Government might have 'embarrassing repercussions' if the Greek Government did not ultimately win. At the same time the Air Ministry was apprehensive that the Greek Government might obtain the material elsewhere. The Foreign Office was therefore asked to approach the French Government with the object of concerting their policy and refusing the supply of war material to the Greek Government.[3] The Air Ministry believed that, though there had never been an explicit agreement with the French, they should share with them the Greek market for aircraft and that

---

[1] Athens Tel. of 3 Mar., and F.O. Minutes, F.O. 371/19504.
[2] F.O. Tel. to Athens, 6 Mar., F.O. 371/19504.
[3] R1426/173/19, F.O. 371/19513.

neither power should try to use the present emergency to squeeze the other out of the Greek market. The Foreign Office approached the French Government with this in mind, and succeeded in bringing them 'into line'. The French, in their eagerness to be co-operative, went even further and approached private firms as well, asking them to 'spin out' any delivery of war material to Greece as long as possible. Interestingly enough, the Foreign Office hoped to bring 'into line' even Germany and Italy, to whom the Greek Government might turn in despair.[1]

The attitude of the Foreign Office was an example of masterly, calculated caution. They considered all eventualities, and left their options open until the very end; so much so, indeed, that the British Minister in Athens was often puzzled by the attitude of the men in London, and expressed the view that they should have shown more sympathy to the Greek Government, which was, after all, the lawful government of a friendly state. The Foreign Office, however, tried to avoid 'getting into the position of having given sympathy or assistance to the loser'.[2] Moreover, policy in the Foreign Office, Waterlow was reminded in reply to his criticisms, was formed by way of *ad hoc* decisions rather than a theoretical examination of general considerations; and, as long as the issue was in doubt, they would prefer to 'sit on the fence'. Finally, the Foreign Office could not possibly be expected to ignore the great influence which the name of Venizelos commanded in Britain, especially in parliamentary circles.[3] Another and more cogent reason behind their cautious policy seems to have been their apparent dislike of the Greek Government. In a Memorandum of 5 March 1935, the Head of the Southern Department explicitly argued: 'The present Greek Government has proved itself not only inefficient and corrupt, but also decidedly inimical to British interests. From the standpoint of the latter, a Venizelist Government could scarcely be worse, and might be considerably better.'[4]

The quick collapse of the March rising in a sense relieved the Foreign Office, but it also caused some quiet resentment. They agreed among themselves that Waterlow had proved himself 'too definitely anti-Venizelist'; and in response to the latter's optimism about the future of Greece without Venizelos, they

---

[1] R1420/34/19, F.O. 371/19504.   [2] R1715/34/19, F.O. 371/19505.
[3] R1829/34/19, F.O. 371/19505.   [4] R1552/34/19, F.O. 371/19505.

commented sceptically that what was in store for Greece was most probably a sort of 'fascist system'. The Foreign Office appeared favourably disposed towards Venizelos, if only for the sake of the days of the Great War. Sir Robert Vansittart in this instance dedicated to Venizelos one of his colourful minutes:

> I always liked M. Venizelos personally; indeed I liked him immensely. But I could never understand the empire that he exerted over the minds of Mr. Lloyd George and Lord Lothian during the unhappy years when I had to act as liaison between the F.O. and the other F.O. at No. 10. I should have thought M. Venizelos one of the most amiable and overestimated men of his day—there were many less amiable—which has dragged on now like an indifferent summer afternoon. Whether dusk is finally at hand, and whether that in itself is a cause for rejoicing I must leave to more expert local knowledge. I should not have thought it would have greatly changed the fundamental defects of Greek character and Greek politics.[1]

The rising presented the eager British Minister in Athens with an opportunity to erase any bad feelings the Greek Government might have had as a result of the refusal to supply aeroplanes. Waterlow called on the Greek Premier during the struggle and, despite the misgivings of the Foreign Office, told him that he followed with 'sympathy' the efforts of the Greek Government to restore order against 'unjustifiable attacks', and that he was sure that His Majesty's Government and the British people shared his feelings and hopes for a quick restoration of order.[2] This expression of sympathy, as well as the presence of a British warship in Greece, produced, according to Waterlow, a wave of feeling in favour of Britain. British influence had become 'predominant', the Minister reported proudly.[3] While there is little doubt that Waterlow was exaggerating in order to impress the men in London and silence their criticisms, he certainly deserved most of the credit for the pro-British feeling in Greece and especially in the Government at a time when there was very little reason for it.

An immediate result of the rising of March 1935, besides the defeat and discrediting of Venizelism, was the reopening of an issue that had remained more or less dormant during the years

---

[1] Athens Disp. No. 94, 16 Mar. 1935, and F.O. Minutes in F.O. 371/19505.
[2] R1503/34/19, F.O. 371/19504.   [3] R1905/34/19, F.O. 371/19506.

of the Republic: the restoration of the monarchy. While it is true that King George II had never renounced his rights to the throne, nor for that matter had ceased to hope for his return to the country, the question of the monarchy preoccupied none of the major parties seriously, and was rather the dream of a number of royalist fanatics and conspirators.[1] There is reason to believe that the issue of the monarchy would never actually have emerged under relatively normal circumstances. The Populist Party, the second largest party in Greece, had recognized the Republic in 1932, and pledged itself to work within its framework. The Republic, therefore, was not in any serious and immediate danger as Venizelos claimed, at least not for the reasons he put forward; the exiled King was not in a position to endanger the Republic, while Tsaldaris and the Populists had no reason to do so, since they were in power. Tsaldaris made it clear shortly after the rising that as far as the Government was concerned there was no question of a change of regime. This was indeed the line of policy that might have been expected from the Populist leader: the rising had discredited the main opponents of the Populists, and had thus secured for him and his party unchallenged power for some years to come. Kondylis was the strong man of the moment, and could afford to wait for the appropriate circumstances to move; for the time being, he was content to rest on his recent laurels as the hero mainly responsible for the suppression of the *coup*.[2] Metaxas, however, could not wait, and resigned from the Government in March, when his advice for strong measures against Venizelism were rejected. In his letter of resignation to Tsaldaris, Metaxas said he was not convinced that the Government were prepared to treat Venizelism according to the 'just demand' of anti-Venizelism; and that he was resigning in order to lead an 'effective' political struggle.[3] In the first

---

[1] Pipinelis in his biography of King George wrote of a meeting of the King and a Greek royalist in Genoa in early 1935. It was proposed that the King should fly to an Ionian island, and effect thus a *de facto* restoration. King George was initially enthusiastic, but on second thoughts rejected it, saying that 'things must be prepared first'. According to another Greek source, a number of royalist officers were in fact scheming for a forced restoration, and so sent to Genoa the emissary mentioned by Pipinelis. P. N. Pipinelis, *George II* (in Greek), Athens, 1951, p. 78; G. Vouros, *Panaghis Tsaldaris* (in Greek), Athens, 1955, pp. 482–3.

[2] S. S. Merkouris, *Georghios Kondylis* (in Greek), Athens, 1954, pp. 116 ff.

[3] Letter of 18 Mar., Daphnis, op. cit., vol. ii, p. 354.

meeting of the Chamber after the rising, Metaxas demanded elections for a Constituent Assembly.[1] Metaxas, incidentally, had been one of the first royalists to recognize the Republic in 1924. While military courts in Athens and Salonika were trying Venizelist officers and politicians, and martial law was still in force, the Government proclaimed elections for 9 June 1935. It was a scandal that irked even Metaxas. In a letter to Tsaldaris, the future dictator accused the Government of scandalous conduct, and demanded the lifting of martial law and censorship.[2] The Government, nevertheless, turned a deaf ear to his accusations, as well as to the threats of the republican parties that they would boycott the elections if the Government did not lift martial law in time. Martial law was actually lifted only on 14 May. The elections were duly held on 9 June, and were boycotted by the republicans. The elections were also suitably rigged, and so returned the Government to power with an unchallenged majority, while the extreme royalists were defeated.[3] Metaxas noted dejectedly in his diary: 'Complete failure. Rigging, pressures, plebiscite issue. I have the impression that the Greek people do not like me; they can see my abilities, but they do not like me. Nevertheless, I go on fighting.'[4]

Metaxas had declared during the campaign that a vote for him was a vote for King George; and he got but few votes. Kondylis, on the other hand, came out in favour of the restoration of the monarchy only after the elections, which secured for him and Tsaldaris a great majority. Kondylis's change of heart was allegedly due to a promise by King George that on his return to Greece he would take Kondylis into his favour.[5] Whatever the truth might be, the Government was subsequently divided on the issue of the monarchy, with Kondylis working openly for the return of King George, while Tsaldaris remained uncommitted and drifted along with events. Parliament passed a law on 10 July for a plebiscite on the issue of the monarchy

---

[1] Daphnis, op. cit., vol. ii, p. 366.   [2] 16 Apr. 1935, Metaxas Papers.
[3] Daphnis, op. cit., vol. ii, p. 370.   [4] *Diary*, vol. iv, p. 153.
[5] On 21 May Kondylis had met N. Papadakis, a friend of King George, and Papadakis read to him a letter from King George in which the King said that he admired Kondylis very much, both as a soldier and a political leader, and that he had in mind even 'higher positions' for him on his return to Greece. Kondylis promised Papadakis to do everything in his power for the return of the King. Vouros, op. cit., p. 483; Daphnis, op. cit., vol. ii, p. 371; Merkouris, op. cit., pp. 197 ff.

to be held in November, and adjourned until 10 October. Tsaldaris then went on holiday to Germany, thus leaving Kondylis free to work towards a restoration by force.

The spring and summer of 1935 in Greece was one of unparalleled confusion and intrigue. The British Minister reported many disquieting symptoms and a drift towards 'irresponsible dictatorship', and tried, along with his French colleague, to stiffen Tsaldaris and the moderates, but to no avail. In May, Waterlow reported that there was a real danger of 'anarchy', and an opportunity for Communism in Greece. He wrote that the question of the monarchy clamoured for settlement one way or the other, since ambiguity would only lead to greater anarchy. Waterlow also expressed his opinion about the issue of the regime. The monarchy, he believed, was essential as a 'stabilizing force', and he suggested that the British Government should lend their influence to promote the restoration of the monarchy. Great Britain, Waterlow explained to the Foreign Office, was expected to play her 'proper part', and this was 'universally' expected and desired in Greece.[1] The Greek Minister in London approached the Foreign Office at the same time, and tried to 'convert' them to the restoration.[2]

The Foreign Office, though not surprised, needed time to formulate its attitude regarding what was clearly an internal affair of Greece. Public opinion in Britain would not necessarily support British intervention in favour of the restoration of the monarchy, and of the Greek Royal Dynasty in particular. Its pro-German attitude during the Great War could not be forgotten. The Greek Minister was told in the Foreign Office that the restoration was an issue for the Greeks to decide, and that the British Government would wish them well, but would not express any opinion, if the Greek people decided to bring back the King. Simopoulos was also told that the important thing was that the return of the King 'should be demonstrated to be the real wish of the great majority of the Greek people', not as the result of a snap vote.[2] In any case, it was decided that the question of the restoration was not a matter in which the British Government should take any part. Sir John Simon, the Secretary of State for Foreign Affairs, replied to Waterlow's

[1] Athens Confid. Disp., No. 202, 13 May 1935, F.O. 371/19507.
[2] F.O. Minutes, 13 May, F.O. 371/19507.

proposal on 30 May, saying that it was doubtful whether public opinion would approve any expression of opinion, much less the taking of any action, by the British Government in favour of such a restoration. The doctrine of non-intervention in the internal affairs of another country, Simon explained, had been given great prominence lately in European affairs, and the British Government found it impossible to do anything which might expose them to the charge of interfering in the internal affairs of Greece. And the Secretary of State concluded:

After careful consideration, therefore, I have come to the conclusion that it would be impossible for His Majesty's Government to take any action or express any opinion in regard to the merits or otherwise of a restoration of the monarchy in Greece. This is not to say, however, that you are precluded from expressing a personal opinion on the importance, if the question of the regime is to be re-opened, of its being settled in a way which would convince the world that the settlement was in accordance with the freely and fully expressed wishes of the Greek people as a whole.[1]

The eager Minister, however, continued his pressure on the Foreign Office to intervene and assist the King to return to his throne. What was at issue in Greece that summer, Waterlow wrote, was whether Greece was to become a constitutional monarchy, or fall into anarchy and 'Communism', which would endanger British interests there. He proposed that an approach should be made to the King and he should be asked to declare that he was willing to return to Greece if he were to be invited by the people. As for the propriety of using British influence, Waterlow repeated his argument that the Greeks always 'looked' to Britain to help them in a crisis, and he reminded the Foreign Office that the King of the Hellenes was the cousin of King George V. The Foreign Office felt, though, that the situation was still too 'fluid' for a move in the direction proposed. Moreover, the King had meanwhile made a declaration along the lines suggested. The Foreign Office, therefore, considered their advice 'unnecessary'.[2]

In fact, the Foreign Office had considered many channels of possible approach to the King as Waterlow had suggested. The most obvious intermediary was of course the Greek

[1] F.O. Confid. Disp., No. 187, 30 May 1935, F.O. 371/19507.
[2] R3597/34/19, F.O. 371/19507.

Minister in London, a royalist and in constant touch with both the King and the Foreign Office. Sir Clive Wigram, another close friend of the King, was also considered.[1] There is no evidence, however, that the Foreign Office actually used an intermediary at this stage. The fact that the King made a declaration on the same lines as those suggested by Waterlow does not of itself constitute evidence that the Foreign Office was behind it. The Minister's idea might well have been passed on by the numerous friends of the King who surrounded the British Minister in Athens.

Following the June elections and the defeat of the extreme royalists, Waterlow reported that there seemed less hope for a restoration. If a plebiscite were held then, it would not give more than 40 per cent in favour of the monarchy, the Minister believed. After the division of the Greek Government on the issue of the monarchy, Waterlow expressed the view that the extreme royalists might try to bring the King back by a *coup d'état*, or as the result of a fraudulent plebiscite. At the same time he suggested the desirability of conveying a warning to the King about the dangers which awaited his return. The Foreign Office was unable to keep track of a situation that changed very rapidly, and of the Minister's equally rapid changes of opinion. They again started the search for intermediaries to approach the King and advise him not to return. Official advice was ruled out, of course, though it was suggested that the Secretary of State should drop the King an 'informal hint'.[2] Again, there is no evidence that such a hint was actually given.

In July Kondylis visited Italy, and on his way back he passed through Yugoslavia where he met Prince Paul. Kondylis gave the Prince to understand that the restoration was a foregone conclusion as far as he was concerned.[3] The following month Tsaldaris also stopped in Yugoslavia on his way to Germany, and at Bled met Prince Paul, Prince Nicholas of Greece, and the Duke of Kent, the last two as the representatives of the King of Greece. Both the Venizelist and the royalist press gave great prominence to this meeting for different reasons: the Venizelists accused Yugoslavia of interference in Greek affairs,

---

[1] F.O. Confid. Disp., 22 June, F.O. 371/19507.
[2] F.O. Memo., R6266/34/19, F.O. 371/19509; R4672/34/19, F.O. 371/19508.
[3] Daphnis, op. cit., vol. ii, p. 373.

while the royalists used it noisily for propaganda, which made the Foreign Office uncomfortable because of the Duke of Kent's presence at the meeting.[1] Meanwhile, the royalists were preparing for a thorough rigging of the coming plebiscite. The British Minister sent some alarmist reports, and the Foreign Office became increasingly concerned about the King's safety, if he were to return to Greece, and felt that he should not do so in these circumstances.[2]

Venizelos, an old and broken man, addressed endless and meaningless threats to the Greek Government from Paris.[3] At the same time, he was in close contact with both London and Athens. Many influential people, both Greek and British, approached him throughout the summer, and asked him whether he would recognize the restoration if King George undertook to return as the King of all the Greeks. Georghios Pesmatzoglou, the Minister of Finance and a moderate royalist, met Venizelos in Paris, and was given to understand that the King had a chance of succeeding in Greece where all the political leaders had failed—that is, in uniting the country— if he returned as the King of all the Greeks after an honest plebiscite.[4] Sir Arthur Crossfield, a close friend of Venizelos, also approached him in September to effect a reconciliation with the King. Venizelos did indeed want a reconciliation since it would do a great deal to unite the divided country; and he was counting on a general amnesty by King George to all political and military leaders of the March rising.[5]

The confusion ended at a stroke on 10 October, when Kondylis carried out the *coup d'état* he had long been preparing. General Papagos, General Reppas, and Admiral Oiconomou stopped Tsaldaris on his way from Kephisia to Athens, and demanded his resignation in the name of the armed forces. In the stormy meeting of the Chamber on the same day, Tsaldaris and another hundred Populist Deputies walked out and what was left of the Chamber elected Kondylis Premier,

[1] Venizelos's letters to Loukas Roufos, 16 and 30 June, Venizelos's Papers, Benaki Museum.   [2] R5640/34/19, F.O. 371/19508.

[3] Venizelos's letters to Loukas Roufos, 16 and 30 June, Venizelos's Papers.

[4] G. Pesmatzoglou, *On the Restoration of 1935* (in Greek), Athens, 1950, pp. 44 ff.; Crossfield letters to Mme Venizelos, 17 and 27 Sept., copies of which Crossfield sent to Simopoulos, Simopoulos Papers, Oxford.

[5] Daphnis, op. cit., vol. ii, pp. 391 ff.

and Viceroy until the return of King George. At the same time, Kondylis and his followers proclaimed the end of the Greek Republic, a state of martial law, and set the date of the plebiscite for 3 November.[1] In great haste the British Government set aside all misgivings, and recognized Kondylis and his regime; the Abyssinian crisis had just broken out, and they could not afford an estranged Greek Government.

The Abyssinian crisis of early October 1935 had serious repercussions on Greek politics, both internal and external. Greece joined Britain and the League of Nations in the sanctions against Italy, and thus initiated a policy that became increasingly opposed to Italy. The Greek Foreign Minister asked to see Anthony Eden in Geneva on 8 October, and assured him that Greece would be prepared to play her part in any economic sanctions that might be agreed on by the members of the League under Article 16 of the League Charter, despite the serious economic and political repercussions which would inevitably follow. Maximos also broached the issue of the monarchy, and told Eden that in the present anomalous situation in Greece, it would be better not to hold a plebiscite, but to effect a restoration by means of a vote of the Chamber.[2]

The *coup d'état* of 10 October presented the British Government with a delicate issue at a most difficult time. Waterlow was of the opinion that, if the King were to return, he would rest on bayonets, a structure as 'fragile' as it would be uncomfortable. He, therefore, advised that the King should be persuaded not to return, and that the Foreign Office should withhold recognition of the new regime.[3] Waterlow also confided that the King was privy to the *coup d'état*, and the Foreign Office took the same view.[4] The Greek Minister in London assured the Foreign Office at the same time that the change of regime in Greece would not affect foreign policy, one indication being that Maximos remained Greece's chief delegate at Geneva. Theotokis, the new Greek Foreign Minister, gave Waterlow similar assurances, and expressed his satisfaction at being able to have 'direct and continuous' relations with the

---

[1] Merkouris, op. cit., pp. 215 ff.

[2] Message from Eden, Geneva Tel. No. 193, 8 Oct. 1935, F.O. 371/19508. The Foreign Office agreed that a restoration through Parliament was preferable.

[3] Athens Tel. No. 244, 11 Oct. 1935, F.O. 371/19508.

[4] Athens Tel. No. 240, 10 Oct. 1935, F.O. 371/19508.

British Government. Theotokis also gave Waterlow official notice of the change of regime in Greece.[1]

The British Government was faced with a serious dilemma: they wished to stay out of the internal affairs of Greece; yet, they needed the co-operation of the Greek Government in the present international crisis, and in a possible emergency in the Mediterranean. Recognition of the new regime, however, was tantamount to recognizing a restoration of the monarchy by force. But from now on the Abyssinian crisis acted as a catalyst in the formulation of British policy towards Greece and Greek affairs. Hitherto, the British Government had followed events and issues in Greece as an interested spectator; thereafter, the British Government became a participant in Greek affairs. The Foreign Office favoured recognition of the new regime, arguing that the British Government should do nothing to alienate it. 'Should a sudden emergency arise in the Mediterranean,' they argued, 'the friendly collaboration of the Greek Government— whether *de facto* or *de jure*, revolutionary or constitutional—may be of vital importance.' Greece seemed to be 'behaving satisfactorily at Geneva', wrote Vansittart.[2] They decided, therefore, that the British Minister in Athens should immediately enter into personal relations with General Kondylis, and they instructed him accordingly.

We think that the present political situation, in which we might at any time require the goodwill and friendly co-operation of the Greek Government, renders it desirable that you should enter into personal relations with General Kondylis and other Ministers, whether there be official recognition of the new regime or not. As for official recognition, the sooner it can be safely effected the better from the point of view of British interests. Delay merely on technical grounds is, in view of the international situation, to be deprecated.

You should acknowledge receipt without delay of the official note from the Minister for Foreign Affairs and in doing so make a suitable response to the remark regarding the establishment of 'direct and continuous' relations with us.[3]

The Foreign Office also approached King George. Sir Robert Vansittart undertook to brief Sir Samuel Hoare on the issue of

[1] Letter from Simopoulos to Sir Samuel Hoare, 12 Oct. 1935, F.O. 371/19509; Athens Tel. No. 245, 12 Oct. 1935, F.O. 371/19509.

[2] F.O. Minutes, Oct. 1935, F.O. 371/19508.

[3] F.O. Tel. 15 Oct., F.O. 371/19508.

recognition, before Hoare met King George. In a note for the Secretary of State, with which the latter agreed 'entirely', Vansittart repeated the argument about the 'good behaviour' of Greece at Geneva, and added that Greece was actually trying to order aircraft in Britain for use against a possible Italian attack. Vansittart then proposed the following line of argument with King George:

> You might say that you would have felt happier on his account if he had been returning on a free vote of the great majority of the population, but that in any circumstances you wish him well and will of course make no difficulties in matters where it is possible to assist him, such as that of recognition; and you hope that he for his part will give us the maximum of co-operation of his country.[1]

The meeting between the Secretary of State and King George took place on 16 October. To the King's inquiry about the attitude of the British Government over his restoration, Hoare replied that, given so many disquieting features in Greece, the British Government could neither encourage nor discourage the restoration; assuming, however, that the monarchy was re-established, the British Government would make no difficulties or delay recognition, and would wish to see it established firmly. The King also inquired whether it was possible to let him have British advisers for the army, navy, and air force of Greece. Hoare assured King George that the British Government would look favourably on such a request, if and when the monarchy was re-established. Summing up the interview, Hoare wrote: 'I gave him [the King] neither encouragement nor discouragement. I take, however, the view that as the restoration is now inevitable, we had much better do everything that we legitimately can to help to make the Monarchy as secure as possible. This should be our line both in London and in Athens.'[2]

From this time forward the Foreign Office developed an attitude towards Greece that depended to a large extent on the position of King George. Their deep distrust of Greek politicians, and the readiness of King George to work in close co-operation with Britain, made the Foreign Office see a useful friend in him. Britain needed a friendly and, if possible, a dependable Greece;

---

[1] Note by Vansittart, 14 Oct. 1935, F.O. 371/19508.
[2] Memo. by the Secretary of State, 16 Oct., F.O. 371/19508.

and the presence of King George would guarantee both considerations, as far as the Foreign Office was concerned. All
previous misgivings over anomalous political developments
were brushed aside. The Greek Minister was told during one
of his frequent calls at the Foreign Office that the British
Government were well disposed towards the restoration of the
monarchy, and they considered the return of King George as
the last *à tout* of Greece.[1]

The notorious plebiscite of November 1935 gave King
George the pretext to return. The plebiscite was rigged in the
best Greek manner: with martial law still on, blue ballots for
the monarchy and red for the Republic. Kondylis and his men
surpassed themselves in their effort to give the monarchy as
large a majority as possible, and announced that the monarchy
had received 97 per cent of the votes.[2] The British Minister in
Athens wrote that the proceedings of the plebiscite were
a 'farce' and the result 'ridiculous'; and the Foreign Office took
the same view, not without some discomfort.[3] Vansittart, when
he was not thinking of Greece in terms of Geneva, always
referred to Kondylis either as 'gangster', or 'ex-commitadji';
and later he wrote of the plebiscite and its result, not without
some truth: 'Any figures were acceptable because no regimes
were.'[4]

Before setting off for Greece King George saw Sir Robert
Vansittart, and discussed with him some matters of immediate
importance. The Greek Government had recently tried to
order aeroplanes in Britain, and the King asked that the British
Government should support the order. King George also
confided that he would be quite alone in Greece, with no
advisers, except those friends he had made during his exile.
He wished therefore to have British advisers in all branches of
the armed forces, instead of the present French Mission. The
French, he said, had destroyed discipline in the Greek army
by their excessive attempts at democratizing it. The Foreign

---

[1] Letter from Simopoulos to the Greek Foreign Minister, 15 Nov. 1935, Simopoulos Papers.

[2] Pesmatzoglou, op. cit., p. 81; Daphnis, op. cit., vol. ii, pp. 390, 391; Linardatos,
op. cit., p. 124; Bert Birtles has a colourful account of the plebiscite in his book
Exiles in the Aegean, London, 1938, pp. 54 ff.

[3] Athens Tel. No. 270, 4 Nov. 1935, F.O. 371/19509.

[4] Lord Vansittart, *The Mist Procession*, London, 1958, p. 557.

Office promised to give him their 'moral support' by way of early recognition, since they could not see much hope for material support, such as aircraft. They therefore instructed Waterlow to show himself as cordial and sympathetic to the King as possible, and to give him help and advice as far as he properly could; and, in conclusion, they explained to the Minister: 'There are so many subjects, ranging from sanctions to Anglo-Greek commercial relations, on which we may hope to profit by the King's goodwill, that we must leave no stone unturned to secure and keep it.'[1]

The British Government was engaged at this time in a parallel policy towards Italy.[2] The British backed the League of Nations in its quarrel with Italy over Abyssinia, and at the same time supported the scheme known as the Hoare–Laval plan. Early in November 1935, Mussolini had approached the British Government to explore the possibility of a general *détente* in the Mediterranean, by which Italy would agree to some sort of limitation in the ratio of British and Italian naval strengths in that area. The Italian approach was tempting, but the Foreign Office, and especially its Southern Department, was very much concerned over the effect of any agreement with Italy on Yugoslavia, Greece, and Turkey. These states were exceedingly sensitive to any alterations in relative British and Italian strengths in the Mediterranean. Even the knowledge that an agreement was being discussed about the actual or potential exercise of British sea-power in the Eastern Mediterranean might have far-reaching consequences.[3] The Abyssinian crisis, however, had revealed to the British Government the glaring deficiencies of British power and potentialities in an uncertain international situation. Faced by Germany and Japan, which were becoming increasingly hostile, Britain, it was argued, could not adopt a policy that ensured a permanently hostile Italy.[4] There were strong arguments for a conciliatory

[1] Note of interview, 5 Nov. 1935, and letter to Waterlow from Vansittart, 11 Nov. 1935, F.O. 371/19509. In his reply on 15 Nov. Waterlow said he had already let the King know 'through more than one channel' that he would find in the Minister of Britain 'a friend sincerely anxious to help him'. F.O. 341/19509.

[2] Viscount Templewood, *Nine Troubled Years*, London, 1954, p. 161.

[3] F.O. Memo., 6 Nov. 1935, F.O. 371/20381.

[4] The deficiencies of British power and arguments for reconciliation with Italy are set out in a report by the Defence Requirements Sub-Committee, 21 Nov. 1935, C.P. 26 (36), Cab. 24/259.

policy towards Italy, and these arguments were put forward throughout the second half of the thirties. The assurances given by the British Government to the small Mediterranean states, Greece included, in December 1935, in connection with their sanctions policy under Article 16 of the League Charter, were always looked on by the British Government and Services without any enthusiasm.

The Greek Government faced a similar dilemma: they wanted to co-operate with the British Government against Italian designs in the Eastern Mediterranean; at the same time, they wished to avoid provoking Italy. The sanctions policy of Greece had already estranged Italy to some extent, and the British assurance of December contributed to this.[1] The Greek Services, especially the Navy, were apprehensive of the Italian menace. The Greek Naval Staff considered the British assurance to Greece during the Abyssinian crisis 'insufficient' and 'vague'. Greece, they argued, could not depend for her safety on Britain's promise to come to her assistance, were she to become a victim of Italian aggression. What was vital for Greece was not belated assistance after an Italian attack, but rather the 'prevention' of such an attack. And as long as British naval and air forces could not be stationed in appropriate positions in Greece, prevention of an Italian attack was impossible.[2]

The Greek Government, however, were never able to impress on the British Government this vital point. Britain needed a friendly Greece, not an allied Greece; and the restoration of a friendly monarch to the throne of Greece had secured to Britain the association desired by the British Government. Internal political developments in Greece since the abortive rising of March 1935 had worked for the return of King George; and the international situation during the autumn of that year contributed to the association of Britain with this restoration, and with Greek affairs in general. It can be safely stated that circumstances, rather than a definite policy, drew Britain towards Greece, though the same cannot be maintained of Greece's policy. The Greek Government deliberately chose to work in close co-operation with Britain, disregarding the

[1] The Greek Prime Minister to Simopoulos, Tel. No. 88038, 9 Dec. 1935, Simopoulos Papers.

[2] Memo. by Greek Naval Staff, No. 18, 27 June 1936, Metaxas Papers.

misgivings of the Chiefs of Staff, in the pursuit of a definite policy, apart from any role played by circumstances. Fear of Italy was of course the main factor; and their wish to get British approval and support for the return of King George certainly influenced their decisions. Both governments considered the King useful in the pursuit of their immediate or long-term interests. The British Government saw in him a dependable friend whose insecure position would depend for stability to a considerable extent on Britain, while the Greek Government saw in him a powerful patron who carried with him a Great Power. King George became thus the key figure in Anglo-Greek relations, and was to remain so as long as the situation in the Mediterranean, as well as the political situation in Greece, did not improve.

British and Greek Political and Strategic Considerations

The war of 1935–6 between Italy and Ethiopia, and the subsequent Italian conquest of Ethiopia caused a major international crisis. The League of Nations, under the aegis of Britain and France, condemned Italy's aggression, and adopted a policy of economic sanctions against the aggressor. Britain, as already mentioned, pursued a double policy towards Italy throughout the crisis, and sought reconciliation with her, despite sanctions. The British Cabinet and the Admiralty wanted this reconciliation because of the tense situation both in the Far East and Europe, especially after the Rhineland crisis of March 1936. The Italian victory, therefore, came as a relief to both Britain and France, and the two Powers gave a prompt lead towards the abandonment of sanctions by the League.

Reconciliation, however, could not be effected easily. Public opinion in Britain was outraged by the Italian aggression, and the small Mediterranean states which had ranged themselves along with Britain and the League were apprehensive of Italian designs. Turkey, Greece, and Yugoslavia looked to Britain for support against possible Italian expansion in the Mediterranean, and regarded an Anglo-Italian settlement with much suspicion and concern. An Anglo-Greek–Turkish Pact might have been one solution for Britain, except that it was bound to alienate Italy further; and present circumstances were not conducive and appropriate for a general Mediterranean Pact that would include Italy.

The immediate problem, however, was how to end sanctions as painlessly as possible. Britain had suffered a serious rebuff in the Abyssinian affair, and the British Government tried to make the best of it. In May 1936 the conquest of Abyssinia was almost complete, and the Foreign Office tried to formulate a policy for the period immediately after sanctions were lifted. They considered possible steps that would reassure the Balkan and East Mediterranean countries, if sanctions were removed in June as was generally expected; for these countries would be automatically deprived of the guarantee by other League members, and more particularly by Britain and France, which they had enjoyed under Article 16 of the League Charter. The simplest way of reassuring Greece and Turkey would be a public declaration by Britain, and if possible by France, both at Geneva and in Parliament, to the effect that if, during the period of crisis, those Mediterranean states which had collaborated with Britain and France in applying sanctions were attacked by Italy they would be assisted by France and Britain in the way contemplated during the sanctions period. It was further argued that, in return for this protection, Britain might be able to obtain from Greece and Turkey valuable concessions regarding the use of their territorial waters and harbours by the British Fleet. Such concessions would greatly restore British prestige in the area, while the commitment to protect them was one which British vital interests would impose on Britain in any case.[1] The Foreign Office finally decided that any declaration should be unilateral and as general as possible. Britain would declare that she would protect her collaborators in case of any aggression consequent on such collaboration. In this way, Britain would be the sole judge as to the time limit of this protection. Public opinion in Britain would understand and even welcome such a declaration as an 'honourable' corollary to Britain's collaboration with these states over sanctions. After this initial step, the Foreign Office contemplated

[1] F.O. Memorandum, 22 May 1936, F.O. 371/20382. See also F.O. Minutes, April 1936, F.O. 371/20381.

the possibility of ultimately 'concretizing' the general declaration into a partial pact.[1]

All these arguments were presented to the Cabinet on 17 June 1936 in the form of a Memorandum.[2] The Foreign Office argued in this paper that a general Mediterranean pact was either impracticable or unsuitable for the immediate objects in view, and it would be more sensible, as far as Britain was concerned, simply to renew the assurances to the lesser Mediterranean states. In return, Greece and Turkey could allow the British Fleet to use their harbours, and an appropriate Anglo-Greek–Turkish scheme could be negotiated as circumstances arose. An Anglo-Greek–Turkish agreement, the Foreign Office argued, would protect British lines of communication, enhance British prestige, and strengthen the Balkan Entente; it would also act as a warning to Italy, would have a stabilizing effect on Egypt, Palestine, and Iraq, and might counteract the growing influence of Germany in Greece and Turkey.

The issues involved were certainly of major importance, and the Cabinet postponed consideration of this Foreign Office Paper until their next regular meeting, by which time they would also have the views of the Chiefs of Staff Committee, which were before the Cabinet at their meeting of 23 June.[3] Meanwhile, Eden had made a declaration in the House of Commons on 18 June, to the effect that the assurances given to the small Mediterranean states under Article 16 of the Covenant in December 1935 would not end with the lifting of sanctions by the Assembly, but would continue to cover the period of uncertainty which was bound to follow the termination of action by the League. Eden added that the British Government regarded an eventuality of the kind that those assurances covered as 'hypothetical' and 'improbable'.[4]

According to the Chiefs of Staff, although Britain wanted a friendly Greece and Turkey, it was most desirable that this end should be achieved without increasing or perpetuating the existing tension in the Mediterranean; and the assistance Britain could expect from these states was very small compared

---

[1] Memorandum by Vansittart, 4 June 1936, F.O. 371/20382.

[2] Memorandum by Eden, 'Problems Facing H.M.G. in the Mediterranean as a Result of the Italo-League Dispute', 11 June 1936, C.P. 165 (36), Cab. 24/262.

[3] Extracts from the Cabinet Conclusions of 17 and 23 June in F.O. 371/20381.

[4] Eden's Declaration in R3565/294/67, F.O. 371/20381.

with what Britain was proposing to give. The Minister for Co-ordination of Defence assured the Cabinet that the Chiefs of Staff had no intention of disagreeing with the statement made by the Foreign Minister in the House about the assurances to the small Mediterranean states. They did object, however, to the assumption of any new commitment in the Mediterranean. It was therefore decided that the Foreign Minister, in his coming declaration at Geneva, should avoid giving any provocation of Italy, and at the same time should reassure Greece, Turkey, and Yugoslavia. The Cabinet also decided that the Chiefs of Staff should further consider an Eastern Mediterranean Pact with Greece and Turkey.[1]

Consequently, the British Foreign Minister made a declaration at Geneva on 1 July 1936, on the same lines as his statement in the House of Commons in June. The Foreign Office also tried to explain to the Italian Government their position in relation to the assurances of December 1935. This position, it was explained, had been stated in the Declarations by the British Foreign Minister; as for the rest, the subject was largely one of 'academic interest', and the eventuality covered by the Declarations was not only hypothetical but improbable.[2] At the same time, the Foreign Office approached the Italian Government with the suggestion that the situation might be greatly eased if Italy gave the three smaller Mediterranean states assurances of her peaceful intentions. Naturally, the Italian Foreign Minister was only too glad to accept this suggestion, and informed the British Government that he was instructing the Italian representatives at the capitals of the three states concerned to make a statement to that effect. Count Ciano also emphasized in his reply to the British Government that he desired to get the question of the British Mediterranean Declarations out of the way in order that normal friendly relations between Italy and Britain could be resumed.[3]

To all appearances, the Italian 'line' of the British Government was alive again. Eden soon made yet another statement in the House of Commons about the assurances to the small Mediterranean states. These assurances, he reminded Members,

---

[1] Extracts from Cabinet Conclusions, 23 June 1936, in F.O. 371/20381.
[2] F.O. Tel. No. 253 to Rome, 11 July 1936, F.O. 371/20382.
[3] Rome Tel. No. 458, 13 July 1936, F.O. 371/20382.

were meant to cover the period of uncertainty following the termination of sanctions by the League. Eden then said that Italy had recently given assurances to Greece, Turkey, and Yugoslavia of her peaceful intentions, and had told them that she had never contemplated, nor was she now contemplating, aggressive action against any of them in retaliation for their past sanctions policy. Therefore, the Foreign Minister stated, this period of uncertainty was at an end; and he concluded that in the view of the British Government there was no further necessity for the continuance of the assurances.[1]

Thus the temporary extension of the assurances, which had been mainly 'face-saving and for home consumption',[2] was brought to an end. The assurances had had an anti-Italian character, and this was opposed by both the Cabinet and the Services, which pressed the Foreign Office for their withdrawal. In fact, the exchanges between Britain and Italy in July 1936 had contributed to a reduction of tension in the Mediterranean. Britain had withdrawn her assurances to the smaller Mediterranean states at the same time as Italy had given assurances of her peaceful intentions to the same states. These exchanges could become the basis of an Anglo-Italian *rapprochement* but the Foreign Office felt that public opinion in Britain would not easily accept an Anglo-Italian understanding at so early a stage. The Spanish Civil War that soon broke out made an understanding even more complicated and difficult to deal with. So the Foreign Office had to content itself with an understanding of no real content in the form of the Anglo-Italian Agreement of January 1937.

The proposed Anglo-Greek–Turkish understanding also ended in a similar result. If British public opinion and the Foreign Office were not prepared to accept an understanding with Italy, the Chiefs of Staff could not recommend an understanding with Greece and Turkey. They gave their views in a Memorandum of 29 July 1936, in which they recommended the report by the Joint Planning Sub-Committee on an understanding with Greece and Turkey—a report drawn at the request of the Cabinet. The Chiefs of Staff argued that the first

---

[1] Eden's Declaration in the House of Commons, 27 July 1936, in F.O. 371/20383. A. Eden, *Facing the Dictators*, London, 1962, pp. 421, 422.
[2] Vansittart in a marginal minute, Oct. 1936, F.O. 371/20383.

desideratum from the strategic point of view was a secure Mediterranean, and that this involved, as the 'primary consideration', the restoration of Britain's former friendly relations with Italy. Any steps that could be taken to renew a peaceful situation in the Mediterranean would be an advantage from the strategic point of view. They felt, however, that any such steps should be subject to this primary consideration, and that no action should be taken which was liable to prejudice it. They further argued that, though it was important to keep Greece and Turkey friendly to Britain, present circumstances were not favourable to the acceptance of fresh military commitments; and assurances 'only too readily could be taken as pledges of support'. Their concluding recommendation was that nothing should be done that was liable to alienate Italy, and that no new military commitments should be undertaken.[1]

The report by the Joint Planners, on which the Chiefs of Staff had based their decision, studied the advantages and disadvantages of a pact with Greece and Turkey. It was very important, as far as Greece was concerned, since it had a major effect on the decisions of the British Government regarding all matters of Anglo-Greek relations of a political or military character, not only in 1936 but from then till the outbreak of the war.[2] The Joint Planners argued that the advantages Britain might hope to gain from an understanding with Greece were the use of harbours and aerodromes in Greek territory in time of war. The geographical position of these bases would simplify the problem of controlling the Central Mediterranean and the Aegean Sea, and would enable the British to launch air attacks against Italy. According to the report, however,

even this advantage is qualified by the probability that internal economic conditions and lack of internal communications in Greece would make the maintenance of our air forces in the country difficult. Moreover, the Greeks are poor fighters and the military problem of protecting their country against Italy in war would be a very difficult one. Greece lies so close to Italian aerodromes that a heavy scale of air attack could be directed by Italy against any military bases established in that country. We should also be

[1] C.O.S. 506, Secret, 'Eastern Mediterranean: Understanding with Greece and Turkey', 29 July 1936, in F.O. 371/20383.
[2] J.P. 164, 21 July 1936, F.O. 371/20383.

committed to the maintenance of Greek sea communications, which would be a commitment, in some respects, greater than maintaining our own, as for us there are routes alternative to the Mediterranean.

An understanding with Greece also entailed the danger that Britain might become involved in hostilities in connection with inter-Balkan quarrels. The Joint Planners therefore concluded that Britain would lose much more than she would gain by an understanding with Greece.

Strategy thus put limits to British policy. Moreover, the Chiefs of Staff themselves made an attempt at formulating policy. In a report of 21 July 1936, they recommended that British policy and liabilities should be freed from the 'vague, wholesale and largely unpredictable' military commitments Britain was at present incurring under the League Covenant. They argued that her problems in the Eastern Mediterranean might best be solved by a strong and friendly Balkan Entente. Greece might be induced to provide Bulgaria with an outlet in the Aegean, and thereby draw that country into the Entente.[1] The response of the Foreign Office to these arguments was justifiably resentful: the Chiefs of Staff could properly answer 'technical' questions on strategy, but ought not to put forward a 'political' assessment or an analysis of British policy.[2]

Britain's association with the small Mediterranean states could not safely depend on either the League Covenant, or the Balkan Entente. A direct solution, however, such as an Anglo-Greek–Turkish pact, or a general Mediterranean understanding, was ruled out, as has already been seen. Britain was still not prepared to enter into definite alliances with foreign states, and continued to search for indirect formulas of associations and alignments until her rearmament programme was sufficiently advanced to allow her to undertake commitments arising from definite combinations.

So far as Greece was concerned, she had ceased by now to count even as a pawn, and the Greek Government increasingly followed Britain's lead in foreign affairs. At the same time, as the lines in Europe began to be drawn, the Greek Government professed a sort of neutralism that was suspect and convinced

---

[1] C.O.S. 497, 21 July 1936, in F.O. 371/19910.
[2] F.O. Letter to the Committee of Imperial Defence, 15 Aug. 1936, in F.O. 371/19910.

neither Italy nor Germany. Greece, it was true, was attracted by economic baits held out in Germany, and was kept in constant fear by Mussolini's demands for 'rispetto timoroso'. But she clung to the illusion that she might be able to buy British support, and work out a political association with Britain. The long tradition of Anglo-Greek co-operation and friendship made the Greek Government take for granted British support in all circumstances, and this prompted it to follow, despite the serious and repeated warnings of the Greek Chiefs of Staff, a policy which depended to a great extent on Britain.

Greece tried to neutralize the dangers that emanated from Bulgaria and Italy, her two potential enemies, by joining the forces thought to be opposed to them. She joined the Balkan Entente in order to meet the Bulgarian danger, and associated herself with Britain against Italy. The Greek Government never seriously considered an alternative or even a parallel policy towards Bulgaria and Italy. It is true that no meaningful reconciliation with Bulgaria could have been effected short of conceding to Bulgaria an Aegean outlet, and this Greece was simply not prepared to concede. Equally, friendship with Italy would have been difficult to achieve in the face of Italian expansionist policy in the Balkans, and the presence of Italy in the Dodecanese. Still, Greece might have been able to evolve a policy towards *i*taly and Bulgaria which they could have interpreted as, if not friendly, at least not potentially hostile.

The position of Greece, as the cohesion of the Balkan Entente decreased, became unenviable. Of the three members of the Entente with access to the Mediterranean, Yugoslavia, reconciled with Bulgaria and courted by both Germany and Italy, was in a relatively good position, while Turkey was comparatively remote from the storm centre. Greece, on the other hand, faced a choice between remaining in an increasingly impotent combination, or withdrawing into isolation which might result in her having to face a possible Bulgarian *revanche* alone.[1] She chose to remain in the Balkan Entente, as she sided with Britain *vis-à-vis* a menacing Italy. By the time war broke out, her association with her Balkan partners had become meaningless, while her hope of securing prompt and adequate support

[1] 'The Loosening of the Balkan and Little Entente', R.I.I.A., *Survey of International Affairs*, 1936, pp. 516, 517.

against Italy by means of an Anglo-Greek alliance became a mirage.

It is essential at this stage to examine the strategic position of Greece as seen by the Greek General Staff. At the beginning of the Abyssinian crisis, they presented the Greek Government with a gloomy picture of the armed forces and the potential power of the country in case of war.[1] The army lacked sufficient supplies in war material, and this made mobilization at the time, or in the near future, problematical. The navy had only a few serviceable destroyers and submarines, and there was no coastal defence at all. The air force was weak, and lacked both modern machines and trained personnel. The Chiefs of Staff were apprehensive that Bulgaria would attack Greece while she was preoccupied in the south against Italy. They reached the following conclusion, which constituted a serious warning to the Greek Government:

The danger from the North is so serious, and the military weakness of Greece so great, that any thought of Greece's participation in an Anglo-Italian war must be ruled out, if the north-eastern borders of the country are not absolutely guaranteed. This danger cannot be compensated for by any support that could be offered.

In January 1936 the Chiefs of Staff further considered the strategic position of the country should war break out between Britain and Italy.[2] The participation of Greece in such a war, they argued, presupposed (*a*) the supply by Britain of war material, such as ammunition, aircraft, and anti-aircraft guns and coastal guns; (*b*) the guarantee of the northern borders; (*c*) the prompt and effective covering of the country by the British Fleet; and (*d*) the protection of the population from air attacks. Any commitment, they warned, on the part of Greece to assist Britain, short of the above assumptions, would constitute a 'crime' against the country.

In the light of this appreciation the attitude of the Greek Government was at best a dangerous gamble. They had repeatedly assured the British that Greece would support them in sanctions against Italy, and in the case of open hostilities

[1] Memorandum by the Greek Chiefs of Staff, No. 3620, Secret, 8 Oct. 1935, Metaxas Papers. See also *Diary*, vol. iv, pp. 615 ff.

[2] Memorandum by the Greek Chiefs of Staff, No. 29231, Secret, 20 Jan. 1936, Metaxas Papers.

with Italy. The Greek Government also accepted the assurances of June 1936, which Britain offered unilaterally in order to preclude bilateral discussions, and to avoid the undertaking of any definitive commitment towards the countries concerned. These assurances, incidentally, became a precedent for the Anglo-French Guarantee of April 1939 to Greece and Romania. As in 1936 the Anglo-French assurances of 1939 were unilateral, and essentially face-saving and for home consumption. The Greek Government accepted the assurances of June 1936 with 'lively' satisfaction, and assured the British Government that Greece was determined to follow Britain's lead in Mediterranean affairs.[1] Metaxas confided to the British Minister in Athens in August 1936 that he was satisfied at the present state of Anglo-Greek relations, and that he was 'grateful' for Britain's friendly attitude towards Greece.[2] It is rather doubtful whether Britain, if it had not been for King George and Metaxas, would have been able to work out an association with Greece, which left Britain unquestionably the lead, and reduced Greece to a state of impotence, and grateful impotence at that.

[1] Athens Tel. No. 27 Saving, 25 June 1936, F.O. 371/20381, and Athens Tel. No. 146, 16 July 1936, F.O. 371/20382.
[2] Athens Tel. No. 269, 6 Aug. 1936, F.O. 371/20383.

II

Political Crisis and Dictatorship

Political Deadlock

On 4 August 1936, and with the approval of King George, Metaxas proclaimed a state of martial law, the suspension of key articles of the Constitution, and the dissolution of Parliament. Thus began four-and-a-half years of dictatorial rule in Greece. Metaxas proclaimed the dictatorship allegedly to forestall an attempt by the Communists to seize power. The threat was certainly not without substance in the minds of the Greek Communist Party, but it is very likely that Metaxas exaggerated its immediate significance and was simply grateful for this convenient pretext to seize power. Lacking popular support or any backing in the army, he was able to establish the dictatorship with the support of only the King and a circle of devoted followers. The political world of Greece, that select coterie of over-clever men, allowed itself to remain paralysed in suspicious silence. Greece slipped into dictatorship, while her political leaders stood by, unable to call the body politic of the country as a whole into action. The general disregard for legality of the previous years had discredited both the political world and parliamentary government. Dictatorship seemed a relatively small anomaly. It was accepted passively, without enthusiasm or protest, but with some uncertain hope of securing order and stability.

On his return to Greece in November 1935, King George dismissed Kondylis, and appointed a caretaker government under Konstantinos Demertzis to supervise the next elections. He also gave an amnesty to the political leaders of the March rising, and pardoned its military leaders. These moves won him much sympathy in both political camps, and would have surely secured the whole-hearted support of the Venizelists if he had extended the amnesty to the military rebels, for pardon

did not carry reinstatement in the army. According to Sir
Sydney Waterlow, King George had a rooted determination,
which amounted to a 'mental block', not to readmit to the
army even a selection of the expelled Venizelist officers.[1] There
is little doubt that he nursed a strong dislike for Venizelist
leaders, politicians and military alike; his decision, however,
not to readmit the Venizelist officers to the army seems to have
been due more to pressure from the royalist officers, as will
be seen shortly, than to his personal feelings. At this stage, he
was in a co-operative and conciliatory mood. He was also
cautious. But time and events soon wore down the King's
apparent cautiousness, and he developed instead an impatience
with Greek politics which led him into rash decisions.

The elections of 26 January 1936, the last in pre-war Greece,
returned both major camps in almost equal strength, and thus
resulted in a political deadlock.[2] The Communists, with only
fifteen seats in the Chamber, became arbiters of the situation,
and their favour was coveted by both camps. The elections had
been held under the system of proportional representation,
since it was thought that the ordinary majority system would
certainly have resulted in a large republican majority.
Demertzis explained to Waterlow a month before the elections
that he had decided to hold the elections under this system, not
out of any preference for it, but because the majority system
would return a 'very large' republican majority, which he
wished to avoid, since it would revive the issue of the 1,200
cashiered Venizelist officers. As Demertzis admitted, Greek
politics in the final analysis turned on control of the army.[3]

The issue of the Venizelist officers separated the two political
camps like oil from water. They each approached the Communists with a variety of offers and enticements. The Venizelists
finally succeeded in clinching a marriage of convenience: it was
the ill-starred Sophoulis–Sklavainas Pact of 19 February.
According to the agreement signed by the two leaders, the

[1] Athens Disp. No. 281, 12 Aug. 1936, F.O. 371/20390.
[2] Of the 300 seats in the Chamber, the anti-Venizelists won 143, the Venizelists
141, the Communists 15. Metaxas, in the anti-Venizelist camp, won 7 seats. Daphnis,
op. cit., vol. ii, p. 402.
[3] Athens Disp. No. 536, 27 Dec. 1936, F.O. 371/19509. Demertzis believed that
the Venizelists would win anyhow, and both he and Waterlow felt that it was
necessary that their majority should be of a 'moderate' size.

Communists undertook to support the Liberal candidate for the President of the Chamber, while the Liberals promised among other things to repeal the anti-Communist Law 4229, to give an amnesty to Communist Members of Parliament, as well as to all political prisoners and exiles, and to dissolve all fascist organizations.[1] It was a successful bargain as far as the participants were concerned, since both sides had secured what they wanted for the moment: the Liberals had won support in Parliament, while the Communists, after many years, would escape from anti-Communist legislation and persecution. As it happened, the notorious Law 4229 had been passed and put into effect in 1929 under the last Venizelos Government, of which Sophoulis was a member. The old foes apparently had little time for qualms or embarrassment.

At this stage the army intervened. On 5 March 1936 General Papagos, Minister for Army Affairs, with the approval of the Chiefs of the Air Force, Navy, Police, and Gendarmerie, visited the King, and informed him that the Armed Forces and the Security Services would not tolerate a government supported by the Communists. It was a challenge that King George accepted without comment. On Papagos's departure, the King called Metaxas, and offered him the Ministry for Army Affairs. The offer was accepted. The Army did not resist, and the King's *coup* was successful.[2] Metaxas had been in touch with King George and seems to have impressed him with what he referred to as his 'solution' of the political crisis.[3] The appointment to the Ministry for Army Affairs was Metaxas's first step to power. On the day of his appointment, he wrote with satisfaction and some pride: '. . . [I am] in complete control of the situation'.[4]

The appointment of Metaxas was greeted with undisguised relief by Venizelos, of all people.[5] It was the old statesman's last public utterance. He died in Paris soon afterwards. A few days later, Metaxas also assumed the key post of Vice-President of the Council, while retaining the Ministry for Army Affairs. On 15 March he made the following statement:

---

[1] *Official Documents of the Greek Communist Party* (in Greek), vol. iv, Athens, 1974, pp. 342–3. See also Daphnis, op. cit., vol. ii, pp. 416, 417.

[2] Ibid., pp. 405–7.   [3] *Diary*, vol. iv, p. 196, 27 Feb. 1936.

[4] Ibid., p. 197, 5 Mar. 1936.   [5] Daphnis, op. cit., vol. ii, pp. 406–7.

We are a provisional Government, which will eventually give place to a government of the parties. Naturally, we are prepared to step down at this very moment if we are denied the Chamber's vote of confidence . . .

For, as far as I am concerned, it is my conviction that Greece cannot possibly abandon the parliamentary system. I strongly believe that it would be disastrous for the country, were it to deviate from the parliamentary system.[1]

Those were misleading words, from a man who never in fact put much faith in representative democracy. Waterlow welcomed the inclusion of Metaxas in the Government, who although his record in World War I had been distinctly unsatisfactory from a British point of view, was devotedly loyal to the King, and seemed prepared to play the part of the 'strong man'. Waterlow also felt that the lack of regular parliamentary government should not be regretted. In the first place, he said, it was in the tradition of Greek politics; in the second place, it gave the King and the Government a 'breathing space' to do constructive work, unhampered by squabbles in the Chamber.[2]

At this time Greece also faced serious labour discontent and strikes, for which the State had no other treatment except force; strikers and demonstrators were its enemies, and were treated in a thoroughly vindictive manner. In early May 1936 the tobacco-workers struck for higher wages, basing their claim on an agreement of 1924 between them and the tobacco industry. On 8 May a body of almost 6,000 tobacco-workers clashed with the Gendarmerie in Salonika, and the rough methods employed to control these disorders prompted other workers, such as the railwaymen and tramworkers, to strike in sympathy.[3] The Government responded with a decree mobilizing the railwaymen and tramworkers: it was a shrewdly conceived measure, since once a mobilization order was issued, workers staying away from work were no longer merely strikers but military deserters and therefore liable to imprisonment.[4] The Government also called in the 3rd Army Corps, stationed in Salonika, to assist the Gendarmerie in containing

---

[1] *Diary*, vol. iv, pp. 198–9, 15 Mar. 1936.

[2] Athens Disp. No. 118, 18 Mar. 1936, F.O. 371/20389.

[3] Daphnis, op. cit., vol. ii, pp. 423 ff.

[4] Birtles, op. cit., p. 259. Mobilization of striking workers and civil servants is in fact an accepted Greek practice.

the demonstrating workers in the city. These measures, however, were the signal for other trades to strike as well, and the number of strikers rose to 25,000. The shopkeepers shut their shops ostensibly in support of the workers, or perhaps in fear of disorders. On 9 May a huge demonstration converged on the area around Government House, and pitched battles between the demonstrators and the Gendarmerie ensued. The toll of the clashes was 12 dead and more than 200 wounded, all of them demonstrators. The Salonika daily press raised a cry against the 'bloodthirsty centaurs' of the Gendarmerie, and attacked the authorities for shedding the blood of 'innocent workers'.[1] The brutality of the Gendarmerie caused a considerable outcry and revulsion throughout the country, and the Government was held responsible for the massacre of the unarmed demonstrators.[2]

On 13 May a general strike was declared by the Trade Unions in protest at the Salonika killings. The previous day the Central Committee of the Greek Communist Party had declared: 'The whole of Greece has been transformed into a gigantic popular volcano. The people are rising against the murderers . . .'[3] But the Communists, for all their high-flown talk, were unable to spearhead a revolutionary struggle, simply because it was a sudden upsurge of popular anger, not a people's revolution. The public, instead, listened to the appeals of the local Members of Parliament for moderation and orderly conduct, and order was, in fact, quickly restored. The Government accepted all the demands of the tobacco-workers, and the strike was over;[4] although labour unrest continued throughout the summer of 1936.

The Salonika events and the brutal treatment of the workers were an ugly warning to many people, not only to workers. It added a new element of social strife to Greek politics. Increasingly labour unrest took on a political colouring which

---

[1] *Macedonia* and *Nea Alitheia*, 9 May 1936.
[2] Birtles, op. cit., p. 225; Daphnis, op. cit., vol. ii, pp. 423 ff.
[3] *Documents of the Greek Communist Party*, vol. iv, p. 366.
[4] Daphnis, op. cit., vol. ii, pp. 425, 426. The British Consul in Salonika reported at the time that labour unrest was due to real dissatisfaction over the present economic evils, rather than to Communist agitation; and that this dissatisfaction was expected to grow, as the Government of Metaxas refused to understand the real causes. Salonika reports of May and June 1936, F.O. 371/20389.

the Government was eager enough to exploit to secure its own position. In a statement after the Salonika riots, Metaxas said that it was clear to the Government that 'the aims of the leaders of the strike movement were political and subversive'.[1] A number of political leaders, Tsaldaris and Papanastasiou among them, attacked the Communists and their aims.[2] Greek politicians now seemed only too ready to give Metaxas enough rope to hang the Left, a convenient scapegoat, as it has so often been in Greece; only they were soon to discover that the aspiring dictator was reserving the other end for them.

Death, however, spared some of them the humiliation of life under dictatorial rule. Kondylis, Venizelos, Tsaldaris, and Papanastasiou died within the year, and left the stage open to King George and Metaxas. In April Demertzis also died, and Metaxas was conveniently installed as Premier. The coincidence of deaths was working in alliance with him. At a most critical period, Greece was deprived of the possible services of many political leaders, her government left in the hands of a non-parliamentary government. Waterlow, observing the Greek scene at this time, wrote to the Foreign Office that there was a possibility that parliamentary government might break down altogether; nevertheless, he was convinced that Greece was fortunate in having at this critical period a King who was impartial, averse to dictatorial methods, yet strong.[3] Sir Sydney, perhaps, could not be blamed at this stage for having left Metaxas out of the account. Quietly and discreetly he was planting his own men in key positions. He appointed old friends and collaborators as Governor-Generals, and Nomarchs (District Governors). On 18 May he also appointed Skylakakis, an old friend with fascist leanings, as Minister of the Interior; and later he introduced Papadimas as Minister for Army Affairs.

As summer approached, the Chamber adjourned, unable as yet to form a government. In mid-June Metaxas invited Sophocles Venizelos, Eleutherios's son, to become Vice-President of the Council in a dictatorial government. Venizelos

---

[1] *Diary*, vol. iv, p. 214.
[2] Birtles, op. cit., p. 331. See also S. Linardatos, *How We Reached the Fourth of August* (in Greek), 2nd edn., Athens, 1974, pp. 221, 228.
[3] Athens Disp. No. 137, 1 Apr. 1936, F.O. 371/20389.

agreed to participate, provided that the dictatorship was not of more than a year's duration, and provided that the Venizelist officers were reinstated. Metaxas accepted. The King, however, opposed the reinstatement of the officers, and when pressed by Venizelos on the issue kept mysteriously silent.[1] On 22 July Sophoulis also saw the King, and announced a recent agreement between the Liberals and the National Populists to form a government when Parliament resumed its sessions in October. King George congratulated the Liberal leader, and the same day informed Metaxas of the agreement. It is alleged that Metaxas summoned Skylakakis, Papadimas, and Diakos, a close friend and collaborator, and informed them that the King had given his consent for a dictatorship, which would be installed within the next fortnight.[2]

Waterlow considered the recent alliance of the Liberals and the National Populists 'unnatural', and he felt that what the politicians really wanted was to prevent Metaxas from putting through any business for which he would get credit, and an almost certain 'rake off' from the large contracts in Germany for war material that were imminent. Waterlow did not anticipate serious trouble, as long as the army remained loyal to the King; and though the prospects of a successful return to parliamentary government were not bright, the alternative of a dictatorship, which was 'repugnant' to the King's disposition, seemed equally impracticable. The British Minister rather felt that the present form of 'semi-dictatorship' would run its allotted course until the end of September.[3]

Metaxas and King George, however, had already decided on the dictatorship. Its date was conveniently furnished by the Workers' Federation, which had declared a 24-hour general strike for 5 August. Dictatorship was evidently not as 'repugnant' to the King as Waterlow believed, or as the King himself maintained.[4] Perhaps he gave his consent for its proclamation,

[1] G. Daphnis, *Sophocles Venizelos* (in Greek), Athens, 1970, pp. 152–3.
[2] Daphnis, *Greece Between Two Wars*, vol. ii, pp. 431, 432.
[3] Athens Disp. No. 264, 30 July 1936, F.O. 371/20390.
[4] Mr. Spyros Markezinis, legal adviser to the King at the time, told the author in an interview of 15 Sept. 1970 that he was present at a meeting between the King and Waterlow a few days before the *coup* of 4 Aug. 1936. According to Mr. Markezinis, Waterlow actually advised the King to establish a dictatorship, while the latter, taken aback by the suggestion, replied to the British Minister: 'Could you dare say that to your King?' It is unlikely that the Minister's 'advice' amounted

sincerely hoping that it would be short-lived. It also looks as if King George panicked as labour unrest mounted, and that he lost his nerve. In any case, he set aside his principles by allowing the suspension of free institutions. It is true that he had been faced since his return to Greece by a thoroughly unstable situation; yet the Constitution and the Parliament he suppressed in August 1936 were realities which he well understood and had sworn to defend. In his proposal to the King for the suspension of the Constitution and the proclamation of martial law, Metaxas maintained that the country was on the eve of a revolution, instigated and directed by the Communist Party. Communist propaganda, he said, had already infiltrated the civil service, and threatened to paralyse the state machinery; and it had begun the process of eroding the discipline of the armed forces.[1] In his declaration to the Greek people on the day martial law was proclaimed, Metaxas again stressed the Communist danger, and said that the Government had proclaimed martial law in order to forestall an imminent bid for power by the Communists.[2] Unfortunately there is no relevant material available, or any serious study, that might indicate the potential strength of the Communists in Greece during the summer of 1936. The numerical strength of the Communist Party in so far as it was revealed in the elections of January 1936 was quite small,[3] and should not be taken as evidence of the potential strength of the Communists at a time of rising labour discontent and public disorders.

The historian of the Greek Communist Party maintains that 'the sudden establishment of the Metaxas dictatorship cut short the *K.K.E.*'s[4] first serious effort to win power'.[5] This cannot be supported by any convincing evidence. According to the same historian, there were 45,000 declarations of 'repentance'[6] by Communists during the four years of the dictatorship;

to more than a casual remark, because he used to think aloud when with the King, and so in fact did King George.

[1] *Diary*, vol. iv, pp. 222–3, 4 Aug. 1936.   [2] Ibid., pp. 225–7, 4 Aug. 1936.
[3] 73,411 votes, or 15 seats in a chamber of 300 seats. Daphnis, op. cit., vol. ii, p. 402.   [4] *Kommounistikon Komma Ellados* (Communist Party of Greece).
[5] D. G. Kousoulas, *Revolution and Defeat: The Story of the Greek Communist Party*, London, 1965, p. 126.
[6] This involved the signing of a paper renouncing Communism. These renunciations meant very little in actual terms, because they were extracted under constraint.

yet he is ready to admit that this number far exceeded the membership of the Communist Party.[1] Contemporary sources, where available, should also be treated circumspectly. Such Communist boasts as the one cited in relation to the events in Salonika in May 1936, if they had any significance at all, went only to show how naïve and unwarranted was the optimism of the Communist leadership. And the rather vague assertions on the part of Metaxas and his men about the imminence of a Communist effort to seize power were never convincing. General Papagos, Chief of the General Staff since August 1936, praised Metaxas and the 'New Order' in 1937 because they had saved the country from Communism.[2] Such expressions of praise, rather profuse during the dictatorship, are understandable, but not convincing. All that can be said with some certainty is that Metaxas's swift action did put an end to a situation that could possibly have led to public disorders. Kafandaris argued later that the Communist threat was not serious, but was used by Metaxas as a pretext to seize power. Kafandaris also argued that the Constitution provided the means, such as mobilization of the workers and martial law, to cope with such threats to the State.[3] Yet Metaxas did act within the accepted mores of the Greek political world, and did use the 'means' at the disposal of the State; only he went further. Once repression of a sector of the community is accepted in principle and becomes the law of the State, it is difficult to draw the line beyond which repression becomes 'unconstitutional'. The last years of the Republic witnessed the first anti-Communist legislation, as well as the exile of Communists to the islands.[4] Metaxas was a product and a representative of the Greek political system; only he played the political game more roughly than was conventionally expected.

[1] Kousoulas, op. cit., p. 130.

[2] Memorandum by General Papagos, submitted to Metaxas, probably in early 1937. It is undated but seems to have been written early in 1937. It is signed by Papagos, and deals with the Greek Army since 1923. Papagos praised Metaxas's strong measures against what he calls the 'scourge' of society, and 'negation' of the Fatherland. Metaxas Papers.

[3] G. Kafandaris, *To the Greek People* (in Greek), Chartres, 1938, p. 3.

[4] Birtles, op. cit., pp. 122 ff. Nikoloudis, Metaxas's Minister for Press and Tourism, maintained that there were 2,300 Communists exiled during the Republic and only 900 during the dictatorship. T. Nikoloudis, *The Greek Crisis* (in Greek), Cairo, 1945, p. 59. The accuracy of these figures, however, cannot be checked.

The 'Technical Illegality'

The news of the dictatorship was received at the Foreign Office with mixed feelings. As might be expected, first thoughts there were about King George and his position in the new situation. The News Department was accordingly asked to see that press comments should be as far as possible sympathetic towards his position. It was generally felt at the Foreign Office that as long as the army remained loyal to the King, the proclamation of a dictatorship might well have a 'stabilizing' effect on internal conditions. Some officials felt that the dictatorship was unlikely to be permanent, though others were more sceptical about an early return to normal political life.[1]

Waterlow initially showed some reserve towards the new regime, and sent the First Secretary of the Legation to make the first contact with Metaxas. The latter explained that he had positive indications that the country was on the brink of a Communist attempt to seize power. According to his information, the strikers intended to converge on the principal streets of Athens, attack Government offices, loot shops, and even molest 'certain' foreign legations. Sir Sydney was sceptical, for he had information that no serious disorders were to be expected on 5 August, and that large sections of organized labour had decided not to participate in the strike. The Minister had little doubt that the real motive of Metaxas, who had always 'hankered' after dictatorial rule, was to put an end to the bickerings and intrigues of the party leaders, and to exploit the Communist threat to this end.[2]

The British Minister, naturally, did not show the same reserve towards the King, whom he saw on 7 August. King George took pains to emphasize that there was nothing he hated more than dictatorship, and that he was determined to return to constitutional government as soon as possible. The King assured Sir Sydney that the present concentration of power in the hands of Metaxas involved only one 'technical illegality', namely, absence of a fixed date for elections. He also brought up the Communist menace, and insisted that the danger had reached that point at which it was necessary either

---

[1] Foreign Office Minutes attached to Athens Tel. No. 158, 5 Aug. 1936, F.O. 371/20390.　　　[2] Athens Disp. No. 272, 6 Aug. 1936, F.O. 371/20390.

to take strong measures or run the risk of something like civil war.[1] It is possible that King George actually believed what he said about an early return to normal political life. And he was probably sincere in his fear of an imminent Communist attempt to seize power.[2] Waterlow felt that Metaxas had exaggerated the Communist menace in his conversation with the King, and had provided him with instances of sabotage which were probably fabricated. Yet, though apparently duped by Metaxas in that respect, the King, Sir Sydney believed, was 'the prime mover in the policy of the late stroke', and it was he, rather than Metaxas, who would be the guiding factor in future developments.[3]

There was yet another, more plausible, explanation of the dictatorship, which both Waterlow and the Foreign Office seemed to accept. Waterlow felt that Metaxas's action was due neither to a Communist threat nor to the deadlock created by the parties; it was rather due to the fact that the parties were about to agree to reinstate the expelled Venizelist officers. This agreement, or the fear of it, brought into play the 'Military League', an organization of royalist officers, who would not allow the readmission of the Venizelist officers to the army at any price. Metaxas is said to have confided to the Yugoslav Ambassador in Athens that, had he not proclaimed the dictatorship, the army would have done so.[4] The Officer corps was composed, in the main, of royalists, and it was inevitable that they should be against the readmission of the Venizelist officers, since it would reduce their prospects of promotion. Also, the King's determination not to readmit the Venizelists adds some credibility to this explanation, though there is no evidence that King George was actually privy to the alleged intentions of the royalist officers.

[1] Athens Tel. No. 162, 8 Aug. 1936, F.O. 371/20390.

[2] Prince George, King George's elderly uncle, allegedly told Argyropoulos in Alexandria in 1941 that the King had 'lied' shamelessly about the Communist threat. P. Argyropoulos, *Memoirs* (in Greek), vol. ii, Athens, 1971, p. 8.

[3] Letter from Waterlow to O'Malley, Confidential, 13 Aug. 1936, F.O. 371/20390. Concerning the instances of alleged sabotage, Waterlow says that the alleged blowing up of a powder magazine was not due to the Communists, but was actually the work of a chemist who had sold most of the powder and had blown up the magazine to cover his tracks; while the attempt on a destroyer was concocted by the officers and members of the crew who had failed to inspect and repair a steam-pipe joint, which eventually burst.

[4] Athens Disp. No. 272, 6 Aug. 1936, Athens Tel. No. 33 Saving, Confidential 7 Aug. 1936, and F.O. Minutes, F.O. 371/20390.

Whatever their feelings about the proclamation of the dictatorship, the Foreign Office took care at this stage to express no
opinion about it either way. Thus the visit of King Edward VIII
to King George and Metaxas, shortly after the August *coup*, is
not necessarily an indication that the British Government felt
favourably disposed towards the new regime. It is true that
both Metaxas and King George seemed to have interpreted the
royal visit in that light. The character and habits of King
Edward, however, lead one to feel that the visit was a royal
escapade rather than a State visit. There is no evidence in the
Foreign Office Papers that the royal visit to Corfu and Athens
was associated with the change of regime. The fact that King
Edward actually expressed political opinions privately to both
King George and Metaxas was rather due to his temperament
and political leanings, which had very little to do with official
British policy. That policy, at least as far as Greece was concerned, was slowly formulated, and was based on the reports of
the British Minister in Greece, and on a realistic appreciation
of Anglo-Greek relations. There is no doubt that the British
Government was relieved in a sense that even the remote
possibility of civil war in Greece had been averted; the recent
events in Spain constituted an ominous warning. On the other
hand there was nothing yet to show that the dictatorship was
more than a stop-gap, and that it would eventually become
a permanent situation.

The royal visit should be treated for what it was worth.
King Edward arrived in Corfu on 20 August 1936, and stayed
as a guest of King George.[1] After their first talk, King George
rushed to telegraph to the eager dictator in Athens: '[The]
King of England expressed himself very favourably about the
situation in Greece.' A week later, Metaxas, too, met King
Edward in Athens. The following is the relevant part of the
telegram Metaxas sent to King George on 27 August:

H.M. the King of England received me for an interview that
lasted one and a half hours. [The] King's reception [was] very

[1] When the British monarch asked King George, 'as one King to another',
how he was getting along in the country, the latter said that he was 'not getting
along at all'. Speaking of the recent events, King George said: 'I might just as
well be back at Brown's Hotel.' *A King's Story: The Memoirs of H.R.H. the Duke of
Windsor*, London, 1951, pp. 307, 308.

cordial. The conversation turned on all subjects, and H.M. showed a lively interest and complete knowledge of Greek affairs. We talked about the traditional Anglo-Greek friendship, which I assured H.M. should last for ever . . . The conversation took place . . . in the presence of the [British] Ambassador, and, at the King's wish, in German . . .[1]

Metaxas also promised to relate the 'details' of the conversation at his next meeting with King George. No doubt Metaxas found this meeting satisfying and reassuring.

Waterlow, at first reserved in his attitude towards the new regime, soon changed. In a long dispatch to the Foreign Office about the dictatorship, he expressed his views, which were forthright. He was inclined to think that the 'master mind' in the situation was the King, and that the dictator merely took 'instructions' from him. He also argued that with a parliamentary system the British Government could not hope for an 'advance in various matters' in which they were interested, such as the foreign debt, and that these had better prospects under the new regime. In due course Sir Sydney was able to convince the Foreign Office of both points: that the King was in charge of the situation, and that the dictatorship held better prospects for British interests. Later, Sir Sydney tried hard to convince the Foreign Office of precisely the reverse; but by then it was too late. For the present, he seemed satisfied that parliamentary government in Greece had been set aside. The following is Waterlow's appraisal of the Greek political scene:

I do not see how anyone with any knowledge of local conditions can shed a tear over the present eclipse of democracy in Greece. The King's return gave the system an opportunity to reform itself and to develop into something better than a pseudo-democratic façade covering a struggle for power with the help of the army; but nine months' patience on the part of His Majesty had merely proved that the very elements of organized democratic vitality were absent. Thus the suspension of free institutions, at a moment when the country urgently needs to be pulled together to face a period of social and economic stress, need not be taken tragically . . .[2]

[1] King George's and Metaxas's telegrams in Metaxas's *Diary*, vol. iv, pp. 246, 247.
[2] Athens Disp. No. 281, 12 Aug. 1936, F.O. 371/20390.

The 'Fourth of August' Dictatorship

The 'Fourth of August' regime was intended to be the 'Third Greek Civilization': more august than Periclean Athens, brighter than Golden Byzantium. Its appeal, however, to the modern Greeks seems to have been very limited, unbelievers in utopias as they have mostly been. Politicians, officers, journalists, artists, men of letters: those were the high priests of the new order, the 'salt' of Greece. George Seferis described them as part of the 'lame', left by the 'sieve of Fate'.[1] Waterlow referred to them as 'pushing arrivistes' given to 'kissing the hand of Metaxas', people who came to believe their own flatteries. 'I cannot but marvel once more at the suppleness of the Greek mind which gives it a limitless capacity for licking the boots of power, for dissimulation and self-deception. Their flattery is Oriental in its shamelessness, and both the giver and the receiver appear to be deceived as it is uttered.'[2]

Published sources for this period of Greek history are for the most part either polemics or apologies for it. They are of very limited historical value.[3] Metaxas unfortunately chose not to record the events of the early period of the dictatorship. On 31 December 1936, after seven months, he resumed his diary to note: 'May God help us. A constant struggle is necessary. Eyes watchful. Never rest. Sword in hand always: For Greece, the King, my friends and myself.'[4] On 6 January 1937 he discontinued writing, only to resume in November of that year, when he wrote:

I stopped. Perhaps, it was better that way. There are many things that cannot be written. Months of suspense and restlessness, without repose. A life full of dangers. The others have not seen those

[1] George Seferis, *Manuscript, September 41* (in Greek), Athens, 1972, p. 25.
[2] Athens Disp. No. 5, 10 Jan. 1939, F.O. 371/23769.
[3] D. Kallonas, *Ioannis Metaxas* (in Greek), Athens, 1938; B. P. Papadakis, *Greece, Yesterday and Tomorrow* (in Greek), Athens, 1946; T. Nikoloudis, *Ioannis Metaxas* (in Greek), Athens, 1941, and *The Greek Crisis* (in Greek), Cairo, 1945; A. P. Tabakopoulos, *The Myth of the Dictatorship* (in Greek), Athens, 1945; M. Malainos, *The Fourth of August* (in Greek), Athens, 1947; I. G. Koronakis, *The Fourth of August Regime* (in Greek), Athens, 1950; S. Linardatos, *The Fourth of August* (in Greek), Athens, 1966; N. Psiroukis, *Fascism and the Fourth of August* (in Greek), Athens, 1974. For Greek titles see the Bibliography.
[4] *Diary*, vol. iv, p. 250.

things, and will never learn about them. Who knows what will become of this notebook, and what hands it may fall into. God knows what I went through. I buried everything inside myself for the well-being of the country. Some day perhaps others who might have noticed something will reveal it. From now on I shall write only what can be written as a record . . .[1]

Metaxas's Papers, now at the General State Archives in Athens, contain a wide assortment of material relevant to the dictatorship: private correspondence; various State Papers, submitted to him in his capacities as President of the Council, Minister for Army Affairs, and Minister for Foreign Affairs; police reports, and recorded telephone conversations of suspected individuals, not excluding Ministers; and many adulatory letters sent to him by admirers of his Government. Waterlow's reports, written with much gusto and style, are usually very informative, if allowance is made for a certain tendency to exaggerate.

Metaxas's allusions to the difficulties he went through during the initial period of the dictatorship might refer to friction with King George, as well as with his own lieutenants. He must have also been disturbed by the apparent coldness and the unresponsive mood of the masses towards his appeals that the Greek people must 'find itself' again, and revive the glorious past. The ideology of the 'Third Greek Civilization' as he preached it made no express appeal to territorial expansion; and if it had contained such an appeal, it is rather doubtful whether the Greek people would have been ready to pay heed: the catastrophe of 1922 had dealt an almost fatal blow to the Great Idea. The people, according to Waterlow, were on the whole 'apathetic', except perhaps the world of banking and business which was delighted to find its activities unhindered by political obstruction.[2]

Metaxas's dictatorship had little resemblance to the existing European models. The dictatorship was not promoted by the army, nor was it pressed upon the country by a political party exploiting the passions of nationalism. Greece had essentially slipped into dictatorship, after a prolonged crisis. Waterlow was even convinced that the dictatorship could scarcely have

---

[1] *Diary*, vol. iv, p. 285, 9 Nov. 1937.
[2] Athens Disp. No. 351, 28 Oct. 1936, F.O. 371/20390.

been brought about, if the King had not returned; and he wondered whether it could succeed:

How can authoritarian government succeed in Greece? It has nothing behind it, and it is merely the chance product of a local paralysis; whereas the genuine dictators have everything behind them and are the product of historical destiny. They are all firmly based on passionate 'ideologies', but the theories that General Metaxas has been proclaiming are not a basis of action, they are merely adventitious drapery, and patchwork at that.[1]

The 'New State', as Metaxas and his lieutenants liked to call it,[2] amounted to the dictatorship of King George and Metaxas and a devoted camarilla. By common consent, the King was the 'Highest Archon' and the 'permanent element' of the regime; and Metaxas, to keep up with the times, assumed the title of 'Archigos' (Chief). Behind them stood supposedly, ever loyal and obedient, the Greek masses. Only '200 families' of politicians and Venizelists were against the new regime, the Minister of Propaganda was later to claim.[3]

Metaxas's political philosophy, as it had developed by the end of his life, can be found in his 'Plan for a Regime',[4] which is a form of political testament. According to this plan, the King should be the highest authority, and should appoint the Prime Minister, who would not necessarily be elected by the people. The King and his Government were to be aided by three 'Councils'—Executive, Legislative, and Judiciary— whose powers should be only consultative. There would be frequent plebiscites and elections, but not political parties. The people would not be 'sovereign', and their role would be 'consultative' only. Finally, society would be a 'Labour Society', in which no Greek would be allowed 'not to work', and all those who lived from the return on accumulated capital would be deprived of political rights, and, from the

[1] Athens Disp. No. 416, 18 Dec. 1936, F.O. 371/20390.

[2] G. A. Mantzoufas and N. D. Koumaros, 'The Fundamental Constitutional Principles of the New State', *To Neon Kratos*, vol. xi (1938). Mantzoufas was Metaxas's son-in-law, and one of the ideologues of the regime. Other prominent theoreticians were A. Kyrou, B. P. Papadakis, and the Minister of the Press himself, T. Nikoloudis.

[3] Nikoloudis, *The Greek Crisis*, p. 60.

[4] *Diary*, vol. iv, Appendix, pp. 862–6. Metaxas drew up this plan in Dec. 1940, one month before he died. It was published separately by his daughter Loukia Metaxas, *The Political System of Ioannis Metaxas* (in Greek), Athens, 1945.

point of view of civil law, would be put 'under tutelage'. Metaxas's 'Plan for a Regime' was never actually put into effect, and remains a historical curiosity only. His authoritarianism and his appeal to populist ideas, however, appeared in his speeches from time to time during his years in power. Metaxas's speeches, published at the time, are full of populist trappings, so dear to dictators.[1] The economic programme of the regime, announced soon after the *coup*, called for 'unity of action through unity of directions'.[2] Greece was to be transformed from a loose body into a compact and efficient corporate state. Obligatory arbitration of labour disputes was practised with some concern for the protection of workers. The Government also intervened freely over the price of bread, oil, and other commodities. A notable achievement of Metaxas's Government was an increase of wheat production and a consequent reduction of wheat imports. Production doubled by 1939, and imports were reduced almost by half by 1940. These were mainly due to Metaxas's drive to make the country self-sufficient in wheat.[3] Metaxas also, much to his credit, instituted Social Insurance.

Metaxas was described after his death by one of his lieutenants as a 'national apostle, reformer, and conservative revolutionary', as well as an 'intellectual', 'social philosopher', and 'prophet'.[4] Another versatile apologist wrote that Metaxas had become for the Greeks 'the Man', and that he could be

---

[1] *Speeches of the First Three Years* (in Greek), Athens, 1939. There are also many speeches in the Appendix of the fourth volume of the *Diary*.

[2] Athens Disp. No. 308, 9 Sept. 1936, F.O. 371/20390. Waterlow hoped that something would come of the grandiose scheme, though he was sceptical about it: 'It took Mussolini more than twelve years to transform Italy, and General Metaxas, apart from being 65 years old, is not a Mussolini or a Hitler. And even if he were, he has against him the intense individualism of the Greek character, with its incapacity for discipline and teamwork, and the difficulty of creating a trained and honest civil service in a country where patriotism is a vogue rather than the reflection of an organic national life.'

[3] Wheat production and imports:

	Production (tons)	Imports
1932	464,502	601,555
1936	531,108	451,068
1938	1,040,000	364,298
1940	—	273,111

A. N. Klimis, *Rural Economy* (in Greek), Athens, 1961, pp. 101, 102.

[4] Nikoloudis, *Metaxas*, p. 17.

compared with Prometheus. He was 'eternal'.[1] During his years in power, poets like Timos Moraitinis sang his praises, and the regimented youth of the country hailed him as 'Great Chief', and declared: 'Loyal, fanatically believing in Your Aims, unwavering, ready for any sacrifice, behold, I abjure decay and pessimism for confidence, energy, and optimism . . .'[2] His private papers are full of adulatory, sycophantic letters from notable people. Marika Kotopouli, the famous Greek actress, wrote to him once to express her profound gratitude because, she said, he had 'rebaptized her in the pure fountains of Greece', and inspired her with new popular Greek 'rhythms and tones'.[3] The venal Greek press flocked to serve the 'New Order'. G. A. Vlachos of the *Kathimerini*, after some estrangement with Metaxas, eventually composed his differences with him.[4] G. Pesmatzoglou of the *Proia* went to the Minister of Press and Tourism some time after the *coup*, and promised the services of his paper to the new regime.[5] The *Estia* went even further and in effect became a principal source of inspiration for the regime.[6]

Metaxas was surrounded by devoted lieutenants, a 'camarilla', as Waterlow called them, which included a grey eminence, Ioannis Diakos, the dictator's closest confidant. Diakos must have wielded great influence, for he is generally referred to as a 'Super-Prime Minister', though he held no official post.[7]

---

[1] Papadakis, *Greece, Yesterday and Tomorrow*, pp. 3, 318.

[2] Linardatos, *Fourth of August*, p. 193.

[3] Letter from Marika Kotopouli to Metaxas, 13 Nov. 1939, Metaxas Papers.

[4] *Diary*, vol. iv, p. 284, 2 Jan. 1937.

[5] Letter from Nikoloudis to Metaxas, 17 Oct. 1936, Metaxas Papers.

[6] The Greek poet George Seferis, who was attached at the time to the Foreign Section of the Ministry of Press, wrote that '*Estia* had not become "Metaxist", but the regime was actually "Estiist" '. With respect to the Liberal press, Seferis wrote that the publishers were doing good business by assuming an attitude of reserve towards the regime, since the public disliked reading praises of the regime. With regard to censorship and the attitude of Greek publishers in general, Nikoloudis used to explain to foreign correspondents: 'I have also been a correspondent, and I know, as well as you do, that the press cannot be muzzled easily. The owner of a newspaper, if he is opposed to the Government and knows that he has the support of the public, will cease to print his newspaper. In fact, from the moment we came to power nobody has acted in that way.' Seferis, op. cit., pp. 30–1.

[7] There are no reliable sources about Diakos, though there is a plethora of references to him in post-war Greek historiography. Madame Lorandos, whose husband was a close friend of Diakos, says that he was a very secretive man, and took care not to leave anything in writing. Interview, Aug. 1970.

Metaxas consulted him on practically every matter, and his diary is full of references to him, tinged with a certain gratitude for his unfailing devotion. An interesting explanation of Diakos's relations with Metaxas is provided by Alekos Kanellopoulos, leader of the Youth Movement. Diakos is said to have been the real power behind Metaxas. Though he lacked Metaxas's idealism, he possessed something that his chief needed badly at times: realism and determination. Diakos was always at Metaxas's side, and took care to dismiss his superior's endless doubts before arriving at a decision. He was a convinced authoritarian, and believed that the dictatorship stood or fell with Metaxas. The dictatorship, he used to say, was like the number 1,000,000, but without Metaxas only six zeroes.[1] Konstantinos Maniadakis, Chief of Security, and Theologos Nikoloudis, Minister of Press and Tourism— a euphemism for propaganda—aped their counterparts in Germany, and could claim some successes. Maniadakis had established a wide net of informers, who were believed to range from men like Napoleon Zervas[2] to vendors of lottery tickets and peanuts, who were instructed in the fine art of eavesdropping on the public.[3] Maniadakis was able to break up the organization of the Communist Party, and, through renegades and police agents, to dominate the local party organizations.[4] He greatly admired Himmler's work in Germany, and tried to borrow German 'scientific' methods in combating Communism.[5] Fortunately, he lacked Himmler's ruthless and inhuman efficiency.

[1] Interview with Mr. Alekos Kanellopoulos, 18 June 1974.

[2] 'Fourth of August', *Acropolis*, 1 Feb. 1972. Zervas was a republican officer and military boss, involved in a number of *coups* in the inter-war period. During the Axis occupation of Greece he was a prominent resistance leader.

[3] Athens Disp. No. 351, 28 Oct. 1936, F.O. 371/20390.

[4] Maniadakis interview published in *Acropolis*, 5 Mar. 1972. See also Kousoulas, op. cit., p. 135.

[5] In 1937 Maniadakis was honoured by Himmler with an invitation for Greek representatives from the police to be sent to Germany to the National-Socialist Congress at Nuremberg in August of that year, where representatives of all the states 'anxious to make war against communism' would, it was hoped, attend. Maniadakis, delighted, accepted the invitation, and in his reply raised the specific questions in which he was interested. These included anti-communist legislation, restrictive police methods, as well as 'the progress of the police in the scientific prosecution of crime', and more particularly, the 'system of treatment and isolation for Communists etc. . . . .' Copies of letters enclosed in Athens Disp. No. 374, 24 Nov. 1937, F.O. 371/21150.

Nikoloudis, the bulky chief of propaganda, aspired to become the archpriest of the 'Third Greek Civilization',[1] besides his preoccupation with the more immediate problems of censoring material for all form of publications. One of Nikoloudis's circulars about censorship was passed to the Foreign Office, and the officials of the Southern Department got a taste of his genius. There was no aspect of life for which Nikoloudis had not provided for the blue pencil or the eraser. Publication of any information affecting political parties and political personages was forbidden, and so was any criticism of the work of the Government. News about Northern Epirus, Cyprus, and the Dodecanese were to be kept out. News or articles about 'the high cost of living, the rise in prices, profiteering', as well as information regarding the Drachma, the exchange rate, the public debt, and the country's credit were also forbidden. Articles with Communist tendencies, or with 'so-called Leftist theories', were forbidden, too. Newspapers, 'on pain of suspension', had to contribute 'enthusiastically' to the work of the Government. Nikoloudis also took care of another aspect of censorship, the appearance of blank spaces in the columns of the Press, which was 'forbidden'. The papers were compelled to fill up the blanks created by the Censor in such a way as not to reveal the exercise of 'precautionary censorship'.[2] Of the rest of Metaxas's men Kostas Kotzias was certainly the most important, or, at least, the most obtrusive. The exuberant Minister-Governor of Athens must have been suspected by Metaxas of scheming to overthrow him, for the latter's papers contain a number of reports by gendarmes and unprofessional spies about Kotzias's meetings and conversations.[3]

[1] In a letter of 13 Aug. 1939, Nikoloudis asked Metaxas for his post to be elevated to that of Minister of Culture. In his reply, Metaxas argued that Civilization was the product of a whole people, 'inspired by one man', who should direct personally all the organs of the State and society. Metaxas naturally kept for himself this supervising function. Letters in Metaxas Papers.

[2] Nikoloudis's circular was enclosed in Athens Disp. No. 344, 28 Oct. 1937, F.O. 371/21148. Waterlow commented that, though a 'believer' in free speech, he considered that censorship in Greece had its 'salutary side', considering the 'degradation' to which Greek newspapers had descended under free institutions.

[3] Metaxas Papers. Kotzias, after a trip to the United States in 1939, got the impression that not many Greek-Americans were 'enthusiastic' about the 'Fourth of August' regime, and suggested that 'only persons, sincerely and unreservedly devoted to the National regime' should be allowed to emigrate there (Memo. by Kotzias, 17 July 1939, submitted to Metaxas).

Andreas Apostolidis, the Minister of Finance, was a man of some significance, as was Alekos Kannellopoulos, the leader of the Youth Movement. The case of Alekos Kanellopoulos is an interesting one. The son of a well-established and respectable industrialist, he joined Metaxas's band out of youthful idealism and sincere admiration for Metaxas. Patriotism, belief in the cause of the Youth Movement, and admiration for the leader were the motives behind Kanellopoulos's energetic drive to inculcate in the young the ideals of patriotism and team spirit. His idealism, however, was not always shared by his subordinates, some of whom were prompted by less admirable motives, while others used questionable means, such as forced enrolment, to achieve the cherished goals.[1]

During his rule Metaxas undertook to ban the goat from the Greek mountains, and his axiom, 'either the forest or the goat', became proverbial. He used the same axiom in dealing with another problem that fell into the category of 'pests', the Slav-speaking minority of northern Greece, and banned the use of their dialect. His eager associates, however, had thought of a more practical solution. General Papagos, Chief of the General Staff, suggested that all sections of the population in the North of 'doubtful national sentiments' should be removed to the interior, or sent away from Greece. Their lands would be given to people from the interior, whose 'Greekness' was unblemished.[2] This resettlement, however, was bound to create land problems, and the Ministry of Agriculture proposed that the undesirables should be encouraged and 'indirectly pressed' to emigrate to South America.[3] There is no evidence that these proposals were considered seriously. Many Greeks from Macedonia actually emigrated to South America at this time, but, it seems, rather out of poverty than through pressure from the Government. It was a piece of great good fortune that Metaxas and his regime lacked the efficiency of non-Mediterranean dictatorships in the work of 'purifying' the race.

[1] Interview with A. Kanellopoulos referred to above.

[2] Memo. by Papagos, Secret, No. 36096, 8 Dec. 1937, 'On the Repopulation of the Border Areas', and Memo. of 15 Nov. 1938, of the same title, in Metaxas Papers.

[3] Memo. by the Chief of Emigration Section, Ministry of Agriculture, 24 Feb. 1938, 'Study Concerning the Emigration of Greek Farmers to Argentina and Brazil', Metaxas Papers.

Britain and Metaxas

The British Government considered the dictatorship a necessary evil, and looked on the methods of the regime with an embarrassed smile, or at times a faint frown. Waterlow never failed to report its less attractive measures and, as early as October 1936, informed the Foreign Office that the system was developing into a full-blown 'Polizeistaat'. The special police were encouraged in brutal methods, and there were alleged instances of forced suicides, secret deportations, and unheralded searches by the police in private homes at all hours.[1] He discussed these disturbing signs with King George, and in explaining his action to the Foreign Office said that the 'hint' dropped to the King should not be interpreted as interference in Greek politics, or that he was proffering his advice 'officiously'. He explained that he felt quite free to 'think aloud' when he was with the King, since the latter always talked to him about local conditions without reserve, 'often unprintably'. Moreover, he considered it useful that the King should get the 'British angle', which included a 'certain concern' about the risks of his position.[2]

These friendly chats caused considerable uneasiness in the Foreign Office, lest the Minister's opinions should be interpreted in Greece as advice offered by the British Government. They quite understood that King George was a 'lonely' man and needed advice. However, they warned Waterlow that he must be careful not to take sides in Greece's internal affairs so that, in need, he could deny 'conscientiously and emphatically' that he had done so.[3] The Foreign Office was understandably uneasy about the liberties he took with the King, in case these came to the knowledge of the Greek Government. At this stage, however, King George himself, as will be seen shortly, was still undecided whether to keep Metaxas, or drop him at a suitable moment; the British Minister's hints must have fallen on ready ears.

Metaxas, for his part, never lost a chance to assure the British Government that he set great store by the traditional Anglo-Greek friendship, and that his Government was determined to

[1] Athens Disp. No. 351, 28 Oct. 1936, F.O. 371/20390.
[2] Letter from Sir Sydney Waterlow to O'Malley, 2 Nov. 1936, F.O. 371/20390.
[3] Letter from O'Malley to Waterlow, Copy, 19 Nov. 1936, F.O. 371/20390.

work in close co-operation with the British. As far as can be
determined from available sources, Metaxas first gave those
assurances in June 1936, in connection with the Mediterranean
crisis.[1] In December 1936, he went 'out of his way', according
to Waterlow, to assure him that Greece was 'irrevocably and
unreservedly devoted to the British connection'.[2] Waterlow
and the Foreign Office must have greatly relished these
protestations of friendship, though they never gave him to
understand that he could be sure of their favour and support.
When allowance is made for Metaxas's sentimental ways, his
assurances, quite unpolitic as far as Greece's position was concerned, must have had something to do with his desire to win
the support of the British Government for his personal position.
A man of better judgement might have shown some reserve
regarding Greece's foreign relations; yet Metaxas was in
a disadvantageous position *vis-à-vis* the British Government
since he depended to a great extent on the King, who was
unreservedly pro-British.

Waterlow, after a long conversation with King George in
March 1937, was reassured that the King had the situation
well in hand, and concluded his observations as follows:
'. . . It is a bull point in the situation that the General, having
no popularity and no personal following among the politicians
or the army officers, can be easily discarded when he becomes
a danger or even when he merely ceases to be useful.'[3] Waterlow
often stressed this 'bull point' regarding the internal situation,
and the Foreign Office must have seen the advantages it
offered them in dealing with Greece. True, the 'Germanization' of Greece was disquieting enough, and the Foreign Office
wondered at times whether it would not be better if King
George actually 'discarded' Metaxas.[4] Such thoughts, however,
were never seriously entertained for long. Moreover, King
George was ready to dispel any British uneasiness about
Greece's position in international relations, and even expressed
the wish to visit England in order to allay doubts as to Greece's
attachment.[3]

[1] Letter from Metaxas to Simopoulos, 6 June 1936, in Simopoulos Papers.
[2] Athens Disp. No. 384, 4 Dec. 1936, F.O. 371/20390.
[3] Athens Disp. No. 95, Confidential, 29 Mar. 1937, F.O. 371/21147.
[4] F.O. Minutes, Apr. 1937, in F.O. 371/21147.

During this time also, King George made his first political proposal to Britain. In a conversation in March 1937 with Lieut.-Col. A. C. Arnold of the War Office, who was on a visit to Greece, he suggested it would be advantageous 'to tackle the whole question of how the two countries stood in relation to each other, politically and militarily', along broad lines. Waterlow felt that King George had used Lieut.-Col. Arnold as a channel for conveying what was in effect a political proposal.[1] His idea of a declaration on Anglo-Greek relations was ruled out by the Foreign Office, for it was thought that this would be bound to 'antagonize' Germany, and therefore do as much harm as good. Cadogan, Vansittart, and Eden agreed on the point; Eden, moreover, felt that the Germans in fact were 'doing' Britain's work. It was decided instead that the King of Greece should be invited by the King of England to visit the country, and this visit in fact took place in November 1937.[2]

The British Government was obliged to make a statement on Anglo-Greek relations soon afterwards. The question was raised in the House of Commons on 22 April 1937, when a member of the Opposition asked that the Government should make it clear to the Greek Government that a continuance of the dictatorship was likely to alienate British sympathies.[3] The following day a Conservative member wrote to the Foreign Office, and said he wished to ask the Secretary of State for Foreign Affairs on 28 April whether he would give an assurance that the policy of the British Government was sympathetic towards 'the friendly monarchy and nation of Greece, irrespective of what form of government, other than Communism', the Greek people wished to have.[4] The question was approved, though not without some mild discomfort,[5] and it was put to the Secretary of State in the Commons in the same wording

---

[1] Record of conversation between King George and Lieut.-Col. Arnold enclosed in letter from Waterlow to O'Malley, Confidential, 29 Mar. 1937, F.O. 371/21147.

[2] F.O. Minutes, Apr. 1937, F.O. 371/21147.

[3] *Parliamentary Debates*, Commons, 1937, vol. 322, 22 Apr. 1937.

[4] Letter by Captain Alan Graham, 23 Apr. 1937, F.O. 371/21150. Captain Graham also wrote in his letter: 'In view of the Anglo-mania of the King of Greece, supported by Metaxas, I do hope a sympathetic answer will be returned. Poor Simopoulos is very upset.'

[5] The word 'irrespective' seemed to have bothered the men in the Foreign Office, but after some consideration they accepted it, since the form of government in Greece was after all a 'dictatorship'. F.O. Minutes, 26 Apr. 1937, F.O. 371/21150.

as in the letter to the Foreign Office. Eden, in replying, assured the House that 'in keeping with the traditional friendship' that united Britain and Greece, the policy of the British Government was 'entirely sympathetic to the Greek people and the Government'. To the Opposition's question whether the Government accepted the exception 'other than Communism', and whether Britain's best friends in the world were 'democracies', Eden replied that the British Government did not base their foreign policy on 'rival ideologies', but on 'peace'.[1]

King George was 'deeply touched' by Eden's statement, as he told Waterlow; and the Greek press went hoarse in its cheers for the British Foreign Minister.[2] *The Times* soon caught up the theme, and in an article of 21 May 1937, argued that an 'unbiased' scrutiny of Metaxas's rule must give him credit for a considerable achievement. 'The abolition of party government and the elimination of the constant political upheavals and squabbles which for many years had been the concomitant of Greek parliamentarism, have restored to the country an unprecedented degree of internal calm and order.' Metaxas was making 'a genuine endeavour to instil a national feeling into his countrymen', and this was not pursued by 'blatantly Fascist or Nazi methods'.[3]

Metaxas could feel a warm satisfaction at these encouraging words, but not King George, who was caught in a difficult position. Criticism of the regime in private had become widespread, and the King was warned by none other than the British Minister, that by putting himself in the hands of an unpopular dictator he was running the risk of being irreparably compromised. The King's reaction is quoted by Sir Sydney in his dispatch to the Foreign Office. King George said that no one was more 'anxious' than himself to return to democracy, but it was difficult to do so. After the usual attack on the politicians, who, he said, were only interested in turning Metaxas out and getting 'jobs' for themselves, King George made the following confession:

[1] *Parliamentary Debates*, Commons, 1937, vol. 323, 28 Apr. 1937.
[2] Athens Tel. No. 67, and Disp. No. 154, 3 May 1937, F.O. 371/21150.
[3] There is some indication that *The Times* article might have been inspired by the Foreign Office. An official of the Southern Department wrote in a minute of 24 May 1937 that he wondered why Simopoulos had not called yet to 'thank' the Foreign Office 'for this'. F.O. 371/21147.

I am quite aware that Metaxas is unpopular, and that the people will not put up for ever with having nothing to grow warm about (except myself, which is not enough), no political catchwords, no grand ideals. There is no danger yet, but a change will be necessary before too long. But what kind of change? Metaxas' talk about a corporative state has, of course, fallen flat and died away. Is any form of elective government possible yet? A government party, with Metaxas at its head? Not a soul would vote for him. Besides, the idea has always been that he should retire when he has done his work . . .[1]

Relations between King George and Metaxas at this time may well have been anything but cordial. Unfortunately, there is no other evidence that might throw light on the relations between the two men. Metaxas resumed writing his diary in November 1937, at the time of the King's visit to England. He read eagerly the Greek Minister's telegrams about the King's conversations, and on 12 November he noted, after reading the telegram of that day, that the British were giving the King 'the entire credit' for the work done since August 1936.[2] Metaxas seems to have been apprehensive during the King's absence in London, and he must surely have been relieved when the King brought back no unpleasant surprise for him from London. On 7 December he noted: '. . . King's return. Everything alright. Disappointment of those who expected a government crisis.'[3] In fact, this visit seems to have brought King George closer to Metaxas. On 8 January 1938, the latter noted briefly: 'King always favourably disposed since his return from England.'[4]

Metaxas and British Interests in Greece

Anglo-Greek relations entered a new phase in 1937, when certain agreements were concluded between the Greek Government and various British companies holding concessions in Greece. What is primarily of interest for this study is not so much the disputes and the agreements themselves as the negotiations in which the British Government was brought in because British policy and wider interests were involved. Economic issues, old and new alike, were dealt with relatively swiftly and in a way that left the British Minister in Athens and the Foreign Office with the impression that Greece at last had

---

[1] Athens Disp. No. 152, Confidential, 3 May 1937, F.O. 371/21147.
[2] *Diary*, vol. iv, p. 289.   [3] Ibid., p. 290.   [4] Ibid., p. 291.

a government that was ready to react decisively without procrastination. What is evident from these negotiations is an unmistakable willingness on the part of Metaxas to be accommodating to British interests, an attitude which had no parallel in Greece under the Republic. On 20 August 1936, two weeks after the *coup* and after fifteen months of default, the Greek Government agreed to pay to the Bondholders 40 per cent of the interest on the foreign debt of the country for the years 1935/6 and 1936/7. Metaxas announced the conclusion of the agreement to King George who was staying at Corfu at the time with King Edward as his guest. King George was delighted, and no doubt his royal guest shared his pleasure.[1]

The issue of the foreign debt, however, was not resolved, and remained a thorn in the side of Anglo-Greek relations. It came up again in the spring of 1937, when the agreement of August 1936 came to an end. The Council of Foreign Bondholders resumed its pressure on the Foreign Office to intervene on their behalf for the payment of a higher percentage of what was nominally due, 50 per cent, or at least 45 per cent. Metaxas was pressed in that sense, but he seems to have reached the limit beyond which he could not go on this issue. Despite the 'strongest possible pressure' by the King to reconsider his attitude, Metaxas refused to do so on political grounds, explaining that public opinion would not accept an increase of payment, and threatened to resign, if the King insisted.[2]

It is possible that Metaxas was bluffing; or that King George used Metaxas's threat as a pretext to silence British recriminations. Waterlow, at least, was much concerned over the way things had turned out. In a letter to the Foreign Office he insisted that it was high time that some sense was drummed

[1] Draft Tel. No. 16217 from Metaxas to King George, 20 Aug. 1936, and the King's reply, Tel. No. 16293 of 21 Aug. King Edward had 'emphasized' to King George during their first meeting 'his hope that the Greek Government should be able to find a way in order to bring the pending economic disputes with England to a satisfactory ending, since this would strengthen the present close relations between Greece and England'. This hint was telegraphed to Metaxas by King George on 20 Aug., at 11.40 p.m., and was received the following day. This telegram bears the same number (16217) as the telegram by Metaxas of the same date, announcing the conclusion of the agreement. It is impossible, therefore, that Metaxas read the King's telegram before he signed the agreement, if the marking of the dates is correct. Telegrams in Metaxas Papers.

[2] F.O. Draft Tel. to Waterlow, 16 May 1937, and reply, Tel. of 28 May, in F.O. 371/21145.

into the bondholders' heads. They overlooked, he said, the fact that 'if and when the politicians came back', they would not get a penny more, and probably nothing. Waterlow thought that Metaxas, however 'unreasonable', offered the most 'any Greek' could do.[1] In a letter to Simopoulos, Metaxas wrote:

I have decided not to retreat a single step. And even if we suppose the impossible, i.e. another government, they (the Bondholders) will not get a single penny, let alone 50%, with the demagogic uproar that would ensue. Therefore, they must realize that I am the most advantageous person to them. Moreover, it must be understood there that Greece is of course a friend of England and she has every intention to remain so; but, if the British also wish to keep Greece as their friend, they must not maltreat her. It is already beginning to be felt here that the British believe they can maltreat us . . . without the slightest consideration for our amour-propre, the elementary [amour-propre] of even the most barbaric nation. Can friendship withstand such conduct?[2]

The Foreign Office, too, became concerned and approached the bondholders in the sense advised by Sir Sydney in order to curb their 'appetites'. It was finally agreed that the Greek Government should send representatives to negotiate with the bondholders in London, without prior conditions.[3] The negotiations started in August 1937, but broke down as neither side was prepared to withdraw from its position. An uproar followed in the British press, which was so vehement against the Greek Government that the Foreign Office was seriously disturbed by the strong language used.[4] King George and Metaxas complained that the hostility of the bondholders and the British Press was out of all proportion, and there the matter rested.[5]

Another issue in which the British Government became involved seriously was the friction between the Greek Government and Cable & Wireless Ltd., the British company that controlled the external communications of Greece, as well as a considerable part of its inter-island and mainland communications. The company had owned cables in Greece for many

[1] Letter from Waterlow to O'Malley, 5 July 1937, F.O. 371/21145.
[2] Letter of 30 June 1937, in Simopoulos Papers.
[3] F.O. Minutes and Tel. to Waterlow of 9 July 1937, and reply Tel. of 12 July, in F.O. 371/21145.   [4] Press coverage of 6 Aug. 1937, in F.O. 371/21146.
[5] Record of conversation between Eden and Simopoulos at the Foreign Office, 7 Oct. 1937, F.O. 371/21146.

years, but now the Greek Government was trying by various techniques to get rid of it and take over the lines and installations. The Greek Government planned to nationalize the telecommunications system of the country, and presented the issue in this light, though it is just possible that they might have been considering selling out the business on more profitable terms to some other foreign bidder. The British Government became seriously concerned over the issue as soon as it emerged, and used every means at its disposal to dissuade the Greek Government from driving out the company. Eden told Simopoulos that he hoped Metaxas would treat the affair in the context of 'wider considerations'.[1] The reasons for this intervention are given explicitly in a Memorandum of the Foreign Office of 30 January 1937, which argues as follows:

... Commercially the Company would like to get out of Greece on the best terms it can, but, acting on the advice of the Committee of Imperial Defence, we have told the Company that it is a very important British interest that these cables should remain in British hands. The reason is that we are able, on them, to intercept a large number of foreign Government messages.[2]

It was decided, therefore, that the strongest possible pressure should be applied to both Metaxas and King George, to whom the issue would be presented as a political question of importance. Metaxas's first reaction to Waterlow's approach was a vehement protest, but he soon quietened down and 'begged' the British Minister to trust him to put the matter 'right'.[3] The Foreign Office felt at the time that they were treating Metaxas rather 'pontifically'; but the treatment had the desired effect. Before long the Greek Government took the first step back, and agreed to suspend action over the installation of a state telephone system, and in April 1937 they reached an agreement with the company.[4]

Under the terms of the Agreement,[5] which was ratified by

---

[1] Dispatch from Simopoulos to Metaxas, No. 324/A/37, Secret, 4 Feb. 1937, Copy. Eden also asked Simopoulos to write to Metaxas that he followed developments in Greece and Metaxas's work with 'great interest'. Simopoulos Papers.

[2] F.O. Minutes by O'Malley, Secret, 30 Jan. 1937, F.O. 371/21143.

[3] F.O. Minutes and Athens Tel. No. 5, Saving, of 13 Feb. 1937, and Athens Disp. No. 50, 17 Feb., F.O. 371/21143.

[4] Athens Tel. No. 35, 24 Feb. 1937, and Tel. No. 23, Saving, of 19 Apr., F.O. 371/21143. [5] Copy of the Agreement in F.O. 371/21143.

legislative decree of 24 May 1937 by the Greek Government, Cable & Wireless Ltd. was granted exclusive control over external telegraphic communications by cable and wireless telephone for a period of sixteen years. It was also agreed that two cable lines connecting the Ionian Islands with Italy were to be closed on the expiry of the company's Italian concession in May 1937, and that the one remaining cable between Greece and Italy (Corfu–Otranto) would be taken over by the Greek Government for terminal traffic between Greece and Italy. It was also arranged that all cables on the Greek interior system worked at the time by the company would be leased to the State at a nominal rental. As might be expected the Committee of Imperial Defence and the Foreign Office were satisfied with these arrangements.[1]

The agreement with Cable & Wireless Ltd. was followed in July 1937 by a settlement between the Greek Government and the Electric Transport Company, the 'Power Company' as it was popularly known in Greece. The company controlled the supply of electricity and electrically powered transport in the Greek capital, and its concession was renewed by the new agreement. Waterlow, who was congratulated on his efforts by the Foreign Office, was distinctly satisfied at this turn of events; he blamed past difficulties on 'Greek parliamentary government', which, he said, had driven the company to bankruptcy. The agreement, he reported, had become possible after the politicians had 'disappeared finally' from the scene.[2]

The Greek Government during this period also came into conflict with various British insurance companies, when it attempted to monopolize insurance interests. Metaxas found himself in a rather unenviable position in that he stood between the British insurance companies and the Greek Army Pensions Fund, which had been granted a monopoly of insurance in Greece. The idea behind the scheme was to find money to raise salaries of army officers without further burdening the budget or risking agitation by some 45,000 civil servants for similar rises.[3] The Director-General of the Army Pensions Fund,

---

[1] Meeting of the Committee of Imperial Communications, C.I.D., 22 June 1937, F.O. 371/21143.
[2] Athens Disp. No. 249E, 24 July 1937, F.O. 371/21143.
[3] Athens Tel. of 4 Nov. 1937, F.O. 371/21149.

Col. Borzonis,[1] approached Waterlow and pointed out that after insurance had been made a monopoly, he intended to place the whole of the Fund's insurance business in Britain. British insurance companies would thus be able to earn larger profits, and it would be other foreign and local companies that would actually suffer. The Army Fund, he promised, would undertake the solemn obligation to effect all their business with British companies over a long period, if the British Government privately informed the Greek Government that they would waive their objections; although naturally they would maintain their official position in order to overcome difficulties with other foreign governments. The Foreign Office refused to become party to such devious proceedings, fearing perhaps that the wily Colonel might be setting a trap for them as well.[2] The project was then abandoned, but was realized later, during the war, when Metaxas was in a far better position *vis-à-vis* the British Government.

In the wave of economic nationalism and the drive towards state control of many interests and services, the Greek Government attempted in 1937 to take over the Blackburn Aircraft Factory at Phaliron. Metaxas had decided not to renew the contract with the company that was to expire at the end of the year, when the State would take over the management and run the factory with the help of foreign experts. At the same time, he assured the British Government that 'under no circumstances' would the Germans be allowed to obtain control of the management, however attractive their offers, although it might be necessary to buy certain materials from Germany.[3] There is no evidence that the Greek Government actually meant to turn over the factory to the Germans; and the settlement of the issue at the end of the year, which left the company virtually in control, with only nominal state management, is evidence to the contrary. During this time, however, there was much talk about a progressive 'Germanization' of Greece. According to Waterlow's sources of information, the Germans had approached the Greek Government in April

[1] Col. Borzonis must have had a finger in many pies for he was also associated with Hellenic Air Lines.

[2] Correspondence between the Foreign Office and the British Minister in Athens in F.O. 371/21149.

[3] Athens Tel. No. 17 Saving, 21 Mar. 1937, F.O. 371/21144.

1937, and asked them to consider the transfer of the factory to German management.[1]

The suspicions and fears of the British Government increased when they read a report by the manager of the Phaliron factory. According to the Greek Air Ministry, fighter aeroplanes were being assembled in a factory attached to the cartridge factory of Bodosakis Athanasiadis, from parts which arrived in Greece in a finished state. The personnel consisted of three or four German supervisors and skilled workmen from the cartridge factory. Ten such aircraft were said to have left Greece for an unknown destination piloted by Germans, while four more were under assembly. The Greek Air Ministry further revealed that Dr. Schacht, when in Greece, had urged the Greek Government to permit the Germans in Greece to export aeroplanes to Spain.[2] The cash for the deal was passing through the British and French Discount Bank in Greece,[3] and this adds more credibility to the report. Later in the year Emmanouil Tsouderos, Governor of the Bank of Greece, informed the British Legation in Athens that Greece had had a 'windfall' that year of over £600,000 sterling from General Franco.[4] There were also many rumours that the Greek Government had been helping the Spanish rebels since the previous year,[5] but they cannot be adequately substantiated. However, all these reports and rumours made the British Government suspicious about the dealings of the Greek Government and Greek firms connected in some way with Germany. It was inferred that Bodosakis Athanasiadis might have been scheming to take over the Phaliron factory,[6] but this cannot be

---

[1] Athens Tel. No. 117, 9 Apr. 1937, F.O. 371/21144.

[2] Report by the manager of Phaliron factory enclosed in a letter from Waterlow to O'Malley of 26 Apr. 1937, F.O. 371/21144.

[3] Letter from Waterlow to O'Malley, 26 Apr. 1937, F.O. 371/21144.

[4] Athens Disp. of 7 Oct. 1937, F.O. 371/21146.

[5] Simopoulos informed Metaxas that there were rumours that the captain of a Greek ship, the S.S. *Sylvia*, though his ship was under contract to carry ammunition to the Spanish Government, had come into contact with the rebels to 'capture' the ship, and this for a generous reward. London Disp. No. 3048/St/36, Copy, 25 Nov. 1936. On 17 July 1938, Simopoulos wrote to King George: '. . . The activities of our ships in Spain . . . cause unfavourable comments. Of course, we do not have the monopoly in such affairs, because others as well are doing the same thing; but we have the monopoly in doing everything worse than everyone else.' Simopoulos Papers.

[6] The manager of the factory informed Waterlow at the time of a scheme by

maintained with any certainty. He had approached the British Government about this time, and offered to supply them with ammunition for their needs in the Middle East, maintaining that he would prefer to be connected with British rather than with German interests.[1]

Throughout these transactions, the British Government moved warily, often bewildered and baffled by what looked like dangerously obscure dealings. The most difficult role, however, must have been that of Metaxas: he was well disposed towards British interests, at least for the sake of Anglo-Greek relations, while trying at the same time to keep up with his programme of state control of various important firms and services in the country. King George at this time, speaking of the nationalist exaltation of the Greek Government, told the British Minister rather unjustly that 'there were no patriots in Greece, only chauvinists', and expressed the hope that the British Government would appreciate that he was obliged at present 'to give them their head until they learned from experience'.[2] Indeed, some of the projects considered might have been uneconomic; yet this did not make them necessarily 'unpatriotic', even if many dubious patriots were concerned in them.

'a local company promoter associated with certain retired officers' to take over the factory and run it with German personnel. Waterlow letter to O'Malley, 26 Apr. 1937, F.O. 371/21144.

[1] Memorandum by Bodosakis, July 1937, F.O. 371/21146. In their reply, the War Office said that they did not regard the firm 'as a source of supply on which they could rely either in peace or in war'. W.O. letter to the F.O., 5 Aug. 1937, F.O. 371/21146.

[2] Conversation between King George and Waterlow, in Athens Disp. No. 95, Confidential, 29 Mar. 1937, F.O. 371/21147.

III

Reconsideration of Anglo-Greek Relations

Unrest in Greece

By early 1938 Greece had experienced one-and-a-half years of dictatorial rule. Metaxas seemed to be as firmly in the saddle as ever, and the regime to be waxing into a full-blown authoritarian state. Then, rather unexpectedly, the politicians broke their silence and moved into the picture. A year earlier, in January 1937, the political leaders had reached agreement on a programme, which included constitutional reforms enhancing the King's powers, and providing for legislation to protect the tenure of Government servants from the uncertain fortunes of party politics, a free but 'responsible' Press, obligatory legislation in labour disputes, and the outlawing of both Communism and Fascism.[1] But their agreement was very late in coming: Metaxas had already stolen the show and imposed his own brand of state.

The politicians, however, had not disappeared from the scene. At least, they now made an effort to remind the public of their existence. In January 1938 they issued a series of manifestos, addressed to the Greek people and attacking the dictatorial regime in unusually strong language. Waterlow felt that the politicians were prompted to take this step by growing public discontent against the dictatorship.[2] This explanation sounds reasonable, but it is difficult to judge whether discontent was widespread in early 1938. It seems more plausible that the paper war was made possible by the fact that the politicians had the opportunity to meet on the occasion of Prince Paul's and Princess Frederika's marriage, which took place on 9 January 1938, and to agree on common action. Theotokis, leader of the National Populists, was allowed to return for the occasion

---

[1] Daphnis, op. cit., vol. ii, p. 441.
[2] Athens Disp. No. 45, 5 Feb. 1938, F.O. 371/22370.

from Corfu, where he had been banished by the regime; and no sooner had he returned to Athens than he got in touch with Sophoulis, leader of the Liberals, and Kafandaris, leader of the Progressives. The result of this contact was an agreement to circulate a manifesto condemning the dictatorial regime. Kafandaris also issued a manifesto separately, and in this case the Government was so much disturbed by its tone that it circulated a forged letter in which the politician condemned his manifesto. Similar action was also taken by other politicians, prominent or otherwise.[1]

Again it is difficult to account for this concerted paper activity, which created quite an impression at the time. Metaxas felt that the politicians wished to become 'heroes'; but that they would only become 'ridiculous'.[2] Whatever the case may be, Metaxas was quick to see that public discontent in a police state could not be effective if deprived of its leadership. Accordingly, he reacted swiftly by arresting and deporting the leaders involved in the affair, thus stifling the movement, at least for the time being. According to the British Minister in Athens, the reason behind Metaxas's strong measures against the politicians was the fact that he was about to leave for Ankara, where the Council of the Balkan Entente would hold its annual meeting, over which he was to preside. Metaxas, therefore, could hardly be expected to leave the country in the midst of a domestic crisis.[3] The deported politicians included Kafandaris, who was exiled to Zakynthos; Theotokis to Paros; Alexandros Mylonas, leader of the Agrarian Party, to Ikaria; Georghios Papandreou to Kythera and then to Andros; A. Livieratos to Zakynthos, A. Melas to Paros, and other less well-known figures to various places. Sophoulis was taken to the Security and, after questioning and some intimidation, was released. An interesting catch was Ioannis Polychronopoulos, the police official accused of complicity in the attempt on Venizelos's life in 1933. Another man arrested was Andreas Michalakopoulos, who was deported on 10 February to Paros, while ill in bed. On 1 March, Michalakopoulos was hurried back to Athens only to die on 27 March.[4] In the previous year

---

[1] Daphnis, op. cit., vol. ii, pp. 445 ff.   [2] *Diary*, vol. iv, p. 291, 8 Jan. 1938.
[3] Athens Disp. No. 45, 5 Feb. 1938, F.O. 371/22370.
[4] Daphnis, op. cit., vol. ii, pp. 449 ff.

Panaghiotis Kanellopoulos was arrested, on account of a manifesto calling on the King to turn out the dictator, and was deported first to Kythnos, then to Thasos, and finally to Karystos, Euboia, where he remained until November 1940.[1]

Waterlow felt that the agitation by itself should not be taken seriously. The politicians, he wrote with some justice, had succeeded at last in forcing Metaxas to make 'martyrs' of them.[2] However, what he was seriously concerned about was the fate of the King in the light of these developments. One result of the recent deportations was that the dictator had decisively strengthened his position, while the King's fate was irrevocably bound up with that of the dictator. In a sense, the disappearance of the politicians from the scene, impotent though they essentially were, had deprived the King of a possible alternative to Metaxas, an alternative moreover which the King could use in order to force Metaxas to lead the country back to constitutional life. These considerations were brought before the King by the British Minister himself, in one of his frequent conversations with the monarch. On 25 January, Waterlow spoke to King George about the current agitation, saying that he was concerned over public discontent against the dictatorship and the inherent threat to the monarchy, since people tended to equate the two. It is interesting that in this instance the King confirmed the Minister's misgivings, and confessed to 'great anxiety'. He realized, as he told Waterlow, that Metaxas was making 'grave mistakes', and something in the form of a 'safety valve' had to be provided soon. All the same, the Minister was left with the impression after this conversation that the King had the situation 'well in hand'.[2] Carrying further this line of argument, Waterlow expressed the view that the King, under the pressure of public discontent, would soon be obliged to 'come into the open' and declare his attitude towards the dictatorial regime. In such a case, he believed, it would be the King, not the dictator, who was bound to win, for the King held 'all the best cards', i.e. the army. The Minister was convinced, and tried also to convince the Foreign Office, that the monarch's position was completely secure, since the army was

[1] Panaghiotis Kanellopoulos, *1935–1945: An Account Sheet* (in Greek), Athens, 1945, pp. 9 ff.
[2] Athens Disp. No. 35, 28 Jan. 1938, F.O. 371/22370.

in his hands. This conviction, as we shall see, was abandoned later in the year, when the Minister would try to convince the Foreign Office of exactly the opposite. At any rate, the Foreign Office on this occasion could only ponder with some concern over the future of Greece. The prevailing feeling in the Southern Department was one of concern and resignation, though one comment ran as follows: 'It will suit our book if the King really becomes master of the situation.'[1]

Metaxas, however, felt otherwise. On 30 January he noted with justifiable satisfaction that 'the deportations had a lightning result', and everyone was 'quiet'. Moreover, he was resolved to 'supplement' the deportations if necessary. He was also satisfied, after a long conversation with the King, that the latter, though 'influenced' to some extent by palace counsels, was 'on the whole in agreement'. At any rate, the dictator had decided to 'go ahead', if need be alone, and that he would allow 'nothing' to stand in his way.[2] The outcome of the whole affair, as far as he was concerned, left little to be desired. Commenting on 19 February, when the dust had barely settled, he noted:

Everyone is now quiet. The rumours came to an end, and so did all opposition. The people are on the whole content, because order has been assured and the Government is strong. The shock of January was due to the people's doubts as to whether the Government was powerful enough to impose its authority, or whether it was hindered by the Palace. All these hesitations, doubts and scepticism disappeared. This has been the result of the display of force . . .[3]

Absolute peace and order reigned; so much so that the dictator felt 'uneasy'.

In late February, and while Metaxas was on his way to Ankara,[4] Waterlow wrote to the Foreign Office, drawing a gloomy picture of the political situation.[5] The dictator, Waterlow wrote, had done some useful work, but he and his regime remained as unpopular as ever; and what was even more disquieting, the popularity of the King was compromised

---

[1] Athens Disp. No. 45, 5 Feb. 1938, and F.O. Minutes in F.O. 371/22370.
[2] *Diary*, vol. iv, p. 292, 30 Jan. 1938.
[3] Ibid., p. 293, 19 Feb. 1938.   [4] Metaxas left for Ankara on 22 Feb.
[5] Confidential letter from Waterlow to Sir Alexander Cadogan, 23 Feb. 1938, F.O. 371/22370.

by his association with the regime. There was little doubt, he believed, that an upheaval in Greece would carry away the monarchy as well as the dictatorship. The Minister went on to say that the British Government had in the Greek case, 'real cause for anxiety; for not only is the Monarchy the only stable element here, but it is clearly in our interest from many wider points of view that the position of so good and steady a friend of ours as King George should be consolidated'. Waterlow felt that there were two courses open to the King: either to declare that he meant to introduce some form of representative government, and that in doing so he would 'either drop Metaxas and act as a dictator himself meanwhile, or impose his own nominees on Metaxas'. But the King's difficulty seemed to be that he could not think of an 'alternative Prime Minister'. Waterlow knew that Kafandaris and Michalakopoulos had been considered for this role, but were both rejected, because the former had made it plain to the King that he would repudiate the Greek foreign debt, while the latter was not dependable in view of his pro-Italian sympathies. But the trouble was that the King was 'nerveless, puzzled, undecided and without a plan'; and worse, he was losing his 'grip'. Clearly, Waterlow was hinting that the King might do well to check Metaxas somehow—or just drop him—and announce that representative government would be reintroduced, and this in the not too distant future. Yet such action was not feasible, because, according to Waterlow himself, the King was simply not in the mood for such action, while he saw no alternative to Metaxas. These points and questions were considered by the Foreign Office, but no easy answers could be supplied. The Southern Department was not convinced that direct Palace government would be any better, since the King would have to accept direct responsibility. Direct palace government, even if acceptable to the people as Waterlow implied, was bound to increase the King's responsibilities and as a result probably undermine his standing in the country. On the other hand, if the King remained aloof and kept away from the actual running of the country, he might be able to claim with some credibility, when the hour of crisis came, that he had been unable to turn the dictator out and reintroduce some form of legal government. A long minute, with which Sir Robert Vansittart, Sir Alexander Cadogan,

and Lord Halifax agreed, concluded with the following suggestion:

> Greece must work out her own salvation. It would certainly be
> most unfortunate from our point of view if things were to drift to
> a climax which would lead to the disappearance of the King who
> is certainly our friend; but there does not seem to be anything that
> we can do to help him and I am not satisfied that we should be well
> advised to urge on him the course of action which Sir S. Waterlow
> seems to favour.[1]

At this point a fuller explanation of British policy is needed,
because this is exactly the time when the Government seemed
to be seriously concerned over the spread of totalitarianism in
central and south-eastern Europe. In a circular dispatch to the
British Ministers in these states, Neville Chamberlain expressed
the fear that the current trend away from democracy and
towards arbitrary government among these states might either
presage a disposition to fortify themselves against German
encroachment, or else denote a conviction that German domination was inevitable sooner or later, with a consequent determination to mitigate its effects by copying in advance the
pattern of the conqueror.[2] Waterlow felt that Chamberlain's
observations could not possibly apply to Greece, because
Greece, he maintained, had submitted to dictatorship neither
in order to fortify herself against German encroachment, nor
in order to curry favour with a power whose domination was
considered inevitable, but solely because parliamentary government had broken down completely. Democracy in Greece,
Waterlow said, was always an 'unreal farce', and the dictatorship could only be understood in terms of the breaking down
of a system grown unworkable under the harsh stresses of the
post-war period. He was also convinced that the presence of
King George as well as the traditional dependence of Greece
on Britain were sufficient to ensure that the continuance of
the dictatorship would not spell a gradual capitulation of
the country to German influence. Moreover, Waterlow and the
Foreign Office believed that ideologically, the Greeks—that

---

[1] F.O. Minutes, Mar. 1938, attached to Waterlow's letter to Cadogan, 23 Feb.
1938, in F.O. 371/22370. Waterlow's letter was sent to King George VI, who was
'sorry' to read the disquieting news.

[2] Chamberlain's Disp. No. 7, of 6 Jan. 1938, F.O. 371/22370.

'non-mystical and cynical race'—were not good material for a Nazi mould.[1] Yet, despite these reassuring observations, there were good reasons for concern over Greek developments, for there were many doubts about the actual strength of King George's position in relation to Metaxas. It is true that the King controlled the army, which he could use in a confrontation with the dictator; the latter, however, controlled the Security Services, and had created a whole machinery of his own in the state apparatus. Moreover, King George had compromised himself and the dynasty irreparably by his association with the regime, and the end of Metaxas might well mean his own fall.

This, then, was the situation in Greece in the early spring of 1938, as far as the British Government was concerned: by all reports an alarming situation and no easy remedy available. The interpretation might of course be questioned, but unfortunately there is very little in the form of dependable evidence on which to base an alternative appraisal of the situation. No doubt, the British Minister was unduly alarmed, and overstressed the gloomy aspects of the situation; at any rate, subsequent developments did not bear out the Minister's fears. Waterlow, like most of his contemporaries, was the least prepared to see the strength of the totalitarian state, which was entrenching itself in Greece. He was a good judge of the causes that led to the downfall of Greek representative government, and could see the appalling helplessness of the political world; but what he was unable to see was the equally appalling helplessness of the people faced with a police state, which in fact accounted for most of the regime's strength. In his expectation of a popular upheaval he was no less unrealistic than the Greek Communists were. As far as alternatives to Metaxas went, it might be argued that the picture was not so bleak. The men packed off to the islands were ready, as the recent events had made it abundantly clear, to assume the responsibility of office. Yet there were many imponderables that conspired against such a solution, even if Metaxas could be turned out of power, which is rather questionable. The key to the whole situation was the army, and a return of the politicians was bound to reopen the issue of the expelled Venizelist and

[1] Athens Disp. No. 23, 24 Jan. 1938, and F.O. Minutes, F.O. 371/22370.

republican officers. There was simply no room for these officers in the army, which was almost completely royalist, and not prepared to welcome them back. Moreover, the royalist army was the source of the King's authority in the country. It is very doubtful whether the army question and the constitutional issue could have been dealt with short of a violent upheaval, for the stakes were indeed high. It was a case of winners and losers again, and the accumulated bitterness made reconciliation almost impossible. Perhaps later and more terrible upheavals might never have come to pass if an attempt had been made at this stage to clean out the Greek stables; but no one who mattered in Greece was prepared to face this task. The army jealously guarded its privileges; the King feared the worst for himself and the country if the army question were to be re-opened; and the politicians were lamentably impotent. What was more important was that the dictator and his lieutenants were increasingly becoming captives of their clumsy fascist gestures and grandiose programmes. Their aim was nothing less than the creation of the 'Third Greek Civilization', and in this they were deadly serious. All these factors were only too well realized by the British Government; and their decision to let Greece work out her own salvation shows to some extent their helplessness over changing the situation. Besides, as far as short-term British interests were concerned, they had very little to complain about, and very much to be satisfied with, in Metaxas.

In early March the dictator returned from Turkey by way of Macedonia, where the public was herded together for a grand welcome, which satisfied his vanity; even so, he expected the welcome to be more 'enthusiastic'.[1] On 19 March he felt 'optimistic' about the situation, but was still puzzled by the probable 'causes' of the January events.[2] A few days later he was still uneasy, and wondered whether the 'storm' had really passed.[3] At this time he had a conversation with Waterlow, and assured the Minister that Greece was 'absolutely bound up with Britain'. This assurance was in fact made in response to the Minister's inquiry about the results of the Balkan Entente Council meeting and the state of Greco-Turkish relations; but

---

[1] *Diary*, vol. iv, p. 298, 12 Mar. 1938.   [2] Loc. cit., 19 Mar. 1938.
[3] Ibid., p. 299, 22 Mar. 1938.

it is possible that the dictator wished to curry favour with the British Minister. Metaxas's uneasiness vanished after attending the celebrations of 25 March. He was satisfied with the appearance of the Labour Battalions, his 'guard' as he called them; and he was overjoyed by the National Youth. After the celebrations he wrote in his diary: 'What a dream, yesterday and today. Yesterday at the Champs de Mars with the National Youth. My creation. A creation which succeeded in spite of so much reaction . . .'[1]

The National Youth Movement, the notorious *E.O.N.* (*Ethniki Organosis Neolaias*), was indeed Metaxas's own creation to a great extent, a creation moreover which provided the dictator with some consolation when popular support was not forthcoming. It is interesting to note that the Youth Movement did not fail to impress at this stage the otherwise sceptical British Minister. Commenting on a confidential circular to district governors of 14 February 1938, Waterlow said that 'the most interesting and encouraging feature' of this paper was that, although the methods for the attainment of the 'reformation' of the Greek character savoured of National Socialism, the end in view was different from 'brutal totalitarianism'. What Metaxas essentially meant was 'the building up of a nation of healthy personalities of the kind that the public school system seeks to produce, and the creation and development of the team spirit as a check to the excessive individuality of the Greek'. Furthermore, this 'reformation' was not to be carried through in opposition to the Church, but in close co-operation with it. Needless to say, Jews were kept out of the *E.O.N.* ranks. The state paper ended with the following:

> The object of the whole organization of the youth in general lines is the same as that for which the State exists: The maintenance of the Greek nation as a strong factor of progress in the future, and the creation of the Third Greek Civilization, a civilization superior to those of the past and capable of keeping our nation among those who wish, are able, and are worthy to live.[2]

---

[1] Ibid., p. 299, 25 Mar. 1938. Uneasiness, however, was endemic with Metaxas. On 31 Mar. he noted: 'I am always uneasy and wavering. I must arrive somewhere. Yet one inch away from dictatorial rule, and parliamentary government is awaiting me. Representation and the like lead to parliamentary government.'

[2] Athens Disp. No. 205, 2 June 1938, F.O. 371/22370. The state paper was signed by Metaxas.

Metaxas's attempts at regeneration of the country preoccupied the British anew, and in particular Waterlow, at the end of the year, when they felt, as will be seen, anything but admiration.

Waterlow soon recovered his optimism about the situation in Greece generally, and the position of the King in particular. King George, it seems, had recovered his 'grip' on the situation. This change of mood on the part of the Minister was reassuring, but caused some sour comments in London. It was not easy, one Foreign Office comment ran, 'to keep up with Sir S. Waterlow'.[1] The position of the King was brought up again in early June by Emmanouil Tsouderos, Governor of the Bank of Greece, a Venizelist who now cultivated the favour of the British Government. Tsouderos suggested that the British Legation should do something to bring the King more into the picture, and this suggestion caused a fresh appraisal of the situation. In other circumstances, the emergence of the King from his habitual aloofness into the open, from the 'shadow' into the 'limelight', would have been desirable; but in this case he would only share Metaxas's unpopularity to an even greater degree. The King's position might have been improved if he had come out with different policies from those that Metaxas was practising, but there was no sign of this, except the hint about a change, already mentioned.[2]

When the storm created by the politicians seemed to have finally subsided, another untoward event suddenly disturbed the otherwise calm surface of the dictatorship. On the night of 28 July 1938, a rising broke out in Canea, Crete, and the rebels broadcast a message from the local wireless station, addressed to the King, the armed forces, and the people, calling for the overthrow of the dictatorial regime and the restoration of representative government. The Government was surprised on this occasion, but reacted swiftly to localize the insurrection. The first step was to drop leaflets inviting the Cretans to disarm the rebels, and this was followed by the dispatch of a small force to the island. A squadron of destroyers and some seaplanes were ordered to the island of Melos, which was to become a base for operations against the Cretan rebels, while an expeditionary force of divisional strength was being prepared. There

[1] Athens Disp., 11 Apr. 1938, and F.O. Minutes, F.O. 371/22370.
[2] F.O. Minutes, June 1938, F.O. 371/22370.

was no need, however, for such forces, since the insurrection collapsed almost by itself. In fact, most Greeks heard of it late on 29 July, when all resistance had already come to an end.[1]

The conspirators included such men as Tsouderos, Pericles Argyropoulos, Aristomenis Mitsotakis, Emmanouil Mantakas, and a host of politicians and cashiered Venizelist officers. A plausible account of the aims and the plan of the insurgents was given to Waterlow by Tsouderos, whose involvement in the affair did not come into the open, despite the fact that he supported the insurgents financially.[2] Tsouderos claimed that the insurrection was neither a local affair, nor inspired from France, as Metaxas wanted people to believe. The affair, according to this account, had been planned by a committee of politicians in Athens, and the end in view was to force a return to representative government by convincing the King, by way of simultaneous demonstrations in many parts of the country, of Metaxas's unpopularity. The movement was not anti-dynastic, nor in favour of Plastiras, as it might be thought, for, as he said, 'there was no desire to exchange one dictator for another—and probably a less efficient one at that'. Tsouderos also took the opportunity to say to the British Minister that, unless the King introduced some change in Greece, there was a real danger of revolution. Waterlow of course dismissed the forebodings of the wily Cretan, and suspected that the latter's confidences might have been the result of private reasons, the nature of which he considered 'useless even to try to guess' at. He accepted, however, Tsouderos's account of the affair, and felt that Metaxas's version, namely that the insurrection had emanated from abroad,[3] was cooked up. Naturally, a rising presented in this light would not be as odious as one that was the result of discontent among the Greeks. Yet the whole truth of the affair could not be ascertained; certain conspirators, he had learnt, had turned traitor, and were perhaps used as *agents provocateurs* by the secret police, and that finally the affair came to an end amidst 'double and triple crossing by all concerned'.[4]

---

[1] Daphnis, op. cit., vol. ii, pp. 457 ff.
[2] Argyropoulos, *Memoirs*, vol. ii, p. 26.
[3] Athens Disp., 3 Aug. 1938, F.O. 371/22370.
[4] Athens Disp. No. 288, Confidential, 15 Aug. 1938, F.O. 371/22370.

D

If double crossings there were, an element of farce was not lacking, either. Following the collapse of the insurrection, a number of arrests were made. They included Stylianos Gonatas, who was deported to Mykonos,[1] P. Rallis, D. Helmis, K. Rentis, General Protosyngelos, Admirals Demestichas and Kolialexis, both prominent in the Venizelist rising of March 1935, and a host of cashiered officers; but the rebel leaders were allowed to slip out of the country. Mitsotakis and most of the other leaders were allowed to board a boat and flee to Cyprus,[2] while Mantakas took to the mountains. The most interesting case was that of Argyropoulos: he was informed by the Minister of Press and Tourism, Nikoloudis, who was related to him, that the Government had decided to arrest him, and was therefore advised to hide. The farce assumed greater proportions when Argyropoulos was visited in one of his 'hiding places' by an emissary of Maniadakis, none else than Napoleon Zervas, who was allegedly active in the resistance, but it is not unlikely that he was at the same time in touch with Maniadakis.[3] Zervas advised Argyropoulos, in the name of Maniadakis, to leave the country; and so he did in fact, but not before meeting the Chief of Security, to whom he 'made it clear' that he did not intend to give up his 'anti-dictatorial' activity.[4] The Greek Communists, who had been in touch with the conspirators,[5] made a belated effort to incite the public to rise against the dictatorship. On 25 September 1938 *Risospastis*, the underground Communist newspaper, carried a manifesto of the Political Bureau of the Central Committee, which was addressed 'to the people, the armed forces, and the new generation', and called on them to express by deeds their solidarity towards 'the liberation movement of Crete'. The rising in Crete, the Communist leadership claimed, expressed 'the will and hopes of the whole of Greece', and was the result of 'the overflowing hatred against the dictatorship'. In March 1939 the Communist Party claimed to have played a 'primary role' in the Canea rising.[6]

---

[1] Gonatas, *Memoirs 1897–1957* (in Greek), Athens, 1958, p. 388.
[2] Daphnis, op. cit., vol. ii, p. 460.
[3] *Acropolis*, 1 Feb. 1972.
[4] Argyropoulos, op. cit., vol. ii, pp. 26, 27.
[5] Kousoulas, op. cit., pp. 136, 137.
[6] *Official Documents of the Greek Communist Party*, vol. iv, pp. 450–1, 466.

The Foreign Office considered the Canea rising 'a purely local affair and not of a true revolutionary type'. They felt that it was a mere incident, which represented the least danger to the dictatorial regime, and made no secret of their conviction that Metaxas was there to stay.[1] All the same, the rising caused a fresh appraisal of the political situation in Greece, which was put on paper. It was felt that the dictatorship, though it did not seem to command the support 'of some of the enlightened sections of the community', was secure, since the existing discontent was not likely to lead to a revolution. The peasants were reported to be satisfied with a good harvest and high prices for wheat, and the workers were content with higher wages, which offset to some extent the rise in the cost of living and social insurance benefits. More important, the loyalty of the armed forces could on the whole be depended on. The dictator, also, had recently assured the British Minister that he had the situation 'well in hand for an indefinite time to come'.[2]

This appraisal also appeared in a Foreign Office letter to the president of the Council of Foreign Bondholders in a reply to his inquiry about the political situation in Greece in connection with a mission the bondholders wanted to send to Greece in order to negotiate a fresh agreement on the debt. To leave no doubts about the attitude of the British Government to the dictatorial regime, Sir Orme Sargent wrote that it was 'in British interests that the present regime in Greece should be maintained and strengthened'.[3] In another letter to the bondholders Sargent wrote to reassure them about Metaxas. Bluntly—almost brutally so—he argued:

. . . What is required in Greece from the point of view of British interests is that the Government should be as stable, efficient and honest as governments in Greece can be expected to be, and that its chief or chiefs should set store by the British connexion. The present Government possesses more or less these qualifications and though we don't hold a brief for it insofar as it is a dictatorship rather than a parliamentary administration, we have had such disappointing experiences of the latter in Greece from the point of view of British

[1] F.O. Minutes, Aug. 1938, F.O. 371/22370.
[2] F.O. Minutes, Aug. 1938, F.O. 371/22355.
[3] Letter from Sir Orme Sargent to Lord Bessborough, 12 Aug. 1938, F.O. 371/22355.

interests, that we are not inclined to attach very much value to that particular type of parliamentarism which is traditional in Greece and which would be the most likely alternative to the present dictatorship. The other alternative would be a purely military dictatorship such as that of General Pangalos in 1926, and such a Government most certainly would not be in British interests.[1]

The Foreign Office further explained that the Government in Greece supported the King, and that this was an assurance that the country would not be divided again over the issue of the regime. Moreover, it was not unlikely that the dictatorial regime would eventually evolve into a government 'of a rather more constitutional nature'. Needless to say, this last represented only a wish, and, as will be seen in another instance, it was expressed with very little conviction.

An Unequal Relation

In the autumn of 1938 the attention of the Foreign Office was turned to a more pressing matter than internal Greek affairs. Anglo-Greek relations, as defined during the Mediterranean crisis of 1935–6, left something to be desired as far as the Greek side was concerned. There was a certain imbalance in these relations, and this Metaxas tried to correct in the autumn of 1938. What was lacking in Anglo-Greek relations, according to him, was a 'sound base' on which these relations would rest. Writing to Simopoulos in May 1938 about relations with Britain, Metaxas said: 'Politically, we shall never cease to be friends; but friendship must rest on a sound base.'[2] Both governments realized the unbalanced nature of Anglo-Greek trade, and it was left to Britain to redress the existing position, particularly in the light of German economic penetration in south-eastern Europe. In April of that year Waterlow had drawn the attention of the Foreign Office to the fact that the British were living on the 'capital' of the investment symbolized by the death of Byron at Missolonghi, and trusted to Greek goodwill to resist German domination.[3]

---

[1] Letter from Sir Orme Sargent to Lord Bessborough, Strictly Confidential, 29 Aug. 1938, and F.O. Minutes, F.O. 371/22355.

[2] Letter from Metaxas to Simopoulos, 31 May 1938, Simopoulos Papers,

[3] Athens Disp. No. 140, 7 Apr. 1938, F.O. 371/22362.

Throughout the period under consideration, the trade balance between Greece and Britain was always in Britain's favour. At the end of 1937, Greece had an unfavourable balance of £1,359,572, and the previous year almost £2,000,000. Greece imported from Britain industrial machinery, various chemical products, and coal, and exported to Britain currants, which amounted to 70 per cent of Greece's total exports of that product, as well as sultanas, figs, and some ores.[1] Greek exports to Britain during this time amounted to 10 per cent of the country's total exports, while imports from Britain amounted to 13·3 per cent of her total imports. At the same time, Greek exports to Germany amounted to 35·3 per cent, and imports 26·2 per cent.[2] Greece therefore exported to Germany more than three times as much as she exported to Britain, and imported from Germany twice as much as from Britain. Germany imported from Greece large quantities of tobacco, a product that topped all others in production and export revenues. Total Greek exports of tobacco in 1938 were 48,894 tons, and this amounted to 50·4 per cent of the total value of Greek exports. Germany imported 25,823 tons, or 52·8 per cent of the total exports of Greek tobacco, while Britain imported from Greece a mere 503 tons, and in the previous year only 203. At the same time, Britain imported close to 100,000 tons of tobacco from the United States, and more than 20,000 from Commonwealth countries.[3]

As far as Greece was concerned, the important step Britain could take to help her break free from economic dependence on Germany would be to take Germany's place as the principal buyer of Greek tobacco. Britain, however, found it difficult to be of any help in this direction. British tobacco companies simply refused to mix Virginia tobacco with Greek tobacco (Oriental), which they considered too 'pungent' for British tastes; and the British Government was never willing to put the necessary pressure on the tobacco interests to reconsider their attitude about a matter that had acquired by then political dimensions. The Foreign Office realized clearly

---

[1] Memorandum of the Greek Foreign Ministry, Nov. 1938, Simopoulos Papers.

[2] B. Sweet-Escott, *Greece: A Political and Economic Survey, 1939–53*, London, 1954, p. 187.

[3] D. Kitsikis, 'La Grèce entre l'Angleterre et l'Allemagne de 1936 à 1941', *Revue Historique*, juil.–sept. 1967, pp. 95–6.

enough that Greece might not be able to resist German domination in the end, unless Britain decided to abandon orthodox trade practices, and fight German methods with 'imitations' of totalitarian weapons. If Germany could use financial pressure to obtain political ends, it seemed surprising that Britain, which was richer than Germany, could not follow the same policy and with greater success. The Treasury, however, felt that they could not possibly 'out-Schacht' Germany in that direction. They were also sceptical about the possibility of Greece being able to obtain any financial assistance from Britain; Greece's credit, according to the Treasury, had sunk low on account of the bondholders' grievances.[1]

The need to buy Greek tobacco preoccupied the British Government in the spring of 1938, when the Foreign Policy Committee held several meetings on that subject. On 10 May the Secretary of State for Foreign Affairs argued in favour of buying Greek tobacco on a massive scale in order to help Greece disengage economically from Germany, but the Chancellor of the Exchequer set out the difficulties involved in such a project, on account of the refusal of the tobacco companies to buy Greek tobacco. The Secretaries for the Dominions and the Colonies argued that the purchase of Greek tobacco would affect unfavourably tobacco imports from Southern Rhodesia and Cyprus. The effect on the trade agreement with the United States was also mentioned, since the purchase of Greek tobacco was bound to affect imports of American tobacco.[2] Halifax repeatedly stressed the political aspect of the question, saying that Greece would be less able and willing to resist German pressure, if nothing was done to help her. But Chamberlain stuck to the business side, arguing that Britain could look for no 'return' from Greece; and that in present circumstances Greece 'could not in fact afford to quarrel' with Britain.[3] The subject of Greek tobacco was discussed again in June, when Halifax persuaded a reluctant Cabinet to make an effort to check German economic penetration in central and south-eastern Europe by aiding these states; but no decision was reached on Greek tobacco.[4]

---

[1] F.O. Minutes and Correspondence with the Treasury, Apr. 1938, F.O. 371/22354.   [2] F.P. (36) 46, Meeting, 10 May 1938, Cab. 27/625.
[3] F.P. (36) 46, Cab. 27/627.   [4] F.P. (36) 30, 1 June 1938, Cab. 27/623.

The question of the Greek tobacco remained unsolved, and made the rounds of various committees and departments. The crux of the matter was the unwillingness of British tobacco interests to buy Greek tobacco, even for resale to the United States. The Foreign Office saw its policy to help Greece being defeated by economic interests. Purchase of considerable quantities of Greek tobacco by Britain would liberate Greece from Germany's economic clutches; at the same time, it would enable the country to work out a settlement with the bondholders, and thus re-establish its credit. It would then be possible for Britain to give Greece a loan, or export credits on a large scale. The purchase of tobacco would thus be the first step in the direction of British assistance to Greece, and both Governments accepted that. But the bondholders demanded as a first step a settlement of the debt, and wished to make such a settlement a prior condition to any negotiations for a loan or credits to Greece. In a sense, they put the cart before the horse, as an official of the Foreign Office observed with dismay.[1]

The easiest way out would have been an Anglo-Greek alliance. It would cut short German penetration in Greece at a stroke, lead to a settlement of the debt issue, and guarantee Greece's independence and territorial integrity. The first hints of a solution on these lines came from the Greek Government, when Apostolidis, Minister of Finance, suggested in May 1938 that Britain should guarantee Greece's frontiers. The suggestion was apparently made in the light of Britain's recent decision to facilitate Bulgaria's rearmament, which had caused much discomfort in Greece. The Foreign Office briefly considered the approach, but felt that Britain could not possibly guarantee Greece's borders, and should rather concentrate on economic aid.[2] Soon afterwards, Metaxas himself proposed to Waterlow that Britain should undertake to guarantee Greece's frontiers, or sign an alliance with her. About the same time, and in the face of Bulgaria's rearmament, King George implored the British to do 'something' for Greece as well.[3]

[1] Foreign Office Memo., 15 July 1938, F.O. 371/22355.

[2] Correspondence and F.O. Minutes, May 1938, F.O. 371/22362. The British Legation in Athens expressed the conviction that the initiative had come from King George.

[3] Athens Tels. Nos. 20 and 21 Saving, 7 June 1938, F.O. 371/22362.

The proposal of the Greek Government, and especially the factors and intentions behind it, were, from the point of view of Britain, beside the point. Evidently, Greece needed the alliance in order to keep Bulgaria at bay, while Britain saw her relations with Greece in connection with German penetration in south-eastern Europe and Italian hostility in the Mediterranean. Even for this contingency, however, alliance with Greece was out of the question. The British Chiefs of Staff had already considered the subject in March 1938, in a report on British strategy towards central and south-eastern Europe. Alliances with these states, the Chiefs of Staff considered, would prove of limited assistance to Britain, and might ultimately constitute 'embarrassing commitments', since Britain had a 'moral obligation' to help them resist a German attack.[1] The Foreign Office decided therefore not to ask the Chiefs of Staff for a reconsideration of Greece's strategic value, and to leave them as yet out of the picture. They wanted first to strengthen Greece's position by economic means; and only if these failed, a consultative pact—not an alliance—might be considered. Alliance with Greece would be far more costly than economic assistance, and would constitute a commitment capable of embroiling Britain in Balkan affairs. Halifax and Vansittart were ready to see the 'indisputable' political value of Greece to Britain. None the less, they were convinced that an Anglo-Greek alliance was out of the question.[2]

But if the British were eager to shelve the alliance issue, Metaxas would not let them. During the Munich crisis of September 1938, Metaxas assured the British Government that in the event of war Greece would remain benevolently neutral towards Britain, and in no case would she side with Italy. Metaxas would define his position no further, until he knew to what extent British forces would protect Greece against an Italian attack. The British Minister in Greece was convinced that British naval requirements in the event of war with Italy would force Greece into an actively benevolent neutrality towards, if not in alliance with, Britain. As might be expected, the Foreign Office was satisfied with Greek intentions in the event of war in the Mediterranean, and considered approaching

[1] C.O.S. 698, Secret, 21 Mar. 1938, Cab. 27/627.
[2] Foreign Office Minutes, June 1938, F.O. 371/22362.

the Chiefs of Staff for an appreciation of Greece's strategic value. The Munich Agreement, however, cut short these exchanges, and the Foreign Office decided not to make to Metaxas any immediate or definitive statement with regard to the issues he had raised.[1]

Shortly after the Munich crisis Metaxas made a fresh approach to the British Government for an Anglo-Greek alliance. In a conversation with the British Minister on 3 October 1938, Metaxas said that he wanted Anglo-Greek relations to become 'more stable'. Waterlow repeated in his telegram to the Foreign Office Metaxas's argument:

An alliance with Great Britain is what I want. And why not? We must assume as a plain fact that in the event of European war the use of the Greek islands and Greek ports will be an imperative necessity to the British Fleet and Air Arm. If you cannot have this automatically as an ally, you will be obliged to take it, but with complications. It is no good blinking geography. And surely Greece will be a force worth having as an ally, and immediately. . . . And an alliance would be the natural thing in the sense that there is not a man, woman or child in Greece who is not whole-heartedly devoted to your country.

Frankly I do not understand your attitude. You need Greece. In the past you have used her in your hour of need and you will do so again in the future, yet while you do much for Turkey, you show no disposition to do anything for Greece, to stand at her side or to help her. I am now thinking not only of our political relations, but also of that economic help, credits and so forth, which we need for our national revival and which we feel, especially in view of what you are doing for Turkey, we have almost a right to expect from you. And you know how Germans are working here. Why do you do nothing?[2]

Naturally, the British Minister was not prepared to give a reply to such a proposal, but speaking personally he said that there were two objections to an Anglo-Greek alliance: (*a*) that it would 'excite' Italian susceptibilities, and (*b*) that British public opinion would object to the assumption of a commitment to defend Greece against Bulgaria. Instead, he put forward the idea of a consultative pact, which Metaxas liked, and the

[1] Athens Tels. Nos. 169 and 171, 28 Sept. 1938, and attached Foreign Office Minutes, F.O. 371/22362.

[2] Athens Tel. No. 177, Confidential, 3 Oct. 1938, F.O. 371/22362.

dispatch of an Air Mission to organize the Greek Air Force, which was received with no sign of opposition. In writing to the Foreign Office, Waterlow expressed the opinion that 'some form of close political relation with Greece' was necessary. At the same time Waterlow felt that it was possible that Metaxas, in making the proposal for an alliance, was moved partly by self-interest, namely the strengthening of his own position, since an Anglo-Greek alliance was expected to be popular in Greece. In the light of internal Greek affairs, therefore, the British Government, by such an alliance, would run the danger of strengthening a dictatorship; on the other hand, Waterlow argued, closer Anglo-Greek relations might very well add to the possibilities of a liberalization of the regime.[1]

Like the British Minister in Athens, the Foreign Office was not prepared to give a reply to this offer, and only instructed the Minister to assure Metaxas that the British Government would give his proposal 'the most careful and sympathetic study'. In non-diplomatic terms, this essentially meant that the proposal would be shelved. Even such 'more practical' palliatives as an Air Mission and non-commercial credits for the Greek Air Force were considered 'far from encouraging', as the Minister in Athens was informed.[2] Despite the unsympathetic treatment of his proposal, Metaxas carried the point still further by handing Waterlow, on 15 October, a Memorandum, the main part of which reads as follows: as a Mediterranean state,

Greece, faithful to the traditional friendship binding her to Great Britain, observes in regard to the Mediterranean question a policy corresponding to that of Great Britain. Consequently, she will be prepared to concert with and to enter into a close contact with His Majesty's Government in the United Kingdom with a view to an agreement on questions of common interest.[3]

The following day Metaxas told the British Minister that Greece 'must be prepared for the possibility of war between Great Britain and Italy in which Greece would sooner or later be involved'; and the reason why he wanted an alliance with Britain was that only on that basis could comprehensive

---

[1] Athens Tel. No. 177, Confidential, 3 Oct. 1938, F.O. 371/22362.
[2] F.O. Tel. to Athens, No. 157, 7 Oct. 1938, F.O. 371/22362.
[3] Athens Tel. No. 196, 15 Oct. 1938, F.O. 371/22362.

defence arrangements be made in concert with Britain, thus avoiding the 'mistakes' of World War I. And if an alliance was simply impossible for the British Government, he urged that they should make available to Greece adequate financial assistance so that Greece could build a strong air force with adequate anti-aircraft and coastal defence. In that case the alliance could become effective in practice. On this occasion Metaxas said something he strongly believed, and something he repeated time and again, namely that control of the Greek peninsula and islands would be 'a vital strategical necessity' to Britain's position in the Eastern Mediterranean. Greece was, indeed, strategically useful to Britain but not vitally necessary. Metaxas was unable, like many Greeks of his generation, to appreciate this difference. At the same time, he explained that if considerable financial assistance was not available, Greece would remain strictly neutral on the outbreak of war and, though she would defend her neutrality against Italian provocation or attack, she 'would yield if necessary to *force majeur*' if this was applied by Britain. But Greece 'in no circumstances' would enter into an alliance with Italy.[1]

Clearly, Metaxas was running after the British, who did not fail to see that they would eventually secure all that Metaxas promised without the obligations of an alliance. In this, of course, they could not have been more correct, but what they failed to see, or appreciate fully, was the usefulness of such an alliance in channelling Greek strategy and war preparations in a direction that would make Greece a worth-while friend. It is worth noting in this context that two-and-a-half years later the British would be sorry to find in Greece an air force not worth the name, an army pinned down in Albania and unable or unwilling to engage the Germans, and the islands, in particular Crete, woefully indefensible. The essence of Anglo-Greek relations and approaches at this time (and subsequently) was that the British underestimated, if not the real, at least the potential value of Greece; while the Greeks overestimated Britain's ability and willingness to come to their assistance, which they, and especially Metaxas, tended at all times and in all circumstances to take for granted. This was also the distance separating Britain's promises of assistance to Greece and the

[1] Athens Tel. No. 200, 16 Oct. 1938, F.O. 371/22363.

latter's expectations, a distance which could never be actually bridged.

In the course of the conversation with Waterlow referred to above, Metaxas refrained from making any threat to the effect that Greece might side with Germany or Italy, if left with no promise of adequate assistance or an alliance. He only said that if the British did nothing for Greece, the latter would be unable to break away from economic dependence on Germany; but this in fact needed no expression, for it was only too well realized by the British. Nevertheless Waterlow felt that what was in Metaxas's 'mind' was an implied threat that if the British remained inactive, Greece would soon be obliged to accept Germany's 'embrace'. This threat, he said, was 'confirmed by a high official source'. Perhaps there was some basis for this allegation, in the sense that a hint might have been dropped by an official; but it is very unlikely that this was the work of Metaxas himself. His forthcoming manner in the exchanges with Waterlow leaves little doubt that he made the proposal in good faith, and that he was sincere, perhaps more than was necessary or permissible for a head of a government.[1]

The Foreign Office considered that an alliance with Greece depended on how Britain's relations with Italy developed, and therefore no decision was possible with regard to Metaxas's proposals until the position of Anglo-Italian relations was cleared up. The attitude of Germany was also considered to be equally important, for any assistance to Greece would be interpreted by Germany as anti-German policy in the Balkans. No 'undue or premature encouragement', it was felt, should be given to Metaxas.[2] The position of the Foreign Office was strengthened by Lord Perth, another 'pro-Italian', who argued, in connection with Metaxas's proposal, that a consultative pact between Britain and Greece, let alone a formal Anglo-Greek alliance, would create the gravest suspicion in Mussolini's mind, and might have 'disastrous consequences' on Anglo-Italian relations.[3] The Foreign Office held fast to these arguments, and decided that strategic considerations came second.

[1] In his diary Metaxas noted two weeks after making the proposal: 'Negotiations with Waterlow. My proposals. I am certain that they will not be accepted. Yet, I am freed . . .' *Diary*, vol. iv, p. 311, 20 Oct. 1938.

[2] F.O. Minutes, Oct. 1938, F.O. 371/22362.

[3] Rome Tel. No. 671, Confidential, 13 Oct. 1938, F.O. 371/22362.

It was believed, and with good reason, that a new appreciation by the Chiefs of Staff would not essentially differ from the one put forward in 1936. And even if the Chiefs of Staff were to give a favourable appreciation of Greece, the Foreign Office assumed that 'strategic considerations should not in all cases be allowed to prevail, but that on the contrary the problem must be looked at from the widest angle'.[1] Waterlow's recommendation that Metaxas's proposal for an Anglo-Greek alliance should be adopted as 'the only solution', fell on unreceptive ears.[2] The proposal was never discussed in a Cabinet meeting.

Halifax then put forward the usual 'second bests'. Writing to Chamberlain on 22 October, he said that in the face of the ample 'goodwill' of the Greek Government and their 'desire to link their policy' with that of Britain, such 'second bests' as the purchase of Greek tobacco and a State visit by King George to England should be considered seriously, lest the Greek Government should feel slighted.[3] But nothing came out of these suggestions. To King George, who was in England on a private visit, the Foreign Office explained that, in view of the inconclusive negotiations between Britain and Italy, any move towards a definite alliance between Britain and Greece would be more likely to do harm than good; an explanation that the King readily accepted.[4] Metaxas's assurances that Greece was irrevocably bound to Britain both in time of peace and war, especially the unreserved manner in which he made them, were in complete accord with Britain's view on the desired character of Anglo-Greek relations. Moreover, Metaxas's profuse and unreserved assurances convinced the Foreign Office that the assurances were to some extent connected with his own position. Among the possible motives behind Metaxas's proposals, they believed, was the 'desire to strengthen his position by adopting a policy of Anglophilia', which the vast majority of the Greek people appeared to approve.[5]

While in London, King George had informal talks with several members of the British Government, the Foreign Office,

[1] F.O. Memorandum, 19 Oct. 1938, F.O. 371/22362.
[2] Letter from Waterlow to Cadogan, Confidential, 17 Oct. 1938, F.O. 371/22363.
[3] R8024/361/19, F.O. 371/22362.
[4] F.O. Letter to the British Legation in Athens, 2 Nov. 1938, F.O. 371/22362.
[5] F.O. Memo., in R10206/361/19, F.O. 371/22363.

the Council of the Foreign Bondholders, and the Export Credits Guarantee Department. In his talks the King maintained that any agreement in the economic sphere should be part of a 'general agreement' between Britain and Greece. This condition, however, was rejected from the start by both the bondholders and the British Government. The debt issue naturally did not concern the British Government directly, and the bondholders were interested only in a settlement of the debt question. In his encounter with Lord Bessborough, the President of the Council of Foreign Bondholders, King George repeated the old arguments of the Greek Government, namely that they were unable to increase the debt payments. The King also took the opportunity to complain about the attitude of the Greek bondholders living either in Greece or in Britain who, when approached by the Greek Government for a separate agreement under which they would be paid in drachmas, turned down the Greek proposals saying that Lord Bessborough 'looked after' their interests. Lord Bessborough put forward the usual arguments of the bondholders, and insisted that any resumption of negotiations should depend on acceptance by the Greek Government of the following prior terms: either a temporary settlement at more than 50 per cent, or a permanent one at 68 per cent. Inevitably, there was no meeting point, and the debt issue remained unsettled.[1]

King George also met Sir Frederick Leith-Ross, President of the E.C.G.D., with whom he discussed the subjects of tobacco and credits. With regard to tobacco, the King said that on his way to London from Hamburg he got evidence, just as the Greek Government had suspected, that some Greek tobacco was re-exported by the Germans via Hamburg to Britain. There is some evidence that such trade was taking place, and it is possible that the Germans re-exported some Greek tobacco to both Britain and the United States in order to get valuable foreign exchange.[2] King George asked whether Britain could buy Greek tobacco on a large scale, and emphasized the

---

[1] Lord Bessborough's record of conversation with King George, 10 Nov. 1938, F.O. 371/22355.

[2] According to information supplied by the British Consul-General at Hamburg, considerable quantities of Greek tobacco were re-exported by the Germans to the United States. Consul's report enclosed in Berlin Dispatch No. 123, 31 Mar. 1939, F.O. 371/23776.

importance Greece placed on exports of tobacco. All he got, however, was sympathy, and some vague promises. Despite all its good intentions, the British Government was simply unable to influence British tobacco interests in the desired direction.[1]

The Foreign Policy Committee considered assistance to Greece twice during November and December 1938, while King George was still in London.[2] Halifax supported the case of Greece, arguing that she was the country which it was most important for Britain to assist at the present juncture; and that no effective assistance was possible unless in some way or other the British tobacco companies could be persuaded to buy at least £500,000-worth of Greek tobacco annually. The Secretary of State also said that repeated representations by himself and Leith-Ross to the tobacco companies had not been successful, and he proposed that the Prime Minister should put greater pressure on them. Chamberlain, however, was reluctant to intervene on these lines, and the Committee decided that the Secretary of State should examine whether the case of Greece could not be met by credits alone. The subject of tobacco was brought up again in a meeting of the Foreign Policy Committee in early December, but the only thing that became apparent was the inability, or the unwillingness, of the British Government to intervene with British tobacco interests and induce them to buy Greek tobacco. The Foreign Office proposal for export credits to Greece was also discussed, and Halifax proposed that a commercial mission should be sent to Greece for that purpose, informing the Committee that King George had in fact asked for such a mission. He said that there was a point on the purely political side, namely that 'the mission would strengthen the King of Greece against Metaxas'. It was finally decided that £2,000,000 for non-commercial credits should be allocated to Greece, and the proposed mission was approved in principle.

At this stage, the Treasury made an effort to connect export credits with the debt issue, but Halifax was able to persuade the obstinate Chancellor of the Exchequer who finally agreed

[1] Note of conversation between King George and Sir Frederick Leith-Ross, 23 Nov. 1938, F.O. 371/22355.

[2] F.P. (36) 33, and F.P. (36) 37, Cab. 27/624.

to waive his objections.[1] Halifax, however, took care to impress this point on the King. Before the King's departure, Halifax wrote to him explaining that, while the British Government did not wish to make the grant of special credits subject to a settlement of the debt issue, they attached 'the highest importance' to such a settlement. Halifax also expressed a hidden warning, saying that failing a resumption of negotiations between the Greek Government and the bondholders, the credits arrangement might not secure 'cordial approval' from Parliamentary, City, and commercial circles.[2]

But the British could not press this point very far, or the whole affair would look like a bargain. Moreover, it was the British Government that had refused in the past to be involved in an issue which they considered to concern primarily the Greek Government and the Council of Bondholders. Also, the export credits allocated to Greece would be spent in Britain on war material; and besides the Garter, these credits were all that King George could bring back to Greece. Tobacco, which was vital to Greece, was shelved, and the proposed alliance was rejected. The grant of £2,000,000 of export credits was essentially alms to a poor relative at the back door.

British Attempts at Intervention

At the end of 1938 the British Government could not possibly have found fault with the attitude of Metaxas's Government towards Britain. The Agreements of 1937 had secured valuable concessions to various British interests; and Metaxas's ample assurances, especially those of October 1938 with regard to Greece's policy towards Britain, were considered satisfactory. Nevertheless it was now, for the first time, that the British Government began to consider the possibility of intervening in Greece's internal affairs to try and do something to make Metaxas's regime less severe and less tyrannical. The British had become concerned over the increasing discontent and resentment caused by the tendency of the regime to tighten control on popular liberties. This popular resentment, it appears, was not felt towards Metaxas only, but towards the

[1] Correspondence between the Foreign Office and the Treasury, Dec. 1938, F.O. 371/22363.
[2] Letter from Lord Halifax to King George, 19 Dec. 1938, F.O. 371/22363.

King as well, because he was identified with the dictator. What the British feared was a situation that might become explosive and lead to a revolution directed against both the regime and the dynasty. Metaxas's attitude towards Britain was of course satisfactory; his treatment, however, of the people's liberties left much to be desired and raised many doubts about the desirability of letting him go on unchecked.

An issue that caused great discontent was connected with the Youth Movement. In late 1938 Metaxas incorporated the entire youth of the country, organized or not, in a nationwide youth organization under his personal aegis and direction. Lacking a popular base, Metaxas apparently sought to create loyal and dedicated followers by inculcating the ideals of the 'Fourth of August' in the young. There is no contemporary account of public opinion by which to judge how far parents really did resent Metaxas's measures. Many Greeks today remember participation in the *E.O.N.* as something imposed on them, but the Youth Movement could not have been so unpopular as all that, to the young at least. It has been argued with good reason that the movement actually appealed to many young boys and girls, because of all that went with it—uniforms, ranks, parades, holidays, excursions to the countryside, free entry to shows, a relative freedom from parental surveillance, and a certain esteem for its members cultivated by the regime.[1] All these were appealing enough to wean many children away from the family, the most sacrosanct of Greek social institutions.

In December 1938 Metaxas decided to make the Youth Movement co-extensive with the State educational system. Accordingly, verbal instructions were given to schoolteachers to tell their pupils that they had to enrol in the *E.O.N.* on pain of expulsion.[2] The resulting distress among Greek families

---

[1] Daphnis, op. cit., vol. ii, p. 471.

[2] Indicative of Metaxas's mood and plans is a circular he sent in February 1938 to the Ministers of Education, Interior, and Public Security, in which he instructed the Ministers to make an effort for the advancement of the Youth Movement. The young must acquire a consciousness of their 'Mission' in the creation of the 'Third Greek Civilization'. They must be steeped in devotion to the Fatherland, the Fourth of August, the King, and the Orthodox faith. The 'spirit of social and State discipline', so markedly lacking among the Greeks, must be developed in the young. Metaxas also expounded the rules and the composition of the Organization, and warned that he regarded it as 'one of the most important in the State'. Copy of Metaxas's circular, No. 3/14/2/33 of 14 Feb. 1938, in F.O. 371/22360.

must have been considerable, if one can believe Waterlow's reports. The British Minister, usually unperturbed by Metaxas's trampling on Greek liberties, was alarmed, and described conditions as desperate. Pupils were being subjected to a form of refined mental torture, and expulsion from the Organization landed fathers in the hands of the police. Sexual scandals were rife, and many compulsory rallies had involved fatal casualties. The number of cases of suffering of which he claimed to have personal knowledge was so great that there could 'hardly be a home in which tears were not flowing'.[1] No doubt, Waterlow exaggerated the viciousness of Metaxas's policy. What is interesting, however, is the Minister's firm conviction that the regime had degenerated into a strong and uncontrolled force for repression and tyranny, and that it was high time to check Metaxas.

Waterlow first tried to influence internal affairs in early October 1938, in connection with Metaxas's proposals for an Anglo-Greek alliance. In a conversation with King George, he pointed out that the harshness of the regime and its continuance in power might endanger the dynasty, and certainly was not calculated to facilitate close relations with Britain.[2] Waterlow got the impression from this conversation that the King was actually considering a change, as he had already hinted on previous occasions. A few days later, however, in a conversation with the British Naval Attaché, King George confessed that he and Metaxas 'had never seen eye to eye more closely than they did now'. The King also said he did not expect trouble from the people, and did not share the fears expressed by both the British Minister and the Naval Attaché. He complained that his Government were often accused of treating opponents brutally. 'But Greece', he ungraciously remarked, 'could not be regarded as a Western country. Greeks were Orientals and looked upon soft treatment as weakness. They were the most democratic people in the world but any one of them given the smallest powers at once

[1] Athens Disp. No. 485, Confidential, 19 Dec. 1938, F.O. 371/22371.
[2] Athens Tel. No. 185, Confidential, 6 Oct. 1938, F.O. 371/22362. Cadogan feared that Waterlow's intervention was dangerous, and that the Greek Government might turn to Germany if pressed hard in this way by the British Minister. Late in the month, while in England on leave, Waterlow assured the Foreign Office that the Greek Government would not turn to Germany out of pique.

became an autocrat and a bully: people expected it and were used to it.'[1]

The British Minister pressed the issue with the Foreign Office, and suggested that the proposed alliance should be made conditional on the institution of some form of representative government in Greece.[2] During November, Waterlow was on leave in England, but there is no evidence that the question was discussed. On his return, however, he took up again the subject of the internal situation, and reported that the outlook seemed bad, unless the King decided to sack Metaxas. He expressed the fear that the latter might soon be overthrown, and violently; and he wondered whether the British ought not to 'go slow' in giving Metaxas any assistance, as this might start an anti-British reaction on the ground that British finance was helping to secure a tyranny. On 20 December Waterlow wrote that he intended to talk to King George on his return from Britain about the situation.[3] Much later recrimination could have been avoided had the Foreign Office tried at this stage to put a brake on Waterlow. Instead, they left things to run their course, believing that Waterlow's attitude was another weathercock 'fit', so frequent with him.

Another disquieting feature of the *E.O.N.* crisis concerned the dynasty. In his drive towards a unified Youth Movement, Metaxas also incorporated the Boy Scouts and Girl Guides, and clashed with their leaders, Prince Paul and Princess Irene. Prince Paul fought hard over the independence of the Boy Scouts and the Girl Guides, but was finally obliged to admit defeat. Prince Paul also had to accept the Commandership-in-Chief of the *E.O.N.*, and the Youth Movement was thus given royal recognition. On 11 December 1938, at a grand parade of the *E.O.N.*, Prince Paul received the fascist salute from the Youth leaders, and presented them with colours. The 'miracle' had happened at last, Metaxas noted with much satisfaction.[4]

[1] Record of conversation between King George and Captain Packer, 12 Oct. 1938, F.O. 371/22371.

[2] Letter from Waterlow to Cadogan, Confidential, 17 Oct. 1938, F.O. 371/22363.

[3] Sir Sydney Waterlow's reports and letters in F.O. 371/22363.

[4] *Diary*, vol. iv, p. 315. There is an interesting account of the ceremony in the Stadium by Edward Wanner, an official of the British Legation in Athens. Wanner described the group leaders of the *E.O.N.* as a 'fearful collection of thugs', heading the long columns of wretched and under-nourished children, whose age ranged

King George was unable either to veto the new policy, or even to save the Scouts and Guides. This was damaging to the dynasty's popularity, which, according to Waterlow, had fallen to 'freezing point'. He reported a widespread conviction that the King and the royal family had definitely sunk to the position of being 'puppets' in the hands of Metaxas, and that they were tied to that position by 'financial interest'. There was a growing belief that the royal family was in Greece to 'feather their nests' by the time of their next expulsion. Waterlow referred to stories of sums remitted to London for their benefit, and certain 'dubious' transactions regarding the indemnification for royal properties confiscated under the Republic. Naturally, these charges found a receptive mood among the people. He dismissed these charges as unfounded, but was concerned all the same about their effect on the public. Another disturbing feature was connected with corruption in the Government. The unpleasant atmosphere, according to Waterlow, was aggravated by a conviction that 'corruption in its ugliest form' was rampant in 'high places'. It was common belief that there was an 'inner gang' surrounding Metaxas, which had a hand in many business transactions. Waterlow mentioned 'two facts' within his knowledge: that high official circles were having a hand in the illicit shipment of Jewish refugees to Palestine, which meant big money to the interested parties, and that the Minister of Finance was allegedly involved in the traffic of drugs.[1]

It is impossible to establish the truth of these allegations. Perhaps corruption was not greater than under parliamentary governments, but now it was monopolized by fewer people, and this made a considerable difference. Under parliamentary government and with the frequent changes of government, spoils—and corruption—could not be monopolized by one

from 6 to 18. To the discomfort of having to stand during the whole day, there was heavy rain and, with no adequate latrine arrangements, the children had to use the parade grounds instead. Prince Paul inspected the heads of the sections, and when they gave him the fascist salute he took the outstretched arm and shook it. As he was a very tall man, the salute usually brought the children's hands to about the right level for hand-shaking purpose. Wanner's report in Athens Disp. No. 485, 19 Dec. 1938, F.O. 371/22371.

[1] Athens Disp. No. 485, Confidential, 19 Dec. 1938, F.O. 371/22371. See also Koronakis, op. cit., pp. 85 ff. These allegations cannot be checked for lack of fair evidence.

group, but changed hands after every governmental change. In fact, this aspect of Greek politics was often pointed out by Waterlow himself. But the difference now was that he was really alarmed by the effect of the accusations of alleged corruption on the public. Moreover, Waterlow had lost his usually cynical attitude towards internal developments, and fell to some extent prey to compassionate feelings for the Greeks, besides being concerned about the fate of the dynasty. In a report of 19 December 1938, Waterlow spoke of a widely held view, which was impressed on him by 'Greek friends', that if the British were to give the Government a loan, they would become unpopular with the Greeks, besides running the danger of losing the money through possible repudiation of the loan by a new government.[1] It is said of Waterlow's attitude at this time, that he had fallen in with a resistance group in Athens, and that his judgement of the situation in Greece was influenced by these people.[2] It seems more probable that he was a victim of his own judgement, as he often reacted to developments in Greece in a manner that was far from cool.

Whatever the truth of these speculations, in late December Waterlow took what he considered from past practice to be the natural course: he saw King George and spoke to him of the situation as he saw it. He told the King that he was convinced that there existed a tense situation due to Metaxas's recent measures regarding the *E.O.N.*, and a general conviction that 'all the real power was now in the hands of a corrupt gang'. He further said that, as far as he could judge, the King had 'lost not only all popularity but also the respect of the great bulk of the population' by his association with Metaxas's regime. He also alluded to credits, and the 'effect' on British public opinion if Metaxas were to continue further along the totalitarian path. He could not take the responsibility, he said, for advising the King to discard Metaxas, for this would be an interference with Greek affairs. He ventured, however, 'to advise His Majesty to follow a formal and transitional course and to insist on the early introduction of some form of legal

[1] Athens Disp. No. 485, Confidential, 19 Dec. 1938, F.O. 371/22371.

[2] Metaxas's daughter maintained at an interview in July 1970 that Waterlow was under the influence of a resistance group of which Tsouderos and Katina Paxinou were members. The same allegation was made by Mme Lorandos at an interview in Aug. 1970.

and constitutional government. British opinion had been expecting it from His Majesty for two-and-a-half years.' Such action seemed necessary if only as a 'safety valve'. Summing up his advice, the Minister said that it had 'become necessary, both for internal and for external reasons, for His Majesty to do something to make it quite clear that he and not General Metaxas was top dog'.[1] King George, according to Waterlow, took his plain speaking 'in very good part', and only said that he was not convinced that things were quite so black as the Minister had described them. Waterlow also felt that he could trust the King to respect his confidence, and he wrote to the Foreign Office that the French Minister had spoken to the King in the same sense.[2]

The Minister's intervention, despite his assurances, shocked the Foreign Office. In the first place, they did not agree with his diagnosis of the situation; or this at least is what people at the Foreign Office said among themselves. In the second place, they questioned the step as such. They felt that Waterlow had gone too far in his confidences to King George and that the manner in which he had spoken was unbecoming to the British Minister in Greece. Greece, after all, was not 'Egypt', and Sir Sydney not 'Lord Cromer'.[3] As will be seen, this objection did not fully represent the views of the Foreign Office. After much deliberation, Sir Orme Sargent wrote to the Minister in a manner that left no doubt as to the reactions of the Foreign Office to his intervention with the King. This step, he said, might lead King George and the Greek Government to deduce that the British Government wanted to overthrow Metaxas and to dictate to Greece another form of government. And he continued:

I think you would be the first to agree that as far as British interests go Metaxas is probably a good deal better than the usual run of the politicians. Your reports have shown that although occasionally it has been suggested that he has pro-German sympathies, our relations with the present President of the Council have run more smoothly than with any of his predecessors and that apart from the debt question we have been able to settle all the

[1] Athens Tel. No. 255, Confidential, 29 Dec. 1938, F.O. 371/22371.
[2] Letter from Waterlow to Sargent, Confidential, 24 Jan. 1939, F.O. 371/23769.
[3] F.O. Minutes, Jan. 1939, F.O. 371/22371.

outstanding complaints which previously rendered our relations with Greece uneasy and even difficult. On the other hand, anything like the old party system would, I fear, mean once again discord and corruption in internal affairs, besides offering new opportunities for German and Italian intrigue and bribery. Apart from this it would be most undesirable that Metaxas himself should acquire the impression that we are hostile to him and are working for his over-throw. Nothing could be better calculated than this to drive him into a pro-German policy and thereby undo all the good that has been done of late.

Waterlow was also asked to report 'shortly' on the effects of his plain speaking to the King.[1]

At this point something more must be said about the attitude of the Foreign Office regarding the whole affair. The men in the Foreign Office did not differ with Waterlow on the essentials, and the reproofs he received were not quite deserved. As will be seen in more detail later on, they were in fact convinced that the harsh measures of the dictatorial regime were causing much resentment among the Greeks, and that this resentment was not limited to the dictator only, but extended to the King who was increasingly identified with the dictatorship.[2] This was essentially Waterlow's appreciation, as we have already seen, and on the basis of this appreciation, the Minister had advised the King to make an effort to relax the coercive measures of the regime. Initially, the Foreign Office was disturbed by the Minister's intervention, fearing that it might be interpreted in Greece as an attempt by the British Government to overthrow Metaxas. However, after further explanations and assurances from Waterlow,[3] it was felt that there was no reason to find 'fault with the arguments or the language used by Sir Sydney Waterlow'. But the most significant—and disquieting—aspect of this affair, which the Foreign Office realized with much apprehension, was that Waterlow's inter-vention with the King had not produced any tangible result, and this because the Minister's word did not carry any weight

[1] Letter from Sir Orme Sargent to Sir Sydney Waterlow, 11 Jan. 1939, F.O. 371/22371.

[2] F.O. Memo., 16 Feb. 1939, F.O. 371/23769.

[3] Waterlow to Sargent, 17 Jan. 1939, F.O. 371/23769. Waterlow assured the Foreign Office that his intervention with the King had not produced any 'un-toward' consequences.

with him. The King appeared no longer prepared to listen to the Minister's advice, nor to accept his views; and as far as the Foreign Office was concerned, this was both unpleasant and disquieting.[1]

Meanwhile, in Athens real trouble was brewing. Waterlow seems to have spoken in the same sense in some other quarters at this time, and his indiscreet remarks reached the Turkish Ambassador, and finally Metaxas. On 31 December Metaxas learned, apparently through the Greek Embassy in Ankara, that Waterlow had expressed to the Turkish Ambassador the opinion that Greece was on the verge of a revolution and a rising of the officers, and that it was useless for Britain to give economic aid under such a regime. Metaxas was furious, and justifiably.[2] On 2 January 1939 he saw the King, and spoke to him of Waterlow's indiscreet remarks. King George told Metaxas that the British Minister had also 'tried to tell him something', but he had treated him 'coldly', and the Minister was obliged to depart.[3]

Waterlow now faced a hostile Metaxas and a critical Foreign Office. In order to soothe the Foreign Office, he wrote that his views were supported by Crown Prince Paul. The Crown Prince was convinced that unless the King took some 'decisive action' soon, he would become powerless and a mere tool of Metaxas. He also believed that the King's prestige, already damaged by his association with the dictator, would be irretrievable before long. It is not clear whether Prince Paul expressed these opinions out of pique against Metaxas, or whether he was aiming them much higher; for he also said that the King's subservience to Metaxas was a 'capital mistake', and that this showed that King George 'either felt unable to govern himself, or that he did not want to'.[4] This was, indeed, valuable support for his position, but Waterlow went further: he claimed that he had 'official authority' for his action and cited a Circular

[1] F.O. Memo., 16 Feb. 1939, and F.O. Minutes in F.O. 371/23769.

[2] *Diary*, vol. iv, pp. 321–2, 31 Dec. 1938. He noted that he had never been so furious at a 'liar' and a 'scoundrel'. He also wrote: 'I make consultations regarding steps to react and avenge. But I feel as if poisoned. He will pay for that. I know who are hiding behind Waterlow.'

[3] *Diary*, vol. iv, p. 347. There is no evidence that the King actually told Metaxas the details of his conversation with Sir Sydney.

[4] Waterlow's interview with Crown Prince Paul, in Athens Disp. No. 7, 10 Jan. 1939, F.O. 371/23769.

Dispatch from the Foreign Office of 6 January 1938,[1] which argued that the British Government could not 'view with indifference, the total extinction of free institutions anywhere', since the transformation of the smaller countries into totalitarian states was a 'long-range threat' to British interests. Waterlow also justified his intervention with the following argument:

I cannot regret, and I hope that the Secretary of State will not regret, that British dislike of the increasingly fascist methods now being imposed on Greece should have been put on record, even if personally and unofficially. If ever the Greeks rise up against those methods, the record will be there to prove the falsity of the belief, which is prevalent here, that His Majesty's Government and myself personally are the upholders of this unpopular regime. This may be useful some day.[2]

Waterlow was certainly looking ahead to future developments in Greece. British policy towards Greece, on the other hand, was conducted to realize relatively short-term aims. What the British Government wanted at this stage was an amelioration of conditions with a façade of constitutionalism to be introduced at some later date, but with Metaxas in power. Lord Halifax was satisfied that Metaxas had proved 'capable of standing up to Germany', and had shown a marked and sincere desire to co-operate with the British.[3] The Foreign Office now came forward with the proposal to make a further approach, not in order to overthrow the Metaxas regime, but to strengthen it. In a Memorandum of 16 February 1939 they argued:

The importance of Greece to us in present circumstances is so great that we would certainly be justified in doing what we can to prevent a revolution at the present juncture. As far as the foreign policy of Greece is concerned the present regime suits us very well, and if, as a result of a revolution, Greece became a prey of competing local politicians, this situation might well afford the Germans and Italians an opportunity of a fruitful intrigue to the detriment of British interests.

This being so, the question arises whether we should not make a further attempt, through the King, to reform the present regime

[1] F.O. Disp. No. 12 to Bucharest, 6 Jan. 1938, R727/64/19, F.O. 371/23769.
[2] Letter from Sir Sydney Waterlow to Sir Orme Sargent, 24 Jan. 1939, F.O. 371/23769.
[3] Note by the Secretary of State, 30 Jan. 1939, F.P. (36) 79, Cab. 27/627.

in such a way as to lessen its unpopularity and increase its general stability. It is no use using Sir S. Waterlow for this purpose in view of the King's suspicions. What is needed is the visit to Greece in the near future of some Englishman in an authoritative but not strictly official position, who is a personal friend of the King and who could gain his confidence and speak to him frankly on the whole subject.[1]

The person chosen for this mission was Lord Lloyd, President of the British Council, and a close friend of the King. In approaching the King, Lord Lloyd was instructed to explain that the British Government was not trying to change the regime just because it was a dictatorship, or to bring about the fall of Metaxas because they did not approve of him or his policy. 'On the contrary', they said, 'our desire is to see the regime strengthened by the removal of the features which are at present rendering it unpopular and therefore vulnerable.'[2] In March 1939 Lord Lloyd met both the King and Metaxas, but he gathered from his talks that there was no prospect of 'liberalization'. King George and Metaxas intended to rule undistracted by constitutional limitations, and dismissed the fears of the British Government as groundless. The Foreign Office decided then that there was 'nothing else' they could do but watch the situation and see how matters developed.[3] Metaxas, at any rate, appreciated Lord Lloyd's visit, and considered his talks with him very satisfactory. Lord Lloyd 'confessed' to Metaxas that his mission to Greece concerned the 'December rumours', and Metaxas took the opportunity of pointing out Waterlow's 'behaviour'. The exchange of views was 'smooth', according to Metaxas, but there is no detailed account of their talks. After their first talk, however, Metaxas got the impression that the British were 'interested' not only in the King, but in him as well.[4]

Lord Lloyd's visit thus took on a new light. What was

---

[1] F.O. Memorandum, 16 Feb. 1939, F.O. 371/23769.

[2] Letter from Sir Orme Sargent to Lord Lloyd, 25 Feb. 1939, F.O. 371/23769. The Foreign Office further explained to Lord Lloyd that the King's frequent and prolonged visits to London had compromised the British Government, and it was possible that if Metaxas's regime was swept away by a revolution the 'British connection' would be repudiated by the succeeding government.

[3] F.O. Minutes, Mar. 1939, in F.O. 371/23769.

[4] *Diary*, vol. iv, p. 358, 4 and 5 Mar. 1939. With respect to Waterlow's prejudiced views, Lord Lloyd in his meeting with King George alluded to a 'pillow' affair. Metaxas, however, regarded this allusion as 'dust in the eyes'.

initially meant to be an approach to King George for the introduction of some form of constitutional government, actually resulted in an exchange of views between Lord Lloyd and Metaxas. In his written instructions there is nothing to show that Lord Lloyd was to have talks with Metaxas as well, let alone broach the subject of Waterlow's indiscreet remarks of December 1938. The Foreign Office had probably asked Lord Lloyd before he left for Greece to sound Metaxas indirectly on his relations with Waterlow after the December incident. Quite possibly, they were thinking by then that Waterlow was no longer the right man for the post of the British Minister.

Metaxas appears to have been preoccupied with the same subject. In the middle of February 1939 he sent Dr. N. Lorandos, a trusted friend and a staunch Anglophile, on a mission to London. Metaxas instructed Lorandos to assure his friends in Britain, Sir Orme Sargent and Lord Harvey among others, that he had irrevocably bound Greece to Britain, and that the British Government ought to trust him in all respects. Lorandos was also told to emphasize to his British friends that Waterlow's relations with Metaxas were no longer what they used to be, for the Minister's views about his person and the regime were now strongly prejudiced. Lorandos met Sir Orme Sargent and Lord Harvey, and perhaps Halifax, and talked to them in accordance with these instructions.[1]

The only indication of Lorandos's contacts with the Foreign Office is a minute of 7 March 1939, according to which Lorandos had said that Waterlow was on bad terms with Metaxas, 'so much so that the latter would not speak confidentially to the British Minister any more'. And the writer of the minute makes the revealing remark: 'This point goes to confirm the wisdom of our recent decision.'[2] The 'recent decision' referred probably to Waterlow's retirement from the Foreign Service; or perhaps only to Lord Lloyd's mission. The two missions however had one subject in common: the British Minister in Greece and his relations with Metaxas. There is no other evidence that Waterlow's retirement was discussed at this time. He actually retired in early June 1939, when the Athens Legation

---

[1] Madame Lorandos in an interview, August 1970. Mme Lorandos had accompanied her husband. See also Metaxas, *Diary*, vol. iv, p. 352, 15 Feb. 1939.

[2] F.O. Minute, 7 Mar. 1939, F.O. 371/23760.

was taken over by Sir Michael Palairet.[1] Sir Michael had better luck than Sir Sydney; the war that soon broke out kept him away from internal Greek affairs. Palairet was the man who saw Greece in war, victory, and defeat, as Waterlow was the man who saw the inner nature of Metaxas's regime at close quarters.

[1] After this book had gone to the printer, Professor John Waterlow, the Minister's son, has made available to the author a number of letters addressed to his father, some of which refer to the Minister's retirement from the Foreign Service. Waterlow's five years' appointment as British Minister in Athens, which ended in November 1938, was extended for a period of one year. The extension was proposed by Eden in February 1938, and was 'cordially approved' in March of that year by Halifax, who succeeded Eden in the Foreign Office. The next document bearing on this issue is a letter from Halifax to Waterlow, dated 20 February 1939 and marked 'Strictly Private and Confidential' in which the Secretary of State explained to the Minister that he had become seriously concerned over the 'legitimate' dissatisfaction among senior First Secretaries and junior Secretaries on account of 'the serious and growing block in promotion'. 'In these circumstances,' he went on to say, 'I have come to the conclusion that it is essential, in the interests of the Service, to apply as strictly as possible the general rule,' which laid down that Heads of Mission should retire from active employment after they had reached the age of sixty. Therefore, he said, 'in view of the interests of the Service . . . , I fear I see no other course but to invite you to relinquish your appointment at Athens at the end of May instead of remaining at your post until November next. I know this decision will cause you disappointment and possibly also inconvenience, but I am sure you will appreciate that I could not make the request of you were I not convinced that it was in the interests of the Service as a whole.' In the light of the circumstances described earlier, Halifax's explanation is not very convincing. Professor Waterlow has confirmed to the author that the real reason behind the Foreign Office decision to terminate the Minister's appointment was the strong disapproval of his strained relations with Metaxas and the conviction that his word no longer carried any weight with the King.

IV

Greece Between Britain and the Axis, 1939–1940

Greece Between Britain and Italy, 1939

The spring of 1939 witnessed the march of the Germans into Prague and the occupation of Albania by the Italians: the dictators had dropped all pretence and inaugurated a new approach in their expansionist policy towards Europe. The Governments of Britain and France, still under the influence of the Munich Agreement, were faced by a situation which they were unable to redress. Instead, they answered the dictators' *coups* by guaranteeing the independence of Poland, Romania, and Greece. It was a weak show of determination to resist further aggression, that no one took very seriously, least of all the potential aggressors. Unfortunately, the Western powers had not decided yet where appeasement should end. Greece watched these developments more or less as a terrified spectator, and received the Guarantee with some relief. The Government, and especially Metaxas, welcomed the Anglo-French gesture for what little it represented in actual terms, but mainly for what they would like it to represent, namely a definite commitment to defend Greece's territorial integrity. There is reason to believe that Metaxas saw the noble but empty gesture as yet one more step towards formalized Anglo-Greek co-operation, a moral obligation on the part of Britain which, it was hoped, could lead to the cherished goal, an Anglo-Greek alliance. The Guarantee did bind the two countries to some extent. Yet what can be said with little room for doubt, is that the British part of the Guarantee of April 1939 was conceived and born somewhere on the busy path between the Foreign Office and the Italian Embassy in London. The scarecrow that was displayed held no surprises for those whom it was supposed to keep at bay.

On 7 April 1939, a Good Friday, Italian troops landed in Albania, and proceeded without serious resistance to occupy the country.[1] The King of Albania had to flee in a hurry, and went to Greece, thus causing some embarrassment to the Greek Government.[2] The Greeks followed the Italian occupation of Albania with great anxiety and Metaxas, obviously alarmed, asked the British for an immediate indication of their intentions, though he made no appeal for assistance should the Italians attempt to seize Corfu or any other part of Greek territory. At the same time, Metaxas informed the British Minister that the Greek Government had made the necessary preparations to meet the danger.[3] Two destroyers were kept ready for action, and coast defence and anti-aircraft guns were being manned, while officers and men of the three services had been recalled from Easter leave. But no special movements of the Greek air force had been ordered, and aircraft remained at their bases in Salonika, Larissa, and Athens; more important, no reservists had been called up as the Greek Government was particularly anxious to avoid giving any offence to Italy.[4] On Easter Sunday Metaxas summoned the British Minister again and announced his decision to resist an Italian invasion of Greece 'to the very end'; he preferred the 'complete destruction' of Greece rather than 'dishonour', he told Waterlow.[5]

In the meantime, Mussolini had already assured the British Government that Italy did not contemplate action against Greece's independence and territorial integrity; and Halifax, in order to pin down the Duce, had explicitly asked that the Italian Government should repeat these assurances to Greece.[6] No sooner was it said than done: Mussolini accepted this suggestion, and repeated the assurances to the Greek Government, 'reaffirming' Italy's intention to respect absolutely

[1] Sir Andrew Ryan, *The Last of the Dragomans*, London, 1951, pp. 334 ff. Ryan was British Minister in Albania.

[2] Athens Tel. No. 113, 8 Apr. 1939, *D.B.F.P.*, 3rd Ser., vol. v, No. 91. Also, Metaxas's Tel. to the Greek Ambassador in Rome, 8 Apr. 1939, in *The Greek White Book*, London, 1942, No. 19.

[3] Athens Tels. Nos. 115 and 116, 9 Apr. 1939, *D.B.F.P.*, 3rd Ser., vol. v, No. 97.

[4] Athens Tel. No. 112, 9 Apr. 1939, F.O. 371/23779.

[5] *Diary*, vol. iv, p. 364, 9 Apr. 1939.

[6] F.O. Tel. to Rome, No. 176 by Telephone, 9 Apr. 1939, *D.B.F.P.*, 3rd Ser., vol. v, No. 101, and Tel. from Simopoulos to Metaxas, 9 Apr. 1939, *Greek White Book*, Nos. 25 and 26.

Greece's territorial integrity, and her desire to develop further the friendly relations already existing between Greece and Italy.[1]

The Greek Government thus received the first assurances from Italy, at the express wish of the British. This arrangement, however, made the Greeks uneasy. Metaxas's Government was anxious in case the Italian assurances to Greece should seem to have been 'extorted' by the British, or be regarded as a 'diplomatic climbdown' for Mussolini.[2] Needless to say, Metaxas's inquiry about the 'intentions' of the British Government had not yet been answered. All the same, he thanked the British Government for their attitude towards Greece,[3] though he does not seem to have been completely satisfied by the way the whole affair had turned out. The Greek Minister in London expressed at this time his personal view that the Italian assurances were not satisfactory to the Greek Government.[4] The Greeks would obviously have preferred a more direct expression of Britain's intentions than the 'extorted' Italian assurances, which were of doubtful value and which the Greek Government had never asked for in the first place.

The British Government, however, was not prepared to give any assurances to Greece, except in close consultation with the Italian Government to avoid giving offence to the latter. When Mussolini's assurances to Greece had been secured, then the way was open for Britain's assurances also. This issue was discussed at a meeting of the Foreign Policy Committee on 11 April 1939. It became evident that the British Government would have liked to find a 'middle road' between provoking Italy and not doing enough to give her a clear warning of Britain's attitude should Italy attack Greece. Besides, Halifax told the Committee, a statement with regard to Greece was desirable to satisfy public opinion in Britain and the United States.[5] Strategic considerations were also discussed, since any definite assurances of Greek territorial integrity were bound to

---

[1] Athens Tel. No. 122, 10 Apr. 1939, F.O. 371/23780. See also Tel. from Metaxas to the Greek Ambassador in Rome, 10 Apr. 1939, *Greek White Book*, Nos. 27, 28.

[2] Athens Tel. No. 121, 10 Apr. 1939, F.O. 371/23780.

[3] Athens Tel. No. 119, 10 Apr. 1939, F.O. 371/23780.

[4] F.O. Tel. No. 130 to Athens, 9 Apr. 1939, *D.B.F.P.*, 3rd Ser., vol. v, No. 112.

[5] Meeting of the Foreign Policy Committee, 11 Apr. 1939, F.P. (36) 41, Cab. 27/624.

affect British strategy. The Minister for Co-ordination of
Defence explained that, as far as British strategy in the Mediterranean was concerned, Greece was valuable only in case of
naval action against Italy; and Britain's 'objective', he pointed
out, should be 'not to save Greece from being overrun', but to
'smash' Italy.[1] Political considerations, however, were given
priority; and in any case the proposed statement would not take
the form of a definite undertaking to go to war over the territorial integrity of Greece. Finally, the statement was drafted,
and was approved by the Committee.[2]

The Italian Government was then informed by Halifax that
'in accordance with the authority conveyed' to him by the
Italian Chargé d'Affaires, the Prime Minister would make
a statement in the House of Commons on 13 April. The British
Foreign Minister further explained that this statement was
'bound' to take account of the extent to which British and
world opinion had been affected by the Italian occupation of
Albania, and it would thus have to include 'some critical
reference' to Italian policy, but this would be 'couched in
a form as little provocative as possible'.[3]

On 10 April the Greek Minister called at the Foreign Office,
and 'begged' them to let him know in advance of any decision
vitally affecting Greece.[4] The following day Metaxas was
informed that the British Government intended to make
a statement that would include a guarantee to Greece. Metaxas
was 'moved' by this communication, and expressed his gratitude for the 'lively interest' of the British towards Greece.[5] The
Greek Government was then informed of the text of the statement on 12 April, and the hope was expressed that it would be
'welcome' to the Greeks.[6] The Greeks in fact seemed to have
mixed feelings about the Guarantee: they welcomed, or at least
Metaxas did, the statement that the British proposed to make;
at the same time, they were uneasy about its effect on the
Italian Government. They informed the British Government

---

[1] F.P. (36) 41, 11 Apr. 1939, Cab. 27/624.
[2] F.P. (36) 42, 11 Apr. 1939, Cab. 27/624.
[3] F.O. Tel. to Rome No. 192, 12 Apr. 1939, F.O. 434/6.
[4] Foreign Office Minute, 10 Apr. 1939, F.O. 371/23780. Halifax wrote in
a marginal note on 11 Apr. about Simopoulos: 'We must not forget him.'
[5] F.O. Tel. No. 144 to Athens, 12 Apr. 1939, *D.B.F.P.*, 3rd Ser., vol. v, No. 145.
[6] F.O. Tel. No. 110, 12 Apr. 1939, *D.B.F.P.*, 3rd Ser., vol. v, No. 136.

that though they did not wish to 'interfere' with the line to be taken by the Prime Minister in the Commons debate, they felt that in view of Mussolini's 'touchiness' it was important that the impression should be given, as clearly as possible, that the Guarantee was not the result of any appeal by the Greek Government.[1] Doubts, and perhaps objections, were raised in the Cabinet meeting of 12 April, after the British Minister handed Metaxas the text of the statement; but Metaxas dismissed the fears of his colleagues as 'unfounded'.[2]

Finally, on 13 April the Prime Minister made the declaration guaranteeing the independence of Greece and Romania, in the House of Commons, and the Secretary of State made the same declaration in the House of Lords. The same day the French Prime Minister made a similar statement. The part of the British statement which came to be known as the 'Guarantee' reads:

... in the event of any action being taken which clearly threatened the independence of Greece and Roumania, and which the Greek and Roumanian Government respectively considered it vital to resist with their national forces, His Majesty's Government would feel themselves bound at once to lend the Greek or Roumanian Government, as the case might be, all the support in their power ...[3]

The British Guarantee did not constitute a definitive commitment to go to war over Greece's territorial integrity, but only an undefined promise of support. As far as British strategy in the Eastern Mediterranean was concerned, Greece was valuable as a neutral State which Britain would not have to defend by committing land forces. This cardinal point of British strategy was pressed, as we have already seen, on the Foreign Policy Committee when the latter discussed the form that Britain's assurances to Greece should take. The Minister for Co-ordination of Defence insisted that Britain's commitment under the declaration should be 'limited' by the use of indefinite words, since Greece had a 'long land frontier' which Britain could not possibly undertake to defend.[4] As will be seen, Chatfield's

[1] Athens Tel. No. 127, 12 Apr. 1939, F.O. 371/23780, and Athens Tel. No. 129, 12 Apr., *D.B.F.P.*, 3rd Ser., vol. v, No. 140.

[2] *Diary*, vol. iv, p. 368.

[3] *Parliamentary Debates*, 5th Ser., House of Commons, vol. 346, Col. 13, p. 197.

[4] Meeting of the Foreign Policy Committee, 11 Apr. 1939, F.P. (36) 42, Cab. 27/624.

strategic considerations of April 1939 proved paramount in October 1940 also, when Italy attacked Greece.

After the scare of April 1939 Greco-Italian relations improved gradually. The attitude of the Greek Government towards Italy was, according to the Italian Minister in Athens, not only 'correct' but 'friendly'.[1] Greco-Italian relations came under reconsideration in September 1939, when the Greco-Italian Pact of Friendship, Conciliation, and Judicial Settlement of 1928 was due to expire. Metaxas, it seems, made the first indirect approach to the Italians on 21 August, when he assured the Italian Minister that he attached the 'greatest value' to Italian friendship, and emphasized his desire for a 'rapid amelioration in Greco-Italian relations'. Metaxas also assured Grazzi that the Greek Government had not promised Britain the use of Greek ports in case of war, nor were they thinking of making such a promise.[2] On 5 September, following Mussolini's declaration of Italian neutrality, Metaxas summoned Grazzi to express again the hope for an amelioration in relations, which would make 'collaboration in the political, economic and cultural fields' possible.[3]

Mussolini's reply to these assurances was prompt and precise. In a note comprising five points and dated 12 September, the Duce promised not to take the initiative in resorting to military action against Greece, and to give substance to this promise he would order the withdrawal of the Italian troops from the Greco-Albanian frontier to a distance of 20 kilometres. The final point of his reply reads: 'Notwithstanding the present situation, the Duce does not exclude the possibility of resuming and stabilizing the policy of Italo-Greek entente, which was previously established by special diplomatic agreements.'[4] Mussolini instructed Grazzi to assure Metaxas that Greece did not stand in Italy's 'way' and that Italy had no plans against Greece. He had 'full confidence' in Metaxas, he said, for the latter had established order in his country. The Duce added that he believed in the possibility of Greco-Italian co-operation

[1] E. Grazzi, *Il principio della fine*, Rome, 1945, p. 45.

[2] *D.D.I.*, Ser. 8, vol. xiii, No. 165.

[3] *Greek White Book*, No. 47. See also B. P. Papadakis, *Diplomatic History of the Greek War 1940–1945* (in Greek), Athens, 1956, p. 34.

[4] *D.D.I.*, Ser. 9, vol. i, No. 166. See also Grazzi, op. cit., pp. 65–7, and *Greek White Book*, No. 49.

in the political and economic field, and that he was prepared to supply the Greeks with arms, especially aeroplanes and guns, if they so wished. Ciano also instructed Grazzi to inform Metaxas that, if the Greek Government wished to draw up a new treaty of friendship and collaboration, he would be prepared to go to Athens in order to sign it.[1] Mussolini's reply was handed to Metaxas on 15 September.[2]

On receipt of the Italian reply, Metaxas telegraphed Simopoulos urgently and instructed him to approach the British Government about the Italian proposals.[3] The same day he also informed Palairet that the Italian Government had suggested renewing the Greco-Italian Pact. Metaxas was suspicious of the Italian suggestion, and confided to Palairet that he would make no reply until he received advice from Halifax, which he was trying to get through Simopoulos.[4] Simopoulos saw Halifax on 15 September and, after informing him of the Italian approach, told him that, before deciding on the attitude to be adopted 'in case' of an Italian proposal for a new pact of non-aggression or renewing the existing one, Metaxas 'wished to ascertain the views of His Majesty's Government on this subject; and he was particularly anxious not to take any action which might be unwelcome to Great Britain'. Halifax's preliminary advice was that any agreement calculated to improve Greco-Italian relations was welcome provided that it 'did not in any way prejudice Anglo-Greek relations and co-operation', and that Greece's national security was not compromised. Halifax added that this also applied to an eventual renewal of the Greco-Italian Pact.[5]

In the evening of the same day Simopoulos called again at the Foreign Office, and announced that the Italians had now made their 'expected' proposals. He seems to have misunderstood the whole affair, for he explained that the Italians had undertaken to withdraw their troops concentrated on the Greco-Albanian border, if the Greeks would agree to accept in an abbreviated form the substance of the Greco-Italian Pact, and supplement it with undertakings of non-aggression, these undertakings to

[1] Grazzi, op. cit., pp. 67–8.
[2] Ibid., p. 69; *Greek White Book*, No. 49.
[3] *Diary*, vol. iv, p. 394.
[4] Athens Tel. No. 399, 15 Sept. 1939, F.O. 371/23780.
[5] Minute by Halifax, 15 Sept. 1939, R7612/31/19, F.O. 371/23762.

be 'subject to existing obligations' on the part of each party. This was bound to cause some annoyance in the Foreign Office. Sargent told Simopoulos that his first impression was that it would not be sufficient for Greece to pledge herself to non-aggression 'subject to no further conditions' than the reserving of existing obligations. For instance, he said, 'Greece had no particular obligations towards the United Kingdom, but the existing close relations between Greece and Great Britain made it essential that Greece should preserve full liberty of action in the event of a conflict arising between Italy and Great Britain.'[1] When Metaxas heard of this, he immediately sent for Palairet, and told him that he was very much hurt by the reception of his message.[2] What had actually happened, he explained, was that the Italian Government had suggested renewing the old pact, and that before replying he had hastened to ask the advice of the British Government. He was much upset, he said, at being treated in any way as open to blame. He told Palairet that he would not renew the pact if the British Government advised him not to do so, and he was ready, in general, to be 'guided by the British Government'.[3]

The whole affair was taking a turn both regrettable and ridiculous. Halifax undertook to clear up the misunderstanding, and assured Metaxas that he greatly appreciated his wish to consult him on the Italian proposal, and promised to send his reply shortly.[4] It is not quite clear who was responsible for the misunderstanding. Simopoulos explained to the Foreign Office that Metaxas had misunderstood his report.[5] It is also likely that Metaxas had not informed Simopoulos of the actual form and contents of the Italian proposal. Simopoulos, however, had certainly muddled things from the start. Finally, the Foreign Office did indeed express annoyance at Simopoulos's second visit, when he announced that the Italians had proposed a non-aggression pact, subject to the existing obligations of the two countries. At all events, Metaxas's impression that his approach had been unfavourably received at the Foreign Office no doubt

[1] Minute by Sir Orme Sargent, 15 Sept. 1939, R7797/1877/19, F.O. 371/23780.
[2] *Diary*, vol. iv, p. 395. Metaxas felt that 'Simopoulos was, to say the least, stupid.'
[3] Athens Tel. No. 407, 16 Sept. 1939, F.O. 434/6.
[4] F.O. Tel. No. 374 to Athens, 18 Sept. 1939, F.O. 434/6.
[5] F.O. Tel. No. 375 to Athens, 18 Sept. 1939, F.O. 371/23780.

gave him a fright, and must have contributed to his promising to be 'guided' by the British Government.

The British looked at the Italian proposal on the Greco-Italian Pact in the light of their desire to keep Italy in play, and to ensure unhindered Anglo-Greek co-operation in case of war between Britain and Italy. The Foreign Office considered that a situation might well arise in which Britain, not Greece, was at war with Italy, and in which the British would need to use Greek harbours. If war between Britain and Italy broke out, Greece would be bound by the Greco-Italian Pact to remain neutral and withhold from Britain the use of her harbours. In a Foreign Office Memorandum of 16 September it was argued: 'It is quite probable that in proposing the renewal of the Pact of Friendship the Italians are simply endeavouring to ensure that, if and when they become involved in hostilities, we shall not be able to use Greece as a jumping off ground for attacks on Italy, and in the meanwhile to reassure tensions, thus lulling us into a false security.' It was further argued that, since Metaxas had of his own accord expressed suspicions about the Italian proposal, it would not be politic for Britain 'to help dispel these suspicions', and encourage him to come to terms with the Italians. At the same time the Foreign Office was concerned over the possible effect on Italy of Greece's refusal to renew the pact or conclude a similar one. Italy could justifiably conclude that behind Greece's unresponsiveness stood the British Government; and she might well be irritated at this. Caution was therefore required by both Greece and Britain. The best course seemed to be for the Greek Government to avoid renewing the old pact, but to consider instead a fresh agreement in more 'general terms', which would not prejudice Anglo-Greek co-operation in any circumstances.[1]

The reply to Metaxas's approach was given on 18 September in an *aide-mémoire*. After expressing 'warm appreciation' of Metaxas's confidence, the British suggested that, although it was advisable to inform the Italians of Greek willingness to conclude a new agreement, 'this new agreement should be in more general terms' than the old pact, and its provisions should comply with the following desiderata: '(*a*) Greece should

[1] F.O. Memo., 16 Sept. 1939, and F.O. Minutes, F.O. 371/23780.

preserve full liberty of action in the event of a conflict arising between Great Britain and Italy. (*b*) Greece should similarly preserve full liberty in the event of her partners in the Balkan Entente coming into conflict with Italy.'[1]

Metaxas was 'relieved' when he received this and thanked Halifax for his advice. He agreed entirely with the recommendations, and told Palairet that he would show him the text of the proposed agreement before communicating it to the Italians.[2] On 20 September a joint communiqué was given out to the Press affirming that Greco-Italian relations continued to be 'sincerely friendly' and inspired by the spirit of 'complete and mutual confidence'. It was also announced that the Italian Government had decided to withdraw the Italian troops from the Greco-Albanian border, and that similar steps were being taken by the Greek Government.[3]

The form of the notes to be exchanged between Greece and Italy was discussed between Metaxas and Palairet on 28 September. The Greek Government, it was felt, should either reply by expressing in very general terms the hope that it would be possible at a later date to place Greco-Italian relations on a 'fixed basis', or it should state that it was difficult for the Greek Government to examine the question of renewal of the pact, or the conclusion of a new one, and that it intended to do so at a later date. Both men favoured the first course,[4] which was also approved by the Foreign Office on 30 September.[5] On the same day the Greco-Italian Agreement was signed, in letters exchanged between Metaxas and the Italian Minister. The exchanged notes were identical in essentials: both referred to the question of the 'fixed' basis of Greco-Italian relations. After mentioning the mutual withdrawal of troops from the Greco-Albanian border, and the common desire for a policy of peace and a 'new period' of friendship between Greece and Italy, the hope was expressed that 'the evolution of the international situation will make it possible for the two Governments in the near future to give their relations a more concrete form'. In the meantime, the two Governments were resolved

---

[1] F.O. Tel. No. 376, 18 Sept. 1939, F.O. 371/23780.
[2] Athens Tel. No. 416, 19 Sept. 1939, F.O. 434/6; *Diary*, vol. iv, p. 396.
[3] *D.D.I.*, Ser. 9, vol. i, No. 297; *Greek White Book*, No. 50.
[4] Athens Tel. No. 446, 28 Sept. 1939, F.O. 371/23780.
[5] F.O. Tel. No. 428 to Athens, 30 Sept. 1939, F.O. 371/23780.

to be inspired by the principles of friendship and collaboration enunciated by the Pact of 1928.[1]

The Greco-Italian Pact was thus allowed to expire, while the two Governments agreed to abide by its principles. Metaxas told Grazzi, during the exchange of notes, that what he really wanted was to place Greco-Italian relations on a better basis than that provided by the Pact of 1928, namely that they should rest on his 'personal sentiments' of admiration for Italy and his devotion to Mussolini.[2] The Italian Government for their part seem to have accepted the form of the exchanged notes without misgivings. Ciano agreed with the wording of the notes,[3] and Grazzi accepted Metaxas's explanations. Grazzi was convinced that the Greek Government could not possibly have accepted a different solution. Greece, he believed, was torn between her desire to be friendly with Italy, and her equal desire not to upset in any way the Western powers, as well as Turkey and the other members of the Balkan Entente.[4]

It is safe to assume, therefore, that the Italians were content with the form and character given to Greco-Italian relations in September 1939. There is little doubt that the Italians were sincere, at this juncture at least, in their desire for better relations with Greece. Mussolini and Ciano seemed well disposed, and they made some friendly gestures towards Greece, the withdrawal of the Italian troops from the Greco-Albanian border being one of them. During this time Mussolini was also prepared to make available to Greece some aeronautical material but the Germans, according to Grazzi, were able to secure the order for a lower price.[5] These gestures undoubtedly reflected the short-lived Greco-Italian 'amicizia', and showed that the Italian Government was in a friendly mood. The unwillingness of the Greek Government, therefore, to seize the opportunity and place Greco-Italian relations on a concrete basis in the form of an agreement of non-aggression seems regrettable. Yet, it is difficult to see how Metaxas could have acted in a way that was clearly undesirable to the British Government. Pipinelis has criticized Greek diplomacy for

---

[1] *D.D.I.*, Ser. 9, vol. i, No. 456, and *Greek White Book*, No. 52. Also *Messager d'Athènes*, 3 Nov. 1939.

[2] *D.D.I.*, Ser. 9, vol. i, No. 546.   [3] Ibid., No. 648.

[4] Grazzi, op. cit., pp. 74, 75.   [5] Ibid., pp. 79–80, 90–2.

'evading' a gesture, which could in no way have compromised Greece's position. This evasion, he believed, was bound to make the Italians suspicious that the Greeks had probably made up their mind about Greece's position internationally.[1] The renewal of the Pact of 1928, or the conclusion of a similar one, could not possibly have stopped Mussolini from attacking Greece in October 1940. Yet it is not impossible that an agreement might have led to different developments in Greece's relations with Italy and Britain. Another Greek Government might perhaps have seized the opportunity to acquire some leverage *vis-à-vis* Britain. Metaxas, however, did not present the British Government with such problems, nor did he waver from his course of co-operation with Britain.

Anglo-Greek Contacts and Agreements, 1939

At this point it is necessary to consider Anglo-Greek contacts and co-operation in the first months of the war. But before that it will be useful to pause briefly and look at Anglo-Greek strategic considerations before the outbreak of war. The first soundings about the possibility of a common or parallel strategy in the event of war in the Eastern Mediterranean took place in early 1939, when Metaxas undertook to explain the essentials of Greek war planning to the British Government. According to Metaxas, Greek defence plans were based on a Mediterranean war in which Italy would be hostile and Greece on Britain's side. Hitherto, Greece had been preparing for a Balkan war, in which the predominant role would be played by the army; but attention had been turned lately to a Mediterranean war, in which the navy and the air force would play the principal part, in close co-operation with the British Mediterranean Fleet and Air Arm.[2]

This appreciation of Greek strategy, however, represented Metaxas's views rather than those of the Greek General Staff. Until April 1939 war planning covered the Bulgarian threat only. The Greek General Staff assumed that any war would be local and static, as the elaborate and costly fortifications on the Bulgarian border clearly showed. General Papagos, Chief

---

[1] P. N. Pipinelis, *History of Greek Foreign Policy, 1923–1941* (in Greek), Athens, 1948, p. 294.

[2] Reports of the British Service Attachés of Jan. 1939, F.O. 371/23760.

of the General Staff, admitted later that the Government had made it clear that the aim of Greek rearmament was to deal with Bulgaria in the event of a Greco-Bulgarian war, in which Bulgaria would have the initiative. This aim was also in accordance with Greece's obligations arising from the Balkan Pact. And he adds: 'The Government had never considered the possibility of a war against Italy to be the purpose of our military preparations.' Greece, he went on to say, did not even possess a plan covering the Italian danger.[1] The April 1939 crisis sounded the alarm, and the Greek General Staff then produced the first plan covering both Italy and Bulgaria, Plan IB, on 4 May 1939. The new plan took into consideration the help Greece might expect from her Balkan partners, in the event of Bulgaria attacking alone; it presupposed British naval superiority in the Mediterranean, and counted on some British and French help; and divided Greek land forces between two lines of defence, the frontiers with Albania and Bulgaria. According to this plan, the fully mobilized forces of Greece were allocated as follows: 5 divisions and 2 brigades for the Albanian theatre of operations, 6 divisions and 1 brigade for the Bulgarian (not including the fort garrisons), and 5 divisions and 1 brigade as general reserves, of which the Albanian theatre received only 2, the rest remaining in the Salonika area.[2] According to Papagos, this allocation, which clearly favoured the Bulgarian theatre, was made necessary by the need to hold Bulgaria at all costs until Turkish help arrived.[3] But this hardly constitutes by itself an explanation of the attitude of the Greek General Staff. It is worth noting in this context that expenditure on the fortifications facing Bulgaria was not reduced after the Italian occupation of Albania, as one might have expected. On the contrary, of the 851,000,000 dr. spent on fortifications between April 1939 and October 1940, the Bulgarian sector received the lion's share, 769,000,000 against 82,000,000 for the Albanian sector, approximately, 90·4 per cent against 9·6 per cent.[4] Total expenditure on defence works in the years 1936–40

[1] A. Papagos, *The Greek Army and its War Preparedness, 1923–1940* (in Greek), Athens, 1945, pp. 325–6.

[2] A. Korozis, *The Wars, 1940–1941, Successes and Responsibilities* (in Greek), vol. i, Athens, 1958, pp. 611–13; Papagos, *The Greek Army*, pp. 327–8.

[3] Ibid., p. 328; Korozis, op. cit., vol. i, p. 613.

[4] Ibid., pp. 154–5, 638–9, 641, 649.

amounted to 1,458,000,000;[1] and more than half of it was spent in the post-April 1939 period. Moreover, there are some indications that the Greek Government—not only the General Staff—were seriously preoccupied with the Bulgarian danger well after the crisis of April 1939, as late as August. During the negotiations of August 1939 about buying aircraft from Britain, Metaxas informed Simopoulos that the Greek Government needed the aircraft in order to cover Bulgaria, as well as Italy. But Simopoulos was told that, in his talks with the British, he 'should not mention Bulgaria'.[2]

The British Government, naturally, disapproved of the emphasis and the general line of Greek strategy: in the first place, they believed that Bulgaria on her own would not attack Greece in the event of a general war; in the second place, they considered that the major danger to Greece was from Italy, and from Britain's point of view this was most certainly the case.[3] The British thus tried to guide Greek strategy to serve their own requirements in the Mediterranean by offering to Greece such war material (coastal defence guns and anti-aircraft guns, mainly) as would enable her to withstand an Italian attack from the air and sea. Those considerations were put before the Chiefs of Staff Committee and they recommended that the Greeks concentrate on aircraft, anti-aircraft guns, coastal defence guns, trawlers for mine-sweeping, and anti-submarine vessels. These armaments, 'mainly designed to protect Greek harbours and bases', were those which would be 'most beneficial' to British strategic requirements in the Mediterranean.[4] These strategic considerations were, of course, an extension of British strategy during the sanctions period. What was expected in the event of a Mediterranean war, in which Italy would be hostile to Britain, was that Greece should adopt a policy of benevolent neutrality towards Britain, and deny her harbours and bases to Italy; and the armaments recommended to Greece by the British Chiefs of Staff were suitable for the defence of those harbours and bases. But the occupation of

[1] Papagos, op. cit., p. 220; Korozis, op. cit., vol. i, pp. 154–5.

[2] Letter from Metaxas to Simopoulos, 26 Aug. 1939, Simopoulos Papers.

[3] Report by the Military Attaché in Athens, 7 Mar. 1939, and F.O. Letter to the W.O., 17 Mar., F.O. 371/23760.

[4] Report by the Chiefs of Staff Sub-Committee of 31 Mar. 1939, in F.O. 371/23760.

Albania by Italy, and the resulting threat to Greece's security changed the strategic realities in the area at a stroke. As has been seen, the Chiefs of Staff of Britain were now faced with a situation for which they had no answer. The Italian presence in Albania had shifted the emphasis in such a way as to put Greece outside Britain's main strategic concerns and interests. All that Britain could now recommend to Greece was to remain neutral if war broke out in the Mediterranean.

British strategy in relation to Greece came under consideration in early September when the British Chiefs of Staff concluded that, with the attitude of Italy and the Balkan states in the balance, Britain's interests would be best served by maintaining the neutrality of Greece.[1] The British Chiefs of Staff were convinced that the intervention of Greece on the allied side could only add to their immediate commitments. From a military point of view, they believed that it was preferable for Greece and the Balkans in general to remain neutral as long as Italy also remained neutral. About Italy's attitude, the Foreign Office was even more explicit: intervention in the Balkans at this time would be 'most unfortunate' because of the disturbing effect it was bound to have on Italy. A violation of Greek neutrality could not be considered unless and until Italy was at war with Britain; and the latter could not at one and the same time pursue a policy of keeping Italy neutral and mobilize the Balkan states against Germany. A neutral, and preferably a friendly, Italy was from the point of view of the Foreign Office more valuable than the Balkans forced into belligerence; and the two seemed almost incompatible. The Foreign Office decided, therefore, that as long as Italy remained neutral and Britain attached paramount importance to that neutrality, British policy should be directed towards ensuring the formation of a neutral bloc in the Balkans.[2]

In the middle of September, and on the occasion of the Italian proposals to the Greek Government regarding the Greco-Italian Pact, the British Chiefs of Staff were asked again for their views on the role to be 'allotted' to Greece, and the co-operation which the Greek Government might expect from

[1] C.O.S. (39) 6, 7 Sept. 1939, Cab. 79/1.
[2] Memo. by the Secretary of State for Foreign Affairs, 'Position in the Balkans', 12 Sept. 1939, W.P. (39) 25, Cab. 66/1.

Britain. In a report of 22 September, entitled 'Greek Co-operation', the Chiefs of Staff gave their first considered views. Old arguments and considerations, as well as new ones, were given in an explicit form, and became the basis of British strategy towards Greece until Greece came into the war. The Chiefs of Staff were convinced that, except in a situation in which Bulgaria and Turkey were both belligerent and on Britain's side, it would be to Britain's advantage for Greece to remain neutral as long as possible, 'even' if Italy declared war against Britain. As a belligerent, Greece would undoubtedly prove a liability, and would tend to absorb allied resources which would be better used in more vital theatres of the war. It was further argued, with regard to British support to Greece, that 'in any event Britain could not provide any British land or air forces to assist Greece unless the neutrality of Italy was assured beyond all possible doubt'. As for the role that Greece was expected to play, the Chiefs of Staff wanted Greece 'in all circumstances' to deny the use of her harbours to Britain's enemies.[1]

The co-operation of Greece, from the point of view of Britain, would be advantageous only in a situation in which Italy was not hostile to Britain; at the same time, Britain could not possibly support Greece if Italy were a belligerent and Britain's enemy. The Italian factor was thus paramount in British strategy towards Greece. Britain was not prepared to hold Staff conversations with Greece, let alone violate Greece's neutrality, because she did not want to upset Italy; and if Italy were in fact to come into the war against Britain, Britain could not possibly commit land or air forces in Greece. Theoretically, Greece and the Balkans in general offered an opportunity to the Allies to hold and wear down enemy forces away from the Western theatre of the war, and could eventually provide a bridgehead for offensive operations. Tempting as these considerations might have been, to France especially, Britain could never entertain them seriously. In the case of a hostile Italy, Britain's first objective would be to eliminate her; and, only after this was achieved, could British forces perhaps be committed in Greece, when there was no danger of their being pinned down in a country difficult to defend and within Italy's immediate reach.

[1] C.O.S. (39) 45, 22 Sept. 1939, Cab. 80/3.

As the year wore on, the British Government decided that all they could do at the moment was to arrange for secret contacts between the Allied Staffs and the Greek General Staff. They also decided that the Allies ought to be 'cautious in regard to Greece, to which country Italy was likely to be particularly susceptible'. The dominant consideration of allied strategy in the Balkans was the avoidance of any action or policy which could antagonize Italy in any way.[1]

The war, however, compelled Britain and Greece to search for alternative ways of co-operation, especially in the economic field. Already in the spring of 1939, the governments of the two countries had negotiated an agreement on the Export Credits, voted by the British Parliament in the autumn of 1938. After hard bargaining about the grant of credits, an agreement was signed in July 1939 to the effect that Britain would provide Greece with export credits for £2,040,900 at 5 per cent interest per annum, to be repaid over yearly annuities in twenty years.[2]

In the autumn of 1939, the British approached the Greek Government with a view to concluding a trade agreement that would restrict Greek exports to Germany and facilitate Greek imports of certain commodities such as foodstuffs, coal, and petroleum. The Greeks in this instance expressed their readiness to co-operate, and only asked that there should be no inter-ference by the British Navy with such trade with Germany as would be permitted under the proposed agreement. This, however, was an undertaking the British Government wished to avoid. The intention behind the agreement was to induce the Greeks to fix a maximum beyond which they would under-take not to export to Germany. This did not necessarily imply an undertaking on the part of the British not to seize contra-band exports to Germany, when they were intercepted by British patrols. The object of the agreement, as far as the British were concerned, was merely to supplement Britain's

[1] Cabinet Meeting, 14 Dec. 1939, W.M. (39) 115, Cab. 65/2.
[2] Relevant correspondence and the Agreement of July 1939 in R5046/5177/5656/5680/31/19, F.O. 371/23761. During the negotiations Simopoulos wrote to Metaxas: 'What predominates here is not the political view, but the business view. Even the miserable credits of £2,000,000, which they have approved, have the appearance of a business transaction, not a political one. They give the impression of fussy merchants and bankers bargaining about the interest and the terms of payment . . .' London Dispatch, Copy, No. 2945/St/39, 23 June 1939, Simopoulos Papers.

contraband control by fixing an upper limit on the amount of goods sent to Germany by routes which Britain could not control, routes overland and up the Adriatic.[1]

The Greeks finally accepted the British terms, and on 9 October 1939 an agreement was signed in Athens by an exchange of notes between Metaxas and the British Minister.[2] The Greek Government undertook to fix a maximum for the export, directly or indirectly, from Greece to Germany, of certain commodities, such as cereals, fruits, vegetables, oil, tobacco, and practically all metals.[3] The Greeks also undertook to supply the British Government with statistics at monthly intervals of Greek exports of these commodities to all destinations in Europe. Pending an agreement about the maximum of each commodity that could be exported to Germany, the Greek Government undertook not to permit the export in any one calendar month of those commodities in excess of one-twelfth of the average annual exports to Germany during the years 1934 to 1938.

The British for their part undertook to put no obstacle in the way of importation into Greece of certain commodities that would be agreed upon later, so long as these goods were used only for domestic consumption. They also undertook to facilitate the supply from their own or other resources of certain commodities needed for domestic consumption. These undertakings, however, did not imply that ships carrying cargo to Greek ports would be exempted from contraband control. Similarly, goods exported from Greece to Germany, which were included in the Contraband Lists of the British Government, would not be exempted from seizure by British vessels, even though they were within the categories and quantities permitted for export to Germany.[4]

The British Government thus secured a considerable limitation of Greek exports to Germany. The Greek Government, in return for effectively abandoning the German market, secured

---

[1] Athens Tel. No. 433, 25 Sept. 1939, and F.O. reply, Tel. No. 417, 27 Sept., F.O. 371/23765.

[2] Metaxas's note, dated 9 Oct., was a reply to the British Minister's note of 6 Oct., F.O. 371/23765.

[3] Other commodities included dairy products, fishery products, meat and meat products, hides, nuts, timber, cotton, wool, flax, hemp, and petroleum products.

[4] R8696/32/19, F.O. 371/23765.

Britain's promise to assist the importation into Greece of certain products, such as cereals, coal, and petroleum, vital for the country's existence. As the war progressed, Greece had more and more to co-operate with Britain in her economic measures against Germany, and became increasingly dependent on Britain for her existence.

Shortly after the War Trade Agreement was signed, the British also approached the Greek Government about the chartering of Greek merchant vessels. Negotiations between the Board of Trade and the Greek shipowners had been in progress since the outbreak of the war, but the Greeks did not accept the terms proposed by the British. The Board of Trade had proposed that the freight should be at the rate current at the time of the charter for British vessels carrying Government cargo, and that the war risk insurance should be undertaken by the shipowners. The Foreign Office was therefore asked to put pressure on the Greek Government in order to bring round the Greek shipowners.[1] The Greek Government was initially reluctant to exert the desired pressure: in the first place, they did not wish to be associated with the negotiations, since they would seem to be taking sides in the conflict; in the second place, they felt that the Greek shipowners could not possibly be treated as if they were of the same status as the British shipowners, and the terms of the chartering therefore could not be the same.[2] What appears to have been the main reason behind Greece's reluctance to intervene, however, is that by the proposed chartering she would lose to Britain one of her main sources of income and free exchange. At a time when she had to make many sacrifices in other fields, it would be hard for Greece to be deprived of a considerable part of her National Income.[3] The Greek Government had also been warned by the Germans that they would regard the chartering of Greek ships by Britain as a serious departure from Greece's neutrality.[4]

The issue of the Greek merchant fleet came up again during the negotiations between the two Governments, which took

[1] F.O. Tels. Nos. 452 and 453 to Athens, 15 Oct. 1939, F.O. 371/23765.

[2] R9286/32/19, F.O. 371/23765.

[3] Letter by the Minister of the Merchant Marine to Simopoulos, 27 Oct. 1939, Simopoulos Papers.

[4] Tel. No. 449/222667 to Athens, 28 Oct. 1939, *D.G.F.P.*, Ser. D, vol. viii, No. 310.

place in London in early 1940, and concerned trade, the debt, tobacco, and other matters of common interest. The effect of the War Trade Agreement of October, and the fact that the British contraband list contained many of Greece's products, would reduce Greek exports to Germany, as compared with 1938, by an estimated £2,500,000. Greece was also very seriously short of primary necessities. The increased price of goods formerly imported from Germany, the rise in the prices of wheat, petroleum, and coal, and the shortage of foreign exchange had created a serious state of affairs. The dislocation of trade had also led to rising unemployment and increasing insecurity of employment. These conditions bore heavily on both the rural and urban population, and seriously affected the economy, precariously balanced even at the best of times.[1]

The British Minister in Athens, alarmed by this state of affairs, entreated his Government to do something for Greece, and soon. The goodwill of the Greeks would lose its value if it became the goodwill of a 'bankrupt country'. Palairet also warned his Government that a financial crisis, which was becoming more possible every day, might lead to the overthrow of Metaxas's Government and its replacement by one which would have little reason to co-operate with Britain. King George and Metaxas also made an appeal to the British Government to make an early announcement of immediate action to increase British purchases from, and supplies to, Greece.[2]

The Foreign Office then decided that the problem of trade with Greece should be regarded as 'political', and not be looked at simply from the commercial angle, or even from the point of view of stopping supplies to Germany. It was further decided that the British Government would consider purchases of tobacco, existing stocks of perishable fruits and minerals, and supply coal, wheat, and sugar to Greece.[3] The British Govern-

[1] F.O. Memo., 14 Nov. 1939, R9927/32/19, and Athens Disp. No. 1, 1 Jan. 1940, R441/441/19, F.O. 371/23914, and enclosed 'Political Review of 1939'. The Political Review of 1939, drawn up by the British Legation in Athens, contained the following warning: 'The standard of living of the bulk of the population is already so low that it can scarcely be further reduced without fear of social disorders.'

[2] Letter from Palairet to the Ministry of Economic Warfare, 7 Nov. 1939, R9790/32/19, F.O. 371/23766.

[3] F.O. Memo., 14 Nov. 1939. The Memorandum was drafted after a meeting of an Inter-Departmental Committee on 9 Nov., F.O. 371/23766.

ment finally decided to act: the Ministry of Food agreed to increase purchases of citrus fruit, the Ministry of Supply to buy quantities of certain minerals, chrome in particular; while the Treasury agreed to buy tobacco to a value of not less than £500,000. At the same time, the Greek Government was informed that the chartering of Greek tonnage was an 'urgent' question, and was asked to bring suitable pressure on their shipowners. If the owners did not accept the terms, the Greek Government was asked to requisition their vessels at the rates applying to British shipping, and then charter them to Britain at higher rates. The British Government also expressed the hope that a settlement would be reached on the debt question, and proposed a definitive War Trade Agreement, which would embrace all outstanding questions.[1]

The Greek Government promptly accepted these proposals, and expressed willingness to start negotiations for a definitive War Trade Agreement. Metaxas also promised his assistance on the chartering of Greek vessels, and asked for information about the number of ships and the rate desired by the British Government. On the debt issue, however, he made it clear that a settlement involving an increase of the current rate of payment (40 per cent) would be impossible.[2] It was finally agreed, at British insistence, that the negotiations should take place in London. In late December, Metaxas sent over the Minister of the Merchant Marine, and early in the new year the Minister of Finance and the Governor of the Bank of Greece. The negotiations were hard going to begin with,[3] since the issues involved were many and often conflicting. The Treasury wanted to make the purchase of Greek tobacco conditional on a favourable settlement of the debt. The Greek Government, however, had for once strong cards: the merchant fleet and the proposed War Trade Agreement. The purchase of Greek tobacco was wanted by the Foreign Office, since it would help Greece to avoid economic dependence on Germany, and would secure the Greek Government's assistance in obtaining favourable terms from the shipowners. The British also wanted to

---

[1] F.O. Tels. Nos. 506, 507, 508 to Athens, 25 Nov. 1939, F.O. 371/23766.
[2] Athens Tel. No. 610, 9 Dec. 1939, F.O. 371/23766.
[3] Metaxas noted in his diary on 23 Dec. 1939 that the British wanted to 'skin' the Greeks. *Diary*, vol. iv, p. 410.

secure the agreement of the Greek Government to restrict exports to Germany for the duration of the war. The issues involved were too important for Britain to risk a breakdown of the negotiations over the debt question, and the Treasury had to submit.[1]

Metaxas followed the negotiations with mixed feelings: he was anxious to secure the goods and provisions which Greece needed, and to find an outlet for Greek products; at the same time, he was concerned over the effect of the agreement on Greece's position. At one point he felt that the British demands, if accepted, would turn the Greeks into Britain's 'slaves'.[2] He was also anxious over the effect on Germany. On 20 January he made a personal request that, in the event of total interruption or a substantial decrease in Greece's trade with Germany, the British Government would undertake to give equivalent help to avert economic ruin. The British Government, however, refused to give this undertaking.[3]

On 22 January the Shipping Agreement was signed by the Ministry of Shipping and the Greek shipowners. The latter undertook to provide thirty-one ships and to ensure that another twenty-nine would be put forward, amounting to about 500,000 tons. The vessels were to remain in the service of the charterers from delivery until January 1941, and the charterers were also to have the option of redelivering any vessel. Rates per deadweight ton ranged from 17s. to 19s. 9d., the higher rate being for vessels of 10,000 tons, and the lower for smaller ones.[4] The War Trade Agreement, really an extension of the October Agreement, was signed on 26 January. The Greeks undertook not to seek, directly or indirectly, maxima in exports to Germany of the commodities agreed upon in October 1939. For their part, the British agreed to help the passage through contraband control, as well as the supply from their own or other sources, of such commodities as petroleum products, sugar, wheat, coal, pig iron,

---

[1] Correspondence between the Foreign Office and the Treasury, Jan. 1940, F.O. 371/24904. The Treasury agreed to a rate of 43 per cent of the interest due to the bondholders for the duration of the war. The debt settlement was not incorporated in the War Trade Agreement.

[2] 17 Jan. 1940, *Diary*, vol. iv, p. 445.

[3] R1149/1150/2/19, F.O. 371/24904.

[4] Shipping Agreement in F.O. 371/24905.

copper, and other metals, which were required for domestic consumption.[1]

The Agreements of January 1940 bound Greece to Britain's economic warfare against Germany, and marked the first stage of her departure from neutrality. The Greek Minister in Berlin explained Greece's difficult position with respect to British contraband control in the Mediterranean, and her dependence on British coal and the income derived from shipping. He also assured the Germans that Metaxas wished not only to maintain, but even to 'expand' Greco-German trade. Naturally, the Germans were sceptical.[2] In August 1940, and as the volume of Greek exports to Germany appreciably dwindled, the Germans informed Metaxas in plain and threatening language that they considered Greece's attitude 'unsatisfactory', and made representations about the fall of Greek exports of chrome, and the chartering of Greek vessels.[3] Finally, on 20 September, the Greek Government had to sign a Commercial Agreement with Germany. In theory, the agreement was an infraction of the Anglo-Greek Agreement of January. But the Greek Government explained to the British that they hoped to live up to the London Agreement in practice even if they could not do so on paper. They laid great emphasis on the fact that the quantities contracted for delivery to Germany were 'purely theoretical', and requested the British to judge them by 'actual performance' rather than by 'paper promises'.[4]

The Greeks had secured an ingenious clause in their agreement with Germany, by which Greek exports to Germany would be sent 'symmetrically' in driblets, rather than the full amount of each agreed quantity at once. By this they hoped to be able to 'apply the brake successfully' on exports to Germany, since transport was becoming increasingly difficult. Thus in October 1940 the Greek Government informed the British Minister that 1,200 German railway trucks were waiting in Greece to be loaded; and as they were held up, Germany would not send coal to Greece, and the latter refused to export the

[1] War Trade Agreement in F.O. 371/24904.
[2] Memo. by E. Weizsacker, 14 Feb. 1940, *D.G.F.P.*, Ser. D, vol. viii, No. 614.
[3] *D.G.F.P.*, Ser. D, vol. x, No. 375.
[4] Athens Disp. No. 239, 28 Sept. 1940, F.O. 371/24914.

agreed commodities to Germany. It was, indeed, an ingenious and quite effective 'performance'.[1]

The Italian Factor, 1940

In 1940 Greek foreign policy was limited by an ambiguous neutrality, which the Government strove to preserve by a policy reminiscent of the ostrich: they were professing neutrality when in fact Greece was closely bound to Britain. Greece, through necessity and the decision of her Government, was gradually drawn towards Britain and closely linked to Britain's war effort. The cumulative forces of the war, and the willingness of Metaxas's Government to co-operate with Britain in all fields, made Greece's neutrality an empty thing. She could stay outside the conflict only as long as any of the great powers chose to let her.

King George and Metaxas were often puzzled by the nature of the war and the issues involved, and at times doubted the correctness of the lines drawn between the combatants.[2] Nevertheless, they never seriously wavered in their decision to hold fast to Britain through thick and thin. The British also never wavered in their decision to stand by Metaxas, despite frequent advice to the contrary. By this time, as we have already seen, King George was either unwilling or unable to effect a change of regime, and exercised little influence over Metaxas. Such thoughts, or hopes, as the Foreign Office may have entertained at times for a possible liberalization of the regime were abandoned. The British Minister in Athens and the Foreign Office decided that it would be wiser for them not to interfere

---

[1] Athens Disp. No. 457, 7 Oct. 1940, F.O. 371/24914.

[2] In Dec. 1939 the King remarked to *The Times* Balkan correspondent: 'I want to know when Britain, France and Germany are going to make war on Russia.' F.O. 371/24909. Metaxas was even more confused, if only because of his old leanings towards Germany, and his anxiety about the regime. On 17 Sept. 1939, he noted: 'Conversation with the King. He is afraid lest we be forced to make concessions in internal affairs, if the people begin to suffer. Perhaps, even worse is in store for us if the Democracies prevail. We shall see.' On 14 July 1940, he noted: 'If the Germans prevail we shall become their slaves. If the British prevail we shall become their slaves. If none, Europe will collapse. Anyhow, she will collapse.' Often he tried to quieten an uneasy conscience: 'It is natural', he wrote on 6 May 1940, 'for maritime countries like ours to be friendly with Britain, and continental ones like Bulgaria with Germany. The difference of regimes does not count, since Britain, too, will follow our road.' *Diary*, vol. iv, pp. 396, 467, 484.

in any way in internal Greek affairs, and that they should shut their eyes to the 'disagreeable elements' in the regime.

The attitude of the British Government towards Greece in 1940 depended on such variables as Germany's policy towards south-eastern Europe, and on Italy's attitude and plans. Germany wanted to leave the Balkans out of the war, (*a*) because she did not want to disperse her forces; (*b*) in order that this area, an important source of supplies for Germany, should remain neutral, at least as long as it provided these supplies; and (*c*) in order not to draw Italy into this area through military action, and so cause a clash of interests between Italy and the Soviet Union.[1] Moreover, if they were drawn into the war, the Balkans could become an Anglo-French base for air strikes against the oilfields of Romania. Germany, therefore, had no reason yet to disturb the neutrality of the Balkans.

Britain and France saw the Balkans, especially from the point of view of possible allied intervention, in a different light. Whereas Britain's view was one of a 'minimum strategic defence', with the defence of Turkey and the Straits as the objective,[2] France preferred decisive action against Germany by establishing an allied bridgehead in Salonika. The British considered that the Allies would gain nothing while risking a great deal, if on their own initiative they brought the war into the Balkans. The case would have been different, of course, if allied military action in the area could have been overwhelmingly effective and decisive. But this was very doubtful, since the Allies lacked the necessary forces. Moreover, successful action would depend on the benevolent neutrality of Italy, the active support of Turkey, and the concurrence of Greece. The first was doubtful, if not impossible. Turkey would fight only when her vital interests were directly affected; and she feared the Soviet Union as much as Germany. Greece, finally, was expected to play her part, but only if adequately aided, and of this there was very little prospect.[3]

---

[1] Memo. by Gen. Jodl, 6 Jan. 1940, 'Policy and the War Effort in the East', *D.G.F.P.*, Ser. D, vol. viii, No. 514.

[2] Report by the Allied Military Committee, 5 Feb. 1940, 'Allied Military Policy in the Balkans', M.R. (40) 10, F.O. 371/24886.

[3] Memo. by the Secretary of State for Foreign Affairs, 'South-Eastern Europe', prepared for the Cabinet in connection with the meeting of the Supreme War Council on 28 Mar. 1940. W.P. (40) 110, F.O. 371/24887.

Britain's position on assistance to Greece depended on the following factors: British forces, if available, could not be sent to Greece, except in the case where Crete was not in Italian hands. Britain, however, could not provide adequate forces for defending the island itself, whose own defences were non-existent. Another governing factor was the relative security of Britain's communications in the Aegean. At the outset of war with Italy, Britain would be unable to secure these communications with her naval forces in the Mediterranean until the Italian threat in the Aegean was reduced. As a first step towards securing them, it would be necessary to neutralize the Dodecanese, and that would not be possible until Britain was able to reinforce her naval and air forces in the Mediterranean appreciably. British assistance to Greece thus depended on denying Crete to Italy and neutralizing the Dodecanese; neither of these requirements was likely to be fulfilled in view of Britain's inadequate forces and vulnerable position in the Mediterranean.[1]

At the end of May 1940, Britain's attitude to assisting Greece could be summarized as follows: in the event of an Italian attack on Greek territory, action would be initially limited to (*a*) the dispatch of an allied detachment to Crete to help the Greeks deny the island to Italy; and (*b*) allied operations to control communications in the Aegean and the Eastern Mediterranean in general. The 'interests of Greece', it was decided, must depend on Britain's ability to 'defeat Italy' rather than to her ability 'to afford local support on the Greek mainland'. In any case, because of vital defence commitments elsewhere and Britain's limited resources, the British could not possibly take Greece under their 'protection'.[2]

In May the British Government also considered the question of an alliance with Greece, as Metaxas returned to the subject from time to time. If Italy were to enter the war against the Allies, Greek intervention would divert Italian forces, and facilitate the dispatch of allied forces to Crete and the use of Greek harbours and bases; moreover, the total allied effort

[1] M.R. (J) (40) 63, 'Military Action open to the Allies in the event of War with Italy', 1 May 1940, in F.O. 371/24942.
[2] F.O. Tel. No. 244 to Athens, 31 May 1940. The Telegram was drafted by the Chiefs of Staff Committee. F.O. 371/24915.

against Italy would be increased. Failing an alliance, Greece might be inclined to come to terms with Italy, while an alliance might keep Bulgaria from joining the enemy camp and encourage Turkey to implement her treaty obligations. An Anglo-Greek alliance would also facilitate Staff conversations between the Allies and Greece.[1]

Yet the alliance had many disadvantages for Britain, since it would increase her 'moral obligations' towards Greece, and constitute an additional commitment, that was 'strategically undesirable'. The Greek Government would also be entitled to demand 'material assistance', which Britain could not spare. Moreover, the alliance would be known to the Italians, who would naturally consider it 'provocative'. They were bound to resent it, and could be driven to seizing bases on Greek territory, or even to entering the war against the Allies. At this point, the Foreign Office seemed prepared to consider an alliance. The Chiefs of Staff, however, wanted Greece to remain neutral, and were not in favour of an alliance. Moreover, they felt that it would be unwise to 'expose' Britain's inability to afford her 'effective direct support'. The issue was briefly discussed by the Cabinet on 23 May 1940, but only to be shelved indefinitely.[2]

The Italian factor also acted as a brake and paralysed action in the Balkans generally. In the last briefing of the British Ministers in the Balkan capitals in April 1940, the Chief of the Imperial General Staff explained that 'the crux of the whole Balkan situation was Italy', and that every effort should be made to keep Italy from joining the enemy.[3] Explorations with the Balkan states could continue, and viewpoints could be expounded; the game, however, according to the British Ambassador in Ankara, had to be played with a 'diminishing supply of trumps'.[4] The Foreign Office, except for the 'Italian line', had nothing new to contribute. As someone cruelly remarked, the Foreign Office was like a 'chameleon' that had

---

[1] Athens Tel. No. 288, 18 May 1940, and C.O.S. (40) 370 (J.P.), 20 May 1940, 'The Role of Greece in the event of War in the Mediterranean', Cab. 80/11.

[2] C.O.S. (40) 370 (J.P.), 20 May 1940, 'The Role of Greece in the event of War in the Mediterranean', Cab. 80/11; W.P. (40) 164, 21 May 1940, 'The Question of an Alliance with Greece'; W.M. (40) 135, 23 May 1940, and F.O. Tel. No. 214 to Athens, 24 May 1940, in F.O. 371/24924.

[3] C.O.S. (40) 299, 18 Apr. 1940. Minutes of Meeting of the Chiefs of Staff with the British Representatives in the Balkans held on 15 Apr., Cab. 80/9.

[4] Sir H. Knatchbull-Hugessen, *Diplomat in Peace and War*, London, 1948, p. 157.

grown tired from sitting so long on the 'dull appeasement stone', and could not brighten up any more.[1]

In late May 1940 a last effort was made to prevent Italy from joining Germany. An approach to Mussolini through President Roosevelt was considered by the Allies: the Allies would undertake to consider after the end of the war 'certain grievances' of Italy about her position in the Mediterranean, and Italy would be admitted as an equal to the Peace Conference. Halifax was in favour of the approach, but the Cabinet was sceptical and confused. Mussolini, however, cut the whole thing short: he had at last decided to burn his boats.[2] Italy declared war on the Allies on 10 June, and in his war speech of the same day Mussolini promised that Italy would not drag her neighbours into the conflict; he warned them, however, that it depended 'on them and only on them' whether that promise could be kept.[3]

Italy's entry into the war presented the British Government with a completely new situation: Italy was hostile, and the position of France was becoming critical. The British Government now considered the possibility of spreading the war to the Balkans. The advantages were considerable: war would adversely affect communications and agricultural and industrial production there, and would damage stocks and supplies. Germany would thus be hard hit, while the Allies had little to lose economically since imports from the Balkans had already been reduced as a result of the closing of Mediterranean shipping routes. On a long-term view, however, intervention in the Balkans would react against Britain, since Germany would swiftly occupy the area and restore communications and production. The Chiefs of Staff considered that the immediate advantages were considerable, and advised that Britain should try to induce Greece and Yugoslavia to intervene on the allied side, while France was still fighting.[4] Methods of 'setting alight' the Balkans, such as Greek and Yugoslav

[1] H. Dalton, *Memoirs, 1931–1945*, London, 1957, p. 371.

[2] F.O. Correspondence in F.O. 371/24958, and Cabinet Conclusions of 27 and 28 May 1940, W.M. (40) 142, 145, Cab. 65/13.

[3] E. Wiskemann, *The Rome–Berlin Axis*, rev. edn., London, 1966, pp. 256, 257; *Greek White Book*, No. 77.

[4] W.P. (40) 200, Report by the Chiefs of Staff Committee, 'Balkan Policy in the New Situation', 11 June 1940, F.O. 371/24948.

mobilization, or the seizure of Crete and Corfu, were therefore considered for a time. The Foreign Office, however, was sceptical: while Italy kept her promise not to attack Yugoslavia and Greece, and as long as the tide on the Western Front did not turn in favour of the Allies, it would be virtually impossible to induce the Balkan countries to intervene in the war on the allied side.[1]

France, however, soon collapsed, and Turkey did not implement her treaty obligations to the Allies. The Soviet Union occupied Bessarabia and Northern Bukovina, and Romania renounced the Anglo-French Guarantee. If Germany was actively engaged in the Balkans it was essential that both the Soviet Union and Turkey should not be estranged by Britain's intervention in the area, and that both powers should side with Britain. In the light of circumstances, however, both desiderata were problematic. Moreover, Germany could very well attack both Britain and the Balkans at the same time, and probably press on towards the Straits, while Britain could not aid Turkey effectively. To spread the war to the Balkans thus became a rather academic prospect, and was abandoned.[2]

About this time, Italian designs against Greece were taking shape. In early July 1940, Hitler assured Ciano that everything concerning the Mediterranean was a 'purely Italian matter', in which he did not intend to interfere.[3] In August the Italians began a press campaign against Greece and staged a series of terrorist attacks against Greek ships. According to Grazzi, these preliminary actions were very much the doings of Ciano and Cesare De Vecchi, the Governor of the Dodecanese, who was convinced that the British Mediterranean Fleet was using Greek naval bases with the connivance of the Greek authorities,[4] and pressed the Italian Government for a more 'aggressive'

[1] F.O. Minutes, June 1940, Cabinet Meeting, 13 June 1940, W.M. (40) 164, and F.O. Memo., 19 June 1940, F.O. 371/24948.

[2] C.O.S. (40) 525, 'Balkan Policy after the French Collapse', 3 July 1940, and F.O. Tel. No. 126, Circular, 5 July 1940, in F.O. 371/24890.

[3] Ciano's conversation with Hitler, 7 July 1940, *Ciano's Diplomatic Papers*, edit. M. Muggeridge, London, 1948, pp. 375–9; *D.G.F.P.*, Ser. D, vol. x, No. 129.

[4] In Aug. 1940, the British Minister in Athens reported the following incident. The captain of the Greek ship S.S. *Hermione* had arranged with the British naval authorities for the destruction of the ship while carrying cargo to the Dodecanese for the Italians. The British Minister feared that this incident might have been known by the Italians, as it was known by the Greek Government. Athens Tel. No. 718, 21 Aug. 1940, F.O. 371/24922.

policy.[1] On 14 August, the Italian Press accused the Greeks of the murder of an Albanian brigand-patriot, Daut Hodja, who had been murdered in Albania, and attacked King George and 'l'amletico Metaxas'.[2] On 15 August, the feast of the Dormition of the Mother of God, the Greek cruiser *Elli* was torpedoed while lying at anchor off Tinos. The Greek Government had no doubt about the nationality of the submarine, but refrained from giving offence to Italy, and announced instead that the cruiser had been torpedoed by a submarine of 'unknown nationality'.[3] All the same, the Italians complained a few days later to the Greek Government about the 'fantastic idea' that seemed to have got around in Greece that Italy was responsible.[4] When asked by the German Government about their intentions towards Greece, the Italian Government replied that their attitude was determined by motives of a 'precautionary character', and that they would consider 'military measures' against Greece, in case Britain proceeded with the occupation of Greek bases.[5] The Italian Chiefs of Staff feared now that Ciano might have 'his war' at last.[6] At this point, however, the Germans intervened and asked the Italians to restrain their actions against Greece for the time being. Writing to the Military Governor of Albania on 22 August, Ciano informed him that it had been decided by 'higher authorities' to slow down the pace of Italian moves against Greece, and instructed him not to take any steps until further orders.[7]

During the August crisis, Metaxas assured the British Government that he was determined to resist any attempt by the Axis against Greece, and that he would prefer destruction to humiliation.[8] The British were naturally satisfied with this determina-

[1] Tel. by De Vecchi to Ciano, No. 658/81, 13 Aug. 1940, *D.D.I.*, Ser. 9, vol. v. See also Grazzi, op. cit., pp. 137, 139, and Mario Cervi, *Storia della querra di Grecia*, Milan, 1965, p. 29.

[2] *Greek White Book*, Nos. 111–18; Cervi, op. cit., pp. 35 ff.

[3] *Greek White Book*, Nos. 120, 129; Grazzi, op. cit., pp. 174–5.

[4] Athens Tel. No. 715, 21 Aug. 1940, F.O. 371/24917.

[5] Berlin Tel. No. 1254, 14 Aug. 1940, and Ciano's reply, Tel. No. 22607/830, 15 Aug. 1940, *D.D.I.*, Ser. 9, vol. v.

[6] Quirino Armellini, *Diario di guerra*, Milan, 1946, 20 Aug. 1940.

[7] Franz Halder, *Diaries*, London, 1950, vol. iv, pp. 166, 170, 20 and 23 Aug. 1940; *Ciano's Diplomatic Papers*, p. 385.

[8] Athens Tels. Nos. 655, 662, 13 and 14 Aug. 1940, F.O. 371/24909, and Tel. No. 684, 17 Aug. 1940, F.O. 371/24922.

tion to remain firm in face of the Italian attitude, but took care also to clear up the matter over which they were mainly concerned: they instructed the British Minister to ask Metaxas whether the Greek Government was intending to reinforce the garrison in Crete. As they explained to Palairet, they preferred to put this question to the Greek Government rather than advise them to take specific precautionary measures since advice might make the Greeks ask what the British were prepared to do for Greece in the event of an Italian attack. If, however, such a question was in fact asked by Metaxas, the British Government had the following answer: 'The greatest assistance that we can give to Greece is to knock Italy out of the war, and to do so we must bring the maximum pressure to bear on Italy at the decisive time and place. Any dispersion of our forces would not assist towards achieving this object. Thus our policy is to attack Italy by air at her most vital spots, i.e. the industrial north.'[1]

On 22 August Metaxas made a 'most earnest inquiry' as to what help Britain could give Greece if she were attacked by Italy.[2] The Chiefs of Staff advised that it was important to encourage Metaxas without giving him promises which could not be fulfilled. If the Italians had to fight, a campaign in Greece would be an 'embarrassment' to them, owing to their commitment in Libya. It was desirable that 'Italy should not achieve her ends without a fight', but Greece would have to resist without any 'real measure of assistance' from Britain.[3] On 24 August the British Government gave their reply to Metaxas. It was the same as that of 17 August: in the event of an Italian attack, Britain's assistance 'must be mainly directed towards knocking Italy out of the war'.[4]

The Foreign Office, however, was anxious lest this 'somewhat negative reply' might lead the Greeks to abandon the resolute attitude they had adopted towards Italy. Britain's strategic position in the Mediterranean and her political prestige in the Balkans and the Middle East would be seriously compromised, if Greece were to submit 'tamely' to Italy. The

[1] F.O. Tel. No. 509, 17 Aug. 1940, F.O. 371/24909.
[2] Athens Tel. No. 727, 22 Aug. 1940, F.O. 371/24917.
[3] C.O.S. (40) 278th Meeting, and C.O.S. (40) 656 (J.P.), 23 Aug. 1940, 'Italian Action against Greece', in F.O. 371/24917.
[4] F.O. Tel. No. 553 to Athens, 24 Aug. 1940, F.O. 371/24917.

British Minister was therefore instructed to do his utmost to ensure that the Greek Government continued to maintain their resolute policy of resistance to Italy 'even to the point of war'. On this last point, the Foreign Office gave the following confidential explanation:

> Italy must if possible be prevented from achieving a bloodless victory over Greece. If she is resolved to obtain control of Greece she ought to have to fight for it and not obtain it by bluff and empty threat. If the bluff is called she may withdraw from her present position and this would constitute a great moral victory for Greece from which we would benefit also. If, on the other hand, Italy persists to the point where she cannot draw back it will be to our advantage that she should get involved in all the uncertainties and complications of a Balkan campaign, especially at this time when she appears to be planning an attack on Egypt.[1]

The British Minister regarded the reply as negative, and expressed the opinion that Britain could not possibly expect Greece to resist alone. The Prime Minister then telegraphed Metaxas on 25 August, expressing his admiration for the latter's 'determination' in handling the crisis. The courageous attitude of the Greeks under Metaxas's leadership, Churchill wrote, had earned the admiration of the British people who, nurtured in the classical tradition, recalled the valour of the ancient Greeks in the face of the 'Persian peril'. Metaxas was 'profoundly moved' by the Prime Minister's message, and was quick to agree with the British that the 'greatest assistance' they could give to Greece in the event of an Italian attack would be to knock Italy out of the war. Metaxas also assured the British that Crete was prepared to offer 'most stubborn resistance'.[2]

The British Government tried at this point, but very reluctantly, to get Turkey to promise help to Greece in the event of an Italian attack. But the Turkish Government refused to be bound by such a commitment, and only promised to make a statement when the National Assembly met on 29 October, to the effect that Greece's fate was of 'vital' interest to Turkey.[3]

---

[1] F.O. Tel. No. 554 to Athens, 24 Aug. 1940, F.O. 371/24917.

[2] Athens Tels. Nos. 688 and 744, 17 and 25 Aug. 1940, F.O. Tel. No. 559 to Athens, 25 Aug., and Athens Tel. No. 753, 27 Aug., in F.O. 371/24917. Metaxas earnestly begged that no publicity should be given to the exchange of messages, apparently in order not to offend Italy.

[3] Cadogan and Halifax doubted whether such pressure should be put on Turkey.

Essentially, the British considered Greece a lost cause, and focused their attention on Crete, which they hoped would be held by Greek forces. If the Greek mainland could be held as well by Greeks, which the British Chiefs of Staff very much doubted,[1] so much the better.

In September 1940 Germany and Italy reaffirmed their agreement to direct their main war effort against Britain, and Mussolini, as he pointed out to the German Government, wished to remain at peace with Yugoslavia and Greece.[2] He is reported to have said that Greece represented a 'problem' that would be solved at the 'peace table'.[3] Perhaps the Italians believed that Greece might after all join the Axis, and make her bases available to Italy. There are indications that the Greek Government was not unanimous on Metaxas's resolution not to yield to the Italians. The British Minister informed the Foreign Office that at the Cabinet meetings after Germany's economic demands of September 1940 Greece's position *vis-à-vis* the Axis was discussed. Nikoloudis alone supported Metaxas, while Mavroudis, Papagos, and Apostolidis, about all of whom Palairet had asked Varvaresos, the Governor of the Bank of Greece, 'were all prepared, if need be, to surrender Epirus to the Italians'.[4] Mavroudis, indeed, was believed by Metaxas to be a 'traitor'.[5]

In late September 1940 during Ciano's visit to Berlin, it was agreed that 'the Greek issue was not of any particular urgency at the moment'. With the failure of Germany's invasion of England, however, Mussolini began considering an attack on

They felt that Turkey's main value was that she was not an ally of Germany's, and that the most important aspect of Britain's policy towards Turkey was the need to maintain unimpaired that 'negative advantage'. Vansittart noted wryly: 'We are getting, *vis-à-vis* Turkey, into the position of a man who is all too understanding not only after but before his wife deceives him. Antlers are a bad national headgear.' F.O. Minutes and Correspondence, F.O. 371/24918.

[1] C.O.S. (40) 656 (J.I.C.), 23 Aug. 1940, Cab. 80/17.
[2] Conversation between Mussolini and Ribbentrop, in the presence of Ciano and the German Ambassador in Rome, 19 Sept. 1940. *Ciano's Diplomatic Papers*, pp. 389–93; *D.G.F.P.*, Ser. D, vol. xi, No. 73.
[3] Armellini, op. cit., p. 95.
[4] Athens Tel. No. 239, 28 Sept. 1940, F.O. 371/24914.
[5] *Diary*, vol. iv, pp. 510, 511. On 25 Oct. 1940, Mavroudis told the German Minister that 'Greece might possibly give sympathetic consideration to a demand for bases in connection with operations against Egypt.' *D.G.F.P.*, Ser. D, vol. xi, No. 226.

Greece as a British 'prop'; and, as will be seen, so did Hitler. In early October the issue of an attack on Greece came up again as an operation for the 'elimination of a British prop',[1] and Mussolini ordered the Italian General Staff to prepare a statement on the forces required for such an enterprise.[2] On 15 October it was finally decided that the attack should take place late in the month, and Ciano promised to create the necessary provocative 'incident' two days in advance.[3] On the 19th Mussolini wrote to Hitler that he was 'resolved to end the delays, and very soon'. Greece was 'one of the main points of English maritime strategy in the Mediterranean', the King of Greece was 'English', the political classes were 'pro-English', while the people were 'immature but trained to hate Italy'. Greece had made available to Britain her naval and air bases, and she was essentially 'to the Mediterranean what Norway was to the North Sea', and so must not escape the 'same fate'.[4] Hitler, therefore, was not vaguely informed about Italy's intentions, as he later claimed, and had all the time he needed to 'persuade' Mussolini to delay the action contemplated.[5] It is rather doubtful, however, whether Hitler would have been willing to hold back Mussolini,[6] even if it had been possible at this late stage.

The British, again asked by the Greeks about assistance to Greece, had nothing to add to their previous replies. The Chiefs of Staff believed it likely that Greek resistance would 'crumple up' under even comparatively light air attack on the cities.[7] Nor did the British Government take seriously repeated warnings from Athens and Washington of an impending attack on Greece. Metaxas none the less assured them once more that he was ready to meet an attack whenever it came.[8] The attack

---

[1] *D.G.F.P.*, Ser. D, vol. xi, No. 135.

[2] Armellini, op. cit., p. 106.

[3] P. Badoglio, *Italy in the Second World War*, Oxford, 1948, p. 26.

[4] Grazzi, op. cit., pp. 206 ff.; Armellini, op. cit., pp. 115 ff.; Badoglio, op. cit., pp. 26–8; Wiskemann, op. cit., p. 274.

[5] *D.G.F.P.*, Ser. D, vol. xi, No. 199; *Les lettres secrètes échangées par Hitler et Mussolini*, Paris, 1946, pp. 81 ff. See also E. Weizsacker, *Memoirs*, London, 1951, p. 244, and *D.G.F.P.*, Ser. D, vol. xi, Nos. 194, 209.

[6] M. L. van Creveld, *Hitler's Strategy, 1940–1941: The Balkan Clue*, Cambridge, 1973, pp. 39 ff.

[7] C.O.S. (40) 365, Meeting of 21 Oct. 1940, Cab. 79/7.

[8] Washington Tels. Nos. 2376 and 2387, 22 and 23 Oct. 1940, Athens Tel. No. 986, 24 Oct., and F.O. Minutes, in F.O. 371/24919.

was launched in the morning of 28 October. On the same day Metaxas noted in his diary: 'War. I call at once Nikoloudis, Mavroudis. I brief the King. I call Palairet and ask for England's aid. I go at 5 [o'clock in the morning] to the Council of Ministers. Everyone, loyal: Mavroudis, too. Everyone, except Kyrou. Tour with the King. The people very enthusiastic. Battles on the Epirus front. Bombings. Sirens. We begin to get settled. May God help us.'[1]

[1] *Diary*, vol. iv, p. 516.

V

Undercurrents

At this point, it is useful to look at internal Greek developments. As we have already seen in a previous chapter, the arrests and deportations of 1938 had cut short a development which, if left unchecked, might have endangered the regime. This action had strengthened Metaxas's position. Moreover, these developments, and Britain's failure to influence the regime in a direction expected to make it more acceptable to the Greeks and therefore less vulnerable, made one point clear to the British: that the regime was there to stay and nothing more could be done to change it, unless they were to take the responsibility of engineering Metaxas's overthrow, which was far from their minds. The British thus resigned themselves to the fact that they were associated with an unpopular regime, although they realized that they ran the risk of becoming unpopular themselves with the Greeks through their tolerance, not to say support, of the regime. This was certainly an uncomfortable position; and explanations to the effect that Britain pursued a policy of non-interference in internal Greek affairs were not very convincing. In the case of Greece it might be argued, as opponents of the regime did argue at the time, that non-interference carried almost the same weight as interference, because close collaboration with the dictatorship from a position of influence rendered such a distinction rather meaningless. These subtle but valid arguments annoyed the British, but not to the extent that it tempted them to change their short-term policy towards Greece. Besides, Greece had had such a record of volatile and anomalous political life that a reasonable dictator was considered to be, from the point of view of British interests, not worse and perhaps better than the probable continuation of instability and the danger of another upheaval in which the army would be involved.

These arguments and dilemmas preoccupied the British

throughout 1939 and 1940; and even if they tried to forget them the Greeks never failed to remind them of these questions. This was particularly true of the Venizelists and the republicans, barred from public affairs and impatient to emerge from the shadows. Since they represented the best part of the traditional Anglophile element in the country, the British watched this element with a certain anxious uneasiness, as many of its prominent members were arrested, deported to the Greek islands, or even imprisoned, as a rule without trial. Incidents like these called forth Foreign Office inquiries at the Athens Legation as to whether they represented an anti-British attitude on the part of the regime. A Foreign Office minute of the time reads: 'By an unfortunate (but quite natural) coincidence Anglophile elements in Greece have got to be hostile to the regime.'[1] This uneasiness became at times serious concern.

One figure who preoccupied the British—and Metaxas even more—was General Plastiras, the prominent Venizelist who lived in France, self-exiled since his abortive *coup* of March 1933. Plastiras was not exactly a person for whom the British could be expected to feel great sympathy, if only because of his past anti-dynastic record. While in exile and having little else to do, he made certain that his name was connected with every conspiracy directed against the regime. Plastiras, as often happens with exiles, had essentially lost touch with Greek realities, and spent his time planning *coups* or landings in Greece, and writing letters to, or reading others from, his fellow conspirators. Some of these letters make pathetic reading now, the space mostly taken up by ciphers, methods of manufacturing invisible ink, or the problems of by-passing the censor. Plastiras was a romantic, innocent of the intricacies of politics, and the least selfish of the Venizelists; for, as will be seen, there were others who were less romantic, but more devious and calculating. In a letter to Alexandros Zannas, another prominent Venizelist, Plastiras wrote at the end of 1938 that he had good reasons to believe that by the spring of 1939 it would be possible for him 'to land at Salonika one day'. If this were to succeed, he wrote, 'I am 99 per cent certain that in 3–4 days I shall be in Athens.' Further on in the letter he said that he would reach Salonika by sea so that his arrival should remain

---

[1] F.O. Minute by Fitzroy Maclean, 18 July 1939, F.O. 371/23761.

unnoticed. But some advance preparation for the landing was necessary.[1] A few days later in reply to Zannas's advice not to be precipitate but rather wait 'till the kettle boils', Plastiras wrote that he could not possibly remain idle and wait for the people to invite him. This, he said, would never happen; while in the meantime 'the country is being corrupted beyond redemption, both morally and materially, and thousands of families of democrats, who have sacrificed everything for democracy, are being subjected to unheard-of humiliations and suffering unimaginable privations. Our fatalistic attitude strengthens the tyranny and before long will make it indestructible.'[2]

Rather surprisingly, Plastiras placed all his hopes on the army, and claimed that he had 'worked' in it since 1935. He was in touch with officers of all political affiliations, and claimed that the Peloponnese garrison and a battalion of the Athens Gendarmerie were in favour of overthrowing Metaxas.[3] Plastiras was also in touch with a number of dismissed officers, with whom he carried on a regular correspondence. In November 1938 he received a letter from General Mantakas, who was still at large after the collapse of the Canea uprising of the previous July. The Cretan rebel was supposed to be active in Crete in organizing resistance to the regime, and urged the exiled leader to proceed immediately to Greece. As a result, Plastiras appointed Mantakas 'Governor of Crete'.[4] The Cretan rebel moved into the picture again in September 1940, but in an unexpected manner: he surrendered to the authorities and begged for Metaxas's clemency.[5] Another officer whom Plastiras claimed had been in touch with him and was planning to overthrow the regime, was General I. Tsangaridis, Commander of 12th division and one of the few Venizelists who

---

[1] Letter of 6 Dec. 1938 to Alexandros Zannas. In the possession of Mrs. Virginia Zannas, Athens. The letter was posted from Cimmiez, France. Mrs. Zannas, who kindly showed these letters to the author, often acted as courier to carry some of them in or out of Greece.

[2] Letter of 12 Dec. 1938, Zannas Papers.

[3] Letter to Zannas, 20 Dec. 1938, Zannas Papers.

[4] Letter to Zannas, 11 Jan. 1939, Zannas Papers.

[5] Letter from Markos A. Mantakas to Metaxas, Canea, 4 Sept. 1940. Markos was the General's cousin, and wrote on his behalf to Metaxas. In view of developments in Europe, and in order to restore unity among the Greeks, he recommended the granting of an amnesty to the Canea rebels.

remained in the army because they had condemned the rising of March 1935. General Tsangaridis and a number of serving and dismissed officers were in fact planning a *coup*, but their plans were betrayed, and the general was arrested in 1938.[1] Among the officers mentioned by Plastiras as participants in the conspiracy there is a familiar figure: Napoleon Zervas. As already seen, Zervas was allegedly in touch with Maniadakis, and therefore it is hard to say for whose benefit he worked, if he did at all, or who benefited most from the alleged collaboration.

Reports about Plastiras's activities and plans reached the Foreign Office rather frequently, for his collaborators were not very good at keeping secrets, even when they did not release them on purpose. In early June 1939 the British Minister in Athens was given certain secret information by opposition circles about the revolutionary activities of Plastiras. This information did not in fact amount to anything specific, and perhaps was passed to the Legation by Plastiras's fellow conspirators in order to remind the British of their existence. It probably concerned contacts between Plastiras and his friends in Greece, especially Tsouderos, of whom more will be said shortly. At any rate the Foreign Office asked Palairet for his views on the importance of these activities of Plastiras, instructing him at the same time to burn the Foreign Office letter after perusal, evidently in order to avoid any possible indiscretion by a junior member of the Legation. Palairet could obtain no evidence of any likelihood of an attempt at a *coup* by Plastiras and his followers.[2]

A few months later some letters to Plastiras from his followers fell in to the hands of the Foreign Office. In early 1940 several letters posted at Famagusta and addressed to Paris (to Mme Marie Canet), were intercepted by the Cyprus censor. The letters were signed by persons using pseudonyms like 'Argyris' or 'Architect', and there is little doubt that the person addressed was Plastiras, and so the Cyprus censor believed. They contain information about conditions in the army and the country in general, police methods and the work of the resistance, but reveal nothing of any importance. These letters were eventually

[1] Daphnis, op. cit., vol. ii, pp. 455 ff.
[2] F.O. Tel. to Athens, Most Secret, 30 June 1939, and Palairet's reply, Tel. No. 293, Secret, 7 July 1939, in F.O. 371/23770.

passed to the Legation in Athens with an inquiry about Plastiras and the likelihood of a *coup*, but the reply was again reassuring. On the evidence so far available, the correspondence revealed nothing likely to endanger the regime.[1]

But the man who preoccupied the British much more seriously than Plastiras was Tsouderos, who played an important role in the conspiracies directed against the regime, and was a prominent Anglophile. It appears that Tsouderos was in touch with a number of the remaining politicians in Athens, while he was still Governor of the Bank of Greece. In time, Tsouderos was persuaded to accept the leadership of the opposition movement and co-ordinate its activities with those of Plastiras.[2] His activities, however, came to the notice of the authorities in late June 1939 after a meeting with General G. Ventiris, a prominent Venizelist. A police search in the house of one of Tsouderos's friends resulted in the discovery of a note in the handwriting of Tsouderos and dated 16 February 1939. The note[3] contained information about developments in Greece, the attitude of the King and the British Legation towards the regime, and the activities of certain politicians. Evidently it was written for the benefit of someone outside the country. This was enough for Maniadakis to take action to secure the necessary incriminating evidence. On 26 June Metaxas was informed of the affair, and began 'preparations' for the dismissal of Tsouderos. On 30 June he invited the unsuspecting victim to see him and showed him the note. A 'scene' followed in which Tsouderos is said to have begged for clemency. Metaxas, though willing to grant this request, demanded his 'immediate resignation', which was of course tendered on the spot.[4]

---

[1] Famagusta letters and F.O. correspondence in F.O. 371/24912. The information about the army amounted only to references to the organizing efforts of the conspirators.

[2] Daphnis, op. cit., vol. ii, pp. 460 ff. The politicians in question were Stephanos Stephanopoulos, Pericles, and Petros Rallis. They in turn collaborated with a resistance organization called M.E.O., the Greek initials for Secret Revolutionary Organization.

[3] The note was in fact torn to pieces during the search, but a conscientious policeman collected the pieces for the benefit of Maniadakis. Daphnis, op. cit., vol. ii, p. 462.

[4] Metaxas, *Diary*, vol. iv, p. 376, 26, 27, and 30 June 1939. See also Daphnis, op. cit., vol. ii, pp. 464, 465.

Writing to the King who was in Rome to attend the marriage of his sister Princess Irene to the Duke of Spoletto, Metaxas took pains to recount the affair in some detail. The conspiracy in question, he wrote, did not amount to anything serious and represented only the 'empty hopes' of the 'known' conspirators abroad. He also informed the King of Tsouderos's dismissal from the Bank, but at the same time assured him that he 'did not intend to prosecute him further'.[1] Obviously, Metaxas was anxious about the King's reaction because of Tsouderos's British connections. His anxiety increased as the eagerly expected reply from Rome did not arrive. On 10 July he cabled to Rome again, but not without a quarrel with the head of the King's political bureau, T. Angelopoulos. Metaxas now 'suspected' that Tsouderos might have been in touch with royalists and even with the palace. The King's reply arrived two hours later, and it must have been reassuring.[2] But a week later Metaxas was still 'suspecting' everyone, except Diakos and Maniadakis.[3]

The British Minister learnt of the dismissal while Tsouderos was under house arrest at his Ekali residence, outside Athens. Palairet avoided communicating with him directly, but could not avoid receiving from him various 'rather hysterical messages' about the regime through Noel Paton, Headmaster of the Spetsai School and a friend of Tsouderos. In these communications Tsouderos stated that the regime was kept in power by British support, and that it would collapse as soon as the British withdrew this support and told the King to do the same. Palairet advised Paton not to see Tsouderos again, and refused to include in the Legation Bag two letters from him addressed to Lord Lloyd and Madame Venizelos. Nevertheless, the Minister drew the attention of the Foreign Office in his report to the fact that Tsouderos's forced resignation, and the various arrests connected with it had 'accentuated [the] intensity of the internal situation', and that discontent against the regime was increasing.[4]

The first reaction of the Foreign Office was to instruct

[1] Metaxas to King George, Foreign Ministry Tel. No. 1617/IΓ' to the Greek Embassy in Rome, 1 July 1939, Metaxas Papers. See also *Diary*, vol. iv, p. 376.

[2] *Diary*, vol. iv, p. 377, 10 July 1939.

[3] Ibid., p. 378, 18 and 19 July 1939.

[4] Athens Tel. No. 301, 10 July 1939, F.O. 371/23770.

Palairet to have nothing to do with Tsouderos's communications, and to suggest the 'utmost discretion' with regard to any personal contacts with him.[1] Obviously, the Foreign Office wanted to stay out of the affair, or at least to be very careful about it, if only because it concerned an avowed Anglophile. All the same, and for that reason, they could not be expected to regard the dismissal in a detached manner. In another telegram of the same date (13 July) the Foreign Office asked Palairet to report on whether he detected in the affair 'any symptom of anti-British feeling or any anti-British intrigue on the part of the influences favourable to the Axis'. If this was the case, Palairet was instructed to seek, if he thought it advisable, an interview with the King 'in order to clear the situation'.[2]

King George was staying at the time in Corfu, and this made matters rather difficult. Palairet found it virtually impossible to reach him, since the Government was bound to deduce from a trip to Corfu that it was connected with the recent affair. The possible alternative of an approach to the King by the British Consul in Corfu was rejected, because the Consul had no secret cipher. At this point, Lord Lloyd called at the Foreign Office, bringing more disquieting news. He had received a communication from Tsouderos, through Paton, in which the dismissed Governor of the Bank said that the armed forces had decided to overthrow the dictatorship, and that this could be accomplished without any great delay. As might be expected, Tsouderos asked the British to lend their support in carrying out the *coup*. This in itself was alarming news, but the Foreign Office was in a position to discount its seriousness. They had little doubt that this was yet another scheme, one of a series that had reached them from time to time for the past year and a half. What was disquieting from their point of view was the possibility of an anti-British 'undercurrent' behind the dismissal of a prominent Anglophile. Lord Lloyd thought that the Foreign Office ought immediately to telegraph Palairet asking his views on this point. Lloyd also asked for a favour: to put in a 'special plea' with the King to the effect that Tsouderos should be allowed to remain as Chairman of the Spetsai School. This was of course a small favour, but the Foreign

[1] F.O. Tel. to Palairet, No. 251, 13 July, F.O. 371/23770.
[2] F.O. Tel. to Palairet, No. 253, 13 July, F.O. 371/23770.

Office wanted nothing to do with it. The school business looked 'very fishy', and Tsouderos was hysterical and demanding. The decision reached after much deliberation was to keep out of the whole business. Palairet was instructed anew on 14 July to hold no communication whatever with Tsouderos, but was nevertheless asked to supply more information as to the possibility of anti-British influences.[1]

Palairet now felt that it was high time to put the affair into its proper perspective to prevent unwarranted concern and possible action that might lead to an undesirable situation. Tsouderos's removal from office, the Minister assured the Foreign Office, was definitely not the result of anti-British influences but only the natural outcome of his connection with the recently discovered conspiracy. For all its good intentions and favourable disposition towards Britain, the Government could hardly have been expected to keep in high office a man who had been proved to be working against the regime. Palairet's relations with Metaxas had never been more cordial and, as far as he was concerned, left nothing to be desired. Metaxas had repeatedly assured him that he was wholeheartedly devoted to Britain, and he could find no valid reason not to accept these assurances at face value. As for the suggestion that he should seek an interview with the King specifically about Tsouderos's dismissal, Palairet was convinced that such personal interventions had better be reserved for a 'serious emergency', in other words when British interests were really at stake; and as far as he was concerned, the recent affair simply did not fall into that category. The Foreign Office could not have expected to receive a more reassuring reply.[2]

Tsouderos, however, would not let the British forget about him. He found ways to pass various communications to the Foreign Office or the Athens Legation. He was a man who refused to take no for an answer; but in his case the answer it seems was never spelt out quite clearly. And almost invariably his forebodings and alarms went along with pleas for personal favours. He now approached Lord Lloyd and asked him to take an interest in the education of his daughter, whom he wanted

[1] F.O. Minutes, 13 and 14 July 1939, and F.O. Tel. to Palairet, No. 255, 14 July, in F.O. 371/23770.
[2] Athens Tel. No. 306, 14 July 1939, F.O. 371/23770.

to send to England for that purpose. Madame Venizelos was supposed to supervise the education of the girl, and this connection further complicated the affair. Naturally, the Foreign Office was not at all enthusiastic about the prospect of Lord Lloyd in communication with Madame Venizelos with the risk of compromising the standing of the British Council in Greece. The plea from Tsouderos was turned down, and his forebodings were dismissed.[1] But worse news from Greece came some days later.

On 5 August 1939 Tsouderos communicated to Palairet yet another memorandum conveying a bleak picture of the situation. This document, along with a recommendation to dismiss Metaxas, was also conveyed to the King. On this occasion Tsouderos's dark prophecies found the Minister in a receptive mood, for he was now ready to admit that the situation was indeed disquieting. It is not easy to point to the possible reasons behind Palairet's change of heart, and it is rather hard to explain in view of his detached attitude. Perhaps the Fourth of August celebrations, which were staged with the usual defiance of public resentment against the Government, made him have second thoughts about the regime and the situation in general. It is also possible that his changed mood was due to certain arrests of Anglophile Cretans following demonstrations in the island on the occasion of a visit from a British naval squadron in May. In fact, these arrests were reported by Palairet in early July, when he took the opportunity to make the sad observation that Anglophile elements in Greece were almost entirely anti-regime. There were similar reactions in London.[2] The Foreign Office had brooded over these arrests throughout July, fearing possible anti-British intrigues; and Tsouderos's dismissal increased these fears. The regime came briefly under reconsideration, and the familiar tortuous arguments were propounded at great length; but the conclusions were only justifications of the policy followed. However shaky the dictatorship and the monarchy might have been, Fitzroy Maclean argued that in the circumstances it would be a 'grave mistake' for the British to recommend any change to the King. The failure of such an intervention would have made an enemy

---

[1] Foreign Office Minutes, 17 July 1939, F.O. 371/23770.
[2] Athens Disp. No. 274, 5 July 1939, F.O. 371/23761.

of Metaxas; moreover, even if the attempt were to succeed, it was by no means certain that they would have been 'substantially better off'. Cadogan thought that the risk was 'rather forbidding'. Palairet felt that an approach to the King might not be unwarranted, but was afraid that Metaxas might get wind of such a step, and that would be 'most unfortunate'.[1] By August 1939 this language came naturally: it had become almost a doctrine when an alternative policy was not available.

About the same time Metaxas for his part was nursing a grudge against Britain, but this had little to do with the British Government. Simopoulos, who dutifully reported articles in the British Press with anti-regime edges in case they escaped the Greek censor, had at his disposal in August a rich crop. Metaxas, as could be expected, was furious, and in a letter to Simopoulos he let off steam:

> I confess to you that now that the Fourth of August regime has completely prevailed, I do not give a brief about the writings of certain stupid British papers. They cannot affect my position at all. But I do resent this, and all the more so in the light of our friendly relations with Britain, and particularly our close relations with the British Government. Portugal, Romania, Turkey, and so on, have similar regimes, but they have never taken the trouble to attack these governments. I cannot help wondering what kind of friendship ours is; they ill-treat the man who runs the affairs of the state, a man moreover who wants to be their friend. Or, do they perhaps believe that I do not run Greek affairs? If this is the case, certainly they must have no brains at all in their heads. As you quite rightly write yourself, the People gave them their answer on 4 August.[2]

At this stage the British Government hardly deserved Metaxas's outburst. Of course, the target was not so much the Government but liberal England in general; but in Metaxas's mind country and government were indistinguishable. As before, and afterwards, he could never bring himself to believe that press criticism in Britain had nothing to do with government policy. In fact, unfavourable articles were occasionally kept from publication at the request of the Foreign Office and favourable queries and comments were arranged in Parliament.

---

[1] F.O. Minutes, 15 and 16 July 1939, and Athens Tel. No. 333, 5 Aug., F.O. 371/23770.
[2] Metaxas to Simopoulos, letter of 25 Aug. 1939, Simopoulos Papers.

The outbreak of war put the Greek situation into a new perspective. Opposition was muffled, and the politicians on the whole refrained from openly attacking the regime. Some hoped that the war would eventually carry away the regime,[1] but generally wanted Greece to appear united in those critical times. War in a sense gave the regime an unchallenged lease of life. In late October 1939 the King told Palairet that now he did not expect any trouble from any quarter. The continuation of the war guaranteed that no dissident voice could be raised.[2] But dissenting voices reached the Foreign Office occasionally in private. On 30 October Alexandros Zannas met Lieut.-Col. Blunt, the British Military Attaché, and brought up a delicate matter, the army. The Attaché was told, confidentially, that there was 'serious unrest' in the army, and that a crisis was inevitable. The unrest was said to be due to the recent partial mobilization, which had proved a failure. The Attaché refrained from commenting on the information, but promised to report on the army shortly.[3] There is little doubt that Zannas's approach was made with a political end in mind, and not only because of concern over the state of the army. As will be seen, the attitude of the army preoccupied the British at a later stage.

Another British preoccupation was the Greek Press, and particularly the censor. This sector of the regime, whose duty until the outbreak of war had been to muzzle critical comments in the Press, was now principally concerned with watching its attitude towards the belligerents. The Greek Government was anxious to maintain the strictest neutrality, and saw to it that the Press followed the same policy. In general, the Press was pro-British in sentiment, and the working of the censorship was therefore inevitably in the German interest. David Wallace, the British Press Attaché, was always quick to see offence in every action of the Greek censor, and so in fact was his German

---

[1] Mr. Konstantinos Tsatsos, Professor of Law at the University of Athens at the time, wrote after the outbreak of war to Mr. Panayotis Kanellopoulos that the time for the tyrants to fall had finally come. The letter was intercepted by the censor, and Tsatsos was in trouble. Along with obvious tyrants like Hitler and Mussolini, he mentioned 'Wotan', and could not persuade the authorities that he did not mean Metaxas—though in fact he did—but the god of German mythology. Tsatsos was deported to Skyros, but was allowed to return early in 1940. Interview with Mr. Tsatsos, May 1974.

[2] Letter from Palairet to Nichols, 31 Oct. 1939, F.O. 371/23770.

[3] Colonel Blunt's interview with Zannas in F.O. 371/23770.

counterpart, Kurt Rösner. Wallace believed that Rösner was on good terms with the officials of the Press Ministry, including the censorship. The British found some support in George Seferis, the poet, who was Chief of the Press Section of the Foreign Ministry at the time; he was 'well-disposed but of little account'. Wallace was suspicious of Nikoloudis's motives, but he could give no convincing reason for this suspicion. On the contrary, the Press Minister seems to have been well disposed towards the British. Wallace's appraisal of individual newspapers is interesting and more or less correct. The *Messager d'Athenes*, which was subsidized by the Foreign Ministry, was not pro-German and on the whole neutral; the *Typos* was consistently pro-German; *Vradyni* was 'suspect'; *Estia*, owned by Cypriots, was anti-Imperial but not pro-German; the *Kathimerini* of G. A. Vlachos was royalist and neutral; *Eleutheron Vima*, the most important paper, was thoroughly Anglophile; *Proia* of Georghios Pesmatzoglou had been 'most helpful' and had in fact published a number of articles by Wallace; and *Acropolis* was 'markedly Anglophile'. The attitude of the Greek Press, Wallace felt, was on the whole 'satisfactory', and more favourable to Britain than to Germany. This was a cheerful note and most welcome to the Foreign Office.[1]

Disquieting news, however, reached the Foreign Office occasionally from various quarters. In late December 1939 *The Times*'s Balkan correspondent submitted to the Foreign Office for approval a record of interviews he had with King George and Metaxas. But the conclusions of *The Times* correspondent were not satisfactory from the point of view of the Foreign Office: Metaxas's regime was more unpopular than ever before and as unstable as ever; the work of the secret police struck 'a high note of Balkan barbarity'; and Metaxas, though undeniably pro-British, was as fascist as fascists went. The article was passed to the Ministry of Information on 12 January 1940 with the comment that, though quite interesting, 'obviously none of it must be published'. On 16 January the Foreign Office was informed that action had been taken to prevent publication of the article.[2]

[1] Memo. by the British Press Attaché, 17 Nov. 1939, F.O. 371/23782.
[2] Memo. by *The Times* correspondent and F.O. Minutes, Jan. 1940, F.O. 371/24909.

In February 1940, two years after the manifestoes of the politicians and a stream of all kinds of disquieting news, the Foreign Office position with respect to the regime was as follows: 'We are wedded to M. Metaxas and so we shall remain until death or the Greeks part us.'[1] For the past two years the regime's unpopularity and the need to reform it in some way had been brought to the attention of the Foreign Office from many quarters, both official and unofficial. But generally, and with the exception of the timid attempt of March 1939 already referred to, the Foreign Office had resisted the temptation to intervene. If there were valid reasons for refraining from doing so before the outbreak of the war, many more were added now, following that event. Metaxas's assurances and the War Trade Agreements provided reasonable assurance that Greece could be depended on to play an important role in case of war in the Mediterranean. Metaxas, however unpopular, followed a policy which met British requirements and promised rich dividends in a future emergency. In March 1940 the Foreign Office reaffirmed its decision to resist the temptation to 'wilt' the regime with 'good advice', and instructed Palairet to refrain from taking any action which might be interpreted as an attempt at intervention.[2]

But there was little need for such advice, because Palairet was in complete agreement with the Foreign Office on the proper policy to adopt towards the regime. Yet, there was one aspect of the whole situation that left much to be desired, namely the attitude of the King. Palairet was on the spot and could not possibly fail to observe this disquieting aspect. For the past two years, and in contrast to his earlier attitude, King George had been unwilling, or unable, to exercise an influence over Metaxas. Another disquieting aspect was the prospect of Metaxas dropping out in one way or another. He was sixty-nine years old at the time, and was surrounded by 'very second-rate individuals'. This was 'unfortunate', but Palairet could think of no remedy for it, for there was none. The regime stood or fell with Metaxas. The Minister became resigned. 'We had better shut our eyes to the disagreeable elements of the regime and not

---

[1] F.O. Minutes, Feb. and Mar. 1940, F.O. 371/24909.
[2] Foreign Office Minutes and Tel. to Palairet, No. 106, 18 Mar. 1940, F.O. 371/24909.

attempt to criticize or modify it unless there should be some glaring instance of what must unfortunately be called "Gestapo" practices by the secret police here.' If the Greeks were to decide to get rid of the regime, they had to do it 'not only unaided, but also unhindered' by Britain.[1]

About this time Metaxas became a prey to grave 'suspicions', which, in fact, never left him until he died a year later. He was continuously and anxiously on the watch to detect possible signs of conspiracies among his collaborators, at the palace, the British Legation, and in the ranks of the opposition. Early in the year he was informed that Tsouderos and Kafandaris were 'intensifying' their activities against the regime;[2] on 16 February he learnt of a 'conspiracy' in Salonika;[3] and a month later he suspected the palace. Crown Prince Paul had told one of Metaxas's men that 'he did not consider it appropriate for the monarchy to be associated with the Fourth of August regime'. As a result Metaxas wondered: 'Who stands behind and teaches them these things?' And the next day, after talking to Maniadakis and Diakos, his suspicions of a 'palace intrigue' were reinforced.[4] On 23 March he wondered about the King's 'attitude', and hoped that it had to do with the 'English lady' who was staying in Athens at the time.[5] The following day, however, he was convinced that it was only a 'family affair',[6] and was happy to find the King 'rather friendly' again.[7] In Metaxas's case, increasing power did not produce, as might have been expected, a feeling of security; on the contrary, as time went on insecurity increased. Long years of tension and intrigue; lack of confidence in most of his lieutenants, who of necessity had to be second-rate in order not to challenge his authority —besides, many able men were unwilling to co-operate with the regime; his delicate position *vis-à-vis* the King; and the mounting responsibilities imposed on him by the war, were not exactly calculated to pacify his fears and make him feel secure.

[1] Athens Disp. No. 48, 20 Feb. 1940, F.O. 371/24909.
[2] *Diary*, vol. iv, p. 445, 20 Jan. 1940.
[3] Ibid., p. 452.   [4] Ibid., p. 457, 14 and 15 Mar. 1940.
[5] King George, according to Pipinelis, had an affair with a 'lady friend from London'. The affair dated from the years of exile, but now the friends found it difficult to meet except on rare occasions. Pipinelis, *George II*, p. 86.
[6] *Diary*, vol. iv, p. 458, 23 Mar. 1940.   [7] Loc. cit., 24 Mar. 1940.

In early April 1940 Metaxas 'suspected' Britain and wondered whether the British were not 'changing' their attitude
towards him. The cause of these suspicions was information
supplied by the King, who had learnt that internal Greek
affairs had been the subject of 'deliberations' in London.
Halifax, he was informed, had 'defended' the regime; 'but why
the debate?'[1] As a matter of fact, deliberations about the
regime in the Foreign Office had never ceased, but now they
were almost a daily affair. The reference to Halifax's defence
perhaps had to do with a letter the Secretary of State addressed
to Palairet. In this letter, dated 18 March 1940, Halifax wrote:

> I entirely agree with you that any internal change which involved
> confusion and division at the present time should be most unfor-
> tunate for us, though I am not oblivious to the danger which lies
> in our being so closely associated with a government which has little
> or no real popular appeal. Undoubtedly the most satisfactory
> development would be if the King could be induced to introduce
> gradually a more democratic form of government. Whether it would
> be possible for him to do this without getting rid of Metaxas is very
> difficult to say, and I assume that in fact the King does not at present
> feel strong enough to try experiments of this kind. Meanwhile you
> will see that we have informed you officially that we share your
> view that you should yourself take no action which could be inter-
> preted as interference with the internal affairs of Greece.[2]

To Metaxas's, or more precisely, to Britain's worries, one
more anxiety was added about this time: the designs of Venizelos's son, Sophocles. Like many a famous man's son, Sophocles
Venizelos was burdened by his father's image, and kept trying
to excel in politics. As we have already seen in connection with
the political crisis of 1936, he had been willing to become
Metaxas's partner in a dictatorial government, although under
certain conditions. Now, he found it politic to oppose the
dictatorship, and plotted its overthrow. On 10 February 1940
Venizelos approached the British Intelligence Centre, Middle
East, and presented them with a memorandum bearing on
internal Greek affairs. Venizelos doubted whether Metaxas
could proclaim a general mobilization in case of emergency,
because he would be faced with 'a nation under arms' and

---

[1] Metaxas, *Diary*, vol. iv, p. 460, 1 Apr. 1940.
[2] Lord Halifax to Palairet, Letter of 18 Mar. 1940, F.O. 371/24924.

ready to turn him out. Greece, he said, needed a government enjoying the confidence of the people and commanding their loyalty and support, not a hated dictatorship. 'A little friendly pressure from Britain and France' on the King was all that was needed, since the King alone was in a position to re-establish normal political life. Therefore, it was necessary that the King should be made 'to realize the sooner the better as to where the interests of his country lay', namely a return to parliamentarianism. Venizelos was ready to furnish detailed information about the regime and the general situation, but the British wanted to hear no more from him. As a result, steps were taken to ensure that no further contact would be made with Venizelos in the future.[1]

The British were by now convinced that they could do practically nothing to change the course of the regime by themselves, and they were not prepared to take the responsibility of advising the King to do otherwise. At this time their attention was concentrated on the King again, for suggestions that he should be brought out of the twilight and his customary aloofness were becoming rather frequent. The King was described as a 'lonely' and 'disheartened' man, who moreover made little secret of his contempt for the Greeks. The British were advised to help him emerge from his seclusion and 'cheer him up' by providing a 'frank and jolly' friend.[2] But Palairet was not very optimistic about the prospect of cheering him up. The King was under the influence of Col. Demetrios Levidis, his A.D.C., a rather domineering man who kept the King inside the palace. According to the Minister, Col. Levidis's influence accounted for much of the King's aloofness which, though desirable since it protected him from rash steps, undermined his image and standing with the people when it was pushed to extremes.[3]

Another matter that was brought to the attention of the Foreign Office had to do with the attitude of the Legation towards the old royalists. This matter was brought up by the

[1] Venizelos's Memo. was passed to the Athens Legation on 26 Feb. 1940. The paper is dated 17 Jan. 1940. F.O. 371/24909. See also Daphnis, *Sophocles Venizelos*, pp. 157–8.

[2] The suggestion had come from Capt. Denne, head of Shell Oil Company, Hellas. F.O. Minute, 28 Mar. 1940, F.O. 371/24909.

[3] F.O. Minute, 11 Apr. 1940, F.O. 371/24909.

Duchess of Kent, who complained to Halifax that the Legation was no longer in close contact with the old royalist families. The complaint obviously referred to royalists who, like Theotokis, strongly disapproved of the King's close association with the regime. These people opposed the regime, and the Legation had good reasons to avoid their company. The Legation, explained Halifax, was in a 'delicate position' since Metaxas might not regard such contacts with much favour.[1]

Very little could have been done to allay the mutual suspicions and antagonisms of the opposing forces. Many royalists were not particularly happy about the King's attitude, and especially his prolonged and close association with the dictatorship. The King, on the other hand, distrusted these people and was on bad terms with the Venizelists and the republicans. He did not particularly like the Greeks. Though it is possible that the King's aloofness had to some extent to do with palace advice, in general there can be little doubt that his attitude was based on the conviction that the course he followed was the right one. As he often confessed to close friends, King George believed that he had undertaken a thankless mission. Certain policies had to be carried through irrespective of present popularity and future consequences. Disheartened, arrogant, stubborn, narrow-minded, and contemptuous of the people, though well-meaning in his own way and devoted to Greece, he was thrown back on himself for company. The cheers he left for the dictator, who craved for the people's affection. His relations with Metaxas were on the whole good, but not cordial; the aristocrat had little use for the clumsy gestures and schemes of the parvenu, and a quasi-fascist one at that. Moreover, he could not be expected to regard the growing power of the dictator without some apprehension. Tacit and unenthusiastic approval was all that Metaxas could expect from King George, and this was primarily the cause of his constant suspicions. These suspicions, fears, and antagonisms were the natural concomitants of the whole situation: a king who remained in seclusion and made no claim to popular affection, but still powerful since his position rested on the army; a dictator who was conscious of his growing power, but regarded the King with a certain awe because of his own royalist inclinations and

[1] Lord Halifax to Palairet, Letter of 18 Mar. 1940, F.O. 371/24909.

the King's powerful connections abroad. The British could only watch the situation and hope that it would not lead in any untoward direction.

In April 1940 the British Government were disturbed to read a report from the Consul in Salonika about labour unrest in that city and at Kavalla. The report was quickly dismissed as alarmist by both the Legation and the Foreign Office, but not before Metaxas learned of the Consul's 'intrigue' and 'false reports'. The incident was smoothed over by the British Government, who gave the necessary explanations to Metaxas. On 21 April he noted: 'Fortunately, they themselves informed us.'[1] But worse news followed, this time from a source that could not be easily dismissed as untrustworthy. Lieut.-Col. Blunt, the Military Attaché, sent in mid-April a rather grim report which bore on the situation in general and the state of the army in particular. The people made little secret of their indignation against the regime, and the army was in bad shape. The report further reads:

The Government are regarded popularly as a set of crooks. Hardly any have a history of government service and it is fair to describe them generally speaking as the political sweepings of the country.

I do not pretend to be able to give a forecast, but it would seem that if the King could bring himself to take a determined line, the country would be saved from another of those upheavals, generally bloodless, which have proved so detrimental to the efficiency of his army and the country in the past. A Government of a semi-military nature would probably prove acceptable to popular opinion in these critical times, and revitalize army administration.[2]

Reports like the above arrived frequently, and the Southern Department became fairly used to them and were not alarmed.

Another Venizelist 'conspiracy' was reported to Palairet towards the end of April by his Polish colleague, but he dismissed it. Conspiracies like this were now reported to him about once a week and sometimes more often.[3] One of these conspiracies must have been connected with Tsouderos, for he was deported at this time. Metaxas hurried to assure the British

[1] Report from the British Consul in Salonika, 4 Apr. 1940, F.O. 371/24911. See also *Diary*, vol. iv, p. 463.

[2] Lieut.-Col. Blunt's report of 14 Apr. 1940 in F.O. 371/24910.

[3] Athens Disp. No. 118, 24 Apr. 1940, F.O. 371/24910.

Minister that, though obliged to deport Tsouderos because of his activities against the regime, 'he had no wish to treat him harshly'. Palairet regretted the deportation, as did Metaxas, doubtless with less sincerity. Tsouderos, in fact, had only been removed to a country residence on the island of Syra.[1] The deportation of Tsouderos was allowed by both sides to pass without further explanations, but trouble came now from another quarter. According to Maniadakis, anti-regime sentiments were being fed to the British Press, and especially the *Daily Telegraph,* by the Greeks in Egypt: by the Greek 'notables', Metaxas wrote angrily, the 'Levantines', who had been discharging their 'venom'.[2] Assurances from the British, though satisfactory, did not pacify Metaxas: he now saw no future for the regime beyond his death. On 9 May he wrote: 'The internal situation will be stable as long as I live. And when I die? This is the problem, for which there can be no solution. Institutions do not survive the personalities identified with them.'[3] Such thoughts now recurred frequently, and he could find no respite.

Similar thoughts also preoccupied the King. In case Metaxas fell ill or died, he told the Military Attaché, he would take over the Government himself until he had made up his mind about a successor to Metaxas. The King's apparent determination was an encouraging sign, but the Foreign Office remained sceptical; his past record argued against such decisive action.[4] As for Metaxas, he was now in a terrible state of mind. He was averse to dispatching a Greek officer to Turkey for consultations with the Allies, as the British had requested. Greece, he thought, ought not to be compromised; moreover, 'Plastiras's men' were in Turkey. On 2 June he was informed by the Crown Prince of certain 'movements by the politicians'. Defence arrangements at the time brought up the question of Crete, the traditional Venizelist stronghold. 'The Cretans?' Metaxas wondered, 'Are they going to betray us?' On 5 July he suspected 'certain officers, one Minister, one Admiral and definitely one General

---

[1] Athens Tel. No. 204, 22 Apr. 1940, F.O. 371/24910.

[2] *Diary,* vol. iv, p. 465, 2 May 1940.

[3] Ibid., p. 467, 4 and 9 May 1940. The meaning of the Greek in the last sentence is not very clear. Metaxas writes: "*Οἱ θεσμοὶ δὲν ἀντικαθιστοῦν τὰ ἄτομα.*" *Ἀντικαθιστοῦν* could be translated as 'replace', but the preceding sentences make this unlikely.

[4] Athens Tel. No. 26 Saving, 1 May 1940, F.O. 371/24910.

and perhaps others, as well', who wanted 'to exploit their Germanophilia of late for their own ends'.[1] No doubt, one of the Germanophiles in question was T. Skylakakis, Metaxas's ex-Minister of the Interior. Skylakakis had been suspected of plotting to overthrow the regime in the German interest, and was deported to an island. Palairet thought that the reason behind the deportation of the prominent Germanophile was that both the King and Metaxas realized that they had not been 'sufficiently compliant' to the Germans in the past to hope for their own future if the Germans were to gain control of the Balkans. They were far too compromised in the eyes of Germany.[2]

Meanwhile, interesting developments came to the notice of the British. These developments concerned the attitude and the activities of the Greek Communists. Their party broken up and infiltrated by Maniadakis's agents, their ranks depleted due to the heavy toll of imprisoned or deported members, and the survivors divided among themselves, the Communists could still manage to hold their plenums. According to the resolution of the 5th Plenum, held in February 1939, the 'primary enemy' of Greece was still 'Monarcho-Fascism', and the first aim its overthrow.[3] But it seems that this policy was not in line with Comintern policy, directed by the Soviet Union. It is said that a Comintern directive of July 1940, or at least a version of it, had it that 'the first duty' of the Greek Communists was to defend their country against the Axis; and since the Metaxas regime was 'fighting against the same danger' there was no reason to aim at its overthrow.[3] This line was accepted by many prominent Greek Communists, among them G. Siantos and N. Zachariadis, the latter still in prison. But the Nazi–Soviet pact of August strengthened the 'Old' party line, which argued against the suspension of activities against the regime. The 'traditionalist' group was saved from the disgrace of becoming the tool of the Axis.[4]

The British followed these developments with a keen interest. Both the Athens Legation and the Salonika Consulate were receiving information regularly about Communist activities,

---

[1] *Diary*, vol. iv, pp. 469, 472, 477, 482, 17 May, 2 and 20 June, and 5 July 1940.
[2] Athens Tel. No. 480, 26 June 1940, F.O. 371/24910.
[3] Kousoulas, op. cit., p. 138.   [4] Ibid., pp. 139, 140.

and had good reason to believe that Communist agents had been placed at the disposal of the German Legation by the Soviet Union. In the light of this collaboration, the labour unrest earlier in the year was believed to have been instigated by Communist agents working for the Nazis with a view to undermining Metaxas's position. Metaxas's pro-British sympathies thus led to strange alignments. The Foreign Office was initially sceptical, but reports from Salonika and Athens left little room for doubt. Information from various sources indicated that former Communist agents were now working for the Nazis.[1] As already seen in an earlier chapter, other Communists collaborated with the authorities. These developments, difficult to credit at first sight, were to some extent the result of Nazi–Soviet relations, but they essentially stemmed from the inherent contradiction in the Metaxas regime: totalitarian in outlook and with unmistakable fascist features, but undoubtedly pro-British in its sympathies.

This contradiction in the policies of Metaxas's regime, and of course the requirements of war led the Foreign Office in early summer 1940 to conclude that a 'shadow mission' in Greece might be necessary. Staff officers, of course, were excluded since they would be unwelcome to the Greek Government; but archaeologists would serve the purpose. Cripps, Pendlebury, Hunt, and N. G. L. Hammond were in turn considered for the job, but Palairet was not enthusiastic about the prospect of having them in Greece occupied in covert activities.[2] The War Office went on pressing this point. They were anxious that officers ought to be distributed in Greece in some capacity, 'with or without the collaboration of the Greek Government', in order to carry out their special duties. The Foreign Office was now becoming more insistent with the reluctant Minister in Athens, although they wanted to avoid staff talks committing Britain in any way.[3] On 3 July they cabled Palairet, explaining the purposes of such a shadow mission, which were (*a*) to make reconnaissances, contact Greek officers and prepare the ground for the military mission, and (*b*) 'in [the] event of disintegration

[1] F.O. Letter to the Athens Legation, 24 Apr. 1940, and reply, 20 May, in F.O. 371/24911.
[2] Athens Tel. No. 413, 9 June 1940, and Athens Tel. No. 471, 24 June 1940, F.O. 371/24922.
[3] F.O. Tel. No. 338, 22 June 1940, F.O. 371/24922.

of [the] State, to maintain contact with pro-Ally military elements and give all possible advice'.[1] Palairet remained hesitant. Military tasks, he thought, could be carried out by the Attachés, more effectively in fact than by 'ex-archaeologists', who had no staff experience. Generally, Palairet was in favour of concealing as little as possible from the Greek Government.[2]

The Foreign Office, however, could not be easily persuaded to abandon the idea, and pursued their arguments notwithstanding Palairet's advice to the contrary. On 26 July, they approached a certain George Northcote Crisford for appointment as a 'Temporary Secretary' at the Legation. On arrival in Greece, Crisford was expected to arrange with the Greek Government for his appointment as Fisheries adviser. In addition to his other duties he was instructed to give advice to the Greek authorities on anti-fifth-column methods and to assist them in countering Italian propaganda in the Dodecanese. Crisford was also asked to gather, in the course of his travels throughout Greece, 'a certain amount of political and military information'.[3] But the project stumbled again on Palairet's objections. The Greek Government, he informed the Foreign Office, could not offer a regular appointment, but only occasional work; besides, Palairet had no work for him as a temporary secretary, while a 'third' honorary attaché was out of the question, since it was bound to arouse the suspicions of the Greek Government.[4]

The subject of undercover activities in Greece with both political and military aims was raised again later on by S.O.E. (Special Operations Executive). In the meantime, the British tried to approach certain personalities in the regime, suspected of pro-Axis sympathies. One man initially suspected of such sympathies was Aristides Dimitratos, Minister of Labour. The Foreign Office wanted to attach someone to Demetratos in order to 'tame him and win him over'. Assurances from the Legation that the Minister of Labour was not hostile to Britain and far from pro-Axis, temporarily satisfied British suspicions. Dimitratos, however, preoccupied the British from time to

[1] F.O. Tel. No. 367, 3 July 1940, F.O. 371/24922.
[2] Athens Tel. No. 508, 5 July 1940, F.O. 371/24922.
[3] F.O. Letter to G. N. Crisford, 26 July 1940, F.O. 371/24924.
[4] F.O. Letter to Palairet, 26 July 1940, and Athens Tel. No. 590, 27 July, F.O. 371/24924.

time, until the Foreign Office had its way. It was arranged in November 1940 that an Englishman was to be attached to the Ministry of National Economy with the task of assisting in the marketing of fish. This interesting job drew a top salary, 10,000 dr. monthly. The post went to none other than Crisford.[1]

But the British had already scored a much more impressive success: they had won over Maniadakis. The Legation fully deserved congratulations from London, for this was the man the British feared most on account of his past pro-German sympathies. On 11 July Palairet reported that Maniadakis, 'with whom we have close (but very discreet) contacts, is excessively friendly and most grateful for all the information we have been able to give him about such things as 5th Column activities'. Contacts with the arch-Germanophile of old, the Foreign Office hoped, would prove 'very useful indeed'. In September Maniadakis obliged the British with the following information: 'Minister for Public Security [Maniadakis] said in strictest confidence yesterday that the only two Ministers who now give trouble by their pro-Axis leanings are Kotzias, Minister for Public Affairs, and Tambakopoulos, Minister for Justice, but that they are both being closely watched.'[2]

The Italian attack against Greece in October changed the scene radically: opposition to the regime amounted to treason. The British could rest relatively assured that the Metaxas Government, which was now fighting one partner of the Axis, was secure. Previous opponents of the regime volunteered to serve in any capacity. Sophocles Venizelos, in New York at the time, cabled his congratulations to Metaxas for his 'manly stand'.[3] Zachariadis, in a letter given to the Press by Maniadakis, wrote: 'In addition to the main front, every rock, every ravine, every village from hut to hut, every town from house to house, must become a fortress for the struggle of national liberation.' Naturally, the 'Old' Communists denounced the letter as

[1] F.O. Letter to the Legation, 6 Aug. 1940, and Legation reply, 20 Sept.; Athens Tel. No. 38 Saving, 23 Nov., F.O. 371/24924.

[2] Letter from Palairet, 11 July 1940, F.O. Letter, 3 Sept., and Athens Tel. No. 882, 20 Sept., in F.O. 371/24922. On 20 Sept. Metaxas had a quarrel with Kotzias, whom he could no longer 'bear' as he wrote; but friction between the two men was not unusual. *Diary*, vol. iv, p. 506.

[3] New York Greek Consulate-General, Tel. No. 1101, 26 Oct. 1940, and Foreign Ministry reply, Tel., 28 Oct., Metaxas Papers.

a forgery.[1] A number of university professors volunteered to fight,[2] but their services were politely turned down; instead, they were advised to contribute to the struggle by using their pens to keep up morale.[3] Panayotis Kanellopoulos was allowed to return from exile in early November; and no sooner was he released than he joined the army in Epirus as a corporal.[4] Other politicians did likewise. Georghios Kartalis, after some training, fought as an anti-aircraft gunner,[5] and Pericles Argyropoulos served on the Albanian front as an Intelligence officer.[6] Junior Venizelist officers were reinstated in the army and allowed to fight, but not senior ones. 'Pettiness', was the comment of a senior Venizelist officer still outside the ranks, and he complained of the injustice to the British Military Attaché.[7] Metaxas was informed at the time of a conspiracy, in which Stephanos Stephanopoulos and Petros and Pericles Rallis were said to be involved. The informer was now Tsouderos himself.[8]

Pressure on the Foreign Office, especially from the Labour Party, to put in a word for the release of political prisoners or deported politicians, was politely resisted. Halifax felt that nothing should be done to 'embarrass' Metaxas at a time when Greece was fighting under his leadership. A revival of the controversy about the regime was 'most undesirable' and contrary to both Greek and British interests.[9] But the Foreign Office was no longer the only Department concerned with policy and the appropriate means to implement it. In a meeting of Foreign Office and S.O.E. officials held on 9 December, internal Greek affairs were discussed on a new basis. The S.O.E. representative stated that one of their members had been at work in Athens 'with the object of promoting a united front'.

[1] Kousoulas, op. cit., p. 141.

[2] In a letter to Metaxas, 30 Oct. 1940, Konstantinos Tsatsos, Ioannis Theodorako-poulos, and Ioannis Kakridis asked him to allow them to join the armed forces. Metaxas Papers.

[3] Interview with Mr. Tsatsos, May 1974.

[4] Kanellopoulos, *An Account Sheet*, pp. 15, 16.

[5] K. Pyromaglou, *George Kartalis and His Times, 1934–1957* (in Greek), Athens, 1965, p. 122.

[6] Argyropoulos, *Memoirs*, vol. ii, pp. 36 ff.

[7] Mazarakis, *Memoirs*, pp. 574, 576.

[8] *Diary*, vol. iv, p. 537, 18 Nov. 1940.

[9] Letters exchanged between Halifax and Attlee and Middleton, Nov. and Dec. 1940, and Foreign Office exchanges with the Athens Legation, in F.O. 371/24910.

In particular, he attempted '(a) to ensure that exiled politicians were allowed to return, (b) to ensure that the Greek Government were aware of the undesirability of having two anti-Italian but pro-German Ministers in the Government, (c) to bring people of Venizelist sympathies into line with the present regime'. The Foreign Office expressed doubts about the 'utility' of these activities, and the S.O.E. representative had to promise that no steps would be taken without the express approval of the Legation.[1]

These 'undercurrents', conspiracies, and covert activities practically never ceased: they were built-in and formed an integral part of the internal situation and the nature of Anglo-Greek relations. As long as Metaxas lived, these undercurrents were held within acceptable limits by both sides; but serious trouble was perhaps inevitable after Metaxas's death. The Government, in the main consisting of mediocrities, then began to fall apart and its members were conspiring for positions in a new political structure. The military were showing unmistakable signs of disobedience and even treason when faced with the German invasion, and nothing could check the appalling disintegration of the army. Essentially, the whole structure Metaxas had built up was collapsing: it stood and fell with him. Could something have been saved? Or would it have been possible, earlier, for Metaxas to come to terms with what was left of the old parties? The months when Greece was fighting Italy, united as a nation after decades of political strife and division, would seem, at first sight, to have offered such an opportunity. But was it possible at all? 'The dictatorship refused to co-operate with the parties', wrote Kanellopoulos, 'because it was simply not for the dictatorship to do so; since by so doing it would have ceased to be a dictatorship.'[2]

---

[1] Minutes of the meeting, 9 Dec. 1940, F.O. 371/24982.
[2] Kanellopoulos, *An Account Sheet*, p. 15.

VI

Friends and Heroes[1]

Greece's war was a relatively small but moving epic of World War II. The historian is hard put to find an explanation for such a marvellous exhibition of human endeavour and the supreme effort of a small people fighting a hopeless war with great spirit and self-denial. The Greeks of '28th October', intoxicated with enthusiasm and defying the logic of superior numbers and power, marched to the front to fight a holy war, a spirited crusade for their native land and the Virgin Mary. Poorly armed and clad, and with frost-bitten limbs, they held fast to the unfriendly mountains of Albania with a tenacity and spirit that won the admiration and sympathy of a world numbed with fear.

The spirited resistance of the Greek soldier was one side of the war, no doubt the bright one. Greek strategy and tactics, however, came under strong criticism after the war;[2] and, though lying outside the context and main interests of this study, these aspects of the Greek war must be dealt with briefly in

---

[1] Olivia Manning's novel of the same title.

[2] A critical source deserving attention are the writings of Gen. Dimitrios Katheniotis, *Account of War Operations, 1940–1941* (in Greek), Athens, 1945, and *The Main Strategic Phases of the War, 1940–1941* (in Greek), Athens, 1946. Both books are based on reports by army, corps, and division commanders, which are not accessible, as the Greek War Archives are closed to public inspection. Katheniotis, along with other senior officers, was appointed by Tsolakoglou, the general who signed the armistice with the Germans in April 1941 against the orders of the Government, to study the reports of the field commanders. Tsolakoglou, as we shall see in the final chapter, had reasons of his own to be critical of Papagos's attitude in April 1941, and this no doubt must account for Katheniotis's strong, almost libellous, criticism of Papagos. The excerpts of the war reports and the orders he cites, however, have a certain value. Another critical work, this time an inside view, is Col. Athanasios Korozis's *The Wars, 1940–1941, Successes and Responsibilities* (in Greek), vol. ii, Athens, 1958. Col. Korozis was a prominent staff officer under Papagos and very close to him before and during the war. Although he does not accept unreservedly Katheniotis's strong censures of Papagos, he nevertheless cites them liberally in order to show a certain temerity on the part of his superior. See particularly pp. 181–8, 237–40.

order to provide a background to Anglo-Greek strategy and military co-operation in the early months of 1941. The Greek General Staff was very little prepared for anything but static warfare on a fixed line of defence; and in the face of the Italian threat, which changed the rules of the game radically, it had no meaningful answer and ran into serious trouble. The most striking feature of the High Command orders before and during the initial stage of the war was their extreme pessimism about the ability of the Greek forces to repulse an Italian attack on an advanced position which was difficult to defend. The General Staff seems to have over-estimated the potential Italian thrust from Albania, and at the same time to have under-estimated the chances of successfully mounting a counter-offensive on a terrain which did not allow the enemy fully to deploy his forces and under weather conditions permitting only minimal use of air support. The line of defence in Epirus and Western Macedonia, thinly manned until mobilization and deployment were completed, was regarded as a lost cause, or so at least it appears from the orders to the field commanders.

This pessimistic mood can be traced back to the spring of 1939, when the first plan to cover the Italian threat had been drawn up. In what concerns the Epirus sector of the over-stretched defences, the general references made by Papagos and the General Staff[1] can be supplemented by the contents of a long report by Col. Drivas, chief of staff of the Epirus division (8th division), drawing on High Command orders since the spring of 1939. Thus, in early May 1939, the Epirus division was expected to fight the enemy only in delaying actions, giving ground southwards up to the lower Arachthos river, where it would engage the enemy in decisive battle. In August 1940 its main task was on the one hand to cover Western Mace-donia, and on the other to guard the road leading southwards to Aitolia–Acarnania. Defence of national territory was desirable only in so far as it did not lead to the dispersal and erosion of the limited forces. A new order, issued on 27 Septem-ber, reaffirmed the same priorities, but left the initiative to the divisional commander. Meanwhile, on 23 September it had

---

[1] Papagos, *The Battle of Greece, 1940–1941* (in Greek), Athens, 1945, pp. 199–202; Greek General Staff, *Causes and Incidents Leading to the Greco-Italian War, 1940–1941* (in Greek), Athens, 1959, pp. 150 ff.

been explained to the division that 'no victories' were expected from it in view of the enemy's superiority, but only 'to save the honour of Greek arms'. On 30 October, the third day of the Italian attack, the division received the following order (No. 13018):

Your mission is to cover the Western Macedonian theatre in the general direction Ioannina–Zygos and to guard the roads leading from Epirus to Aitolia–Acarnania. Of these, the guarding of the road leading to Zygos should have priority, and its execution must be the task of 8th division. Your efforts to defend national territory in Epirus must in no way lead to wearing down the effectiveness of forces, which could make fulfilment of above tasks problematic.

The following day, the same objectives were repeated: 'Covering of the roads leading to Metsovon (Zygos), primary objective. Covering of roads leading to Aitolia–Acarnania, secondary objective.' Once more the division was ordered not to engage the enemy on the advanced line Elaia–Kalamas, which ran parallel to the Greco-Albanian frontier. In the face of these orders, the divisional commander's decision to stand and fight on the Elaia–Kalamas position is only something to marvel at. On 30 October Gen. Katsimetros issued an order to his officers and men calling on them to look forward not backward: 'Everyone's eyes ought to be directed forward at all times; and in everyone's thoughts and actions the spirit of decisiveness and offence, not retreat, ought to prevail.'[1]

At this point an explanation of G.H.Q.'s priorities is needed in order to see the situation as it appeared from Athens. The road Ioannina–Zygos leads to both central Greece and Western Macedonia, to Larissa and Salonika respectively; and concern for its safety is quite understandable, because both cities were vital centres of mobilization. To the east of the Epirus division, the Western Macedonian army, which consisted at the time of barely two deployed divisions, was given the task of guarding the road leading from Korytsa (Albania) to Florina and thence to Salonika. As far as G.H.Q. was concerned, completion of mobilization and deployment had to receive priority, and all else, not excluding defence of national territory, came second. Tactics, therefore, had to assume the following order: delaying

[1] Katheniotis, *Account of War Operations*, Part I, pp. 52–6, 58; *Strategic Phases of the War*, p. 41. See also General Staff, op. cit., pp. 143 ff.

action on successive lines of defence in a south-easterly direction until mobilization was complete and the main Greek forces were transported to the front. What G.H.Q. dreaded most was the belated completion of mobilization and deployment at a time when the enemy had unchallenged air superiority and might be in a position to prevent the Greek war machine from ever getting into action. Greek strategy therefore was generally sound and based on a realistic appraisal of the situation.[1]

But others felt otherwise. 'Never before', it is stated rather unjustly, 'had Greece's fate been entrusted to the hands of a more incompetent General Staff.'[2] Field commanders, it is maintained, were called upon to fight a war 'decided in advance', in which their main duty was to save the honour of Greek arms. The High Command in Athens, said Gen. Tsolakoglou, commander of 3rd army corps (Western Macedonian army), had no brighter idea than 'heroic resistance and quick collapse'.[3] It lodged itself at the Grande Bretagne Hotel, and was never quite affected by the spirit of the front. 'G.H.Q.', wrote Tsolakoglou later, 'was never baptized in the font of the front and therefore lacked its mentality.'[4]

Of course, it was easy to pass judgement after the war; when it had been proved that air superiority in extremely mountainous terrain and under unfavourable weather conditions was of little practical use, and after Mussolini's eight million bayonets had been tested and found to be not so terrifying. But in late October 1940, these were imponderables, which the General Staff had to take at face value. Moreover, offensive action was not particularly the meat of the inter-war Greek officer corps, Papagos's critics included. The Eastern Macedonian fortifications, the famous 'Metaxas Line', were their pride, even after 1939, when they discovered a gap on the Albanian flank. The General Staff, though not exactly the pick of the Greek military at the time, did not differ a lot from any other senior officers when it came to strategy. The only difference was that it fell to it to see its prestige, when the test came, resting on a defensive position which belonged to another age.

---

[1] Papagos, *The Battle of Greece*, pp. 199–202; General Staff, op. cit., pp. 150 ff.

[2] Katheniotis, *Account of War Operations*, p. 49.

[3] Katheniotis, *Strategic Phases of the War*, Part II, p. 13.

[4] G. Tsolakoglou, *Memoirs* (in Greek), Athens, 1959, p. 16.

As far as tactics were concerned, however, Papagos and his staff pursued a sound policy in the initial stage of the Italian attack, a policy which was lamentably missing when it came to resisting the Germans.

We must return, however, to the diplomatic field, the main concern here. For Italy, as we have already seen, the invasion of Greece was a pre-emptive strike against a probable British base from which Italy could be seriously threatened. It was also an attempt to secure a position in the Eastern Mediterranean, from which alignments favourable to Italy could be established. As far as Britain was concerned, the attack on Greece created an inconvenient commitment; but she welcomed the opening of a new front which was bound to create a diversion of Axis forces away from more vital theatres. Britain could count on a friendly and loyal Greece to prosecute the war against the Axis with minimum support from British resources.

Britain had given Greece a solemn assurance that she would come to her assistance if she became the victim of aggression and chose to oppose the aggressor; at the same time, Britain was not bound by an alliance. This she had systematically avoided, in order not to incur the commitments it would certainly create for her. The two countries were essentially allies, as long as they fought against the same enemy, namely Italy, but not allied in a formal sense. They were fighting a 'common foe', the Prime Minister wrote to Metaxas after the Italian attack on Greece. Britain, Churchill also promised, would give Greece 'all the help' in her power.[1]

But help was more easily promised than given. At a meeting of the Chiefs of Staff Committee on 28 October, at which the Prime Minister was present, help to Greece was urgently discussed. Before the Committee were the Italian ultimatum to Greece and the Greek refusal to comply, Metaxas's request that Britain should defend Corfu from a possible Italian landing and Athens from air attacks, and his appeal for arms and financial assistance. The attack on Greece was no surprise to the Chiefs of Staff, and they were prepared to meet it, but not exactly in the way the Greeks wanted. Their thoughts were first and foremost about Crete, not the Greek mainland. A recent memorandum covering the case of an Italian attack

[1] 28 Oct. 1940, F.O. 371/24919; Metaxas, *Diary*, vol. iv, p. 526.

on Greece was conveniently at hand. Considering this eventuality, the Chiefs of Staff had written: 'Our naval position in the Eastern Mediterranean would be weakened by an Italian occupation of Greece, but on the other hand, Italian aggression in Greece would give us an opportunity of securing a valuable prize in Crete and a naval and air base.'[1] As was natural, the question of Crete received primary consideration at the meeting of 28 October. From Britain's point of view, 'it was most important to deny Crete to the enemy'; and with this in mind a telegram had already been sent to the Commander-in-Chief, Mediterranean, instructing him to do everything in his power to forestall any Italian attempt to seize the island. At the same time, the Commander-in-Chief, Middle East, was instructed to send a battalion to the island immediately. But the Greek request ran into serious trouble. Metaxas's appeal for arms, particularly A.A. guns, could only be met by denuding Egypt, where British deficiencies in both heavy and light A.A. guns were extremely grave. The Prime Minister suggested that an A.A. cruiser should be stationed at Piraeus, but this would not do very much for the protection of Athens from air attacks. As for the defence of Corfu, it was felt that there would be no objection in exposing the fleet to air attacks from mainland Italy since denial of the island to the Italians was very important. Finally, Churchill proposed, and the Committee agreed, that since Athens had been bombed, towns in northern Italy must also be attacked.[2] In general, the Chiefs of Staff were rather pessimistic about the prospect of sending adequate help to Greece, and even more about Greece's prospects of repulsing the Italian attack. In the past the Chiefs of Staff had failed to guard against inspiring 'over-confidence', the campaign in Norway being a typical example of over-optimism resulting in bitter disappointment. This lesson had now to be applied to events in Greece, and this was conveyed to the Ministry of Information. The Press was accordingly directed not to encourage expectations of what British assistance could do for Greece.[3]

---

[1] C.O.S. (40) 871, 1 Nov. 1940, Cab. 80/21. This paper is wrongly dated. It must have been written before the Italian attack on Greece.

[2] C.O.S. (40) 362 Meeting, 28 Oct. 1940, Cab. 79/7.

[3] C.O.S. (40) 364 Meeting, 29 Oct. 1940, Cab. 79/7.

But Crete was a completely different matter. On 29 October the defence of the island was again discussed, this time by the Joint Planning Staff. Churchill was optimistic about the availability of forces and material means for the defence of Crete, and pressed the matter with much vigour. The token force (one battalion) already on its way to the island was not enough, and he hoped that at least two brigades would be provided. At the same time, landing grounds must be developed, and Suda Bay must be developed as a refuelling base for the Mediterranean Fleet, and at least a limited scale of A.A. defences must be installed. The future garrison of Crete could be squeezed out of Middle East resources, because an Italian attack on Egypt did not appear to be materializing. Malta also could run a temporary risk, since the establishment of an additional refuelling base and advanced landing grounds would greatly increase British power to strike at the Italians. These sacrifices on the part of the Middle East and Malta were expected to produce considerable dividends in the near future. Churchill also brought up the question of the Dodecanese, and instructions were given to plan an operation in the islands. As far as Crete was concerned, the Prime Minister reiterated the view that 'every effort should be made to assist the Greeks to defend Crete'.[1] It was now left to the Joint Planners to match Churchill's undaunted spirit with exact figures on paper. As might be expected, the Chiefs of Staff had some reservations and did not share his confidence. Besides the problem of finding forces to defend Crete, the full scheme for the development of a base would take time to materialize.[2]

At the same time prospects for helping Greece did not improve. When it came to helping the Greeks in their fight against the Italians, reservations increased, and not only on the part of the Chiefs of Staff. Such help as might be provided could only be indirect. The defence of Crete was the main objective, and the Greek war effort necessarily received only peripheral attention, even at the level of strategic planning. Here the views of London and Athens, within the British camp, diverged. The British Minister and Attachés in Athens did not consider Crete in any immediate danger, and urged instead

[1] J.P. (40) 119 Meeting, 29 Oct. 1940, Cab. 80/21.
[2] C.O.S. (40) 882, 30 Oct. 1940, Cab. 80/21.

that assistance should be concentrated on the Greek mainland. The Minister therefore suggested that the defence of Crete should be abandoned for a 'more forward objective', direct help to the Greeks in knocking out the Italians. At the risk of seeming 'importunate' and 'impertinent', Palairet wondered whether Britain was not losing a chance offered by airfields in Greece to bomb Italian bases and troops in Albania. Metaxas, in a personal message to Churchill, had urged the British to send as many aircraft as could be spared for operations on the Albanian front.[1] The British Government felt that the Minister in Athens did not appreciate their difficult position, as far as the availability of forces was concerned, and did not really understand the main line of British policy towards Greece. No explicit pledges of support had been made, Churchill telegraphed to Palairet on 31 October, except that Britain would do her best. The Prime Minister instructed the Minister in the following lines: 'You should not encourage vain hopes when forces to execute them do not exist. You should, if challenged, point out that our guarantee was given in conjunction with France, and that our position in the Middle East has been terribly injured by the French desertion, leaving us to face the whole attack of Italy through Libya . . .'[2]

The case for help to the Greeks was now supported by the British Military Mission. In a personal message to Sir John Dill and Gen. Wavell, Gen. Gambier Parry, head of the Mission, pointed out the need to help the Greeks in their fight against the Italians. The King was dissatisfied with the British attitude towards the Greek war effort. Of course he realized Britain's difficulties and her goodwill; but Greece, King George complained, could not possibly 'live on goodwill alone'. Metaxas expected the next ten days to be critical. It was not a question of battles won or lost; Greece, he said, was fighting for her existence at that moment. Was it not possible for the British to provide at least some air support? The appeal for air support was supported by the King. Gambier Parry felt obliged to press home this recommendation: 'Apart from the practical military aspect, maximum cooperation now, repeat maximum cooperation *now*, will have immense morale effect

[1] Athens Tels. No. 1019, 30 Oct. 1940, and No. 1023, 31 Oct., F.O. 371/24919.
[2] F.O. Tel. No. 806, 31 Oct. 1940, F.O. 371/24919.

and will go far towards removing the regrettable impression that British Military assistance in widest sense, as proclaimed in the world press, is taking the form of words rather than deeds.'[1]

Anthony Eden, Secretary of State for War, who was in Cairo at this time, was apprehensive 'lest the cries from Greece' should result in an order to divert forces from the Middle East to Greece.[2] After consulting Wavell, he telegraphed Churchill that they were unable to send sufficient assistance to Greece, since a diversion of British forces from the Middle East would jeopardize Britain's position in that vital area.[3] Surprisingly enough, Churchill argued back saying that the Greek situation should 'dominate' others. So Eden decided to return to London and give a clear picture of the situation in the Middle East, and to stop the 'folly' of diverting British forces to Greece. Naturally, he was dismayed at the dangerous 'improvisations' and the 'high-sounding phrases' of the Prime Minister.[4] As will be seen in the next chapter, a few months later, it was Eden who improvised dangerously in the face of the German invasion of Greece.

The cries from Greece were left unheeded at this stage except for one squadron of Blenheims which was already on its way to Greece. At a Cabinet meeting on 1 November it was suggested that the war material due to be dispatched to Turkey might very well be diverted to Greece, but to no avail. Though immediate help to sustain the Greeks was important, in the long run Turkey was considered to be 'more important' to Britain than Greece.[5] Fifteen aircraft—for that was the initial British assistance—amounted to very little, Metaxas felt; and he prayed to God.[6] Meanwhile, the initial force to Crete was

[1] Message from Gen. Gambier Parry to Sir John Dill and Gen. Wavell, 2 Nov. 1940, F.O. 371/24919.

[2] A. Eden, *The Reckoning*, London, 1965, p. 126. Eden says that he was told by Churchill: 'If you lose Khartoum your name will live in History.'

[3] Ibid., pp. 166 ff.

[4] Ibid., pp. 169, 170. In his diary Eden noted on 3 Nov. 1940: '. . . The weakness of our policy is that we never adhere to the plans we make. If we had ever thought to help Greece, we should long since have laid our plans accordingly. Instead of which we took a deliberate decision not to do so, and then go back on it and seek to improvise out of air, at the expense of air-power! High-sounding phrases only make matters worse . . .'

[5] W.M. (40) 281, 1 Nov. 1940, Cab. 65/16.

[6] *Diary*, vol. iv, p. 527, 2 Nov. 1940.

being augmented. A second battalion and brigade H.Q., eight heavy and twelve light A.A. guns, one field company, and one troop command were ready to sail from Egypt on 2 November. The previous day ten light A.A. guns had already sailed from the Middle East, one 6-inch coast defence battery from home stocks via the Cape, expected to reach Egypt in mid-December, and a number of light artillery pieces and heavy machine guns.[1]

The plans for the defence of Crete were also ready on 2 November. For the refuelling base, needed as soon as possible, there would be one infantry brigade plus adequate A.A. defence (estimated strength: twenty-four heavy and twenty-four light A.A. guns), a number of C.D. guns, searchlights, underwater defences, and one fighter squadron to operate from a base near Suda Bay. These defences could provide sufficient cover to enable the Fleet to make 'occasional' use of Suda Bay, at least at night. For unrestricted access, however, the number of A.A. guns had to be doubled. With respect to landing grounds, the picture was rather bleak. The only existing aerodrome was 70 miles away from Suda Bay, and unsuitable for bombers in its present state.[1] As for assistance to Greece, the Joint Planners could think only of indirect ways. In their report of 1 November, under the heading 'Assistance to Greece', they could find very little even to put on paper. One recommendation was to block Durazzo and Valona, perhaps using fire-ships. Both towns could also be attacked from the air. As for military action, they recommended that some engineers might be dispatched to assist the Greeks in demolitions, 'to delay the Italian advance'. But steps were taken in another direction. S.O.E. was consulted on the subject of underground activities in Albania, and the reply was encouraging. S.O.E. had set in motion plans prepared in advance 'for the stimulation of revolt in Albania', and had reason to believe that these plans were meeting with some success.[2]

[1] J.P. (40) 614, 2 Nov. 1940, F.O. 371/24920.
[2] C.O.S. (40) 25 (o) J.P., 1 Nov. 1940, Cab. 80/106. Julian Amery, *Sons of the Eagle*, London, 1948, p. 40, writes that British agents were in touch with Albanian refugees in Belgrade, who were preparing to launch a revolt against the Italians. The plan was approved by London and the British Military Mission in Athens, but the Greek General Staff did not allow the passage of rifles and ammunition to the Albanians, arguing that they could be better used by Greek soldiers than Albanian irregulars. Activities in Albania seem to have preoccupied British agents since the summer. Col. Korozis writes of an incident worth mentioning here. On

Churchill, however, was not at all satisfied with the rate of assistance. On 3 November he pressed the point to the Chiefs of Staff, expressing the wish that four bomber squadrons due to go to Egypt had better fly immediately to Greece and Crete. In a letter of the same date to the Chiefs of Staff Committee, he wrote: 'perhaps you will say that all I propose is impossible. If so, I shall be very sorry, because a great opportunity will have been missed, and we shall have to pay heavily hereafter for it. Please try your best.'[1] The Prime Minister's word seems to have had a salutary effect, for on the same day the Chiefs of Staff were reconsidering assistance to Greece. But there was some hard thinking to be done. A.A. defences in the Middle East were inadequate, and had been further weakened by the dispatch of two batteries to Crete. The allocation of two more batteries for Greece would be a 'serious drain' on the dangerously limited resources. The implications of assistance to Greece were felt to be more serious when it came to consider the dispatch of aircraft. A drain on fighters would leave the British Isles in a 'dangerously weak position' *vis-à-vis* Germany. The situation with bombers was not much better. The number of bombers proposed for Greece would reduce the force in Egypt by 50 per cent for some weeks. But political considerations prevailed. 'It is necessary', the Chiefs of Staff Committee argued, 'to balance these implications against the very strong reasons for affording assistance to Greece and, equally so, against the consequences which would result from the over-running of Greece with its dire effects upon our relations with Turkey.'[2]

The reluctant Chiefs were grudgingly giving in to political pressure. They recognized 'the paramount importance of giving Greece the greatest possible material and moral support in the shortest possible time'. Maximum emphasis naturally fell on air support, but certain problems arose at the receiving end.

16 June 1940 a Greek doctor was arrested in Epirus, carrying 100 lb. of dynamite and intending to cross over to Albania. According to the findings of a secret inquiry, the doctor, who is referred to only by the initial K, was a Greek from northern Epirus and an agent of British Intelligence (Organization D). Doctor K was in touch with Col. Cripps, and wanted to carry out acts of sabotage in Albania. Korozis, op. cit., vol. ii, pp. 77–82.

[1] C.O.S. (40) 896, 3 Nov. 1940, Cab. 80/21.
[2] C.O.S. (40) 897, 3 Nov. 1940, Cab. 80/21.

Even if the aircraft were available, not more than five squadrons could be operated in Greece for lack of suitable aerodromes. Of the existing airfields, only those at Tatoi and Eleusis were serviceable, while the one at Larissa was 'too exposed'; and all badly needed A.A. defence. Nevertheless, the Chiefs of Staff proposed on 3 November the dispatch of three squadrons of Blenheims, one already on the way, and two squadrons of Gladiators, all five from the Middle East. Two more squadrons of Wellingtons were to be provided from Malta.[1] The next day the Commanders-in-Chief, Middle East, were instructed on the lines of these proposals. Three Blenheim and two Gladiator squadrons had to be sent to Greece, but no mention was made of the two Wellington squadrons, obviously for lack of operating facilities in Greece. The cable included this explanation: 'It has been decided that it is necessary to give Greece the greatest possible material and moral support at the earliest possible moment. Impossible for anything from United Kingdom to arrive in time. Consequently only course is to draw upon resources in Egypt and to replace them from United Kingdom as quickly as possible.'[2]

At a Cabinet meeting on the same day Churchill said that public opinion in Britain was 'most anxious for British intervention in Greece'. Besides, the alliance with Turkey could not be preserved if reinforcements to Greece were on a smaller scale than those proposed. Therefore, it was of the utmost importance to help the Greeks to resist the Italian attack. 'Strategically,' he said, 'the loss of Athens would be as serious a blow to us as the loss of Khartoum, and a more irreparable one.'[3]

The above remark was perhaps made for the benefit of Eden, who was still in the Middle East and trying hard to dissuade the Government from draining Middle East forces and war material. But by 6 November, the Secretary of State for War had waived his reservations, as the Prime Minister was happy to inform the Cabinet the same day. Eden and the British

---

[1] C.O.S. (40) 898, 3 Nov. 1940, Cab. 80/21.

[2] C.O.S. (40) 372, 4 Nov. 1940, F.O. 371/24920. The idea of dispatching four squadrons of Hurricanes and four squadrons of Wellingtons was considered by the Chiefs of Staff, but rejected. Even if the aircraft were available, there was no prospect of improvising aerodromes to operate so many modern aircraft. W.M. (40) 282, 4 Nov. 1940, Cab. 65/16.

[3] W.M. (40) 282, 4 Nov. 1940, Cab. 65/16.

Commanders there agreed to the measures proposed, and accepted the risks involved in the Western Desert in view of 'the political commitment to assist Greece'.[1]

By the end of the first week of November, political considerations had prevailed over the reluctant military, and assistance to Greece was agreed upon by everyone concerned. As far as general policy was concerned, however, the British Government considered that support to Greece, though desirable, must not jeopardize Egypt and Britain's commitment to assist Turkey. The Italian attack offered the opportunity to establish bases in Greece from which Italy and the Romanian oilfields could be bombed; Egypt and Turkey, however, had priority of support. As far as the general war effort against Italy was concerned, it was decided (a) to secure control of sea communications on the coasts of Greece; (b) to operate as many aircraft as possible against Valona and Durazzo from Greek bases, but not against Italian air forces, in Albania; and (c) to dispatch 'technical units' to Greece (engineers, A.A. guns, A.T. guns, and personnel) in order to assist in air defence, to 'delay' the enemy's advance by demolitions, and, in the last resort, to destroy stocks and facilities.[1]

Meanwhile, the Greek forces on the Albanian Front went into counter-attack, and turned the Italian attack into retreat. In the light of these achievements, British policy by the middle of November envisaged supporting Greece with the object of securing a foothold in the country, when adequate forces had reached the Middle East, in order to intensify the British offensive against Italy, and eventually to take air action against the Romanian oilfields. The British Minister in Athens, who followed developments very closely, pressed these points on the Foreign Office with remarkable persistence. According to Palairet, the question, as seen from Greece, was whether the British or the Axis would be able to take advantage of the new situation created by the Italian attack. The unexpectedly successful resistance of the Greeks had given the British the initiative; and if they hesitated to press home this advantage, they would allow Germany to retrieve the difficult position in which Italy had placed the Axis. Germany, he thought, would not attack, whatever the provocation, until she was ready; and a

[1] W.M. (40) 283, 6 Nov. 1940, Cab. 65/16.

'most powerful deterrent' to such action would be the presence of a large air force, partly based at Salonika.[1]

At this stage, these views were also shared by the Greek Government. On 16 November Metaxas explained the Greek position to Admiral Turle, the naval member of the Military Mission, in the following terms: '(*a*) Transferance of Britain's war operations to the Balkans through Greece; (*b*) In order to prosecute the war, [dispatch of] aircraft, anti-aircraft and anti-tank guns; (*c*) Trucks; and (*d*) Tanks. I assured him that we shall continue [the fight] during the winter, and that we anticipate a German attack.'[2] The next day, 17 November, King George wrote to the King of England, and complained about the attitude of the Military Mission. Whenever the Greek Government approached the Mission for a more forward strategy, they always thought 'what would Egypt think?'. For better or worse, the King said, Britain had a 'Balkan front', but Cairo could not grasp the political implications of the situation. And he further wrote: 'As I see it, if you can establish yourselves in Greece with a strong air striking force you may not only deal the Italians crippling blows, but you may even deter the Germans from moving against Greece during winter for fear of losing Romanian oil and of difficulties of communication at this time of year.'[3]

British policy, in theory at least, was similar to the Greek position. In their instructions to the Military Mission on 15 November, the Chiefs of Staff explained that British policy was based on the hope that Greece would continue to resist the Italians 'by arms', and on the assumption that the Germans would not invade Greece 'in the near future'. Though the instructions did not cover the eventuality of German invasion, a general explanation was nevertheless given:

[1] Athens Tel. No. 1133, 14 Nov. 1940, F.O. 371/24921.
[2] *Diary*, vol. iv, p. 534.
[3] Letter from the King of Greece to the King of England, 17 Nov. 1940, F.O. 371/24921. In a draft letter, intended as reply to the King, Halifax wrote that Egypt was 'still in danger' and if Egypt were to be lost the whole position in the Middle East would have collapsed. Churchill wrote in a note for the Foreign Minister that this was 'not true' and there was no reason why the King could not be told the truth. British authorities in Egypt were on the verge of an offensive and naturally were loth to release aircraft for Greece. The draft was therefore changed in the sense of Churchill's note, and sent to Greece on 13 Dec. F.O. 371/24921.

'The object is to secure a firm foothold in Greece, when adequate forces have arrived in the Middle East in order to extend and intensify our offensive action against Italy, and possibly eventually to take air action against Romanian oil-fields and communications with Germany.' But commitment of land forces was simply ruled out.[1]

Generally speaking, aims at this stage did not diverge; but there was a crucial difference of approach to the problem of Germany. As far as the Chiefs of Staff of Britain were concerned, the possibility of air attacks launched from Greece against Romanian oil was within the bounds of over-all strategy and possible moves against the enemy. But for Greece the problem was of vital concern, one of sheer existence. If the Greek Government did want the presence of British air units, that was to ward off German invasion: attacks against German interests in Romania were desirable so far as the common war effort was concerned, but were better dispensed with. What was essentially meant by a Balkan front was a deterrent to Germany, not so much a theatre of offensive operations, for which the British simply lacked the means. Metaxas made the Greek position clear to Palairet on 17 November, in connection with an invitation to Greek representatives to attend a conference of allied states in London. The British Government pressed for Greek participation, but Metaxas was extremely reluctant to send representatives. Did the British want to 'provoke' a German invasion of Greece? he asked Palairet point blank. If so, he was willing to go along with their wishes, but they had to share responsibility for such a step. And how could they possibly help the Greeks against the Germans, when they were not able to help them sufficiently against the Italians? In a note for the Foreign Ministry, Metaxas wrote:

. . . I replied to the British Minister that, though we have every good intention to please the British Government, we must nevertheless draw their attention to the possible consequences of our participation, which would provide Germany with the pretext she is waiting for to attack immediately. I also added that, though we are convinced that this attack will materialize sooner or later, we feel that its postponement even by a fortnight would be greatly advantageous to us. The British Minister accepted this. If, despite all this, I said,

[1] C.O.S. (40) 942 J.P., 15 Nov. 1940, F.O. 371/24920.

the British Government believe that it is opportune to provoke such
an attack, he must state that categorically, aware as he is of the
consequences and the responsibilities we have accepted in common.
If that was the case, he must see to it that we are supplied with
aircraft, not only against the Italians—inadequate in the first
place—but against the Germans as well, whose air attacks against
us must be given very serious consideration.[1]

As we shall see, no explicit reply was given. Unlike Metaxas,
the Foreign Office evaded such inconvenient inquiries. But
German aims in the Balkans were increasingly to preoccupy the
British.

Germany's intervention in the Balkans before she was prepared for such action would be an advantage to Britain.
Moreover, a German advance there might reduce the chances
of any resumption of the attack on Britain. The British, however, did not wish to see the Italians 'rescued' by the Germans.
The Albanian front was pinning down considerable Italian
forces, and draining Italian supplies. The only danger was that
Germany might try to mediate in the Greco-Italian conflict.
In late November, the Foreign Office feared that such a move
was possible in the near future, if Italian reverses continued.[2]

German policy and strategy on Greece are now fairly easy
to trace. When the plans for the invasion of Britain were finally
shelved, Hitler began considering a 'peripheral strategy',
essentially a series of strikes against Britain in the Mediterranean. In the light of this strategy, Greece became an important objective, or rather a springboard from which attacks
could be launched against Britain's position in the Eastern
Mediterranean. Thus initial German strategic considerations
on Greece had a distinctly offensive character. It is not surprising therefore that Hitler sounded his military chiefs in
early November in this sense, and the first preliminary war
plans were drafted with this objective in mind. After the Russo-
German talks in Berlin on 12–13 November, however, and the
realization on the part of the Germans of the differences that
separated them from the Russians with respect to the Balkans,
besides other parts of the world, Hitler set his mind on a war
against Russia, from now on his great adversary and the enemy

---

[1] *Diary*, vol. iv, p. 537, 18 Nov. 1940.
[2] F.O. Memo., 28 Nov. 1940, and F.O. Minutes, F.O. 371/24892.

most to be feared. In the light of the new priorities, therefore, the 'peripheral strategy' against Britain was dropped as hurriedly as it was devised, and Greece was to be considered from now on mainly in relation to German plans and preparations for an invasion of Russia. Hitler of course would have been happy to deal with Russia and Britain at the same time, but this was simply not feasible since the necessary forces and resources were not available. The German General Staff and Hitler therefore had to settle for a limited undertaking in order to secure the right flank of the German forces directed against Russia, that is a pre-emptive strike against Greece as a probable British base.[1]

In the light of these German plans, the Italian action against Greece, which from the start had been unwelcome to the German General Staff,[2] now became an extremely annoying and inconvenient factor in the shape of a general military reverse, which threatened the very position of Italy in the war. The Germans feared that the Italian reverses offered Britain the opportunity to establish herself in Greece, and this was undesirable in the light of the planned action against Russia in the coming spring. A British foothold in this corner of the Balkans could have very well endangered Germany's venture in the East in more ways than one. Besides the real and immediate danger to the Romanian oilfields, to which the Germans had always been alive, Britain's position in Greece was a potential threat to the right flank of the German forces, if this were to develop into something similar to the allied Salonika front of World War I.[3] It is not out of context to mention here this veritable 'bogy', a Salonika front, which so much preoccupied not only French strategists, but the Germans as well. Considering Britain's limited forces in the Eastern Mediterranean as well as her actual interests in the area, the German fears of a British bridgehead in northern Greece on a scale similar to the allied front of World War I may now seem unrealistic. Yet, the very presence of Britain in Greece could not but revive memories of their defeat on that earlier Salonika front,

---

[1] Creveld, *Hitler's Strategy*, pp. 55 ff., 81 ff.

[2] Halder, *Diary*, vol. v, p. 4, 1 Nov. 1940; *Fuehrer Conferences on Naval Affairs, 1940–1941*, London, Admiralty, 1947, pp. 112 ff., 4 Nov. 1940.

[3] Creveld, *Hitler's Strategy*, p. 84.

and this was a danger the Germans believed they could not afford to take lightly at a time when they planned to invade Russia. At any rate, this much can now be reasonably maintained with respect to Germany's planned action against Greece: it was not so much in support of Italy's deteriorating position in Albania as a pre-emptive move against Britain's position in Greece. Thus, Operation 'Marita',[1] the German code word for military action against Greece, had very little to do with Italy and very much to do with Britain.

In the meantime, the Germans made an effort to mediate in the potentially dangerous Greco-Italian conflict. If the German right flank could be secured through a cessation of hostilities this would be a considerable relief. If the Greco-Italian war came to an end, the British would probably be compelled to withdraw from Greek territory, since the presence of their forces in Greece could be associated solely with the Italian threat to that country. The origin of the initiative for this mediation is not entirely certain, but on existing evidence it appears to have come from Germany. According to this version, the approach for a German mediation came from the head of the German Intelligence Service through the good offices of the Hungarian Minister in Madrid, who in turn approached the Greek Minister in the Spanish capital. A parallel approach came through the German Cultural Attaché in Athens to Maniadakis, the Greek chief of Security. Also, the German Minister in Ankara seems to have been preoccupied with similar activities.[2] The possibility of German mediation was freely aired in the Press, and appeared as persistent rumours in Balkan capitals, as well as in Berlin and Madrid.[3] There is no question that Germany would have been delighted to see an end to this rather irrelevant war between Greece and Italy, and it is logical to argue,[4] that the reason for the rejection by Metaxas of the offer of mediation must be sought in Britain's

---

[1] *Hitler's War Directives, 1939–1945*, ed. H. R. Trevor-Roper, London, 1965, pp. 46 ff.; Creveld, *Hitler's Strategy*, pp. 92 ff.

[2] E. Schramm von Thadden, *Griechenland und die Grossmächte im Zweiten Weltkrieg*, Wiesbaden, 1955, pp. 217–18, 150. For the most recent and complete account see Martin van Creveld, 'Prelude to Disaster: The British Decision to Aid Greece, 1940–1941', *Journal of Contemporary History*, vol. ix (1974).

[3] F.O. Minutes, 4 and 6 Dec. 1940, F.O. 371/24921.

[4] Creveld, 'Prelude to Disaster', pp. 71 ff.

obvious interest in preventing such a development. The Greek sources support this argument but they also introduce other complexities. It appears that Metaxas, although he subsequently cut short approaches emanating from Germany, was not initially opposed to them, and perhaps even favoured the idea of German mediation. Despite the initial brilliant victories in Albania, Metaxas had few illusions about the ultimate outcome. Yet, he was determined to fight it out with the Italians to the bitter end.

The Greek counter-attack of mid-November 1940, which officially ended on 6 January 1941, had lost its impetus by early December and for all practical purposes came to a standstill about the same time. Certain factors conspired against a vigorous offensive by the Greeks: bad weather, lack of transport and supplies, and Papagos's extremely cautious tactics. Metaxas followed the slow progress of the advance with increasing anxiety. As early as 28 November, the Under-Secretary of State for Army Affairs, Papadimas, complained to Metaxas about the slow advance. Metaxas, although he shared the Under-Secretary's concern, explained the situation on the front in terms of insufficient transport and supplies, and for the first time made some reference to complications. At the same time, he got wind of Germany's intention to settle the conflict by force. As a result of this information, and in the presence of King George, he told Papagos that, unless the Italians were knocked out soon and the war in Albania brought to an end, Greece ran the danger of being attacked by Germany. On 1 December he pressed Papagos again for vigorous action.[1] The next day Papagos left for the front, accompanied by Crown Prince Paul. But the visit to the front did not change the situation; despite the unanimous agreement of the field commanders on the need for a vigorous offensive, Papagos settled for only limited offensive action against the enemy.[2] Metaxas was seriously concerned over the shortage of supplies, and on 3 December wondered whether it would not be advisable to 'stop' after all.[3] The weather improved on the 5th, and the problem of supplies was temporarily solved. On the 6th the Greek army captured Santi Quaranta, but this was small

---

[1] Metaxas, *Diary*, vol. iv, p. 540. 27, 28, 29, 30 Nov. 1940.
[2] Katheniotis, *Strategic Phases of the War*, pp. 71–6; Tsolakoglou, pp. 45–8.
[3] *Diary*, vol. iv, p. 541. 1, 2, 3 Dec. 1940.

relief to Metaxas who considered the advance unsatisfactory; and on the 8th, when Argyrokastro fell to the Greeks, he was unable to share the general elation; he saw 'no way out'.[1] As time went on, his concern over the slow advance increased; and so did his dissatisfaction with Papagos's 'attitude'. Nevertheless, his determination to go on fighting remained strong.[2]

Evidence that Metaxas had initially sought German mediation, which cannot be verified from written sources and must therefore be tentative, is provided by Georghios Pesmatzoglou, an old friend and political associate.[3] According to his account, Pesmatzoglou was sent by Metaxas to Berlin in December 1940 on a secret mission to sound the German authorities regarding mediation. Pesmatzoglou met Schacht and Kordt, as well as Prince Erbach, the German Minister in Athens, and explained that Metaxas wished to see an end to the Greco-Italian war, and was prepared to ask the British to leave Greece, on condition that Greece kept the occupied territories in Albania, as well as Valona. Schacht, according to the same account, doubted whether the British could be persuaded to leave Greece, even if the war with Italy was brought to an end. Kordt, whom Pesmatzoglou met in Berne, and Erbach were less sceptical than Schacht of the prospects of this approach.

Whatever the case may be, the question of German mediation should be treated briefly as it finally materialized, and mainly in the context of Anglo-Greek relations. According to press reports in early December 1940, emanating from Spain, Switzerland, Yugoslavia, and Turkey, Germany had let it be known that she was anxious to bring the conflict to an end, and was about to take steps to effect a reconciliation between Greece and Italy.[4] On 7 December Metaxas 'most emphatically' assured the British Minister that 'he would never agree to any attempt to drive a wedge between Britain and Greece'. He also told the Minister that, after knocking out Italy, Britain

[1] *Diary*, vol. iv, p. 542.   [2] Ibid., pp. 544, 546. 16, 21 Dec. 1940.
[3] Pesmatzoglou to the author in an interview of 18 Sept. 1970. Pesmatzoglou was a close associate of Metaxas, their association dating from the days of World War I. Both were prominent in the royalist party of that time, and were exiled, along with others, in 1917, soon after the King's exile.
[4] F.O. Minutes, 4 and 6 Dec. 1940, F.O. 371/24921. The Foreign Office warned the Greek Government to be 'on their guard', but decided not to 'expose' these reports for there was a danger that Britain would appear to be keeping Greece fighting for 'Britain's interests'.

and Greece must turn their attention to Germany. Naturally, the Foreign Office took the chance to nail Metaxas down, and expressed their 'warm appreciation' of his assurances about his attitude towards Germany.[1]

The first German approach was made indirectly through Madrid on 17 December. The Hungarian Minister there called on his Greek colleague, 'on behalf of an official German personality', with the proposal for an eventual armistice between Greece and Italy. According to this proposal, the Greek forces would occupy the Albanian territory they had conquered, and a neutral zone between the opposing forces would be occupied by the Germans so as to prevent incidents. A condition would be the evacuation of the British units stationed in Greek territory. The proposal was telegraphed by the Greek Minister to Metaxas, but rejected by the Cabinet. According to this account, Metaxas informed the German Government that such proposals must come through the regular diplomatic channels; the matter, however, rested there.[2]

The Foreign Office considered that the position of Greece in the event of Italy's defeat and elimination from the war, would be 'anomalous'. The same would also be true if Greece

---

[1] Athens Tel. No. 1289, 7 Dec. 1940, F.O. Minutes, and F.O. Tel. No. 1110 to Athens, 14 Dec., F.O. 371/24921. The Foreign Office feared such mediation soon after the Italian attack. As the Italian Minister in Athens was delaying his departure, the Foreign Office telegraphed Palairet, instructing him to speak to the Greek Government and press them 'to get the Italian Minister out of the country with the least possible delay', since German propaganda was making much play of it. Metaxas assured the British that there could be no question of German mediation. F.O. Tel. No. 1041, 1 Nov. 1940, F.O. 371/24920.

[2] Schramm von Thadden, op. cit., pp. 150 ff., 217 ff. According to the same source, the Greek Minister had recommended to Metaxas the proposed German mediation in order that Greece should avoid Germany's armed intervention in the future. This source is dubious, or the Greek Minister misinformed the author of the above book. P. Argyropoulos, the Greek Minister in Madrid, gave Sir Samuel Hoare, his British colleague, on 5 Dec. an account of a conversation between the German Ambassador and the Hungarian Minister, passed on by the latter to the Greek Minister. The German Ambassador, who evidently wished his views to be communicated to the Greek Minister, said that Greece should approach Germany with a view to the latter's mediation to end the conflict on terms favourable to Greece. At this point, the Greek Minister told his Hungarian colleague that a separate peace was 'unacceptable' to Greece, and that the only chance of a general peace was the complete defeat of Italy. The Greek Minister, it seems, gave Sir Samuel Hoare a different account; or, he was probably sincere, and only changed his opinion by the time of the second approach by the Hungarian Minister, if there was a second approach. Madrid Tel. No. 399 Saving, 5 Dec. 1940, F.O. 371/24921.

concluded a separate peace with Italy. Greece had not declared war on Germany and, once the Greco-Italian war was over, she was likely to revert once more to neutrality. In that case, Britain would have to evacuate Crete and abandon the Greek naval and air bases. This, according to the Foreign Office, would be both an 'immediate loss' for the navy and the air force, and a 'potential loss' in case Britain were to embark on a Balkan campaign in the spring. It was decided, therefore, in spite of Metaxas's assurances, to press the Greek Government 'with a view to ensuring that Greece shall not make a separate peace with Italy', and to raise the question of 'future collaboration' between Britain and Greece in the war.[1] This approach, however, was bound to bring up delicate questions. Metaxas might very well demand, in return for not concluding a separate peace, specific undertakings on aid to Greece, or perhaps ask for territorial acquisitions which the British Government might find it difficult to agree to. The British Minister was therefore instructed to 'encourage' Metaxas to 'elaborate' on what he had already said about continued co-operation and to leave nothing undone to ensure this collaboration.[2]

Meanwhile, on 20 December Metaxas was visited by the German Minister, who endeavoured to elicit Greek plans for the future. Metaxas told Prince Erbach that his first object was to defeat Italy and that, while he had no claims in Albania, he was determined that Italy should never again have a foothold in the Balkans. After the visit, Metaxas told Palairet that 'he had made it perfectly clear to the German Minister that the alliance with England was the basis of his policy'.[3] On the following day Metaxas further told the British Minister that Italy must be defeated first and then Germany, implying, according to Palairet, that Britain and Greece would continue their military co-operation 'even when dealing with Germany alone'. The British Military Attaché was also told by Metaxas that 'England and Greece must remain allies after the war'. The British Minister thus decided not to press Metaxas further in the sense

---

[1] F.O. Memo., 'Possibility of Greece Making a Separate Peace', 14 Dec. 1940, F.O. 371/24922. See also F.O. Minutes in F.O. 371/24921.

[2] F.O. Tel. No. 1167 to Athens, 21 Dec. 1940, F.O. 371/24922.

[3] Athens Tel. No. 1394, 20 Dec. 1940, F.O. 371/24914. See also *Diary*, vol. iv, pp. 545 ff., 20 Dec. 1940. On 23 Dec. Metaxas noted: 'Halifax congratulates me for my attitude towards Germany.' *Diary*, vol. iv, p. 546.

the Foreign Office wanted, since he considered these assurances sufficient; he only feared that Metaxas might not have realized 'the full implication of such an intention', namely that Greece should remain Britain's ally throughout the war.[1]

By late December the issue had subsided but the Foreign Office was still anxious about the future position of Greece. If Italy remained in the war there was no fear of Greece concluding a separate peace; if Italy did not stay in the war Greece could remain on Britain's side only by declaring war on Germany, unless Germany attacked her. The Foreign Office seriously considered that Britain's object must be to get the Germans to 'commit' an act of aggression against Greece, and this they were of course more likely to do if the British 'established' themselves in Greece 'well and truly'.[2] Although these were simply views agreed upon by the Foreign Office, it is interesting that the dispatch of British forces was initially considered not as a response to the impending German attack on Greece, which they learnt about only later, but rather in order to have the Germans 'commit' an aggressive act against Greece. This 'scheme' was perhaps just another academic scheme of the Foreign Office. It is not unlikely, however, that these considerations did influence the decision of the British Government to dispatch General Wavell hurriedly to Greece in mid-January 1941, and Eden and Sir John Dill in February with proposals to send British forces.

Meanwhile, the Greek offensive in Albania was meeting with impressive successes. After taking the measure of the Italians, the Greeks were giving them a sound thrashing. The Western Macedonian army pushed ahead, until Korytsa fell on 22 November.[3] Enthusiasm in Greece ran high, and Metaxas shared the general mood.[4] In a radio speech the same day he said, among other things: 'We fight, not only for our existence, but also for the other Balkan peoples and Albania's

[1] Athens Tels. Nos. 1405, 1419, 1420, 21 and 25 Dec. 1940, F.O. 371/24921.

[2] F.O. Minutes, Dec. 1940, F.O. 371/24922. The Foreign Office correspondence regarding the possibility of German mediation in the Greco-Italian conflict was submitted to the Chiefs of Staff at this stage.

[3] Greek General Staff, *The Greek Counter-Attack, 14 Nov. 1940–6 Jan. 1941* (in Greek), Athens, 1966, pp. 66–71. See also Tsolakoglou, op. cit., pp. 33–6. Tsolakoglou was at the time Commander-in-Chief of 3rd army corps, to which Korytsa fell.

[4] *Diary*, vol. iv, p. 538, 22 Nov. 1940.

liberation as well.'[1] This remark caused trouble, since there were certain circles, in Britain especially, which were not enthusiastic about the 'liberation' of Albania, for the term could be interpreted in more than one way. Concern for the fate of the conquered part of Albania was expressed the previous day, even before the capture of Korytsa. On 21 November the Ministry of Information put in a word with the Foreign Office and asked whether it would have been possible for Metaxas 'to make a declaration confirming the integrity of the existing Greco-Albanian frontier and asserting that Greece in combating Italian aggression [was] also fighting for Albanian independence'. In the Albanians Britain had a 'very powerful potential ally' against the Italians. The Ministry of Information was also concerned about specific matters. The present Greco-Albanian frontier was from the British point of view a 'very satisfactory one' and had better be left as it was.[2]

The Foreign Office was rather sceptical about the desirability of bringing up such a delicate question with the Greeks: after all, they were waging a war and had much on their shoulders. The last thing they would have asked Metaxas was to make a declaration on the lines suggested by the Ministry of Information. Finally, on 25 November, three days after Metaxas had made his speech, Simopoulos informed the Foreign Office that Metaxas had referred to the desirability of Albanian 'independence'.[3] No doubt the Greek Minister had misinterpreted Metaxas's utterance, for there was no reference to 'independence' but to 'liberation'. Palairet was instructed to telegraph the exact words used by Metaxas, and the reply left no doubt: Metaxas had referred to 'liberation'.[4] This caused further argument, but the Foreign Office reached the conclusion that nothing could be done in the direction proposed by the Ministry of Information, and that they had better 'keep in line' with Greek policy towards Albania. The Ministry of Information had now to accept the Foreign Office conclusion.[5]

[1] Metaxas, *Diary*, vol. iv, p. 857, 22 Nov. 1940.
[2] Oliver Harvey to Sir Orme Sargent, 21 Nov. 1940, F.O. 371/24866.
[3] F.O. Minutes, 23 and 25 Nov. 1940, F.O. 371/24866.
[4] F.O. Tel. to Athens, No. 988, 26 Nov. 1940, and Athens Tel. No. 1219, 27 Nov., F.O. 371/24866.
[5] F.O. to the Ministry of Information, 29 Nov. 1940, and Ministry of Information reply, 4 Dec., F.O. 371/24866.

But the Ministry of Information was not the only party interested in the fate of Albania. On 25 November the Foreign Office was approached by Philip Noel-Baker, member of a committee which looked after Albanian interests, who suggested that a declaration ought to have been made by the British Government for Albanian independence, and that care should be taken not to encourage Greek 'irredentist' claims.[1] This approach had a sequel. On 27 November the Opposition brought up the matter in the Commons. The Under-Secretary of State for Foreign Affairs was asked whether any arrangement had been made as to the form of administration that was to be established as a result of Italian 'withdrawal' from the southern part of the country. The reply to this question was a curt 'No'. Noel-Baker inquired whether the Government had taken notice of Metaxas's recent reference to Albania's 'liberation', to which he received a curt 'Yes'. Already, an inquiry about whether the Government aimed at the restoration of an independent Albania, which was submitted to the Foreign Office for approval, had been withdrawn.[2] A few days later, Noel-Baker urged the Foreign Office to see to it that their policy did not put 'wrong ideas into the Greek head' about frontiers. But the Foreign Office feared that these ideas were already present in the Greek mind.[3]

Towards the end of November, the Foreign Office position was that the Greek Government ought not to be pressed in any way about Albania. Albania could never stand alone and would always be dependent on some power for protection, but Italy should never again be allowed to be her protector.[4] The most interesting part of this policy was what was left unsaid; and it was this that worried those who saw some advantage in winning Albanian sympathies at this stage. A rising in Albania was felt by certain circles to be desirable, and the Special Operations Executive was supposedly at work towards this end. On 24 November the Chiefs of Staff were asked whether it would be possible to provide arms for an Albanian legion to be organized by King Zog in Constantinople. But the reply was negative.

---

[1] P. Noel-Baker to R. A. Butler, 25 Nov. 1940, F.O. 371/24867.
[2] F.O. Minutes, 27 Nov. 1940, F.O. 371/24867.
[3] F.O. Minutes, 5 Dec. 1940, F.O. 371/24867.
[4] F.O. Minutes, 28 Nov. 1940, F.O. 371/24867.

If there was any equipment to spare, 'even of the kind suitable for Albanians', there were other aspirants with prior claims. At any rate, nothing could be released until the Albanian organization had taken shape 'a little nearer the seat of operations'.[1]

But secret organizations had their own ways. According to a Greek source in a position to know, British Intelligence agents had moved to Korytsa as soon as the city was captured by the Greeks, ostensibly to organize a clandestine network of informants in Albania; but their aim was, in fact, to foil Greek attempts to organize a resistance movement in the Albanian interior.[2] It is not unlikely that Greek army circles had ideas of their own about the conquered part of Albania. Metaxas in fact refers to some friction he had with the General Staff who wanted the administration of the occupied territories placed under military jurisdiction.[3] According to a British source, Greek army circles wanted to annex the region and did everything to prevent British attempts at inciting a revolt, mainly through a prohibition on running arms to the Albanians.[4] While there is little doubt that the Greeks did cherish an ambition to annex the region in the future it is very doubtful whether they actually foiled the naïve attempts of British agents to incite a revolt. The British Chiefs of Staff showed no enthusiasm for this enterprise. In fact, the Greek Government actually favoured the idea of guerrilla warfare by small bands as Palairet surmised from conversations with Government officials. But a British declaration concerning Albanian independence was bound to arouse Greek 'misgivings', and was ruled out by the British Minister. In a conversation with Gen. Heywood, head of the Military Mission, Metaxas had 'said spontaneously that he neither wished nor intended to occupy Albania permanently but that a future settlement must secure certain strategic points to Greece to protect her against a recurrence of the recent attack'. Metaxas also said that in his public utterances he had been very careful 'not to go beyond a general statement about the liberation of Albania'. The Foreign Office decided that this was enough 'to put the lid' on the idea for a declaration. They

[1] F.O. Letter to the War Office, 24 Nov. 1940, and W.O. reply, 28 Nov., F.O. 371/24868. [2] Korozis, op. cit., vol. ii, pp. 77–82.
[3] Metaxas, *Diary*, vol. iv, pp. 544, 547. [4] Amery, *Sons of the Eagle*, p. 40.

had no wish to go any further than Metaxas in this matter, and the S.O.E. was informed of this decision.[1] Fear of offending Albanian susceptibilities, however, remained alive.[2]

In the meantime, the question of air action against Romanian oilwells remained very much an issue, and made the rounds of various departments. The Foreign Office engaged in endless but, on the whole, academic discussions about such a prospect; and although everyone agreed that it would have been to Britain's interest to involve Germany in the Balkans, they realized perfectly well that the British were not in a position either to prevent or compel the Germans to embark on a Balkan campaign. One action open to Britain, however, was the occupation of Salonika. This was expected to provoke German intervention, but there was not sufficient ground to believe that the Greeks would have consented to a step calculated to incur German retaliation; besides, as far as the Foreign Office knew, the British were simply in no position to occupy Salonika.[3]

It is interesting to note that at this time the Chiefs of Staff were not pessimistic about their prospects in this area, at least when it came to academic considerations of this kind. In a study by the Joint Planning Staff, dated 11 December, there is much that could have made the Joint Planners want to swallow past staff studies if they cared to read them. According to this study, under present conditions at least seven more squadrons of aircraft could have been accommodated and maintained in Greece, bringing the total to twelve. As far as land forces were concerned, two British divisions could have been maintained in Albania during the summer months and four in the Salonika bridgehead. In the event of Greek reverses and retreat, four British divisions might have been maintained on the defensible line of Mt. Olympus, if the Greeks were to decide to make a stand there; or two divisions in the Lamia area, if they were to fall back further to the south.[4]

[1] Athens Tel. No. 1337, 14 Dec. 1940, and F.O. Minutes, 15, 16, and 18 Dec., F.O. 371/24868.

[2] When Metaxas, in cutting a new year cake, cut one section for Korytsa and another for Argyrokastron, the Foreign Office feared that the gesture would have a 'bad effect' on the Albanians. F.O. Minutes, 9 and 10 Jan. 1941, F.O. 371/29818.

[3] F.O. Minutes, 2 and 5 Dec. 1940, F.O. 371/24982. In a marginal minute R. A. Butler wrote: 'Surely it is important for us to aim at involving part of the huge German army somewhere.'

[4] C.O.S. (40) 1032 J.P., 11 Dec. 1940, Cab. 80/24.

On the specific question of a possible front in northern Greece the Chiefs of Staff now wanted to move ahead, but they had difficulties with a reluctant Greek Government. The Military Mission pressed the point, but to no avail. In the middle of December an effort was made to send a small reconnaissance party to report on aerodromes in northern Greece, with a view to operations in the spring. But both Metaxas and Papagos were reluctant to allow this step, because they were unwilling to provoke the Germans. The Military Mission believed that the matter called now for a Cabinet decision. If Metaxas were to be pressed to withdraw his objections he was very likely to inquire as he had often done in the past whether the British Government would have been prepared to face an immediate attack. But this was an extremely delicate matter, which had better be left alone. Nevertheless, academic treatment of the matter went on unabated. From the military point of view, the Chiefs of Staff attached the 'greatest importance' to the preparation of further aerodrome facilities in Greece. The Prime Minister was excited by the prospect of large-scale air attacks launched from Greek bases. He envisaged the operation of modern bombers and fighters, and pressed the matter on the Chiefs of Staff. Advance preparations in Greece were vital: he would not like to see the British surprised 'by events'.[1]

In accordance with instructions from the Prime Minister, the Chiefs of Staff instructed the Air Officer Commander-in-Chief, Middle East, to prepare plans for basing a large air force in Greece. But the reply was far from cheerful. Plans stumbled on political difficulties, because the Greeks were disinclined to incur the risk of a German attack. On 20 December the Chiefs of Staff were in turn captivated by the idea. Great importance was attached to the extension of landing grounds in Greece. In addition to the possibility of hitting Germany in the Romanian oilfields, Turkey could have been assisted, if the need arose. Finally, the aerodromes would have been of considerable value if the Germans were to attempt a move south-eastwards.[2] Again, the Chiefs of Staff were looking ahead, but no headway could be made with the Greeks.

---

[1] Athens Tel. No. 1349, 16 Dec. 1940; Churchill to the Chief of Air Staff, 15 Dec., F.O. to the Chiefs of Staff, 19 Dec., W.O. to F.O., 20 Dec., F.O. 371/24921. [2] C.O.S. (40) 434 Meeting, 20 Dec. 1940, F.O. 371/24921.

At a Cabinet meeting of 27 December, Churchill dealt with the matter both from the strategic and the political points of view. Though German intervention was to be anticipated in the long run, Britain 'had no wish to draw Germany down on Greece'. Nevertheless, construction of aerodromes south of the Mt. Olympus–Arta line could proceed. With respect to the bombing of Romanian oilwells from Greek bases, Churchill was very explicit: nothing of the kind could be attempted without first having obtained the permission of the Greek Government.[1]

As the year came to its end, the matter was referred to the Foreign Office, where persuasive arguments were not lacking. King George's letter of 17 November, in which the British were pressed to send planes to Salonika, was a convenient text, and Palairet was instructed to make use of its contents. As to the question of the possible provocation to the Germans by turning Salonika into an air base, the Foreign Office was inclined to believe that the Germans did not want to invade the area during the winter months. Besides, failure by the Greeks to prepare for a German attack could not be expected to spare them from such an attack. If Metaxas were to inquire whether the British Government would have been prepared to face the risk of an immediate German attack upon Greece, Palairet was instructed to reply that the British Government 'do not rate this risk high'. And they added a further persuasive argument: the measure of assistance to Greece depended on aerodrome facilities prepared before the German attack.[2]

The first approach came from the Military Mission on 30 December. Metaxas now withdrew his objections, and accepted the British proposal. The relevant entry in his diary reads: 'Question of Salonika to be used by air force. Despite all the danger from the Germans, I decide, after day long thought, to accept it. Excuse for the benefit of the Germans: today's bombing of Salonika.'[3] But the next day he drew back, quite unexpectedly:

This morning I virtually withdrew yesterday's consent for the establishment of British air forces at Salonika. First with D'Albiac

[1] W.M. (40) 310, 27 Dec. 1940, Cab. 65/16.
[2] F.O. Tel. No. 1212 to Athens, 29 Dec. 1940, F.O. 371/24921.
[3] Metaxas, *Diary*, vol. iv, p. 549, 30 Dec. 1940.

[Air member of the British Military Mission], and then on his advice with Palairet. I explained my position clearly and sincerely to Palairet. We will provoke a German attack. Is this to our advantage? If the British have the air forces required to repulse it and attack Germany, it is to our advantage. If they do not have them, it is not; in fact, failure to check the Germans becomes dangerous. The resulting shock in the Balkans will be detrimental to Britain's cause. With Palairet I clarified the question of our policy after the defeat of the Italians: that we shall help the British against the Germans as well. These explanations took a long time. I set as the basis of our relationship long term ties with the British. For the present I hope to avoid the question of Salonika, and therefore German intervention. This morning it weighed heavily on my conscience . . .[1]

Palairet gave a similar account of Metaxas's sudden change of heart. When he put to Metaxas the Foreign Office argument that British assistance to Greece in the event of a German attack would largely depend on how far aerodromes had been prepared beforehand, Metaxas observed that that applied only to preparatory measures. What was now suggested was the establishment of an air base at Salonika, and Metaxas had received intimations that it was this which would provoke German action. There was a 'distinct risk' involved, and until the British Government had considered that risk he could not authorize the establishment of British air force units at Salonika. Generally, Metaxas was of the opinion that the British must do nothing to provoke Germany until Italy had been dealt with and the attitude of Turkey and Yugoslavia had been ascertained. It would then be possible to strike at the Romanian oilfields. This would induce the Germans to advance through Yugoslavia which might then be expected to resist.[2]

It is difficult to draw a line indicating where Greek timidity, on the one hand, and British optimism on the other, became unjustified. On the subject of the German threat to Greece, words carried little weight, and the British had very little else to put into the scales besides words. If British assistance was inadequate in support of the Greek effort against the Italians, nothing could go very far to assure the Greeks that they would receive adequate assistance in time to face the Germans. Again, it is difficult to say where strategy ended and diplomacy began

---

[1] Metaxas, *Diary*, vol. iv, p. 550, 31 Dec. 1940.
[2] Athens Tel. No. 1456, 31 Dec. 1940, F.O. 371/29818.

on both sides. As far as Britain was concerned, considerations about the desirability of establishing air bases with a view to operations against Germany were both strategic and political: crippling blows might have been dealt against German interests in Romania, and at the same time Britain's position in the Balkans would have been strengthened to a considerable extent. From the Greek angle, things looked somewhat different. The common war effort against the enemy was one thing, and Greece's existence as an independent state another. Though the Greeks had few illusions at this time about German intentions, they hoped, even against hope, to avoid the invasion from the north, or at best to postpone it. This attitude became a way of life for Greek leaders, and paralysed all action. The more imminent the German threat became, the more Greek leaders, and particularly the army leaders, made an effort to concentrate their attention on the Albanian front: it was an enterprise which was felt to be honourable and within their capacities. As far as Metaxas's attitude is concerned, it is not easy to explain his change of heart from one day to the next. His sincerity in the instance of his decision on 30 December is under a shadow of doubt, for he never actually put his heart into the project: he was in a position to know that the means for its realization were not forthcoming. Perhaps he only gave in to British pressure, and meant to think the matter over, as he actually did, on the next day.

More reassuring was Metaxas's response to a British inquiry as to his aims after the defeat of Italy. Palairet put the question 'frankly'. He knew that if Germany attacked Greece, she would resist; but if Germany did not attack, 'would Greece declare war on her?' When Metaxas said 'yes', Palairet asked him whether public opinion in the country would not consider that, once Italy had been defeated, war against Germany was an unnecessary risk. 'You can leave that responsibility to me', Metaxas replied undisturbed. He was certain that he had some 'authority' over his compatriots, and a 'dossier' against Germany which he had not yet published would support it. He assured Palairet that 'it was the duty of Greece to stand by England against Germany, as England had stood by Greece against Italy'. Besides, there could be no peace for any country until Germany had been defeated. Metaxas also waved aside

Palairet's suggestion that a war with Germany might not have been popular in Greece. The war, he assured the Minister, 'would not be finished until Germany as well as Italy was defeated'; and he was perfectly prepared to provoke Germany when the moment came. Palairet was satisfied that Metaxas gave no hint that Greece might require undertakings from Britain in return for remaining in the war until the defeat of the Axis.[1]

On 2 January 1941 the British Chiefs of Staff considered the situation after Metaxas's refusal to allow the establishment of an R.A.F. squadron at Salonika until he knew that the British Government had considered the project in all its implications. After a full discussion of the implications it was agreed that 'as the issues to be decided were of the highest political and military importance, it would be necessary to refer the question to the Prime Minister' before a reply could be sent to Athens. In the meantime the Foreign Office was asked to send an interim reply to Palairet to the effect that the points raised by him and Metaxas were under consideration by the Government. Evidently the Chiefs of Staff were still not prepared to tackle the wider strategic aspects of the proposed establishment of an air base at Salonika, let alone its political aspects. Palairet raised the matter again on 6 January, and so did Simopoulos the next day. The only reply given was that the matter was still being considered by the Government.[2]

[1] Athens Tel. No. 1457, 31 Dec. 1940, F.O. 371/29825.
[2] C.O.S. (40) 3rd Meeting, 2 Jan. 1941; F.O. Tel. to Athens, No. 21, 3 Jan., Palairet Tel. No. 30, 6 Jan.; and F.O. Minutes, 8 and 9 Jan., F.O. 371/29818.

VII

Grim Decisions

The German Factor

At the beginning of 1941 Germany became the main concern of Anglo-Greek relations, while Italy was relegated to the background. On 1 January, wishing to anticipate events, Mussolini ordered the new Commander-in-Chief in Albania to prepare for 'energetic' action in order to silence world 'speculation' on Italian military prestige, before the Germans advanced south in the spring.[1] Mussolini was determined to wash off the 'stigma of defeat'.[2] But the centre of gravity shifted from Albania to northern Greece, as Germany prepared to invade Greece with overwhelming forces. Though the initiative now passed to the military, and strategic considerations seemed to be paramount, diplomats still played an important role; indeed, in the end, political considerations proved to be decisive.

The concentration of German troops in Romania since early January was an ugly warning to Greece. Reports of the concentration of troops reached Athens from Bucharest and Berlin, but German aims were as yet difficult to assess. Simopoulos informed the Greek Government on 3 January that according to Foreign Office information the Germans did intend to invade the Balkans.[3] The next day Metaxas received a telegram from the Greek Military Attaché in Berlin saying that the Germans aimed at seizing Salonika in a drive through Yugoslavia.[4] This information went a considerable way towards dispelling Metaxas's doubts about German intentions. He was now in a position to interpret certain approaches, which had recently come through various quarters, recommending him to yield to

[1] U. Cavallero, *Commando Supremo*, Bologna, 1948, p. 45.
[2] D. Alfieri, *Dictators Face to Face*, London, 1954, p. 93.
[3] Demetris Kitsikis, *Greece under the Fourth of August and the Great Powers* (in Greek), Athens, 1974, pp. 106, 107.
[4] Papadakis, *Diplomatic History*, p. 130.

Hitler. But he stood by his decision to resist Germany. To the Greek Minister in Berlin he telegraphed: 'Better we die.'[1] All the same, he instructed Simopoulos to make further inquiries at the Foreign Office about German aims. A second telegram to London, dated 5 January, reads: 'Please see the Foreign Secretary and impress on him the very serious danger facing the Balkans as a result of the concentration of German forces. If attacked, Greece will unhesitatingly defend herself to the finish.'[2] Evidently, Metaxas wanted to leave no doubt at all about his determination not to give in to the Germans, even though he was disappointed with the small amount of British aid. On 4 January he noted: 'Abandoned by the British. Attacked by the Germans. Menaced by the winter. Courage! Courage! Let us fall like men.'[3]

But Metaxas's main concern was for the war he already had on his hands, and this demanded all his energy and attention. On 4 January he presided over a war council to consider Greek requirements for the Albanian front. Those present, besides Metaxas, were Papagos, Papadimas, and the members of the British Military Mission. Metaxas proceeded to give a lengthy account of the war situation, and then asked the British to supply Greece with additional aircraft for strikes against the Italian bases in Albania, Durazzo and Valona in particular. He also asked for transport vehicles as soon as possible, and an increased effort on the part of the British to damage Italian communications with Albania.[4] From Metaxas's notes of the meeting it appears that the German threat was left out, and the only matter of discussion was assistance for a more vigorous offensive against the Italians. Metaxas came out of the meeting rather pessimistic. The attitude of the British representatives was by no means encouraging and their replies were 'indefinite'. The prospects of air support were 'doubtful'. Metaxas foresaw serious trouble, and wondered whether Britain had not 'abandoned' Greece in favour of the war in North Africa. 'What shall we do? Are we going to hold out?' he noted with understandable anxiety about the future.[5]

[1] Papadakis, op. cit., p. 131.
[2] Ibid., pp. 132–3; Metaxas, *Diary*, vol. iv, pp. 555–6, 4 Jan. 1941.
[3] Metaxas, *Diary*, vol. iv, p. 556.
[4] Athens Tel. No. 26, 5 Jan. 1941, F.O. 371/29818.
[5] Metaxas, *Diary*, vol. iv, p. 555, 4 Jan. 1941.

The Greek advance in Albania had slowed almost to a standstill as a result of bad weather, Greek deficiencies in transport and air support, and heavy reinforcements for the Italian forces. At no stage had the flow of men and munitions to Durazzo and Valona been seriously hampered, and the strength of the Italian forces in Albania was twice what it had been at the beginning of the war. King George expressed grave concern at the situation to the British Military Attaché. He feared that, although the forces' morale remained high, it would be shaken by the evidence of increasing enemy strength in Albania, where the Greeks expected to continue their rapid progress. The King emphasized that it was essential to prevent the present slow-down from developing into deadlock or even retreat. Immediate air and naval action against Albanian and Italian ports was therefore vital. Late on 4 January, Metaxas impressed on Palairet the urgent need for motor vehicles, increased air support, and a greater effort to prevent the Italian forces in Albania from being reinforced.[1]

Meanwhile, important developments were being initiated in London. The question of assistance to Greece had been referred to the Prime Minister, who in turn informed the Cabinet on 7 January that he had invited the Chiefs of Staff to consider whether Britain could afford more assistance to Greece, and, more particularly, air support.[2] The next day Palairet was informed that the British Government were giving 'most careful consideration' to the Greek requirements and doing what they could in the circumstances. The same day the Defence Committee once again considered the Greek war effort and decided to help the Greeks and to approach them to consider the possible dispatch of British forces to Salonika. This important decision had been reached in the light of information that a German attack on Greece was imminent. If the Greek Government agreed, the British Government would be ready to instruct Wavell to proceed to Athens in order to confer with Metaxas. Palairet was instructed to telegraph the Greek reply to the Foreign Office and to the Middle East Command.[3]

[1] Athens Tel. No. 26, 5 Jan. 1941, F.O. 371/29818.
[2] W.M. (41) 3, Conclusions, 7 Jan. 1941, Cab. 65/17.
[3] F.O. Tel. No. 57 to Palairet, 8 Jan. 1941, F.O. 371/29818. See also W. S. Churchill, *The Grand Alliance*, Boston, 1950, pp. 15, 16; Eden, *Reckoning*, pp. 186, 187.

Metaxas promptly complied: he would warmly welcome a visit from Wavell at once or whenever it was convenient to him; but to avoid speculations he asked that nothing should appear in the Press.[1]

The decision to dispatch an expeditionary force to Greece completely reversed all previous plans and strategy, but satisfied political considerations and needs. According to Churchill, the decision was a 'political' one.[2] What is not clear is Metaxas's attitude in agreeing so promptly to confer with Wavell. In the Foreign Office instructions to Palairet referred to above, the Minister was expected to inquire whether the Greek Government would agree to 'confer' with Wavell. There is no mention of the Defence Committee decision to dispatch an expeditionary force to Greece, let alone of the expected size of that force. Metaxas refers to the matter as a proposal by Eden that Wavell should proceed to Athens for 'consultations'.[3] It is not unlikely that he expected the consultations to concern his previous appeal for assistance against the Italians. But as we have already seen, his telegram to Simopoulos about the German threat and his determination to resist a German attack had been dispatched at the same time as he had appealed to Palairet for help. It is possible that the British and the Greek sides had differing expectations from the meeting, but both were in agreement that top-level military consultations were necessary. As far as the Greeks were concerned, opinion about the visit was divided. Some members of the Government, and particularly Mavroudis, feared that the visit would provoke the Germans; but Metaxas had his way. Papagos, who had left for the front on 8 January, was recalled to Athens for the occasion.[3]

As the day of the conference approached, Metaxas grew restive and did a considerable amount of soul-searching. British help, when it did arrive, was insignificant. The British, he felt, were not really willing to provide even financial assistance. As well as being disappointed with the British attitude, and anxious about the top-level meeting, he had to deal with yet another problem: a proposal by Papagos to promote low-

[1] Athens Tel. No. 39, 9 Jan. 1941, F.O. 371/29818.
[2] Churchill, *Alliance*, p. 16.
[3] Metaxas, *Diary*, vol. iv, p. 557, 9 Jan. 1941.

ranking Venizelist officers, who had been readmitted to the army during the war. As if this was not enough, information about the attitude of the other Balkan states was rather discouraging. The arrival of a number of lorries and other war material was the only cheerful aspect of the generally bleak picture for Greece in early 1941. The Greek advance on the Albanian front was at a standstill, and frost-bite was taking a terrible toll of the troops. Metaxas felt that everything would be lost, and that there were but few hopes for Greece. 'Are we seeing the end of Greece?' he wondered on 12 January.[1]

In London, the decision to dispatch forces to Greece was quickly implemented: there was little soul-searching there. Churchill was impatient to see the Empire forces engage the Germans in a country whose independence Britain had solemnly guaranteed. As a result of the decision of 8 January, the Chiefs of Staff warned the Middle East Commanders on the 10th of a possible German attack against Greece, perhaps by the end of the month, and informed them of the decision to send British forces to Greece's aid. Once Tobruk was taken, Greece had priority over all other operations. The Middle East Command was therefore authorized to allocate one squadron of infantry tanks (heavy), one regiment of cruiser tanks, ten regiments of artillery and five squadrons of aircraft for operations in Greece. Middle East doubts as to whether the Germans really intended to invade the Balkans at that time of the year were silenced by Churchill. The defence of Greece, he telegraphed Wavell, was the top priority after the fall of Tobruk. The destruction of that country would 'eclipse' Wavell's victories in Libya, and adversely affect the attitude of Turkey. Wavell was expected to show 'prompt and active compliance' with the recent decision of the Defence Committee and to proceed with preparations. At the same time he was ordered to visit Athens at the earliest possible moment for consultations with the Greeks in order to study appropriate forms of assistance.[2]

The Middle East Command was not particularly happy about the 'strategical switch' from North Africa to the Balkans. Turkey and Yugoslavia, important factors when it came to

[1] Ibid., p. 558, 11 and 12 Jan. 1941.
[2] Churchill, *Alliance*, pp. 17–19. See also Sir Llewellyn Woodward, *British Foreign Policy in the Second World War*, vol. i, London, 1970, pp. 519 ff.

planning help for Greece, were uncertain quantities. The standing of the Greek army was also a consideration, because clearly no forces ought to be sent if the fighting capacity of that army in operations against the Germans was in doubt. Moreover, the amount of shipping available and the capacity of Greek ports were matters of concern, and so was the time factor, which was difficult to assess. Would there be sufficient time to transport and concentrate the British forces before the Germans started their southward advance? For if the British were caught on the move the undertaking was doomed to failure, and a disastrous failure at that. The planners in the Middle East were faced with a very 'unattractive' operation, whose advantages moreover appeared to be 'nil'.[1]

But the military had to fall in with the decision of the Government. In the afternoon of 13 January, Wavell arrived in Athens. That evening he had a meeting with Metaxas, which was taken up by a briefing about the military situation in Greece. The following day another meeting was held. Those present were Metaxas, Wavell, Papagos, Air Chief Marshal Longmore, Commander-in-Chief of British Air Forces, Middle East, and Palairet. A lengthy review of the situation convinced Metaxas that the British had very little to spare for Greece. He thought that it was a 'miracle' that the British had persevered and even won victories in North Africa. Besides air force units and other war material, they had little else to offer in the form of aid against the Germans. At the same time, information about German aims was contradictory. From Greece it seemed that the Germans would probably force their way into Bulgaria by one method or another, but news from both Germany and Bulgaria was now more reassuring. Turkey seemed to be optimistic, when she did not evade direct inquiries about her attitude from both London and Athens. The Greek Ambassador in Ankara was hard put to assess the attitude of the Turkish Government, but felt that in the event of German intervention in the Balkans, with or without the collaboration of Bulgaria, Turkey would find herself at war with the aggressor. Saraçoğlu, the Turkish Foreign Minister, spoke to the Greek Ambassador in similar terms on 15 January, but at the same time he was not inclined to believe that the Germans really intended to

[1] F. de Guingand, *Operation Victory*, London, 1947, pp. 49 ff.

invade the Balkans. The Greeks were naturally puzzled by Turkey's attitude, and wondered whether Turkey was not already on the slippery road towards giving in to German pressure. The Yugoslavs were also evasive for reasons which will shortly become clear. Metaxas was informed by the British representatives that Yugoslavia would prefer not to see British forces in Salonika.[1]

On 15 January the decisive conference was held. Wavell put together tanks, anti-aircraft and anti-tank guns, but the sum total did not impress the Greeks. Metaxas's notes of the meeting run as follows: 'We reject [the offer] for obvious reasons. They said that their Government set great store [by the acceptance of the offer].' These are the Commander-in-Chief's words:

'You differ radically from our Government.' He repeated that three times in the course of the protracted, but otherwise smooth, conference. But I prevailed. I reassured them that we shall never agree to a separate peace, and that we fight, not for victory, but only for our honour; and that we would prefer destruction [to dishonour]. Palairet shook my hand, and Wavell congratulated me. Both were moved. It would be interesting to see, after all that, whether I shall be called a Germanophile in London.[2]

At noon Metaxas had another meeting with Palairet, and spent the rest of the day conferring with other members of the Government and the Greek military leaders at the Foreign Ministry and the G.H.Q. Late that night he was convinced that he had done his duty in turning down the British offer; but some doubts still remained:

The thought recurs: If we were to allow the dispatch of even a small force to Salonika, would this not sweep along the other Balkan states? Wouldn't it? Of course not; because Britain's weakness is known to everyone! But if we dared? Shouldn't we have dared? A terrible dilemma! But what am I supposed to do? The Germans, although they might quieten down now, will start afresh in the spring. If only the British had even five divisions and plenty of equipment. But they have next to nothing.[2]

Wavell and the British Military Mission gave more complete, if less sentimental, accounts of the conferences. As might be

[1] Metaxas, *Diary*, vol. iv, p. 559, 15 Jan. 1941; Kitsikis, *Greece under the Fourth of August*, pp. 114, 115.
[2] Metaxas, *Diary*, vol. iv, p. 559, 15 Jan. 1941.

expected, the needs of the Albanian front were given priority by the Greek side. Papagos gave a formidable list of the Greek army's requirements for the Albanian operations: transport (lorries and pack animals), clothing, aircraft, A.A. and A.T. guns. Wavell tried to meet Greek needs but not to the extent that the Greek representatives wanted. Two hundred lorries were on their way to Greece, and Wavell hoped to send 200–300 more soon. Pack animals he had none. As far as clothing was concerned, he had little to add to what had already been shipped to Greece: 180,000 pairs of boots, 350,000 pairs of socks, and a considerable number of blankets and other articles. As for the remaining items in the Greek list, very little could be spared. Wavell offered to send a combined A.A. and A.T. regiment for use on the Albanian front, but the offer was 'politely but quite definitely' turned down by Metaxas. Similarly, a company of light tanks for use on the Albanian front was turned down. Interestingly enough, Metaxas said in rejecting these offers that he would consider them if the situation became 'really urgent'; which is hard to explain in view of his urgent appeal for help earlier in the month. Wavell felt that the Greek refusal to accept the units offered for the Albanian front might have been due 'to false pride or some other political reason'. In any case, in view of the obvious reluctance of the Greeks, Wavell did not press them further.

The discussion then turned to the 'Salonika problem', which revealed a 'complete divergence of views'. Wavell stated that he could spare two or three divisions for dispatch to Salonika. These forces would enable the Greeks to offer 'strong resistance' to any German advance, which in view of the mountainous terrain 'could not be in overwhelming numbers'. The dispatch of these troops would convince the Turks and the Yugoslavs of Britain's 'determination to support Greece to the utmost and to resist any advance on Salonika'. Moreover, this step might discourage the Germans from undertaking an advance southwards. If nothing was done, Wavell said, the Germans would be encouraged to attempt a *coup de main* against Salonika, and Turkey and Yugoslavia would be discouraged from taking any action in favour of the allies.

Metaxas took an 'entirely opposite' view. The dispatch of these forces, while not sufficient to defend Salonika, would provoke Germany to take action against Greece. His view was that the British should make preparations for landing an expeditionary force at Salonika and neighbouring ports with the utmost secrecy, 'but should not land any troops at all until [they] could land in sufficient numbers to act offensively as well as defensively'. Material and stores had to be consigned to the Greeks, but the British should not appear 'at all if possible'. Wavell laboured hard to press the British views, but the Greek representatives remained unmoved. Metaxas produced telegrams from the Greek Ambassador in Belgrade to show that the effect on Yugoslavia of the proposed landing of British troops would have been precisely the opposite of what was desired.

Metaxas then put on a show of bravery and loyalty to minimize the effect of the divergence of views:

> The President concluded by saying that we must not interpret his attitude as a refusal to accept assistance at Salonika but as a request for postponement. Once [the] Albanian situation was cleared up large Greek forces would be available for [the] Salonika front and he would then welcome assistance. He then said with great emphasis that, though these were his views, if Salonika was attacked [the] Greeks would fight to [the] last and that we could rest assured [that] they were with us to the end, whether [the] Germans came in against them or not. There was no question of separate peace. He did feel strongly however that [the] best present policy was to prepare bases as secretly as possible, but on no account to land any troops.

Wavell felt that in view of the Greek attitude and the 'apprehension of Yugoslavia', as well as the 'apparent general easing of the situation', it would be 'inadvisable to press [the] Greeks at present as regards landing of troops'.[1]

When seen in detail and in the light of the circumstances, the British offer carried even less weight. In view of the scarcity of shipping, the British forces were not expected to reach Greece before two months had elapsed. The forces which Wavell could immediately dispatch were one artillery regiment, one combined A.A. and A.T. regiment, and 60–65 tanks. Metaxas was convinced that he had little choice but to turn the meagre offer down: it fell far short of Greek estimates of the forces

---

[1] British Military Mission to the War Office, Personal for C.I.G.S. from Wavell, Tel. No. P. 26 cipher 15/1, Most Immediate, 15 Jan. 1941, F.O. 371/29813.

needed to strengthen the front in Macedonia. Papagos was of the same opinion. On 16 January he was visited by Wavell and Heywood, who explained that they had received a signal from London ordering them to try and persuade the Greeks not to turn down the offer. Naturally Papagos was not prepared to give a reply, and only promised to submit the British advice to Metaxas, which he did shortly afterwards. In presenting the case to Metaxas, he said: 'An attempt ought to be made to persuade the British Government that the offer of assistance to Greece would not only fail to produce substantial military and political results in the Balkans, but would also, from the more general allied point of view, be contrary to the sound principles of strategy, as far as the war in the Mediterranean was concerned.' If, in spite of all these arguments, the British Government insisted on acceptance for 'political reasons', Papagos said that it was not advisable to turn the offer down outright.[1]

The British offer fell short of Greek General Staff estimates and plans concerning the German threat and ways to meet it. In a memorandum of 11 January, which was submitted to Metaxas, Papagos dealt with the prospect of British assistance against the Germans, but he began with two important desiderata: (*a*) that the Albanian front should not be stripped of any forces, and (*b*) that the line of defence against the Germans should be along the Eastern Macedonian fortifications. In order to cover Salonika and Eastern Macedonia it was necessary to make an effort to repulse the enemy first on the line of fortifications and then on the River Nestos. The Greek forces in Eastern Macedonia, which could not be reinforced from the Albanian theatre of operations, amounted to barely three divisions, plus the garrisons of the forts, while the forces required to hold the line of defence effectively was estimated at no less than nine divisions. Also, to avoid the danger of being outflanked from the west by way of a move south along the River Axios, from two to three divisions were required. Therefore, from eight to nine additional divisions were needed, besides aircraft, and A.A. and A.T. guns in sufficient strength. These forces had to be supplied by the British, and could land simultaneously at Salonika, Amphipolis, Kavalla, and other Macedonian ports,

[1] Papagos, *The Battle of Greece*, pp. 257–9.

thus minimizing the time needed for landing and deployment, which were estimated to take a fortnight, provided that there were no delays caused by enemy air attacks. In order to deal with this danger, sufficient A.A. defences were required at the landing ports.[1] In his appreciation of the German threat, Papagos told the British representatives at the conference that the rapid landing of these British forces, in combination with the Greek forces present in Macedonia, would allow the formation of a good defensive line stretching from the River Axios to the River Evros.[2] According to his appreciation, not an inch of Greek soil was left undefended and the Albanian front was left intact.

The Greek refusal to accept the limited forces which Britain could spare was a disappointment to the British Government; but nothing could be done to make the Greeks reconsider their position. The War Cabinet was informed of the Defence Committee's view that there could be no question of 'forcing' British assistance on the Greeks, if they were unwilling to receive it; and the Cabinet agreed that 'the decision lay with the Greeks'. Churchill was disappointed by the turn of events, and laid the blame on the Yugoslavs. It was clear, he said, that Prince Paul had told the Greeks that if they accepted the British forces he would allow the Germans to pass through Yugoslav territory.[3] But the Foreign Office could not take 'no' for an answer. They did not share the Greek view that the British would, by taking this or that action, provoke Hitler to attack Greece, or, indeed, take any action which he would otherwise not take. Palairet was thus instructed to try 'to disabuse' the Greeks of this idea, which was after all what German propaganda aimed to encourage.[4]

But Metaxas could not be easily 'disabused' of that idea now that he knew the size of the force the British were prepared to send to Greece. On 18 January he handed to Palairet the following memorandum:

We are determined to resist by every means and at all costs a possible German attack, but in no case would we provoke this attack, unless Great Britain were in a position to make the necessary

---

[1] Ibid., pp. 327–9. [2] Ibid., pp. 255–7.
[3] W.M. (41) 8, Conclusions, 20 Jan. 1941, Cab. 65/21.
[4] F.O. Tel. No. 135 to Athens, 18 Jan. 1941, F.O. 371/29818.

assistance available to us in Macedonia. We have expounded in detail to General Wavell what the size of this assistance ought to be. What has been offered to us is absolutely insufficient. Therefore, while the transportation of this force to Macedonia would amount to a provocation and would bring as a result an immediate German, and perhaps also a Bulgarian, attack against us, the insufficient strength of this force would condemn our resistance to failure. Moreover, we have been categorically assured that Yugoslavia, although disposed today to resist the passage of German forces through her territory, would withdraw this assurance if the German attack were to be provoked by the dispatch of British forces to Macedonia.

Metaxas went on to say that the Greek Government would prefer to study, together with the British, the necessary preparations for the transportation of British forces. Landings should not take place unless German troops entered Bulgaria. In order to land forces in Greece at short notice, a strategic reserve had to be organized in Egypt, as well as air forces and A.A. defences for the Macedonian ports. In concluding his note, Metaxas drew the attention of the British Government to the fact that 'the problem of South-Eastern Europe' could not be met with the forces at present in the Middle East. The Greeks would of course do their duty to the end; but it was left to the British Government to take into consideration the views of 'loyal and devoted friends'.[1]

As a result of the Greek refusal to accept immediate assistance, the Defence Committee reconsidered British policy in the Eastern Mediterranean. The capture of Benghazi was now of the greatest importance, and the next objective would be the capture of the Dodecanese. At the same time a strategic reserve had to be created in the Middle East 'with particular reference to rendering assistance to Turkey or Greece within the next two months'. It was hoped that this force would soon be equal in strength to four divisions.[2] Metaxas's suggestion for creating a strategic reserve for landing in Macedonia was apparently seized by the Defence Committee in the hope of salvaging something out of the planned project. This decision proved very useful in February, after a change of guard in

[1] Metaxas, *Diary*, vol. iv, pp. 560–1.
[2] C.O.S. to Commander-in-Chief, Middle East, Tel. No. 49, 21 Jan. 1941, Premier 3/209.

Athens, and when important decisions were taken by both the Greeks and the British.

For on 29 January Metaxas died. The significance of his passing, both for Greece and the Anglo-Greek connection, at this critical juncture, hardly needs to be emphasized. While alive, he kept under control his frightened Ministers and prodded on his military chiefs.[1] The last entries of his diary make a moving document of a man whom circumstances and his undoubted abilities had placed very high in the finest hour of the Greeks. Purged of his usual conceit and vanity, and freed from what he called his 'demons', he saw the 'truth' just at dusk. He cleared his conscience by dissociating himself from Hitler and Mussolini, whom he considered 'false' and 'liars'; and on 5 January he admitted with much humility: 'Will God forgive us for 1915?[2] We are all to blame! And Venizelos, too! Now I realize how much I was to blame!'[3]

Change of Guard

For both the British and the Greeks the selection of a successor to Metaxas posed a number of serious problems. On 28 January, after a week in bed with influenza and an abcess in the throat, Metaxas suddenly became extremely ill owing to an internal haemorrhage. A blood transfusion did not improve his condition appreciably. Although strict secrecy was kept about the illness, measures had to be taken in case the worst befell. On the same day King George summoned the Cabinet to discuss the advisability of appointing a Vice-President of the Council. By evening, Metaxas's condition had deteriorated, and late at night Palairet telegraphed the Foreign Office that the President of the Council was not expected to live through the

[1] Metaxas's daughter Loukia and Col. Korozis maintain that Metaxas considered the replacement of Gen. Papagos as Commander-in-Chief, because Metaxas always suspected that the general was not equal to the task. He sent Miss Metaxas on 14 Jan. to the front with a personal letter to Gen. Lavdas, the commander of the 2nd division, asking the latter's advice on the issue of the military leadership. When Miss Metaxas returned to Athens, her father was on his death-bed. She had brought him a letter from Gen. Lavdas recommending that Metaxas should take over the supreme command of the Armed Forces with Gens. Pangalos and Manetas as his aides. Interview with Col. Korozis, 27 Mar. 1972, and with Miss Metaxas, referred to in an earlier chapter.

[2] Metaxas of course refers to the National Schism.

[3] Metaxas, *Diary*, vol. iv, pp. 552 ff. 2, 4, 5, 7, 8, 12 Jan. 1941.

night.[1] Soon after midnight Palairet s̆aw the King and asked him what he intended to do, saying that he hoped the King would excuse the question: it was 'caused by anxiety', which he knew the British Government would feel 'as to the future'. King George intimated to the Minister that he intended to appoint an immediate successor to Metaxas 'as proof that there was no change in policy', and that he had thought of Alexandros Koryzis, Governor of the National Bank and former Minister of Social Welfare under Metaxas. Palairet was not satisfied with the King's decision, and suggested that the King himself should assume the government provisionally, stressing that 'he was the only person in Greece who could in the present circumstances immediately take over [the] immense prestige and authority of General Metaxas and that to appoint a mere figure-head would be unsettling to Greece and would not be understood abroad.' But the King hesitated to take such a step. Palairet hoped that the Foreign Office would not disapprove of his action. He felt bound to discover the King's intentions, because he believed that the shock of Metaxas's death, for which the country was completely unprepared, 'was fraught with danger'; and he was not convinced that the appointment of a 'nonentity' in Metaxas's place was the right solution or that it would not lead to internal dissensions. Metaxas, he said, was 'unfortunately irreplaceable'.[2]

The Foreign Office approved Palairet's action in encouraging the King to assume the government provisionally. Approval was cabled soon after receipt of Palairet's telegram. But in view of the fact that the appointment of Koryzis was certain, the Minister was instructed not to press his suggestion further.[3] Nevertheless, the Southern Department was dissatisfied with the King's decision. It was feared that the members of the Government would be jealous. This could have been avoided by making Koryzis Vice-President and giving the titular presidency to Papagos, if the King was not prepared to assume the position himself. It was also feared that the effect of the appointment on the Venizelists would be 'most untoward' in a situation where they might reasonably have expected to be

[1] Athens Tels. Nos. 126, 130, 133, 28 Jan. 1941, F.O. 371/29862.
[2] Athens Tel. No. 134, 29 Jan. 1941, 1.40 a.m., F.O. 371/29862.
[3] F.O. Tel. No. 201, 29 Jan. 1941, F.O. 371/29862.

included in a national government. Cadogan drafted a telegram to Palairet, in which he suggested the appointment of
a 'National Government' including Venizelists, but Eden
stepped in and prevented the telegram from being sent. He
preferred to leave the matter to Palairet, for Palairet was in
a position to know better. Moreover, it was dangerous to interfere in what would certainly be 'a rapidly changing situation'.[1]
Instead, a telegram to the King from the Prime Minister was
immediately dispatched, expressing 'heartfelt sympathy' on
the loss Greece had suffered. The message went on to say that
the knowledge that King George was there to carry the burden
of prosecuting the war would be a 'comfort' to the Greeks and
a 'consolation' to the British.[2]

Palairet regretted the King's decision to appoint Koryzis,
who, he said, lacked strength of character and thus was not the
appropriate choice for the times. But he hoped that the King
would govern in reality if not in name. Indeed, the King had
hinted as much to him when he saw him on the night of 28/9
January. But this was small comfort to the Foreign Office. The
appointment of Koryzis was the least likely to appeal to the
Greeks: as the leader of a totalitarian State, he would work
under all the disadvantages from which Metaxas had suffered,
without enjoying the reputation Metaxas had won in the past
few months. As for the factors behind his appointment the
Foreign Office was completely in the dark. It seemed possible
that Koryzis had been nominated by Metaxas as his successor
in the hope that he would continue his programme of social
reforms. Possibly, Koryzis's administration was merely an
interim one to pave the way for a national government later.
Concerning a national government, everyone in the Southern
Department was in agreement that it would have been most
suitable for Greece at this crisis. But before venturing on the
dangerous ground of intervening in internal Greek affairs and
authorizing Palairet 'to drop a discreet word of advice in this
sense', further information was needed. Cadogan agreed with
this line of policy, and so did Eden.[3]

[1] F.O. Minutes, 29 Jan. 1941, F.O. 371/29862.
[2] F.O. Draft Tel., approved and dispatched by the Prime Minister, 29 Jan.
1941, F.O. 371/29862.
[3] F.O. Minutes, 29 and 30 Jan. 1941, F.O. 371/29839.

In the late afternoon of 29 January, Koryzis received Palairet and begged him to convey his assurances to the British Government that he was 'determined to pursue his predecessor's policy of closest co-operation with Greece's great Ally until final victory'. For the moment Koryzis retained all offices held by Metaxas, including that of Foreign Affairs. Palairet's impression of the new President of the Council, notwithstanding his assurances, was that he lacked energy and initiative. This impression and a rumour he had heard that an undesirable appointment was being considered for the post of Foreign Affairs prompted Palairet to ask Col. Donovan, who was seeing the King that evening, to impress on him the importance of not entrusting the key post to anyone 'considered weak enough to yield to German mediation proposals or intimidation'.[1] The delicate mission was duly carried out, and King George assured Col. Donovan that Koryzis would not listen to German approaches. The King was absolutely certain of the new President's integrity and he knew that Metaxas had a high opinion of him, though he had not designated him as his successor. The King, however, admitted that Koryzis was not a strong man; and to Donovan's remark that he would be 'His Majesty's mouthpiece', he reluctantly agreed, but said he would find it difficult to exceed his constitutional powers. Palairet saw future dangers in this attitude. While interested in military matters, King George did not particularly concern himself with internal and external affairs. Palairet feared that the King might not exercise the authority needed.[2]

On the basis of these initial impressions of the men on the spot, it seemed as if Koryzis would merely be the King's 'mask'; but would this mask always have the King behind it? Palairet and the Foreign Office did not feel confident that it would. Greek politics had had many surprises, and even more so at changes of leadership. A few days later the Foreign Office still found it hard to assess the situation and merely put forward more inquiries. On 4 February they telegraphed to Palairet, asking for his views on 'possible alternatives' to Koryzis. Palairet was also asked to report on whether there was a strong popular desire for a national government to carry on the war effort. And

[1] Athens Tel. No. 143, 29 Jan. 1941, F.O. 371/29839.
[2] Athens Tel. No. 150, 29 Jan. 1941, F.O. 371/29839.

if so, would such a government be likely to be more efficient in prosecuting the war? Naturally, unimpeded war effort was what mainly concerned Britain. The Foreign Office also needed information about such influential members of Metaxas's regime as Kotzias and Diakos, particularly the latter. What were their reactions to the appointment of Koryzis? The Foreign Office also wanted to have the Minister's opinion about the possibility of appointing Papagos as titular President of the Council if Koryzis proved to be a failure and no more suitable person could be found. Finally, one had to take into account the attitude of the Venizelists, who could be expected to want a broadening of the basis of the Government.[1]

Palairet put off replying to the Foreign Office until he had ascertained the position and views of Maniadakis. 'I now know', he wrote on 8 February, 'that it was he, with Diakos (who continues to exercise the same influence as before) who was responsible for the choice of Koryzis as President of the Council and that he proposes that the Government should be carried on with no changes at all.' Palairet believed that Maniadakis aspired to take Metaxas's place and to run the country on the same lines as before, excluding from the Government all those whom he suspected of being Venizelists. He feared that this course was dangerous and proposed to warn the King about it. Neither the army, which was the most important factor, nor the people would be prepared to accept Maniadakis as dictator. As for the existence of a popular desire for a national government combining all the talents, Palairet said there certainly was such a desire; and he was convinced that such a government 'would no doubt be a more efficient instrument for prosecuting the war than the present one'. He did not think that Papagos would have been a good choice, and would rather prefer Koryzis but with the Cabinet strengthened by the inclusion of new elements.[2]

The first assurances came from the King himself. On 8 February he told Palairet not to worry about anything Maniadakis said. As to the formation of a national government, this was out of the question. The King, after consultations with

[1] F.O. Tel. No. 227, Important, 4 Feb. 1941, F.O. 371/29839.
[2] Athens Tel. No. 182, 8 Feb. 1941, F.O. 371/29839. Regarding Koryzis's appointment, Mr. A. Kanellopoulos has stated to the author that the responsibility for the appointment rested with Diakos. Interview with Kanellopoulos referred to in a previous chapter.

army commanders at the front, was convinced that the only way to preserve unity and determination to prosecute the war was to make no change of government at present. Army commanders had told him that 'they had been greatly relieved that he had not changed the Government: if representations of other political parties had been brought in they could not have guaranteed support of the army'. The King might perhaps include a few Venizelists in the Government, 'but on their personal merits and not because of their politics'. His main concern for the present was to make certain that the present Government represented 'a continuation of former war policy', and was convinced that the formation of a national government would endanger both that continuation and national unity. Both Palairet and the Foreign Office accepted the King's policy, but were not completely convinced that his reasoning was sound. If Greece was likely to be faced with great trials in the future, it might prove unfortunate that the country did not have a national government.[1]

An unlikely victim of the change at the top was Alekos Kanellopoulos, head of *E.O.N.* Kanellopoulos was removed from his post because he had issued instructions to *E.O.N.* members that they were to obey any government as long as it followed the policies of the 'Fourth of August' regime. Obviously, Koryzis regarded this as a challenge to his authority. The post went to Spyros Louvaris, Kanellopoulos's lieutenant.[2] It is said that the new head of *E.O.N.* surrendered to the Government the *E.O.N.* revenues, which amounted to 10,000,000 dr., along with a considerable number of blankets, quantities of tinned food and other supplies, as well as fifty machine guns, 50,000 rifles, and other arms. Kanellopoulos was keeping these stores for use by *E.O.N.* members against the enemy, if Greece were to collapse and be occupied by the Axis, which he and others in the Government expected to happen sooner or later.[3] Another member of the Government, Nikoloudis, who was opposed to the appointment of Koryzis, consented to stay after pressure from the King in order to show that the Cabinet remained united.[4]

---

[1] Athens Tel. No. 189, 8 Feb. 1941, and F.O. Minutes, F.O. 371/29839.
[2] Athens Tel. No. 205, 12 Feb. 1941, F.O. 371/29839.
[3] Interview with Mr. Kanellopoulos.
[4] Athens Tel. No. 139, 29 Jan. 1941, F.O. 371/29862.

King George and Koryzis seemed to be determined not to allow dissension. On 22 February Gen. Pangalos and Col. Gonatas with several others were taken to the Security for questioning, but were subsequently released on the understanding that they would remain in their homes, which were watched.[1] It seems that the charge against them was that of undermining confidence in the Army Command; but it is not unlikely that in the case of Pangalos his confinement might have had something to do with approaches to Germany.[2] There also seemed to be some discontent among Venizelists, but from the point of view of the Foreign Office such discontent was not very dangerous. Venizelist discontent, it was felt, was not as 'serious' as dissent among the adherents of the right wing would have been. For the latter might be expected to give the Germans an 'opening'. It was understandable that royalist officers should advise against admitting Venizelists to the Government, but this advice hardly reflected rank and file opinion, let alone public opinion.[3]

In fact, discontent had always been the case in Greece since 1936; but it was the absence of Metaxas from the scene that made all the difference. The British had trusted him, and were always confident that he could deal with discontent at home and at the same time prosecute the war in close collaboration with them. Though it may sound like an overstatement, Britain could never again find a more trusted friend in Greece than Metaxas, with the exception, of course, of King George. One of Palairet's dispatches is an eloquent memorial to Britain's lost friend:

The death of John Metaxas on the 29th January, at the age of 72, closes a very glorious chapter in the history of Greece. We have every reason to hope and to believe that the succeeding chapters will be equally glorious, and will lead to a victorious conclusion; but no future events can ever obscure the honour due to General Metaxas for the wisdom and prudence with which he prepared for the danger; for the courage with which he met it on that early morning of the

---

[1] Athens Tel. No. 271, 25 Feb. 1941, F.O. 371/29839. See also Gonatas, *Memoirs*, pp. 392–3.

[2] It is said that Pangalos approached the German Minister on 6 Mar. with a plan to establish a pro-Axis regime, join the Tripartite Pact, and end the war with Italy. Creveld, op. cit., p. 133.

[3] F.O. Minutes, 27 Feb. 1941, F.O. 371/29839.

28th October, 1940; and for the skill and tenacity with which he used the amazing courage and dash of the Greek forces to repel and vanquish the invader. There can be little doubt that the future historians will place him among the great men of Greece and, indeed, of Europe, whose actions and personality have vitally influenced the course of the war.

From the moment of my arrival in Greece in June 1939 I felt convinced of General Metaxas' sincerity in his expressions of goodwill and friendliness towards Great Britain; and when war broke out in September of that year he at once made it clear to me, not only that his sympathies were entirely with us, but that he knew that the interests, indeed the very existence of Greece as an independent State, were bound up with our victory. Throughout the difficulties imposed upon him by Greece's neutrality during the first year of the war he never wavered in that conviction: and when the moment came to put it into effect he did not hesitate for a moment. He rejected the Italian Minister's ultimatum without even consulting the King or the Cabinet, and his first act after M. Grazzi left the house was to appeal for our help.

In the course of the three months which have elapsed since then he made it perfectly clear that he was determined to pursue the war, side by side with us, not only against Italy, but also against Germany, without whose defeat he recognized and declared that there could be no real peace.[1]

Palairet then paid tribute to Metaxas's qualities: 'He was not only an accomplished statesman and soldier, possessed of rare gifts of vision and imagination, but a man whose humanity, generosity and consideration for others inspired real affection.' Palairet felt that in him the British had lost a 'true friend' to whom they owed gratitude and respect. Not long afterwards, when the British came to deal with Metaxas's successors, they must have longed for the days when he was in charge of Greek affairs, and must have appreciated even more his unfailing loyalty and friendship.

[1] Athens Disp. No. 41, 1 Feb. 1941, F.O. 371/29839.

VIII

Unfortunate Misunderstanding

The Tatoi Conference

Koryzis inherited from Metaxas a most difficult situation and very little of his indomitable spirit. He had too much on his shoulders, which were not made for such a weight. He was an honest and honourable man, but honesty and honour were not the only qualities required of a Greek Premier in the first months of 1941. And like many Greeks at the time, he hoped, even when there was little ground for hope, to avoid a German attack. On 8 February 1941 and after a visit from Palairet, at which he was asked to state whether the Greek Government stood by Metaxas's declaration of 18 January, Koryzis handed the Minister a note, which confirmed the resolution of the Greek Government to resist a German attack at all costs. The note went on to say that Greece was bound to Britain, and that she would go on fighting at her side until final victory. And it added:

We repeat the declaration made on 18 January by the late President of the Council, according to which the dispatch of a British force to Macedonia has to take place only if German troops cross the Danube or Dobrudja and enter Bulgaria. It remains to settle the size and composition of the British force which would be sent to Macedonia in that event, in order that the British Government may be in a position to judge whether, in spite of the sacrifice which Greece is prepared to undergo in resisting the aggressor with the weak forces at her disposal on the Macedonian front, the British forces to be sent would be sufficient with the forces at Greece's disposal to check the German attack and to encourage at the same time Yugoslavia and Turkey to participate in the struggle. For it is certain that the premature dispatch of insufficient forces would be considered by Germany as a provocation and would have the immediate consequence of precipitating the launching of the German attack on Greece, thus destroying even the faint hope that this attack might be avoided.

The only object of the considerations set forth above is to afford the British Government the opportunity of examining the question seriously from this point of view; we exclude any reservation on our part in regard to the obligations assumed by us in accordance with the aide memoire of 18 January 1941. The Royal Hellenic Government would be happy to know the point of view of the British Government on the above.[1]

Writing to the Greek Minister in London two days later, Koryzis tried to elaborate on the Greek position with regard to the German threat and the dispatch of British forces to Greece. The arguments contained in the note he had handed to Palairet were repeated, but with further explanations. The assistance Wavell had offered in January fell short of the forces which were required to check the Germans, and would do more harm than good in the direction of Yugoslavia and Turkey. Koryzis also said something else, which revealed the secret thoughts and hopes of the Greek Government:

No doubt, no one can be certain that Germany would not advance further after entering Bulgaria. Nevertheless, since the main object of Germany's present drive is to keep the Balkan states from forming a common front under British auspices, and since she perhaps considers that this object might well be achieved by her mere presence in Bulgaria, it is not unlikely that she may not want to advance against Greece, at least for the time being . . . [This] would afford Greece the time needed to bring the war in Albania to a victorious end . . . For this reason, I would like to stress the very urgent need to expedite supplies of munitions and aircraft, which we have already requested.[2]

The hope of avoiding a German attack was therefore kept alive by the Greek Government; and so was their resolve to prosecute the war in Albania, unimpeded by any obstacles. As we shall see, the Albanian front received top priority until the very end.

The Foreign Office was hard put to it to answer Koryzis's note. They had evaded the issue when Wavell was in Athens, and had put off replying to Metaxas's note. It would have been 'somewhat embarrassing', they thought, to give a cut-and-dried

[1] Papadakis, *Diplomatic History*, pp. 144–6; Athens Tel. No. 194, Immediate, 9 Feb. 1941, F.O. 371/29813.

[2] Kitsikis, *Greece of the Fourth of August and the Great Powers*, pp. 133–5. The dots indicating omission of words or sentences are in the form presented by the author of the book.

answer to the Greek Government, as had been requested.[1] The question was whether Britain would come to Greece's assistance when Greece appealed to her and with sufficient forces to check the Germans. Naturally, the issue at hand was one for the Cabinet and the Defence Committee to decide. In fact, the Defence Committee was about to consider the question from the point of view of over-all strategy, while the Foreign Office tried in vain to find an answer. The Greek inquiry had come at a very propitious moment: Benghazi had been captured. Churchill informed the Cabinet on 10 February that the situation in the Eastern Mediterranean had been altered by the early capture of Benghazi. 'In what way should our forces in the Middle East now be employed?' Churchill asked. As a result the Cabinet invited the Defence Committee (Operations) to discuss this matter at a meeting which would be held that night.[2]

Important decisions were now being taken in London; but Athens was kept in the dark. So far as the note of 8 February was concerned, graver doubts as to the desirability of accepting a small force could not have been expressed in diplomatic language, except by virtually rejecting the offer. It is possible that in different circumstances an outright refusal might have been the Greek reply to Palairet's inquiry; but not with a war in progress and the need for British supplies extremely urgent. At this point it is questionable whether the Greek Government wanted British land forces more than the British Government tried to make them want them. The strategic and political aspects of British policy with regard to assistance to Greece can hardly be separated, for they were two sides of the same coin. It was necessary to help Greece, because if she was left on her own and wilted before the pressure from the Axis the effect on the Balkans would be disastrous. In view of the unexpectedly early capture of Benghazi and the Greek request pressing for information about the size and composition of the forces which Britain could send to Greece, the Defence Committee reviewed over-all strategy in the Middle East. The position had also been altered by a Turkish refusal to accept

---

[1] F.O. Minutes, 10 Feb. 1941, F.O. 371/29813.

[2] W.M. (41) 15, Conclusions, 10 Feb. 1941, Cab. 65/17. See also L. Woodward, *British Foreign Policy in the Second World War*, vol. i, London, H.M.S.O., 1970, p. 522.

immediate British assistance. Greece now became the focal point of British strategy in the area:

The Defence Committee consider that if Greece were to yield to Germany without fighting, Turkey also would not fight, and consequently that the only way of making sure that the Turks do fight is to give sufficient support to the Greeks to ensure that they fight. Accordingly, the Defence Committee have decided that it is essential for us to place ourselves forthwith in a position to send the largest possible land and air forces from Africa to the European Continent, in order to assist the Greeks against a possible German attack through Bulgaria.[1]

In a telegram to Wavell Churchill said: 'If Greece is trampled down or forced to make a separate peace with Italy, yielding also air and naval strategic points against us to Germany, [the] effect on Turkey will be very bad. But if Greece, with British aid, can hold up for some months [the] German advance, [the] chances of Turkish intervention will be favoured.' Wavell was therefore ordered to earmark for transfer to Greece troops and material from the existing garrison in the Middle East, stretching the drain 'to the limit'. The expeditionary force would, it was hoped, consist of at least four divisions, including one armoured division, together with munitions and additional air forces to the capacity of Greek airfields. To expedite matters with the Greeks, Eden and General Dill, C.I.G.S., would fly to the Middle East. If unable 'to reach any good agreement with the Greeks and work out a practical military plan', then the British had to make the best of the situation; they would keep Crete and occupy Greek islands which were of use as air bases.[2]

Churchill went on to say that it was not known what the Greeks would say to 'a great offer of this kind', nor what their means of resisting the Germans were. This assertion, however, does not hold much water, for as we have seen already, this 'great offer', that is four divisions, fell short of the nine to ten divisions originally estimated. As to the forces at the disposal of the Greeks, again there could have been little doubt: three divisions plus the garrisons of the forts. Metaxas and Papagos

[1] Chiefs of Staff to the Commander-in-Chief, Middle East, Tel. Secret, 11 Feb. 1941, Premier 3/209.

[2] Churchill, *Grand Alliance*, pp. 65, 66.

had left no room for doubt about their estimates concerning the forces required to check the Germans on the frontier. Either the British were not convinced by Greek estimates, or they believed that the Greeks could be persuaded to waive their objections to the British offer, or both. Of course, the Greeks had made no secret of their misgivings about British help; but at the same time they had been emphatic about their determination to fight the Germans, even if left on their own. It is not unlikely that the Greek Government did not want to sever the British link by turning down an offer which, though unsatisfactory from the Greek point of view, the British seemed to set great store by. No doubt the Albanian front was a soft spot, which made the Greek Government vulnerable to pressure or persuasion: if only the Greeks could be persuaded by stick or carrot, or by a ruse, that British help, after all, was not so negligible! Churchill, at least, wanted to believe that it was not.

On the same day that Churchill cabled Wavell to prepare for possible action in Greece, the Greek Chargé d'Affaires called at the Foreign Office to deliver Koryzis's note, which had already reached the Foreign Office by telegraph from Palairet. In this connection Romanos was instructed to raise certain points, which he did with Cadogan. Although the Greek Government recognized, he said, that the decision to send a force to Greece rested with the British Government, they hoped that the British would bear in mind that 'to send an insufficient force might be worse than nothing at all'. The British would only be sharing in a disaster, and that would discourage Yugoslavia and Turkey. Another point concerned the timing of the British help. 'Monsieur Koryzis questioned whether it would not be better, instead of sending help immediately after the Germans had entered Bulgaria, to wait until they actually committed an aggression against the Greek frontier.' Cadogan was puzzled: would it not be waiting too long? Romanos thought that 'Koryzis still had a hope that the Germans, even if they occupied Bulgaria, might stop there and not actually proceed to attack Greece'. Finally, Romanos said that the Greek Government were anxious for 'an exchange of views' between the two Governments or their General Staffs on the degree of help that could be given and the moment at which it should be given. The Greek army in Albania would undertake large-scale operations that week, and if these were successful the Greeks would be able to spare a number of troops to reinforce the Macedonian defences. Romanos was told that the British for their part 'were actively examining the situation which had been produced by the recent successes in North Africa', and that soon they would be in a position to give the Greek Government a clearer picture of British dispositions. As for an exchange of views on strictly military matters, this of course would take place between the General Staffs.[1]

The Foreign Office was thus confronted with what seemed to be a reconsideration of policy by the Greek Government. Churchill saw the record of the conversation between Cadogan and Romanos, and the Chiefs of Staff were informed of its subject-matter. The following day, 13 February, Romanos called again at the Foreign Office, where he was questioned on the change of Greek attitude with regard to the time when the Greek Government would be prepared to receive British help in Macedonia. He now said that it was not a change of attitude. Koryzis adhered absolutely to Metaxas's declaration: the Greek Government would appeal to Britain for help as soon as the Germans entered Bulgaria. The object of the oral communication was merely to suggest that 'perhaps it might be wiser' to send help when the Germans arrived on the Greek frontier and not earlier; but this was for the British to decide. Koryzis would not press his point, if they decided to send help as soon as the Germans crossed into Bulgaria. Besides, this was a matter for the General Staffs of the two countries to discuss. The Foreign Office found this an 'egregious proposal' and difficult to reply to.[2] Koryzis's point about the timing of British help, though not pressed on the British, made plain a serious divergence of views.

At this point it is useful to see how the situation looked from the British Legation in Athens. The Greek army was preoccupied on the Albanian front; and in the face of the German threat its position was precarious. Papagos staked everything on the defeat of the Italians. All his troops except three divisions were concentrated on the Albanian front. If Germany were to obtain a passage through Bulgaria for an attack on Greece,

---

[1] Record of conversation, 12 Feb. 1941, F.O. 371/29813.
[2] F.O. Minutes, 13 Feb. 1941, F.O. 371/29813.

Salonika would be endangered and difficult to defend. It might have been different, of course, if Yugoslavia were to rally to the side of Greece; but it was very doubtful that she would actually do so, although both she and Greece had admitted that Salonika was of vital importance to them. Britain, it seemed to the Legation, should aim 'to get the Yugoslav Government to rescind their warning to the Greek Government against the dispatch of British troops to Macedonia'.[1]

As far as the internal situation was concerned, things were not any better. Metaxas's death had left the country without an outstanding political leader to impose his will on the rest of the Government and the people. To bring Greece into a war with Germany and to maintain her will to fight two great powers on two fronts was, according to the Legation, a 'serious undertaking'. To maintain Greece's will to fight Germany two things were necessary: (*a*) that the Greek army would remain satisfied with the political leadership, and (*b*) that outside help would come 'in sufficient quantity to make it something better than a forlorn and desperate hope for Greece to resist a German attack'. With regard to the first point, the army seemed to be satisfied with the Government, but the latter left something to be desired from a more general point of view. As for sufficient help, its importance could hardly be exaggerated, if Greece were to remain united in her resolve to resist Germany as well as Italy. Clearly the Legation understood Greek realities and difficulties much better than London did. But Greece was now part of a bigger game: a key to British strategy in the Balkans. From Britain's point of view, it was imperative that Greece should fight the Germans at all costs.

The delicate mission was entrusted to a top-ranking party: Eden and Dill. Churchill handed to Eden sealed instructions, which amounted to a great deal but left him practically free to make decisions. The Secretary of State would represent the British Government 'in all matters diplomatic and military' in his talks with the foreign governments; and although he was under instructions to keep the Government informed of his actions, he could act as he thought best 'in an emergency'. The main object of the mission was to find, along with the Commander-in-Chief, Middle East, and the Governments of Greece,

[1] Memorandum by the British Legation, 13 Feb. 1941, F.O. 371/29798.

Turkey, and Yugoslavia, ways of sending help to Greece at the earliest possible moment. To this end, it was necessary to concentrate in Egypt 'the strongest and best-equipped force', which could be sent to Greece at short notice. Eden was fully empowered to negotiate and formulate with the Greeks plans for common action, and to get in touch with the Turks and Yugoslavs with the object of inducing them to fight, preferably on a common front.[1] For their part, the Foreign Office took care to remind the Secretary of State of Koryzis's point with regard to the moment when Greece would be prepared to receive British help.[2]

On 20 February Churchill informed the Cabinet of Eden's arrival in Cairo, and explained the purpose of his mission:

If the Greeks decided to oppose a German advance into their country, we shall have to help them to the full extent of our power and Mr. Eden would inform them of what help we could give. It might well be that a German thrust toward Salonika would be irresistible; but if the Greeks decided to fight, we should do what we could. It was possible, of course, that before making their advance the Germans would offer the Greeks such attractive terms that they would feel bound to make peace. In that case we could not very well blame them, nor should we take such a decision on the part of the Greeks too tragically. We should have done our duty and should then have to content ourselves with making our position in the Greek Islands as strong as possible. From these Islands we could wage air war against Germany, which in turn might eventually turn in our favour.

He then read to the Cabinet his instructions to Eden, which were 'generally endorsed'.[3]

The same day Eden and Dill held a meeting with the Commanders-in-Chief, Middle East, to discuss the proposed enterprise. From the political point of view, there was general agreement to help Greece at the earliest possible moment. But doubts were raised as to the 'military expedience'. Admiral Cunningham expressed 'grave uncertainty' about the soundness

[1] Enclosure to Tel. No. 4617 cipher 18/2, Most Immediate and Most Secret, from Governor and C.-in-C., Gibraltar, to C.-in-C., Middle East, 18 Feb. 1941, F.O. 371/29813. See also Churchill, *Grand Alliance*, pp. 66–9; Eden, *Reckoning*, pp. 192–3.

[2] F.O. Tel. No. 451 to Cairo, 19 Feb. 1941, F.O. 371/29813.

[3] W.M. (41) 19th Meeting, 20 Feb. 1941, Cab. 65/21.

of the decision from the military point of view, and Dill doubted whether it was the 'right one'. But Wavell, although he doubted that adequate forces could reach Greece in time to hold the Germans, recommended the enterprise, and advised proposing to the Greeks that Salonika should be defended. After the meeting, Eden cabled to Churchill that agreement had been reached to do everything 'to bring the fullest measure of help to [the] Greeks at [the] earliest possible moment'. If the Greeks were to accept the offer, there was 'a fair chance of halting a German advance and preventing Greece from being over-run'. As to a line of defence, opinion differed: although Wavell was prepared to contemplate a line covering Salonika, doubts were expressed as to whether so advanced a line could be held. The forces available for action in Greece in the immediate and near future were one armoured brigade and the New Zealand division, to be followed by the Polish brigade, an Australian division, an additional armoured brigade, and a second Australian division. In his telegram to Churchill, Eden added: 'My present intention is to tell the Greeks of the help we are prepared to give them now, and to *urge* them to accept it as fast as it can be shipped to them. If they will accept this help and brave any risk it may entail of involving them in early hostilities with Germany there is a fair chance that we can hold a line in Greece . . .'[1]

Dill had even fewer doubts about the decision than Eden. He had gone to the Middle East with the 'firm idea' that the dispatch of forces to Greece was inadvisable, and that it was preferable to send these forces to Turkey. But after he had talked with the Middle East Commanders, who believed that there was 'a fair chance of successfully holding a line in northern Greece' if the British were to act at once, he concluded that the only chance of preventing the Balkans from being overrun by the Germans was to send forces to Greece at the earliest possible moment. As to the defensive line, Dill, like Eden, was uncommitted. In a cable to the V.-C.I.G.S., Dill said: 'It is not yet possible to decide what line we should aim at holding in Greece

---

[1] Churchill, *Grand Alliance*, pp. 70–2. This crossed telegrams from Churchill, in which Eden was told not to consider himself obligated to the Greek venture if he and the others felt that it would only be 'another Norwegian fiasco'. Woodward, *British Foreign Policy*, vol. i, p. 526.

but I doubt very much whether Salonika could be covered. If this proves to be so after our discussion with [the] Greeks tomorrow we may still be able to hold a line covering northern Greece and giving Yugoslavia a bolt-hole through the Monastir Gap.'[1]

By 21 February, therefore, important decisions had been taken in Cairo. First, it was decided to send forces to Greece at all costs and at the earliest possible moment. Second, the size and composition of the expeditionary force were agreed upon by the local Commanders-in-Chief and the party from London. Third, the line of defence was left to be decided after the talks with the Greeks; and though serious doubts were raised about the ability to cover Salonika, a line covering that city was not ruled out off hand. With regard to the first two, the position was clear; the British representatives intended to argue the Greeks into accepting the expeditionary force. So far as a line of defence was concerned, its location was left to be decided in common with the Greek representatives. One factor that weighed heavily in the Cairo talks was the desirability of inducing Yugoslavia and Turkey to fight on the side of Britain and Greece. It was hoped that both Yugoslavia and Turkey could be induced to fight by the presence of British forces in Greece, and Yugoslavia in particular, by holding a line covering Salonika.

Churchill subsequently explained that the word '*urge*' in Eden's telegram was meant to apply, 'not to the principle of acceptance by the Greeks of British help, but to the timing of their acceptance if that was their resolve'.[2] As we shall see, the urging was not limited to the timing of help. The decision to help Greece was reaffirmed on 21 February; and so was the size of the force. Eden sent Churchill a second telegram that day. With regard to the prospects of a campaign in Greece, he said nothing could guarantee success. The venture was a 'gamble'; but the decision was based on what had been agreed upon by the Defence Committee: 'to run the risk of failure' and rather 'suffer with the Greeks than to make no attempt to help them'. Moreover, the attitude of both Turkey and Yugoslavia depended on British help to Greece. It was

---

[1] Eden, *Reckoning*, pp. 197–8, 21 Feb. 1941.
[2] Churchill, *Grand Alliance*, p. 72.

possible, however, that the Greeks might turn down the British offer. In that case, the matter could be reconsidered; but Eden intended to concentrate all his efforts 'on trying to induce [the] Greeks to accept our help now'. One important matter awaiting decision was the line of defence. Everyone would have liked to hold the Germans on a line covering Salonika, but Longmore and Cunningham seriously doubted the feasibility of the project. Eden and Dill therefore preferred not to take a final decision until they had discussed the matter with the Greek Government.[1] The very serious objections of the planners in the Middle East were put aside. Political considerations prevailed.[2]

The line of approach to the Greeks agreed on in Cairo on 21 February was the following: according to British information the Germans intended to occupy Greece. Their aim was to obtain a foothold on the Greek mainland from which to prosecute with greater advantage the war against the British. The Greeks had asked the British for help, and the British were prepared 'to give it in the fullest measure'. The note went on to say:

> The Greek Government have expressed misgivings lest the premature dispatch of insufficient forces would be regarded by Germany as provocation. As regards the insufficiency of our forces, we hope that the size and quality of the forces we are ready to make available will convince the Greeks that we have fair chances of checking and holding a German attack. As regards sending a premature force, if we are to send troops, they must be sent at once. Every day is of value and it is vital that the British forces should be established before weather enables the Germans to move. Our object is to forestall, not to precipitate, a German attack.

The question of the line to be held could then be raised. The Greeks would be asked for details of their own plan and for information with regard to the forces, which they would be able to release from Albania to form a line against the Germans.[3]

The strategic situation from the Greek angle presented many problems. There were two desiderata, which though not

---

[1] Eden, *Reckoning*, pp. 196-7.
[2] De Guingand, *Operation Victory*, pp. 54, 55.
[3] 'Note on Approach to the Greeks', 21 Feb. 1941, F.O. 371/33145.

explicitly stated in January, were present in the minds of the Greek General Staff: (*a*) to prosecute the war in Albania unimpeded by other campaigns, and (*b*) not to abandon Eastern Macedonia without a fight. Therefore any act which might provide the Germans with the pretext to attack, ought to be avoided, in order to finish with the Albanian front, which was a running sore and sapped the country's strength. But if the German invasion could not be avoided, as there were unmistakable signs that it would not be, then everything should be done to make certain that the battle would be fought in Eastern Macedonia, where the General Staff had built through the years a formidable defensive wall. Two factors, however, had to be taken into account: British assistance and the attitude of Yugoslavia. The first left much to be desired, and the second was difficult to assess and always remained an uncertain quantity. In the light of these factors the Greek General Staff had to do the best they could to accommodate their priorities.

A line of defence on the Macedonian fortifications presented formidable problems, because these forts had been built to face Bulgaria in a static war and not a blitz attack, in which concentrations of armour with air support were thrown in. The principal flaw in Papagos's thinking is in his judgement that the enemy could be held on the fortifications at all, even by employing twelve divisions, as he maintained. The string of forts had as a southern flank a narrow strip of land, beyond which was the sea, and this precluded any tactical manœuvre; in fact, the area constituted a trap where an army stretched along the border could be dealt with piecemeal by parallel enemy thrusts at different points, while air attacks would gravely disrupt supply lines and troop movements. Salonika, the main port of supplies, was open to air attacks, and could be easily reached by a thrust southward along the River Axios. The capture of this vital base would make the Greek position in Albania untenable. But this brought in the Yugoslav factor, since Salonika could be easily reached by way of southern Yugoslavia. In this respect the Greek General Staff were faced with an extremely difficult problem, and their strategy depended on this uncertain factor. Here was a gap, which could not be ignored, at least in theory. If withdrawal from Albania was undesirable and was therefore ruled out, and the Macedonian fortifications could not be abandoned, it was necessary to make the best of the situation, essentially a compromise, and a very poor one at that. Papagos considered those eventualities, and adjusted future strategy to their demands. In case Yugoslavia actively joined Britain and Greece, Macedonia and its port base of Salonika would not be abandoned, since it constituted the only effective way of supplying Yugoslavia; therefore, the Anglo-Greek forces had to hold the Germans along the Greco-Bulgarian border, on the fortified line. If Yugoslavia remained neutral and did not allow the passage of German troops through her territory, Eastern Macedonia would be evacuated and the line of defence would be moved to the west on a line running north-eastward—Mt. Kaimaktsalan–Mt. Vermion–Mt. Olympus. This line left Salonika to the enemy, but was short and defensible. Finally, if Yugoslavia remained neutral but was forced to allow the Germans to pass through her territory, or simply collaborated with the Germans, the Kaimaktsalan–Vermion–Olympus line was undesirable, since it ran the danger of being out-flanked from the west by a German thrust through the Monastir Gap and down the Florina plain. The Greek position in Albania ran the same danger. In that case the best line of defence would be one running in a westerly direction along Mt. Olympus, River Aliakmon, River Venetikos to the Ionian Sea close to the Greco-Albanian frontier. This line was rather long but nevertheless defensible, and it would be a joint concern, the Greek armies of Epirus and Western Macedonia holding roughly the western half and the Anglo-Greek forces the eastern half.[1] The British favoured the second line, that is, the Kaimaktsalan–Vermion–Olympus line, the 'Aliakmon line', as it became known: it was short, based on defensible ground, and not far away from Larissa, both a centre of communications and an air base.[2] Consultations about Anglo-Greek strategy and a common line of defence were to stumble on a serious divergence of views, which was not admitted until it was too late: the British had set their minds on the Aliakmon line, while the Greeks were unwilling to abandon the advanced line based on the fortifications, and the hope that the Yugoslavs would eventually join the allies.

[1] Papagos, *Battle of Greece*, pp. 262–3.
[2] De Guingand, *Operation Victory*, p. 54.

Two factors made it almost impossible for the Greeks to formulate realistic plans. These were: (*a*) the uncertain attitude of Yugoslavia, which influenced Greek dispositions and lines of defence; and (*b*) the Albanian front, which was sacrosanct to the General Staff. Papagos was convinced that to evacuate Macedonia and abandon Salonika were steps which, if carried out 'prematurely' and before Yugoslavia's attitude was ascertained, might well strengthen the objections of the Yugoslav Government to joining Britain and Greece, and even provide them with grounds for collaborating with Germany. This strategy therefore would defeat the political ends of Britain and Greece. Equally, to divert forces from Albania was out of the question, since there would be inadequate forces to maintain a successful resistance against the Italians. For these reasons the High Command decided that in the event of a German attack, 'the main Greek effort should continue to be exerted on the Albanian front', irrespective of developments on the Macedonian front. The Greek army would not 'jeopardize its position as the victor against the Italians'.[1]

At the same time as Eden, Dill, and the Commanders-in-Chief, Middle East, discussed the Greek enterprise, the Greek High Command and the British Military Mission held last-minute consultations. All possible lines of defence were considered, but none was found satisfactory.[2] With regard to the German threat, Papagos gave the following appreciation: 'The uncertain attitude of Yugoslavia made it very difficult for him to decide on [a] fixed plan of defence.' If Yugoslavia were to collaborate with Greece, the possibility of holding the Germans on the Greco-Bulgarian frontier 'might be seriously considered'. But if Yugoslavia remained neutral 'Salonika would have to be abandoned'. He went on to say that a German attack 'before the present situation in Albania had been cleared up would be [a] catastrophe'. For this reason it had been decided to avoid doing anything that might precipitate a German attack before the Greeks could capture Valona. After achieving this objective the Greeks would be able to withdraw troops from Albania for the defence of Eastern Macedonia. The Mission concluded

---

[1] Papagos, *Battle of Greece*, pp. 254, 263.

[2] British Military Mission to the C.-in-C., Middle East, Tel. No. 58 cipher 20/2, Immediate and Most Secret, 20 Feb. 1941, F.O. 371/29818.

the telegram by saying: 'Capital importance of Yugoslav position being clarified cannot be overestimated.'[1]

Eden's decision to visit Athens for talks with the Greek Government was cabled to the British Minister on 21 February.[2] The following day, a high-powered British party flew to Athens, and at 5.30 p.m. the first Anglo-Greek meeting was held at the Tatoi Palace, the King's country residence outside Athens. Those present were, on the Greek side, King George, Koryzis, Papagos, Col. Kitrilakis, Director of Operations, General Staff, and two officials from the Foreign Ministry; and on the British side Eden, Dill, Wavell, Longmore, Palairet, Heywood, who acted as interpreter, an officer representing Cunningham, and Pierson Dixon of the Foreign Office.[3] Before the talks started, and in order to dispel any doubts as to Greece's determination to fight the Germans even if left alone, the King insisted that Eden should first have a word with Koryzis. The King alluded to certain rumours and speculations about his resolve to resist the Germans, and assured Eden that such allegations were false. Eden was reluctant to see Koryzis alone, but finally consented to do so. This meeting amounted to a reaffirmation of Greece's determination to continue the struggle, not only against Italy, but against Germany as well. It was a 'display of courage', Eden wrote.[4] In fact, it was more than that. Koryzis also said that against a German attack Greece could count, besides the three divisions at her disposal on the Macedonian front, only on British help. The Greek Government ignored the intentions of Yugoslavia and Turkey, let alone their military plans. 'This question, therefore, is not only exceptionally important, but also extremely urgent.'[5]

Eden gave an account of the situation in the Balkans in view of the concentration of German troops in Romania and their infiltration into Bulgaria. It appeared that these German moves aimed to 'subdue' Greece and 'immobilize' Turkey. Their ultimate aim was to strike at Britain's position in the

[1] Brit. Milit. Mis. to C.-in-C., Middle East, Tel. P59 cipher 20/2, Immediate and Most Secret, 20 Feb. 1941, F.O. 371/29818.
[2] Cairo Tel. No. 347, Immediate, 21 Feb. 1941, F.O. 371/29798.
[3] Record of Anglo-Greek conversations, 22 Feb. 1941, 5.30 p.m., F.O. 371/33145.
[4] Eden, *Reckoning*, p. 199.
[5] Note handed to Eden by Koryzis, 22 Feb. 1941, F.O. 371/33145.

Near East. He went on to say that after the Greek appeal of 8 February for 'help and counsel', the British Government had decided 'to offer the maximum possible help to Greece at the earliest possible moment'. The forces available after the British victories in North Africa would, if the Greeks and the British were to agree on a good plan, give them 'a fair chance of halting a German invasion of Greece'. Eden then indicated what forces could be made available. These forces would be sent in three sections: (*a*) One division, one armoured brigade, and supporting arms including two regiments of medium artillery and some A.A. guns; (*b*) a second division and one Polish brigade; and (*c*) a third division and, if required, a second armoured brigade. The total strength of these forces would be: 100,000 men, 240 field guns, 202 A.T. guns, 32 medium guns, 192 light and heavy A.A. guns, and 142 tanks. Disembarkation of the first contingent would be completed by the thirtieth day after the decision to send the forces. Already shipping was being assembled for their transport. For the command of the British force, Wavell had decided to recommend General Wilson, commander in the recent victories in Libya; a recommendation that was promptly accepted by the Greek representatives. In the air the position was as follows: existing forces consisted of one Hurricane squadron, two Gladiator squadrons, four Blenheim squadrons, and one night squadron on a temporary loan basis. The British were prepared to send an additional Blenheim squadron at the end of February and in early March, re-equip the two Gladiator squadrons with Hurricanes during March, add two more Gladiator squadrons at the end of March, and possibly two more fighter squadrons. Furthermore, a total of twenty night-bombers could be operated from Athens at short notice. Finally, a number of modern aircraft were being supplied. Summing up, Eden said that this was the position as the British saw it, and that they 'could not look beyond a certain period', since it was impossible to foretell future developments.

Koryzis reaffirmed Greece's determination to defend herself against any attack, and said that any help from Britain 'was warmly welcomed'. But he took care to introduce the now customary note of prudence: the danger of precipitating a German attack. It was essential, he said, to consider 'whether the forces which Greece could make available and the forces which Great Britain could provide would, taking into account the dubious attitude of Yugoslavia and Turkey, be sufficient to provide effective assistance to Greece against German attack'. He raised this point, he said, 'as a purely military and not as a political question', and suggested that the military representatives should discuss it. But he asked for the British view on the attitude of Yugoslavia and Turkey and the contribution they might make towards resisting the Germans. Eden admitted that the British Government were not in a position to know the attitude of the two countries, but hoped to obtain an indication of Turkey's attitude during his forthcoming visit to Ankara. He emphasized, however, that the British and the Greeks should take their decisions 'independently of the attitude of Turkey and Yugoslavia'; otherwise 'it might be too late to organize an effective resistance to a German attack on Greece'. Koryzis's suggestion to avoid action which might provoke the Germans meant that the dispatch of British assistance must wait till Greece had been attacked. 'The British view was that the action must be taken at once, or it would be too late to send effective aid.' It was desirable to decide in principle 'whether the British forces would come or not', so that plans could be agreed upon. But Koryzis reiterated his view, and suggested that the military aspect should be discussed first. The British could do nothing but agree, and the conference adjourned so that the military representatives could hold a separate meeting.[1]

At the military conference Papagos, after briefly reviewing the situation on the Albanian front, gave an account of Greek plans and present disposition of forces. Greek forces in Eastern Macedonia consisted of three divisions, and in Thrace of thirteen battalions. There were no A.A. or A.T. guns in these areas. He then proceeded to discuss the choice of a defensive line. This depended on Yugoslavia's attitude, which was a political matter. The Greeks aimed 'to establish a front behind which forces from Albania could withdraw, since the moment Germany attacked, operations in Albania would have to be

[1] Record of the first Anglo-Greek meeting, 22 Feb. 1941, F.O. 371/33145. See also Eden, *Reckoning*, pp. 199–200; Papagos, *Battle of Greece*, pp. 264–5; Woodward, *British Foreign Policy*, vol. i, pp. 526 ff.

restricted to the defensive'. If Yugoslavia were to come in, 'the
line to be held would be one covering Salonika'. Otherwise,
there could be only one possible line: the Aliakmon line
(Mt. Olympus–Mt. Vermion–Mt. Kaimaktsalan). 'If this was
held, all troops to the east of it must be pulled in to hold it', or
they ran the danger of being cut off by the enemy. Papagos
also realized 'the extreme importance of time, which made it
impossible to wait for Yugoslavia and Turkey to declare
themselves'. He had therefore asked his Government for
permission to begin the withdrawal of troops from Macedonia
and Thrace before a German move made the withdrawal look
like retreat. When asked how he would propose to employ the
British force, 'if it were accepted as offered', he replied that
'it would all be needed on the Aliakmon line'. But Papagos
returned to the question of the Yugoslav factor. 'If Yugoslavia
said tonight that she was going to fight, the Greeks would hold
the Nestos line (the Metaxas line) and ask the British to land
at Salonika and Kavalla.' The British representatives were in
agreement with Papagos on the military views expressed by
him.[1] The least that can be said about Papagos's attitude at
this meeting is that it was ambivalent. In principle and in the
light of Yugoslavia's uncertain attitude, he seemed to prefer
the Aliakmon line, on which he was prepared to withdraw all
Greek forces to the east of that line. Yet, the prospect of Yugoslavia eventually deciding to join Britain and Greece made him
very reluctant to abandon the forward line based on the Nestos
River and the fortifications.

At the final plenary meeting, held at 10.45 that night,
Papagos gave a résumé of the military appreciation agreed
upon by the Greek and British representatives, which was that,
'in view of the dubious attitude of the Yugoslavs and the
Turks, it was not possible to contemplate holding the line
covering Salonika, and that the only sound line in view of the
circumstances was the line of the Aliakmon'. But he stressed
anew the importance of Yugoslavia's attitude, 'on which
depended the choice of the line to defend Greece'. Wavell
stated the British view that, in the light of the dubious attitude
of Yugoslavia and Turkey, 'the only reasonable course was to
make certain of the line indicated by Papagos (i.e. the Aliakmon

[1] Record of meeting, 22 Feb. 1941, F.O. 371/33145.

line)'. At this point Eden joined in to bring up certain 'political questions', since the military were in agreement, in principle, on what constituted the best line of defence. This effort to separate political from military considerations was unfortunate, because, as we have already seen, according to Papagos's appreciation of the situation, political and military considerations were, from the Greek point of view, tightly bound together. But the Greek Commander-in-Chief failed to raise this point, which was crucial to the strategy he had laid down himself. The attitude of Yugoslavia, Eden said, 'made it desirable, from the military point of view, to organize the Aliakmon line at the earliest possible moment'. Koryzis expressed agreement with this view. Eden then went on to say that 'military requirements demanded an immediate withdrawal of Greek forces in Eastern Macedonia to the Aliakmon line'. In view of the 'political aspect', there were three alternatives:

(*a*) To withdraw the troops without waiting for Yugoslavia to declare herself.
(*b*) To begin the withdrawal concurrently with an approach to the Yugoslav Government.
(*c*) To wait until Yugoslavia had made her intentions clear.[1]

It is necessary to pause briefly to consider these alternatives. The first was preferred by the military of both sides, by the British because it satisfied military considerations, and by the Greeks for the same reason, but only in principle. The third was contrary to the British decision to send forces to Greece at the earliest possible moment for reasons which have been described earlier. This alternative, however, corresponded with Greek plans and disposition of forces; and, although Papagos did not explicitly express his preference for this alternative, there is very little doubt that he preferred it to the other two. The second alternative was essentially a subtle combination of the first and the third, but it conflicted with the political end in mind and was therefore self-defeating; because the withdrawal of Greek forces from Eastern Macedonia ruled out any co-operation with Yugoslavia. As we shall see shortly, the agreement reached at the end of the conference included elements of all three alternatives.

[1] Record of meeting, 22 Feb. 1941, F.O. 371/33145.

To return now to the proceedings of the meeting, Eden said that he was not hopeful of obtaining a 'satisfactory indication of Yugoslavia's attitude too soon', but he was prepared to approach her by sending a staff officer to Prince Paul. Both sides, however, were doubtful as to how much could be disclosed to the Yugoslavs, and readily agreed to disclose as little as possible for security reasons. This was another weak point which, interestingly enough, failed to draw the attention of the representatives—if they did not intentionally turn a blind eye to it: the Yugoslavs were not prepared, and naturally so, to declare themselves, unless they knew as much as possible about Anglo-Greek aims and actual plans. Finally Eden suggested that 'decisions' should be taken on the following three points:

(i) Whether a British Staff Officer should be sent to Belgrade to see Prince Paul.

It was agreed that this should be done. (This decision was subsequently revoked, and it was decided instead to convey a message through the British Minister in Belgrade.)

(ii) Whether preparations should at once be made and put into execution to withdraw the Greek advanced troops in Thrace and Macedonia to the line which we should be obliged to hold if the Yugoslavs did not come in.

It was agreed that this should be done.

(iii) Whether work should at once be begun on the improvement of communications in Greece in order to facilitate the deployment of our mechanized forces.

It was agreed that this should be done.[1]

Eden's account of the Tatoi conference of 22 February, although it omits many important points, is an abbreviated version of the official British record and in agreement with it.[2] But Papagos has given a different account. He later maintained that before arriving at the grave decision to abandon Macedonia and Thrace it was necessary to ascertain beyond all doubt Yugoslavia's attitude; and that 'according to the reply received, the order for the evacuation would be issued or not, as the case might be'.[3] This divergence of views, besides the serious impact it had on the organization of defence against

---

[1] Record of the final plenary meeting, 22 Feb. 1941, F.O. 371/33145.
[2] Eden, *Reckoning*, pp. 200-1.   [3] Papagos, *Battle of Greece*, p. 265.

the Germans, involved the honour and good faith of the two allies. Did Papagos go back on his word? From the British records of the conference it seems that he did. But the records were not signed by the two parties, and this is perhaps what may account for the misunderstanding. All the same, Papagos's case is a poor one, even on the basis of his own account, and particularly in the light of the second round of Anglo-Greek talks in early March. There can be little doubt that from the military point of view the Aliakmon line was preferred by both parties: it was naturally strong and defensible. But was the attitude of Yugoslavia the deciding factor for withdrawing, or not, Greek troops as Papagos has maintained? According to Eden's and Dill's cables of 21 February, a line covering Salonika was not ruled out but left to be decided upon in common with the Greeks. But Papagos was the first to support the Aliakmon line, ruling out one in Eastern Macedonia on military grounds, notwithstanding even a favourable attitude on the part of Yugoslavia. Therefore, the second part of his argument—that decision on a defensive line depended on Yugoslavia's attitude—is not very convincing.

Papagos refers to the conference in rather general terms, and it seems that he was writing from memory or with the assistance of notes, if he did not intentionally pass over many important details referred to earlier.[1] One important omission concerns the actual decisions taken at the conference. As we have already seen, a decision was taken separately on each one of the three points agreed upon, that is the approach to Yugoslavia, the withdrawal of Greek forces to the Aliakmon line, and the improvement of communications. Thus, the decision to start withdrawing Greek troops at once to the Aliakmon line stood, irrespective of the approach to the Yugoslavs and their reply to that approach. Yet, it is not unlikely that Papagos did come away from the February talks with the impression that preparations

[1] The fate of the Greek record of the Tatoi conference remains a mystery to this day. In the official History of the Greek Army in the Second World War it is mentioned in passing that 'the official record, or copy of it, has not been found in the Foreign Ministry Archives, or in the General Staff Archives, and nor for that matter in any other State Archives'. *Struggles in Eastern Macedonia and Western Thrace, 1941* (in Greek), Athens, 1956, p. 47 n. Korozis, op. cit., vol. i, pp. 7–8, says that the record in question, along with the papers of the Commander-in-Chief's office and a selection of G.H.Q. papers, were put away into safety in April 1941 by order of Papagos.

I

for the withdrawal of Greek troops should await a clarification of Yugoslavia's attitude. The wording of the second—and
controversial—point leaves some room for misinterpretation.
It was agreed to start preparations for the withdrawal of Greek
troops to the line which would be held 'if the Yugoslavs did
not come in'; and it is possible that Papagos did interpret the
eventuality in quotes as a condition for starting the withdrawal. Moreover, although the decision to send a British staff
officer to Belgrade to sound Prince Paul was subsequently
revoked, an approach to Yugoslavia was not ruled out, and
was in fact made by the British Minister in Belgrade. Eden's
telegram to Churchill after the conference was over goes some
way to support Papagos's case. From the talks, Eden said,

it emerged that in view of the doubtful attitude of Yugoslavia the
only line that could be held and would give time for withdrawal of
troops from Albania would be a line west of the Vardar, Olympus–
Veria–Kaimaktsalan. If we could be sure of Yugoslav moves it
should be possible to hold a line further north from the mouth of
the Nestos to Beles covering Salonika. It would be impracticable,
unless Yugoslavia came in, to hold a line covering Salonika in view
of exposure of Greek left flank to German attack.

In full agreement with the Greek Government the following
detailed decisions were reached:

(a) In view of the importance of the Yugoslav attitude as affecting
the deployment of troops in Greece, it was agreed that I should
make a further effort to attempt to persuade the Yugoslav
Government to play their part.

(b) That the Greeks should at once make, and begin the execution of, preparations to withdraw the advance troops to the
line which we should have to hold if the Yugoslavs were not
willing to come in.

(c) That work should immediately be started on improving
communications in Greece to facilitate the occupation of this
line.

Eden went on to say that the British representatives were
impressed by the 'frankness and fair dealing' of the Greek
representatives, and were convinced of their determination to
resist the Germans. The British recognized the risks of the
undertaking, but they had to accept them.[1] Essentially, the

---

[1] Secretary of State to the Prime Minister, Athens Tel. No. 262, 21 Feb. 1941,
Cab. 105/2. This telegram is wrongly dated. The date must be 23 Feb. 1941.

two sides approached the issue from different points of view, and the fact that no agreement or records were signed left some room for different interpretations. Eden was determined (*a*) to urge the Greeks to accept the British forces as soon as possible, and (*b*) to persuade them to join the British in holding the Germans on the Aliakmon line. The British wanted to form a strong defensive line and to make the fight worth the serious drain on Middle East resources. In principle, the Greeks seemed to be in agreement with the British. But Papagos had already had to face grave pressures and material losses. The Albanian front was draining Greek resources, and a new war effort on the scale contemplated was almost beyond Greece's ebbing strength. In the circumstances, while there is no doubt that the Yugoslav factor preoccupied the Greek High Command, it is not unlikely that it was only an honourable pretext for not withdrawing the agreed forces to the Aliakmon line. The Greek army of Epirus was exhausted and ill supplied and, after four months of arduous fighting, was not in a position to undertake a further campaign. Moreover, the Greek General Staff did not look favourably on a withdrawal from Epirus and the occupied territory of Albania, thus turning the hard-won victories into ignominious retreat. On the other hand, withdrawal from Eastern Macedonia would be a serious blow to public morale in Greece, since a great segment of Greek territory, along with Salonika, would be abandoned to the enemy. Finally, the Greek military leadership, and particularly Papagos, could not easily bring themselves to abandon the defence works in Eastern Macedonia without a show of resistance; they had invested money and professional judgement in them and wished to prove that the works had not been constructed for nothing.[1] Only a week before the Tatoi conference, the commander of the Eastern Macedonian army had written to Papagos: 'The Greek army and people are convinced as a result of propaganda, films, etc., that this line is strongly fortified, and consider it, if not impregnable, at least hard for an enemy to break through, let alone capture. Consequently, its capture by the enemy without serious resistance would have a disastrous effect on the morale of both the army and the public.'[2]

---

[1] Papagos, *Battle of Greece*, pp. 261 ff.

[2] Report by Gen. Bakopoulos, commander of the Eastern Macedonian army, to

No doubt, the conference of 22 February was a success, so far as the British—or Eden at least—were concerned. The Greeks had accepted the British offer, and appeared to have agreed to hold the Germans on the Aliakmon line. Eden and his aides were triumphant: the part of their mission that concerned Greece was crowned with success.[1] A country whose independence Britain had publicly guaranteed had accepted the forces offered and on Britain's terms. The presence of British forces in Greece held out some hopes that Yugoslavia and Turkey would finally decide to join Britain and Greece against the Axis. But from the military point of view, there can be little doubt that the enterprise was unsound. The Greek army was exhausted and as ill supplied as ever; and Greek generals were preoccupied with the prosecution of the war against the Italians. British forces, though impressive on paper, were insufficient to check the Germans. Finally, the Germans were firmly fixed in their intention to extinguish any focus of resistance in the Balkans: the concentration of German troops in Romania was not a secret, nor by this time was it intended to be.

Eden had taken a grim decision in the teeth of many imponderables. Sceptics in the Foreign Office were not very happy about his having 'plumped' for helping Greece.[2] But the Chiefs of Staff endorsed Eden's proposals for sending an expeditionary force to Greece. In a report of 24 February they said that though the enterprise was a 'gamble' they accepted the opinion of the advisers on the spot, who felt that there was a reasonable prospect of successfully holding up a German advance. By sending forces to Greece, the British were taking 'the only chance of forming a Balkan front'. The formation of a Balkan front would have the following advantages: (a) it would make Germany fight at the end of a long line of communications and expend valuable resources uneconomically; (b) it would interfere with Germany's trade with the Balkans and particularly with oil supplies from Romania; (c) it would enable Britain to establish bases from which to launch air

Papagos, 16 Feb. 1941, included in his report to the Greek General Staff after the war, 14 Jan. 1942, War Archives, Greek General Staff, vol. F628. For a description of these Papers see p. 265 n.

[1] De Guingand, *Operation Victory*, p. 59.

[2] A. Cadogan, *Diaries, 1938–1945*, ed. D. Dilks, London, 1971, p. 358, 23 Feb. 1941.

attacks against Italy and the Romanian oilfields; and (*d*) it 'would keep the war going in Albania, and prevent Italy devoting her energies to re-establishing her position in North Africa'. If Britain were not to help Greece, Germany would seize control of the Balkans, and would (*a*) acquire air bases from which she could threaten Britain's Middle East position, (*b*) concentrate her efforts against Turkey, and (*c*) run oil from the Black Sea to the Adriatic.[1]

The disadvantages of the enterprise, according to the Chiefs of Staff, were many. The British were undertaking a commitment the extent of which they could not foresee. If all available forces were to be sent to Greece, nothing would be left for Turkey. Moreover, British forces in North Africa would be depleted; and the Axis, after building up their own forces, would seriously threaten Britain's position there. The dispatch of forces to Greece would also strain shipping; and if naval units had to be evacuated from the Mediterranean, the British forces in Greece would be stranded. Finally, once British forces were established in Greece, the Germans might well decide to attack Turkey instead. But there were weighty political considerations which tipped the balance in favour of sending forces to Greece:

> Politically, it seems to us that there would be serious disadvantages if we were to fail to help Greece. The effect on public opinion throughout the world, particularly America, of our deserting a small nation which is already engaged in a magnificent fight against one aggressor and is willing to defy another, would be formidable.

The conclusions of the Chiefs of Staff report to the Cabinet read:

> Our considered opinion is as follows: The possible military advantages to be derived from going to the help of Greece are considerable, though their achievement is doubtful and the risks of failure are serious. The disadvantages of leaving Greece to her fate will be certain and far reaching. Even the complete failure of an honourable attempt to help Greece need not be disastrous to our future ability to defeat Germany. A weighty consideration in favour of going to Greece is to make the Germans fight for what they want instead of obtaining it by default. On balance we think that the enterprise should go forward.

[1] W.P. (41) 39, Secret, 24 Feb. 1941, Cab. 66/15.

At a Cabinet meeting of the same day (24 February), Churchill said that it was necessary to decide whether to send forces to Greece. He was in favour of the enterprise, which might bring Turkey and Yugoslavia in and would force Germany to disperse her forces. Moreover, the effect on the United States would be favourable. To the Australian Prime Minister, who suggested that the venture had better be abandoned if it was only a 'forlorn hope', Churchill said that this was for the Australian Government to decide. In his opinion, the dispatch of forces to Greece was a risk which the Cabinet had to undertake. Besides, the enterprise in question was only an 'advance position', which the British could try to hold without jeopardizing their main position. Before deciding on the issue, Churchill invited the Cabinet to express their views. 'The views expressed were, without exception, in favour of sending military assistance to Greece.' Therefore, the Cabinet authorized Churchill to cable Eden that they approved the dispatch of help to Greece on the basis outlined by him.[1] Accordingly, Churchill gave the order: 'Full steam ahead'.[2] Cadogan now thought that 'on all moral and sentimental (and consequently American) grounds' the decision was perhaps the right one: the venture was bound to be a failure, but failure in a 'decent project' was better than no action whatever.[3]

The die was cast, but Eden's mission was only beginning. His Balkan interlude took him next to Ankara to inform the Turkish Government of the recent decision to send a British force to Greece and to enlist Turkey in a common effort against the impending German advance. The Turks approved of the British decision to help Greece, but were extremely reluctant to commit themselves. Turkey, they explained, lacked sufficient war machinery and aircraft, and could not possibly undertake offensive action. A less convincing explanation was their fear that the Germans might well aim to invade Turkey instead of Greece. None the less, they promised to fight back if attacked, and even considered concerted action if Yugoslavia was brought in. No doubt the Turks were unimpressed by the force the British proposed to send, much as

[1] W.M. (41) 20, Conclusions, 24 Feb. 1941, Cab. 65/21.
[2] Churchill, *Grand Alliance*, p. 76.
[3] Cadogan, *Diaries*, p. 358, 24 Feb. 1941.

they praised the decision in principle.[1] A similar approach to Yugoslavia produced no better results. The Yugoslav Government was too prudent, and hoped to avoid a German attack by not giving any provocation.[2] They had much to lose from a German attack, and something to gain as the prize for doing nothing at all, namely Salonika. With the exception of Greece, the Balkan states were not prepared, as Churchill wanted, to act at the wave of Britain's 'wand'.[3]

Extorted Agreement

On 1 March the first German army formations entered Bulgaria, and the following day Eden and his party flew from Ankara to Athens, where they were in for an unpleasant surprise. Papagos had not yet commenced the withdrawal of Greek troops to the Aliakmon line, as had been agreed on 22 February; and after the German entry into Bulgaria he was even less willing to order his troops to withdraw. Papagos had told Heywood that it was now too late to start this operation: it would take twenty days to complete the withdrawal and there was a danger of the troops being caught on the move by the Germans. Moreover, withdrawal from Eastern Macedonia in the face of the German presence in Bulgaria would alarm the local population and perhaps lead to a mass exodus. No troops had been withdrawn from the Albanian front either, because Papagos feared that a similar move would have had a disastrous effect on the morale of the troops.[4] He had been waiting for the Yugoslavs to clarify their position, and this was why he had kept postponing the withdrawal of troops. Papagos has subsequently maintained that he had repeatedly asked Heywood whether a reply from the Yugoslavs had been received, and on each occasion he had been informed that no such reply had materialized.[5]

Eden was convinced that there had been an 'unfortunate misunderstanding'. As far as he was concerned and according

[1] Eden, *Reckoning*, pp. 207, 208.

[2] Ibid., pp. 208, 209; Churchill, *Grand Alliance*, pp. 98 ff.

[3] Churchill, *Grand Alliance*, p. 95; Woodward, *British Foreign Policy*, vol. i, pp. 530 ff.

[4] Record of meeting held at the British Legation in Athens, 2 Mar. 1941, F.O. 371/33145.

[5] Papagos, *Battle of Greece*, p. 266.

to the agreement reached at the Tatoi conference, withdrawal of Greek troops must have commenced immediately after the conference. Dill was of the same opinion. Asked as to the line to take with the Greeks, he said: 'It would be militarily unsound to attempt to hold any line other than the Aliakmon line, or to hold that line with less than eight divisions (plus one division in reserve)', the necessary minimum agreed upon on 22 February. The British troops would be insufficient to hold this line, and therefore the Greeks had to provide the balance. Eden agreed that it was essential to get the 'minimum requisite troops' for that purpose, and said that he would bring up the subject at his audience with the King that day.[1]

At 10.45 that evening (2 March) a series of meetings commenced, which lasted two hours; but no agreement was reached. Asked by Koryzis about the attitude of Turkey and Yugoslavia, Eden took pains to explain the result of his approaches. The Turks had accepted the decision to send all available British forces to Greece, but were reluctant to commit themselves, fearing that the German attack might be delivered at Turkey. Eden had suggested that Turkey should declare war on Germany if Germany were to attack Greece, but the Turkish attitude on this question was 'indefinite'. He was convinced of the determination of the Turks 'to play their part', but their forces were not in a condition to undertake offensive action. As for the attitude of Yugoslavia, he had insufficient information and therefore could not possibly count on her. The Yugoslavs were 'unsettled and frightened', but the British Minister in Belgrade thought that they might be more willing to come in if they knew about British plans. This, although appreciated at the Tatoi conference, had been considered too dangerous for fear of leakage to the Germans. Eden was prepared to send a further message to Prince Paul, but the British Minister in Belgrade, who was present at the meeting, had now very little hope that the Yugoslav reply would be favourable. Eden said: 'We need not despair of Prince Paul but cannot count on him.'[2]

Koryzis reiterated Greece's determination to resist Germany

---

[1] Record of meeting held at the British Legation, 2 Mar. 1941, F.O. 371/33145.
[2] Record of meeting held at the Presidency of the Council, 2 Mar. 1941, F.O. 371/33145.

and Italy, but said that the negative attitude of Turkey and Yugoslavia was a 'great disappointment'. From the Turks the Greek Government had received a statement that they would declare war on Germany if she were to attack Greece. 'As regards Yugoslavia, the Greek Government had been convinced that she would help too.' The Greeks, Koryzis said, had 'counted' on Turkey and Yugoslavia; but despite their disappointment, they were resolved to fight the Germans and continue the war against the Italians. 'For the purpose of facing a German attack in Macedonia the Greeks had only three divisions plus whatever troops the British could send.' Eden checked Koryzis saying:

This very question had been examined the previous week at Tatoi and . . . both General Papagos and General Wavell had thought that there were good chances of Anglo-Greek forces holding the Aliakmon line. Moreover, when the matter had been discussed at Tatoi and it had been agreed to hold the Aliakmon line, we had taken our decision on the basis that the Turks and Yugoslavs would not come in. There was thus no change in the situation, and [the British] were at a loss to understand the disappointment which the Greeks now expressed at the attitude of the Turks and the Yugoslavs.

Koryzis had little to say as an answer to Eden. He only said that whatever had happened, even if both the front in Albania and that in Macedonia were to collapse, 'the Greek Government would go to Crete or some other island and would continue the struggle at the side of Great Britain'. But Eden was mainly concerned about the present, not the future. With regard to a defensive line, he thought, things did not look so black as Koryzis had implied; and his military advisers thought that the Aliakmon line had good chances of being held. Koryzis must have sensed Eden's desire to hold the Aliakmon line at all costs, for he turned the conversation in another direction. The Greek people needed evidence of effective help. 'The soul of Greece is brave but sensitive', he said. In order to continue their heroic resistance, the Greeks needed moral and material encouragement. And he asked whether the British could meet the Greeks on the following points: (i) The abolition of the International Financial Commission; (ii) The promise that the question of Cyprus would be settled according to

Greek desires; (iii) An undertaking to use the Greek Dodecanese Legion in any operations for the capture of the Dodecanese.

Eden was caught unawares and was hard put to it to reply to these awkward points. He said that the first 'could be examined' by the Greek Government and the British Legation. As for the second, 'he was not prepared to discuss such a wide political question in connection with the present problem which was the purely strategical one of putting up the best possible combined resistance to a German attack'. Finally, Eden was prepared to discuss with Wavell the third point raised by Koryzis. After dealing with the political questions, Eden went on to say that on the assumption that it was agreed to hold the Aliakmon line, the British had already started sending troops; but now they were told of 'difficulties' in holding that line. Koryzis tried to counter Eden's charge with an argument that was new and left something to be desired. The Greeks, he said, 'had only accepted the Aliakmon line on the assumption that the necessary withdrawals of troops from Albania and Macedonia could be made in time before the Germans arrived. They now thought that there was not enough time.' This was a poor display by the Greek President of the Council. The meeting then adjourned for the military to decide whether there was still time to form a defensive line on the Aliakmon, or not.

At the military meeting Dill pressed the British position that they should push on with preparations to hold the Aliakmon line. The transport of British troops to Greece, he said, 'was being accelerated as far as possible', and General Wilson, commander of the expeditionary force, was due to arrive in Athens the following day. As to the Yugoslav attitude, there was simply not enough satisfactory or definite information; and therefore there was no sense in waiting for further information from that quarter. Now, he went on, it was even more important than before to carry out the agreed plan. But Papagos used the time factor to support the Greek position. Was there enough time to concentrate and deploy the troops on the Aliakmon line? German troops were already in Bulgaria, and a German attack could be expected in about ten days' time. He needed at least fifteen days to move troops from Thrace and Macedonia to the Aliakmon line. Naturally, no troop movement had yet commenced: 'he had been waiting, as agreed at Tatoi, for a firm reply from Yugoslavia'. As might be expected, Dill supported the opposite view. Some bitter exchanges followed. Papagos dug his heels in. He had understood that they must wait for a reply from Yugoslavia since, if Yugoslavia did enter the war on the allied side, the Aliakmon line was not the best line to hold, because it would drive Yugoslavia into Germany's arms. The conversation was leading nowhere.

Dill wavered before Papagos's unaccommodating mood. Where, then, he asked, should British forces be disembarked? At Salonika and Kavalla, was Papagos's prompt reply; so that, if these forces were not to deploy on the Aliakmon line, they could have gone to the Bulgarian frontier to stiffen Greek resistance on the fortified line. Asked by Dill whether the Greek offensive in Albania was given up and if so whether some troops could be transferred from that front, Papagos said that the army had passed 'from the offensive to an offensive–defensive' but no troops could be withdrawn; the Italians were greatly superior in numbers. Dill tried to explain the danger to the ships and troops in the event of landing troops in Macedonia. But Papagos pursued his own line. An attempt to defend Salonika would have a favourable effect on Yugoslavia, and might have influenced her to come in. And to Dill's point that the British forces might be too late in arriving on the Macedonian front, Papagos said that he preferred to fight on prepared positions with a better chance of holding them than on unprepared positions and with a chance of being caught on the move back to them. The Generals were unable to reach agreement at this stage, and joined the civil representatives to reconcile their positions.

But the full meeting did not produce any better results. The main point of discussion concerned the 'misunderstanding', and both positions were stated with equal force. The meeting broke up to allow Dill and Papagos to discuss anew the question of a defensive line. The British position was that if the Greeks tried to hold the Germans on the Macedonian front and the British tried to do the same on the Aliakmon line, allied forces would have been weak on both lines and would be defeated comprehensively. Papagos agreed, but reiterated his position that the Greeks could not withdraw from Albania or from Macedonia without 'grave risks'. And he repeated his justification for what was really closer to his heart; if the Yugoslavs were to fight, the Greeks would have to stand on the forward line. The meeting broke up with Dill saying: 'General Papagos will have to fight the battle.' It was a statement which was left without comment.[1]

Faced with a serious deadlock and a possible breakdown of the talks, Eden summoned Wavell to Athens on 3 March. A new meeting was held at 6.30 p.m. the same day at which the British and Greek military representatives tried again to smooth out their differences and reach an agreement on the defensive line to hold against the Germans. But the presence of Wavell simply added one more voice in favour of the British interpretation of the Tatoi agreement. There were some bitter exchanges between Wavell and Papagos, which only went to increase the existing tension. Papagos refused to withdraw any troops from Macedonia, and recommended instead that the British troops should go, if time permitted, to Macedonia as well as to the Aliakmon line. Dill stressed the risk he was taking in using the only strategic reserves of Britain in the Middle East, and the certain disaster they faced if they were dribbled into an 'uncoordinated battle'. 'The problem was insoluble', Papagos said, and came very close to relieving the British of their promise to help Greece: 'Greece was now facing two great Powers; she had fought one of them for four months and had reached the limits of her power and endurance; she was most grateful for the help which Great Britain had already afforded and now proposed to offer, but this help was limited.' The discussion could not be carried any further, and the matter was referred to Eden.[2]

At 11.00 a.m. the next day the military representatives met again. In the meantime, advice or pressure from above had produced a telling effect on Papagos. He now said that 'he had re-examined the problem in the light of the great importance attached to the arrival of British forces in Greece', and offered three divisions for the Aliakmon line. Apparently, the King had spoken to Papagos, who had been obliged to back down. As a result of the new situation, Dill and Wavell left the meeting

[1] Records of meetings, 2–3 Mar. 1941, F.O. 371/33145.
[2] Record of meeting held at the British Legation, 3 Mar. 1941, F.O. 371/33145.

to re-examine Papagos's proposals; and after discussing them with Eden, they concluded that the troops offered represented too small a force. In announcing the British decision, Dill also said that Eden, Wavell, and himself had in the meantime asked for an interview with the King, who had agreed to meet them at the British Legation in the afternoon. Papagos must have sensed trouble, for he brought up again the question of the 'misunderstanding'. He insisted on what he had said at the meeting of 2 March, 'that the plan for the Aliakmon line had been based on waiting for a clarification of the attitude of Yugoslavia and that he had daily asked, after the conversations at Tatoi, whether any reply had been received from Prince Paul'. The meeting came to an end with Dill saying that no doubt a misunderstanding had occurred, and that it was now necessary 'to take the situation as it was and re-examine it'.[1]

At the next meeting, at which King George was also present, Papagos went back to the attack and reiterated his previous position. He opened the proceedings by giving an account of the situation as it appeared to him. The only sound plan was 'to build on the existing three divisions in Macedonia and resist the Germans on the fortified and organized position along the Nestos–Rupel line [the Metaxas line]'. From the political point of view also it was necessary to hold this line since the Yugoslav attitude was still undecided. Dill resented this departure from the morning proposal which, though unsatisfactory from the British point of view, provided some ground for discussion. Papagos now veered round again to his morning position, adding seven battalions to the initial offer of three divisions. If the British would agree to accept this offer, he would make the forces available, though he still did not regard it as the best solution. This was probably the best the British could hope for, and Dill promptly snatched at it. He accepted the offer saying that 'the British generals thought it a reasonable plan'. A show of determination on both sides was now called for. Papagos gave an assurance that he would carry out his mission as Commander-in-Chief of the Anglo-Greek forces with 'confidence and determination'. Dill said that the British were 'confident' of holding the Germans on the Aliakmon line. And King George joined in with an unexpected salvo: 'His Majesty

[1] Record of meeting, 4 Mar. 1941, F.O. 371/33145.

the King said that General Papagos, *now that he had decided to face the Germans,* would do it with the same determination whatever the troops available and whatever plan was adopted.'[1] A more explicit charge of wavering in the presence of foreign representatives could not have been made. Papagos left the King's charge unanswered. Eden then announced, after consulting Dill in private, that the British Government would be prepared to accept Papagos's plan, provided that the Greeks would concentrate on the Aliakmon line three divisions and seven battalions, as Papagos had proposed. It was finally agreed to draw up a note, embodying the decisions which had been reached, for signature by Papagos and Dill, 'in order that no misunderstanding might arise in the future'. Papagos and Wilson then discussed the details of the plan with regard to concentration and deployment of the Anglo-Greek forces on the Aliakmon line.

The decisions taken as a result of the discussions between the Greek and the British High Commands were put on paper and were signed by Papagos and Dill. Thus, the Greeks would leave in Macedonia only three divisions to fight on the fortified line, and would concentrate on the Aliakmon line with all possible speed the 12th division and seven battalions from Thrace, the 20th division from Florina, and the 19th motorized division from Larissa. The British forces would be dispatched as rapidly as shipping would permit, and would concentrate on the Aliakmon line, on which the combined forces would give battle. The command of all the forces on the Aliakmon line would be entrusted to General Wilson under the high command of General Papagos. In case Wilson disagreed with Papagos, the matter would be referred to Wavell; and if he in turn were unable to settle the matter with Papagos, it would be referred to the British Government.[2] It was a pitiful compromise, but something for Eden to take home.

In a telegram of 5 March to Churchill, Eden informed the British Government of the agreement reached by the Greek and the British High Commands. He explained that the British representatives had to accept the Greek forces offered by Papagos for the Aliakmon line. They recognized the dangers

[1] Record of meeting, 4 Mar. 1941, F.O. 371/33145. Italics added.
[2] Text of the Anglo-Greek agreement of 4 Mar. 1941 in F.O. 371/33145.

involved, but 'did not consider it by any means a hopeless proposition to check and hold the German advance' on the Aliakmon line. To have accepted Papagos's proposal to send British forces to the Metaxas line would have been disastrous; while withdrawal of the British offer of assistance altogether would have led to the rapid elimination of Greece from the war and would have had an unfavourable effect on the Middle East, the Near East, the Empire, and America. It was a 'correct decision' in a changed and difficult situation, Eden said.[1] But in London the decision was received with mixed feelings. The Cabinet agreed that the situation had changed for the worse since February, and that it might be necessary to 'reconsider' the recent decision. At the same time it was agreed that no immediate decision was called for, at least until the Yugoslav attitude had been assessed. The Cabinet further decided that Churchill should cable Eden 'setting out the doubts expressed in [the] decision in the War Cabinet as to the wisdom of proceeding with the enterprise'.[2]

Writing to Eden on 6 March, Churchill expressed grave doubts about the Athens agreement and the circumstances under which it had been reached. The new situation, he said, made it difficult for the Cabinet to believe that the British had now any power 'to avert [the] fate of Greece', unless Turkey and Yugoslavia were to come in: the British had done their best to promote a Balkan front against Germany. Of Eden's strenuous efforts in Athens he said: 'We must be careful not to urge Greece against her better judgement into a hopeless resistance alone when we have only handfuls of troops which can reach [the] scene in time.' Moreover, the commitment of New Zealand and Australian troops to a hazardous enterprise raised 'grave Imperial issues', and the assent of the Dominion Governments was doubtful. The Greeks, he went on to say, should be liberated 'from feeling bound to reject a German ultimatum', unless on their own they were resolved to fight, in which case the British had 'to some extent to share their ordeal'. Churchill also sent a Chiefs of Staff commentary which said: 'Our conclusion is that the hazards of the enterprise have

---

[1] Athens Tel. No. 313, 5 Mar. 1941, Cab. 105/2. See also Eden, *Reckoning*, pp. 211–12; Churchill, *Grand Alliance*, pp. 99–100.

[2] W.M. (41) 24, Conclusions, 5 Mar. 1941, Cab. 65/22.

considerably increased. Nevertheless, despite our misgivings and our recognition of a worsening of the general situation, we are not as yet in a position to question the military advice of those on the spot, who in their latest telegram describe the enterprise as not by any means hopeless.'[1]

More serious doubts were raised at a Cabinet meeting on 6 March. Churchill stressed his anxiety lest the Greeks felt that the British had put 'undue pressure' on them and had persuaded them against their better judgement. Sir Robert Menzies, the Australian Prime Minister, was dissatisfied with Eden's decision. 'The War Cabinet had not', he thought, 'been well informed of the facts; and the action of the Foreign Secretary regarding the military agreement between General Dill and General Papagos was embarrassing.' He had had difficulties in persuading his Government in February, when the military advisers in the Middle East considered that the operation, though hazardous, offered reasonable chances of success. Now, he said, all kinds of difficulties had been brought forward, but no reason had been given why the operation would succeed. Churchill was shaken by the force of Menzies's arguments, but personally felt that the British Government could not possibly 'go back' on the Athens agreement, unless the Greeks themselves released them. As a result, it was decided to defer a decision until Eden's reply to Churchill's telegram had been received. At the same time, Eden was informed of the Cabinet decision.[2]

Eden stood firm by his decision. Replying to Churchill, he said that he and the others were 'unanimously agreed' that, despite the risks involved, the 'right decision' had been taken. For support, he referred to Palairet's views, who was unreservedly in favour of honouring the Athens agreement.[3] Palairet felt strongly that there could be no way back, for the effect of withdrawing from the agreement would have been disastrous. The British could not possibly abandon King George after the assurances given to him as to the reasonable chances of success.

[1] Churchill to Eden, Tels. Nos. 607 and 608, 6 Mar. 1941, Cab. 105/2. See also Churchill, *Grand Alliance*, pp. 101–2; Woodward, *British Foreign Policy*, vol. i, pp. 532, 533.

[2] W.M. (41) 25, Conclusions, 6 Mar. 1941, Cab. 65/22. Also Churchill, *Grand Alliance*, p. 104.

[3] Churchill, *Grand Alliance*, p. 104.

There was no question of liberating the Greeks from feeling duty bound to resist the Germans, because they were determined to fight alone if necessary. Besides, both King George and Papagos were now confident that there was a chance of the Germans bloodying their nose in Greece.[1] Replying to another telegram from Churchill, dated 7 March, in which the Prime Minister said that he needed something more in the way of concrete facts, besides reasons of *noblesse oblige*, to justify the operation, Eden stressed that the Greeks had made plain their determination to resist the Germans, and had consistently maintained this attitude. There was no question of their feeling duty bound to fight, but simply their realization that there was no way out by way of honourable peace when the Italians and the Germans menaced their country. He also did not fail to refer to the calamitous effect of Greece's collapse on Yugoslavia and Turkey, if Britain were not to help.[2]

The Cabinet reluctantly gave in, and endorsed Eden's action. The military advisers on the spot were convinced that the Greek campaign would not be a hopeless venture, and the Chiefs of Staff were prepared to accept their judgement and adhered to their former opinion that the enterprise should go forward. Churchill saw a fair prospect of reaching the Aliakmon line in time to check the Germans; and, though the Yugoslavs were adopting a 'cryptic' attitude, he had not lost hope entirely. His view was: 'We should go forward with a good heart.' Menzies questioned the soundness of the decision, but agreed with Churchill that the operation should go forward. The Cabinet, therefore, confirmed the decision to send military assistance to Greece, and decided that all necessary arrangements to this end should proceed forthwith.[3]

The decision of the British Government to send troops to Greece satisfied the need to make a gesture of support to a country publicly guaranteed by Britain, a country moreover resolved to resist the Germans even alone if necessary; and at the same time it made it more likely that Yugoslavia and Turkey might finally decide to join in a common effort against Germany. The presence of British forces in Greece satisfied both political and military considerations, which in this case were closely

[1] Ibid., p. 103.   [2] Ibid., pp. 105–6.
[3] W.M. (41) 26, Conclusions, 7 Mar. 1941, Cab. 65/22.

linked. By the end of the first week of March, however, any military advantages that might have been expected looked more theoretical than real. The allocation of forces agreed upon on 4 March made it almost certain that the British and the Greeks would lose everything except their honour. This applied especially to the Greek Government and the High Command, who were resolved to make a last stand and fall honourably before abandoning an inch of Greek soil. But this attitude was not shared by everyone in Greece. The staff of the Western Macedonian army put forward on 1 March a plan covering the possibility of German invasion. To guard against the danger of being outflanked by the Germans, the Western Macedonian army would retire to the south on a line running from east to west, Aliakmon–Venetikos–Pindus Range, while the Epirus army would hold the line to the west. The fall back from the Albanian front would be facilitated by placing three divisions to guard the approaches from the east, on a position roughly the same as the Aliakmon line. It was believed that if this plan was carried out in good time, there were reasonable chances of successfully defending Old Greece throughout 1941, and that the Greek army would remain 'an important factor in the Balkans'. This plan was submitted to the Greek High Command on 4 March, but was rejected.[1] A fresh effort in the same direction later in the month did not fare any better.[2] The High Command would prefer to leave the army victorious against the Italians and have it fight against the Germans only to save the honour of Greek arms. Papagos's initial position remained unchanged: in case of German invasion, the main Greek effort would still be made on the Albanian front, so that the Greek army would always preserve its position as victor against the Italians.[3]

At the same time, the Greek High Command had to deal with criticism of the Anglo-Greek agreement by Cabinet members, especially Maniadakis. As a colonel in the Asia Minor campaign, Maniadakis considered the Anglo-Greek plan had no chance at all of holding up the Germans on the Aliakmon line, and feared that the Greeks would be forced to abandon the mainland after a short fight. While still in Athens

---

[1] Katheniotis, *Strategic Phases of the War*, pp. 122–6.
[2] Tsolakoglou, *Memoirs*, p. 63.   [3] Papagos, *Battle of Greece*, p. 254.

and on being informed of Maniadakis's views and his 'very defeatist mood', Eden saw the King on 5 March. Eden pointed out that 'it was deplorable if Greek Ministers, especially one so influential as Monsieur Maniadakis, were in so defeatist a state of mind', and persuaded the King that Maniadakis should have a talk with Dill and Wilson. As a result of this intervention with the King, the British generals and Maniadakis met the same day, but not before the King reproved his Minister, who arrived at the meeting in a 'much firmer frame of mind' than earlier in the day. Maniadakis assured the British that they 'could rely on him for entire co-operation in all matters'.[1]

About the same time, the Germans decided to liquidate Greece at all costs, their hopes of making her give in without a fight having vanished by early March. The Anglo-Greek Staff talks of January, February, and early March did not pass unnoticed, and the landing of British troops at Piraeus in early March strengthened Germany's decision to proceed with the plan for the attack and occupation of Greece. Throughout the first half of March several Greek attempts to ward off German invasion through diplomacy were cut short by the German Government. Similar approaches were made by General Pangalos, the dictator of the mid-twenties, who proposed to establish a pro-Axis Government and bring the war with Italy to an end, as well as by Mavroudis, who sounded the Germans about the possibility of an honourable peace with Italy and the withdrawal of British forces from Greece. It is said that Greek army circles made a similar, though unofficial, approach to the Germans. But Hitler was now determined to throw the British out of Greece by force;[2] and when the Yugoslav Government finally signed the Tripartite Pact on 25 March, the road to Greece became wide open and safe.

In Greece, notwithstanding the resolve of the Government to make a stand at all costs, the situation became more and more desperate following the entry of German troops into Bulgaria. The withdrawal of the Greek forces from Thrace sounded the alarm for the local population and the authorities, who started deserting the area for the interior. To pacify the

---

[1] Minute by Pierson Dixon, Eden's Foreign Office aide in the mission to Greece, 5 Mar. 1941, F.O. 371/29855.
[2] Creveld, *Hitler's Strategy*, p. 133.

people, who were overcome by panic, a team of Ministers, headed by Kotzias, hurried to northern Greece. In Kavalla, unemployed workers were promised increased unemployment benefits, and farmers were informed of a number of beneficial measures. In Komotini, strenuous efforts were made to pacify the population, especially the poorer classes, and to check the looting of shops and storerooms. In Alexandroupolis, 3,000 rifles were distributed among the people to protect themselves against possible inroads of Bulgarian 'comitadjis'.[1]

On the Albanian front the German threat had a disastrous effect on the morale of both officers and men, especially after the enemy had entered Bulgaria. The dismissal of two corps commanders and other changes in the army commands[2] did not go very far to raise deteriorating morale. It was not so much defeatism, but rather the fear of being attacked from the rear, an eventuality which became more real every day, and to which the High Command seemed to be oblivious. In Eastern Macedonia the Greek forces waited for the onslaught determined to give battle for the honour of Greek arms. On 25 March a last attempt was made by the British to induce Papagos to order the Greek forces in Eastern Macedonia to retire to the Aliakmon line, offering to provide the necessary transport facilities to rush the troops to the line.[3] At a meeting in Athens on 26 March, General Kotoulas, commander of the Greek forces on the Aliakmon line, and General Bakopoulos, commander of the forces on the Metaxas line, supported the British proposal to withdraw the forces from the advanced line. They were convinced that to abandon the troops there was tantamount to condemning them to captivity. Papagos, though he recognized this danger, stood firmly by his initial decision and made it clear that what was expected of the troops on the Metaxas line was to fight only for the honour of Greek arms.[4]

The Belgrade coup of 27 March, which overthrew the Government and deposed Prince Paul, radically changed the situation in the Balkans, or appeared to have done so. Eden and his team rushed to Athens and held yet another round of

[1] K. Kotzias, *Greece, Her War and Glory* (in Greek), 3rd edn., Athens, 1947, pp. 241 ff.

[2] Tsolakoglou, op. cit., pp. 60 ff.

[3] Papagos, *The Battle of Greece*, p. 269.

[4] Katheniotis, *Strategic Phases of the War*, p. 150.

talks with the Greeks, in view of the new Yugoslav attitude. Papagos gave his view of the strategic requirements in the new circumstances. As a first phase he envisaged 'a solid and continuous defensive front from the Adriatic to the Black Sea'. For that purpose rapid decisions in both political and military spheres were necessary. Yugoslavia would have to lend a hand in Albania, and this would go a long way in clearing up the situation on the Albanian front. As a result, Greek troops would be released for employment in the Macedonian sector. With regard to the Macedonian front, Papagos maintained that it was now advisable to reinforce it with all available Anglo-Greek forces.[1]

Papagos's grandiose plan did not go very far towards convincing the British. It was necessary first to make arrangements with the Yugoslavs and to induce the Turks to come in. Eden's approaches to the new Yugoslav Government had not as yet produced a reply, and reports from the British Minister in Belgrade suggested that the situation there was still fluid. As for the Turks, it was more than doubtful that they would be willing to fight for Salonika or to take the initiative with the Yugoslavs. Dill also pointed out the difficulties in constituting a continuous front, as Papagos wanted. The country was good for the full employment of the enemy's armour; the Macedonian and Thracian ports were vulnerable to air attacks; and the front had very little depth. Neither side was prepared to move from its initial position, and the military representatives were once more left alone to square their differences. The British now tried to secure what little they had gained at the beginning of the month. The military meeting produced no concrete results except agreement on the line to be taken with the Yugoslavs.

The mission to Yugoslavia was entrusted to no less a person than the C.I.G.S. But the Yugoslavs were evasive to the new British approach. Dill pressed them to promise that they would launch an attack against the Germans in southern Bulgaria, if the Germans were to attack Greece at the Greco-Bulgarian frontier, but the Yugoslavs did not consider that such an attack on Greece was likely. They expected instead a German attack in southern Yugoslavia, and therefore asked the British to

[1] Record of meeting, 28 Mar. 1941, F.O. 371/33145.

threaten the enemy left flank from the south-east. As to Yugoslavia's attitude with regard to the Tripartite Pact, the Yugoslavs were again evasive. The Prime Minister told Dill that he would neither denounce nor implement the pact. The Yugoslavs also ruled out staff talks on a political basis, and only agreed to send a staff officer to concert plans with the British and the Greeks. Dill returned from Belgrade almost empty-handed.[1] And the Anglo-Greek–Yugoslav talks the next day (3 April) did not produce any concrete results either. The Yugoslavs were simply left unimpressed by the size of the British forces in Greece.[2] The German threat had paralysed all action in the Balkans, and last-minute attempts by Britain to form a block under her auspices were of no avail. The Balkan countries were soon to pay for their past mistakes, or simply because they were small and weak and in Germany's way; and the British would pay for attempting to do something that ought to have been attempted long before and with more substance in it.

[1] Record of meeting held at the British Legation in Athens, 2 Apr. 1941, F.O. 371/33145.

[2] Record of Anglo-Greek–Yugoslav talks held on the Greco-Yugoslav frontier, 3 Apr. 1941, F.O. 371/33145.

IX

Military and Political Crisis, April 1941

The story of the battle of Greece has been told often and with
varying success. We must leave to military historians the task
of providing an accurate account of the fighting and of making
an evaluation of the tactical and strategic decisions that were
taken. We do not possess, as yet, a wholly satisfactory exposi-
tion of these problems. Here attention will be focused on the last
act of the Greek drama, when army, regime, and country
collapsed in defeat, humiliation, treason, and chaos. The
account will not be exhaustive—much more than the available
Greek sources is needed for that; but it will attempt to provide
glimpses of what happened in the fateful April of 1941, as the
army disintegrated and authority broke down. Metaxas's
pride, the flimsy structure he had built through four-and-a-half
years of hard work, repression, propaganda, and tightrope
tactics collapsed like a house of cards. Death saved him the
anguish of seeing Greece defeated and occupied by the enemy
he had admired all his life. Like Metaxas and King George,
many Greeks felt that small and poor countries like Greece
should at least save their honour; but claims to honour, as we
shall see, were conflicting. Even now it is not easy to say
whether the King or the army leadership had a better claim
to honour. At the time, judgement was made more difficult by
the unprecedented disaster. The attitude of the King and many
of his subjects was eloquently expressed by Aghnidis, the Greek
Under-Secretary-General of the League of Nations. Speaking to
Bova Scopa, the Italian Minister in Lisbon, who tried in early
March 1941 to make him see 'sense' and intervene with the
Greek Government to come to terms with Italy, Aghnidis said:

My countrymen are an obstinate and uncompromising lot when
it comes to matters concerning their country's independence and
honour. Maybe . . . we shall disappear as a nation, as you seem to
imply, but even then it would be in a good cause; it would be

preferable for the Greek survivors to be able to relish the fact that honour was saved and that modern Greece had done something to justify its ancient origins and existence rather than live dishonoured and despised. Nothing is ever really lost and our example may still be useful in rousing people to their duty, even if everything is at stake.[1]

In April 1941 the battle of Greece was in its last and most dramatic stage. The Greek and British allies were reaping the bitter harvest of vacillation, unsound strategy, and hasty decisions, as well as having to fight against great odds. On 6 April the German Twelfth army opened the attack from Bulgaria against southern Yugoslavia and northern Greece. Two German army corps attacked the Metaxas line in Eastern Macedonia, but met with stiff resistance. The campaign, however, was decided in southern Yugoslavia, where the Germans faced a single Yugoslav army corps. On 7 April the Germans broke through the Yugoslav defences. German units now advanced in the direction of Monastir, while to the east other units moved down the Axios valley. On the 9th German advance units entered Salonika: the fate of the Metaxas line was sealed. The following day hostilities in Eastern Macedonia ended as the Greek forces on the Metaxas line laid down their arms. The Germans now threatened to turn the right of the Anglo-Greek forces (W Force) deployed on the Aliakmon line, as they prepared to advance south along the Aegean coast. In the west, German units advanced south in the direction of Florina threatening to turn both the left of the Aliakmon line and the right and rear of the Albanian front, where the Greek army, some fourteen divisions strong, held a wide front against the Italians. The only sound decision on the part of Gen. Papagos, the allied Commander-in-Chief, at this point would have been to order the retreat of the Greek forces facing the Italians to link up with W Force, before the enemy advance drove a wedge between them. The order to retire south was only issued on 12 April, too late as we shall see. W Force faced a similar danger. As early as 8 April, it had become apparent that the disposition of W Force needed adjustment in order to face a German thrust through the Monastir Gap.

---

[1] Record of conversation, 3 Mar. 1941, supplied to the Foreign Office by the British Legation in Berne, F.O. 371/29843.

On 10 April, Papagos ordered the withdrawal of W Force to an intermediary position to protect its left. The following day the Germans began to probe the line, and launched an attack on the 12th, which in fact started the long and arduous retreat of the defenders from one position to the next. The brief period from 12 April, when the Greek forces in Albania were ordered to retire south, until the 23rd, when the King and Government of Greece left the capital for Crete and Gen. Tsolakoglou signed the final protocol of armistice, was a time of serious military and political crisis, the details of which are still very little known.[1]

The military situation on the Albanian front had become by 12 April very critical. The will to fight had been broken under the strain of fighting a six-month winter campaign, in which the Greek army had performed prodigies of valour. What the Greek forces, officers and men alike, feared most and were eager to avoid at all costs was humiliating surrender to the Italians whom they had defeated and held in contempt. By this time it was commonly felt that to continue the war against the new and more formidable aggressor was futile. Battle-weary and demoralized, but determined all the same to avoid surrender to a defeated enemy, the Greek army in Albania saw capitulation to the Germans as the only honourable solution. This was proposed to Gen. Pitsikas, commander of Epirus army (1st and 2nd army corps), by the commander of 1st army corps, Gen.

[1] The best source for the period under consideration are the War Archives of the Greek General Staff, which unfortunately are closed to public inspection. The present author was given permission to read a number of volumes in the summer of 1975, on the understanding that the notes would be submitted at the end to the Historical Section of the General Staff for inspection. A considerable number of notes referring to desertion, disintegration of units, irregular activities of local authorities, and particularly critical opinion of Gen. Papagos's attitude were withdrawn by the Historical Section. The War Archives include a large number of lengthy reports by field commanders submitted to the General Staff after 1941. Attached to these reports are many G.H.Q., army, corps, and divisional orders. Also included are diaries of various units, but in a typed form. A considerable amount of material is missing, lost in one way or another or burned during the evacuation of the Government in April 1941. The volume of the official History of the Greek Army in the Second World War, *To telos mias epopoiias, Aprilios 1941* (The End of an Epic, April 1941), Athens, 1959, which covers this period, is based primarily on information drawn from a number of field commander reports. It has the merits and shortcomings of most official histories, in this case the shortcomings being more obvious, as the volume covers a most critical and tragic period of modern Greece.

Demestichas, as early as 1 April. This was also the view of the commander of 2nd army corps, Gen. Bakos, who believed that withdrawal from the Albanian front at that late stage would lead to the disintegration of the army. Pitsikas's reaction to the proposal put forward by Demestichas was to reprimand the general; but on 11 April, and after renewed pressure from his commanders, he sent the following cable to G.H.Q., Athens: 'Corps commanders inform me that recent developments, following German invasion, have affected troops. They believe that a retreat in depth may lead to shameful disintegration of the army, and make an appeal for solution securing salvation and prestige of our victorious army.'[1]

Gen. Tsolakoglou, commander of the Western Macedonian army (formerly 3rd army corps), was also in favour of a 'solution' and he pressed Pitsikas and G.H.Q. for a decision at the earliest possible moment. The Western Macedonian army held the right of the Albanian front and was the first to feel its right and rear threatened after the German breakthrough in southern Yugoslavia. On 9 April G.H.Q. ordered Tsolakoglou to evacuate Korytsa, turning a deaf ear to his frantic appeals for an early general withdrawal. All the same, Tsolakoglou planned for a general retreat to be executed on receipt of a new order, which he expected at any moment. Two days later, however, he thought that orderly retreat was impossible. When Papagos asked him on 11 April for his views on that matter he received the following reply: 'The opportunity for a withdrawal has been irrevocably lost. Now it is unfavourable to the army, which, although victorious, has been made to remain a mere spectator watching the enemy march on its rear.'[2]

Despite this negative—and critical—reply, Papagos issued the long expected order for a general retreat on 12 April at 9.30 a.m. The withdrawal would start as of the same day and the forces would eventually occupy a line whose right would be based on the western Aliakmon.[3] Oddly enough, Papagos felt the following day that he owed some explanations to the field

[1] Epirus army to G.H.Q., No. 9113/1111, 11 April 1941, Very Urgent, General Staff, vol. F634. See also *End of an Epic*, p. 98.

[2] *End of an Epic*, pp. 98–9; Papagos, *Battle of Greece*, pp. 301–2; Tsolakoglou, *Memoirs*, pp. 70–2. Tsolakoglou says that he interpreted the delay in ordering the retreat as a sign that the Commander-in-Chief no longer needed the services of the Western Macedonian army.   [3] *End of an Epic*, p. 289.

commanders for the decision to evacuate the occupied territories and retire south. 'Reasons of supreme national interest', he said in a signal, 'as well as military considerations made it imperative to order the retirement of the forces from Albanian soil and the evacuation of all occupied territory.' He went on to say that 'retirement' did not mean 'defeat'; on the contrary, 'a successful withdrawal and the continuation of fighting under present circumstances would amount to a rare military achievement and add new glory to our army'. Papagos concluded by reaffirming his unshakeable belief in final victory.[1]

We now know, however, that Papagos never seriously considered dismantling the Albanian front, except as a last and desperate move. Proposals for withdrawal from the Albanian front had been made as soon as Germany's intentions to invade Greece became apparent. Specific plans for withdrawal were put forward in early March, when the Western Macedonian army proposed to retire south; but the proposed retreat, as already seen in the previous chapter, was rejected by Papagos. Papagos had decided to leave the Greek army victorious against the Italians and have it fight against the Germans merely for the honour of Greek arms. Indicative of his attitude regarding resistance against the Germans is a conversation he had with Gen. Bakopoulos, commander of the Eastern Macedonian army, on 12 March. In the course of the conversation Bakopoulos asked for reinforcements from the Albanian front, but Papagos ruled it out since it would have weakened the Greek position and given the Italians the opportunity to score 'a success, even a minor success', something he would not allow. To Bakopoulos's remark that the Albanian front would be threatened primarily by the Germans after the collapse of the Macedonian front, 'the Commander-in-Chief stated that his main concern was, as far as History and World public opinion were concerned, that the Italians should remain till the end defeated by the Greek army, which would be the case only if the Greeks held their present positions in Albania until the moment of attack by the German army'.[2]

---

[1] G.H.Q. to Epirus and Western Macedonian armies, No. 1512, 13 Apr. 1941, General Staff, F623/A/407.

[2] Report by Gen. Bakopoulos, 19 Dec. 1941, submitted to the General Staff 19 Jan. 1942. General Staff, F628, Part II, pp. 80-1.

On 12 April, while the Greek forces were retiring south, German formations broke through the 'sensitive boundary'[1] between the Albanian front and W Force: the road to central Greece lay open and the fate of the Greek forces in Albania was sealed. Events now moved fast. The British forces holding the left of the Aliakmon position wheeled south, while the two Greek divisions of W Force moved slowly west. The commander of the Greek forces was informed by the British that very little mechanized transport could be provided for his troops. Strained and failing signals communications in a rapidly changing situation added to the bitterness felt by the Greek troops who were essentially abandoned to their fate.[2] Gen. Wavell, who was on a visit to his forces in Greece, informed his commanders that all reinforcements for the Greek theatre would be held up: the disaster in the Western Desert and the threat to Egypt itself were convincing enough reasons. The Middle East Command was already considering the extrication of the British expeditionary force from the Greek mainland with the least possible loss. While in Greece, Wavell decided to rename the hard-pressed 6th Australian division and the New Zealand division, the 'Anzac Corps'.[3] The expeditionary force would fight from now on only rearguard actions and these against great odds.

The German breakthrough sent the Greek Government into a panic. As early as the evening of 11 April King George had warned the British Minister that in case of a German breakthrough between the right of the Western Macedonian army and the left of W Force, Athens would become untenable as the seat of government, owing to the increasing panic in the capital and to the proximity of the Salamis naval base. The King then went on to say that if the Government had to abandon the mainland, he would prefer to go to Crete; but since the island was vulnerable from the air and therefore unsafe, he proposed Cyprus as the seat of the Greek Government. The King also asked whether some 50,000 recruits under training in the Peloponnese could be evacuated, preferably to Cyprus, to

[1] I. S. O. Playfair, *The Mediterranean and the Middle East*, vol. ii, London, H.M.S.O., 1956, p. 84.

[2] C. Karassos, *The War against the Germans in Central Macedonia, 1941* (in Greek), Athens, 1948, pp. 77–8.

[3] J. Connell, *Wavell, Scholar and Soldier*, London, 1964, p. 414.

finish their training and be ready for use in the Dodecanese or elsewhere.[1] Rarely has so serious a matter been put forward so naïvely.

The Foreign Office was quick to see the real motives behind the Greek proposal, but refrained from giving a reply before consulting the Governor of Cyprus and the Chiefs of Staff, if only to procure convincing arguments against the proposal. Interestingly enough, Eden's initial reaction was positive. He was in favour of the Greek Government being allowed to establish itself in Cyprus, if the occasion arose, and could not see why some Greek recruits should not be evacuated to the island. The Chiefs of Staff also favoured the Greek proposal. But the Governor of Cyprus was opposed, and provided all the arguments needed to return a well-argued negative reply. The presence of the King and his Government on Cyprus would render the position of the British authorities almost impossible, since all loyalties would be centred on the King; and no matter how carefully he and his Government acted, the tendency would be to disregard the British authorities and to consider the Greek Government as the *de facto* if not the *de jure* government of the island. The Greek proposal, he further argued, would also intensify the latent hostility between the Greek and Turkish communities which, as the result of Turkey's failure to enter the war on Britain's side, was increasing. These arguments, even when phrased in more diplomatic terms, did not go very far toward satisfying the Greek Premier, when Palairet communicated the British reply on 13 April. A renewed appeal the same day on similar lines left the British unmoved. Koryzis instructed Simopoulos to press the proposal on Churchill and Eden, but the British Government tactfully shelved the matter, and when it arose in the hectic days that followed made it a point to say as little as possible about it.[1]

On the front the rot had set in. The disintegration of Greek army formations after 15 April was terrifyingly rapid, and withdrawal took the form of disorderly retreat. War-weariness

---

[1] Foreign Office Correspondence and Minutes, 12–14 Apr. 1941, R3817/11/19, F.O. 371/29839 and R3882/3888/11/19, F.O. 371/29840. Also Tels. Nos. 2777/2792/St/41, 13 Apr. 1941, from Koryzis to Simopoulos, Simopoulos Papers. See also Papadakis, *Diplomatic History*, pp. 189–93.

and the conviction that further resistance was futile had broken the will to fight. Failing signals communications contributed to the growing disorder. The commander of the Western Macedonian army was in the dark about the outcome of the fighting on his right and of the German breakthrough, and it was only brought to his attention late on 13 April by the commander of the Central Macedonian army (12th and 20th divisions), which marched slowly towards Epirus. The next day the two divisions of this army were placed by a G.H.Q. order under the command of the Western Macedonian army; but by the afternoon of 15 April these divisions ceased to exist as organized units.[1] Early in the afternoon of the same day the commander of 12th division reported to Gen. Karassos, commander of the Central Macedonian army, that 'all units of the division had disintegrated during the retreat south of the Aliakmon, the officers being unable to hold back the fleeing men; and that his division consisted of only himself, his staff and the regimental commanders'. The 20th division, the other Greek division originally part of W Force met with a similar fate.[2] The commander of the Western Macedonian army, his new H.Q. now established at Kalabaka, was cut off from the commands of his retiring units due to inadequate communications. On 15 April he reported this situation to G.H.Q., which endorsed his recommendation that the retreat of his units should be directed westwards, in the only free direction, not southwards, as originally intended by the order of 12 April for general retirement.[3] For all practical purposes, the Western Macedonian army was allowed to march into the Epirus trap.

The Epirus army was in far worse shape, and its prospects of withdrawal bleak, as the road system in its rear was inadequate and in bad condition. The morale of the troops was declining rapidly, especially of those units which had gone through heavy and continuous fighting throughout the winter. The 8th division, the famous Epirus division which had been fighting the Italians since the previous October, was battle-weary and demoralized. Retreat meant abandoning their homes to the

[1] *End of an Epic*, p. 121.
[2] Report by Gen. Karassos, 7 July 1942, General Staff, F627, p. 73.
[3] *End of an Epic*, pp. 122–3.

despised enemy.[1] Disintegration in the Epirus army seems to
have started in the 2nd army corps, and more specifically in the
5th (Cretan) division. In a signal to Pitsikas, dated 15 April,
at 4.05 a.m., Gen. Bakos, the corps commander, gave a dramatic account of the 5th division:

> Since nightfall yesterday the division began disintegrating, and
> no unit can now be considered organized. This was reported to me
> by the commander of the division, who used the phrase: 'there no
> longer exists a 5th division'.
> The same was reported to my chief staff officer by Col. Papadon-
> gonas, the division's infantry commander, who said that neither he
> nor any other officer, colonels included, were able to keep order
> among the troops, some of whom turned their rifles against the
> officers . . .[2]

The same day Bakos replaced Gen. Papastergiou in the command of the division by Col. Papadongonas; but replacement
of commanders could no longer stem the tide.[3] Serious acts of
disobedience were also reported to Bakos by the 15th division;
and soon the infection spread to the entire corps.[2] The 1st army
corps, although not as badly affected as the 2nd, faced a similar
danger. The corps held the westernmost section of the front
and was pinned down by a general Italian attack, while
awaiting the 2nd corps to complete its withdrawal.[4]

Pressure on Pitsikas from both corps commanders to seek
an end to hostilities now increased. Demestichas reported to
both the Epirus command and G.H.Q. that the army was
faced with complete and humiliating disintegration which it
least deserved, and that the officers of his corps considered
a negotiated capitulation to the Germans to be the only
solution, on the condition that the Italians would not be
allowed to cross into Greek territory. The same day, 15 April,
Pitsikas held a conference, at which both Demestichas and
Bakos were present. The two commanders reiterated their view
that further resistance was impossible. At the end of the conference a report on these lines was drawn up and signed by Pitsikas,

---

[1] Ibid., pp. 123 ff.

[2] 2nd army corps to Epirus army, No. 8598, 15 Apr. 1941, 4.05 a.m., General
Staff, F634.

[3] 2nd army corps to 5th division, No. 8596, 15 Apr. 1941, General Staff,
F634

[4] *End of an Epic*, pp. 138, 139.

Bakos, and Demestichas, and was entrusted to a senior officer, Col. Grigoropoulos, to carry to Papagos. The messenger was also instructed to report orally to the Commander-in-Chief and try to get his consent for an armistice.[1]

At this point it is necessary to pause briefly to examine the factors behind the demoralization and disintegration of the military units in Epirus. The official *History of the Greek Army in the Second World War* deals in passing with the causes of the 'astonishing change in the picture' in the space of one week, without the Epirus army even contacting the Germans:

> The attack from one more great power; the collapse of Yugoslavia; the heroic but brief resistance of the Eastern Macedonian army; and, finally, the collapse of the Anglo-Greek line of defence in Central Macedonia convinced the men of the victorious Epirus army that further resistance was futile. But, at the same time, they were eager to avoid at all costs the humiliation of being taken prisoner by the Italians, whom they had beaten in many defensive and offensive engagements. These feelings were shared by both the officers and men of the Epirus army; and the weight of these feelings was such that ruled out a clear and objective analysis of the situation . . .[2]

A more immediate cause of the disintegration must have been the war-weariness of certain units which had been fighting the Italians under appalling conditions. The 5th division, the first to disintegrate, had gone through several campaigns since the beginning of February under heavy bombardment and extremely harsh weather conditions. For the last few weeks the men of the Cretan division had done without cooked rations.[3] Another cause must have been the resentment felt by the Cretan soldiers against the Government and the military leadership of the country, which were doing practically nothing for the defence of the island. It seems that strong pressure was put on the authorities to send the division to Crete, but the unit was kept in Epirus. Indicative of the ill-feeling common among the Cretans is perhaps an incident which took place after the capitulation. In late April the commander of the division was shot dead on return to Crete without his troops by a Cretan.

[1] Th. Grigoropoulos, *From the Top of the Hill* (in Greek), Athens, n.d., pp. 183 ff.; *End of an Epic*, pp. 140–1.
[2] Ibid., p. 142.   [3] Ibid., p. 127.

The murderer was not arrested as no one would give him away.[1] In Epirus there were also units from Thrace and Macedonia, which had already been occupied by the Germans, and whose men felt that fighting while their homes were under the enemy was an unnecessary sacrifice. Another reason was certainly the failing spirit of resistance among many military and political leaders.

Symptoms of defeatism or panic in government and military circles began to appear about this time, if not earlier. According to a report of 14 April, the King had difficulties with panicky and defeatist officials, had forbidden the Cabinet to frequent G.H.Q. (Grande Bretagne Hotel), and summarily dismissed them to their offices with the order to spread optimism.[2] The British Minister thought of a more drastic measure. After bringing to the King's attention the deplorable attitude of a number of his Ministers, who had been subject to panic, he suggested: 'had not the time come for [the] creation of a small and resolute Cabinet which would exclude all except really reliable Ministers from any share in the conduct of the war?' But this was already happening in practice: all important decisions were being taken by a small body and were communicated by Koryzis to the rest of the Cabinet every evening 'without comment or discussion'. The King assured Palairet that the morale of the ordinary man was excellent, and it was only in circles near the Government that panic was to be feared. He had decided to dismiss immediately any Minister who showed panic.[3] The King appeared to be in firm control, and determined to make his army acquit itself well till the end. To revive the weakening morale of the armed forces King George issued on 15 April an order of the day, which also defined the general course of Greek policy:

. . . The honour and interest of Greece and the fate of the Greek race preclude all thoughts of capitulation, the moral calamity of which would be incomparably greater than any other disaster. In view of this, I appeal to your patriotism as soldiers and as Greeks, enjoining you to do your duty to the end in the above spirit. It

[1] Tel. from Palairet, Canea, No. 15, 30 Apr. 1941, F.O. 371/29830.

[2] Tel. from Lincoln MacVeagh (U.S. Minister), No. 229, 14 Apr. 1941, after conversation with the King. F.R.U.S., 1941, vol. ii, pp. 717–18.

[3] Athens Tel. No. 708, Most Immediate, Most Secret, 14 Apr. 1941, F.O. 371/29840.

must not be forgotten that the British Army continues to fight in defence of Greek soil.[1]

But the King's resolute attitude was not shared by some of his Ministers and military leaders. On the same day that this order was issued, unauthorized orders for leave were also issued. On 15 April two weeks' leave was given to the men of certain reserve units, which came from enemy-occupied territories, and Papadimas asked that the measure should apply to all reserve officers and men no longer needed. At the same time Papadimas ordered preparations for the removal to Crete of two classes of fresh recruits and the Cadets. On 16 April he issued another order giving two months' leave to another class of recruits recently called up and one month to certain classes of reserve officers.[2] These orders were ostensibly issued to ease congestion at the centres of mobilization,[3] but their effect on morale was disastrous, since they were interpreted as a prelude to general demobilization. According to one account, an unauthorized order was also issued from the Air Ministry grounding all aircraft and instructing that petrol tanks at Tatoi and Eleusis aerodromes should be destroyed. This order had been countermanded by the King, who had only heard of it through the British Military Mission.[4]

On 16 April pressure on Papagos to seek a solution was renewed. But the Commander-in-Chief made it plain to his subordinates at G.H.Q. that capitulation while British forces were fighting on Greek soil was out of the question.[5] Put differently, this meant that the evacuation of the British forces would open the way to capitulation; and that was exactly what Papagos wanted: to see the British out of Greece at the earliest possible moment. Late in the afternoon of the same day Papagos met Wilson, to whom he suggested, after a brief review of the situation, that as the situation might soon become critical the British should re-embark their forces 'and save Greece from devastation'. Wilson was of the same opinion.

[1] Pipinelis, *George II*, p. 106; L. Archer, *Balkan Journal*, New York, 1944, p. 179; A. S. G. Lee, *The Royal House of Greece*, London, 1948, p. 85.

[2] *End of an Epic*, pp. 212–13.

[3] Ibid., p. 212. See also Archer, op. cit., p. 182.

[4] A. Heckstall-Smith and H. T. Baillie-Grohman, *Greek Tragedy '41*, London, 1961, pp. 62–3.

[5] *End of an Epic*, p. 173.

Papagos then asked Wilson for his opinion about the Greek Government leaving for Crete, to which Wilson replied that 'it was advisable to do this at once'. These exchanges were telegraphed to London in a personal signal for the C.I.G.S. from Wavell, who asked for instructions as to what action he was to take on Papagos's suggestion to re-embark the British forces, as he presumed that the request to this effect from the Greek Government should be obtained before the actual re-embarkation began. Wavell recommended at the same time that preparations be started for the evacuation.[1]

The reply to Wavell came directly from Churchill in the early hours of 17 April: 'We cannot remain in Greece against [the] wish of [the] Greek Commander-in-Chief and thus expose [the] country to devastation. Wilson or Palairet should obtain endorsement by the Greek Government of Papagos' request.' All the same, Churchill endorsed Wavell's recommendation to start preparations for evacuation.[2] Palairet's reaction to the suggestion made by Papagos was one of feigned anger. 'It is not a question of [the] Greek Commander-in-Chief requesting [the] British troops to leave Greece to avoid devastation of this country', he cabled to the Foreign Office. But he concluded: 'It is fortunate that the idea was first raised by General Papagos, thus relieving General Wilson of the necessity of proposing it himself.'[3] If Palairet was at heart delighted by what he considered a timely approach from Papagos, Churchill certainly was not. He was unable to understand the Minister's inference that 'Wilson would or could have proposed re-embarkation of [the] British forces as sound tactics', if Papagos had not suggested it himself. With Churchill, honour came first. To everyone concerned he made it plain that, before the British could commit themselves to re-embarkation, the specific endorsement of Papagos's suggestion by the King and/or the Greek Government was absolutely necessary.[4]

Papagos's 'timely' approach for the re-embarkation of the British forces seems to have been the result of pressure from the

[1] C.-in-C., Middle East, to W.O., Most Immediate, No. 0/57341, 16 Apr. 1941, 7.15 p.m., F.O. 371/29818.

[2] F.O. Tel. No. 836, Immediate, 17 Apr. 1941, 3.25 a.m., F.O. 371/29818.

[3] Athens Tel. No. 738, Most Immediate, 17 Apr. 1941, 6.50 a.m., F.O. 371/29818.

[4] F.O. Tel. No. 854, Most Immediate, 18 Apr. 1941, 3.15 p.m., F.O. 371/29818.

field commanders to open the way for a ceasefire. Although it cannot be established with absolute certainty, it appears that Papagos's meeting with Wilson late in the afternoon of 16 April was preceded by another meeting he had with the officer carrying the recommendation of the field commanders to end the war. Col. Grigoropoulos met Papagos around 7.00 p.m. the same day, and read to him the report of the commanders. Papagos explained to this officer that, although he was fully aware of the critical situation in Epirus, capitulation was out of the question as long as the British were fighting in Greece.

However, taking into consideration the position of the Greek forces, the Commander-in-Chief recognized that capitulation was necessary, though without compromising himself in the eyes of the British, adding that in two or three days a solution would be possible after the departure of the present Government and the assumption of power by a new one, which would authorize the Commander-in-Chief to start negotiations with the Germans.

When the emissary of the commanders pressed him to allow what he had just said to take place as soon as possible, Papagos promised to make an effort in that direction so that a solution could be found the following day. He then left to see the President of the Council. Papagos saw Grigoropoulos again at 8.30 p.m., and it is quite likely that in the intervening time he saw, in addition to Koryzis, Wilson as well.[1]

When he met Grigoropoulos for the second time that day, Papagos announced that the Government would under no circumstances agree to capitulation as proposed by the field commanders, while the British were fighting in Greece, for it would dishonour the country. 'The Government', he said, 'would prefer the disintegration, destruction and captivity of the army, even its dishonouring, if it could not be avoided, to capitulation to the Germans through the Government.' This way Greece would safeguard her honour, and would be assured of Britain's full support after the war. He finally said that, since the forces in Epirus would soon be encircled, things must be left to run their course. Papagos then ordered Grigoropoulos to report the above to Pitsikas as his reply to the appeals from the commanders. But this officer implored him to make yet

---

[1] *End of an Epic*, p. 174.

another effort to get the consent of the Government for an armistice, saying that 'the honour of the Greek army was the honour of fighting Greece'.[1]

These exchanges continued. Grigoropoulos met Papagos a third time late that evening. At this meeting, besides Papagos, Grigoropoulos, and a number of senior officers, Diakos, Papadimas, and Maniadakis were also present. The Government representatives argued at length trying to justify the decision not to allow capitulation as long as the British forces were fighting in Greece. Papadimas recognized the tragic position of the Greek army, and stated that 'capitulation, the solution proposed by the army, would be possible as soon as the Government departed'. Both Papagos and Maniadakis expressed agreement with this view. His mission completed, the officer proceeded to communicate with Pitsikas to whom he conveyed the position of the Government and the Commander-in-Chief. The result of this was an order issued by the Epirus command late on 16 April, stressing the need to prevent the dissolution of the army for 'a few days' in the expectation of 'certain developments', and appealing to the patriotism of the troops not to abandon their positions.[2] By this time, however, general orders like that had no effect at all, and probably reached only a handful of officers and men.

On 17 April trouble started in yet another quarter. There was a mutiny on a destroyer and serious incidents on other vessels of the fleet.[3] The same day the Minister of Marine Papavasileiou was dismissed after a quarrel with the President of the Council. The reason for the quarrel, according to Papavasileiou, was the absence of his name from the list of Ministers and officials to be evacuated;[4] but it is not unlikely that this was only a pretext to get rid of an undesirable Minister, who had been practically dropped from the Cabinet two days earlier.[5]

In Epirus the field commanders were getting out of control. On 17 April Tsolakoglou talked to Papagos on the telephone

---

[1] Ibid., p. 174.   [2] Ibid., pp. 175–6.
[3] A. E. Sakellariou, *Greece's Position in the Second World War* (in Greek), New York, 1944, p. 213.
[4] I. Papavasileiou, *Our Navy in the Pre-War and War Period 1936–1941* (in Greek), Athens, 1945, p. 30.
[5] Sakellariou, op. cit., p. 212.

and, after describing the tragic situation, implored him to seek a solution in order to prevent the complete disintegration of the army. Papagos's reply was to hold on for two more days. Shortly afterwards, Tsolakoglou learnt that a number of senior commanders intended to sign an armistice, without the approval of Papagos. He then got in touch with Pitsikas, who agreed that an armistice was necessary, adding that he expected an order to that effect from G.H.Q. soon. The same day the Western Macedonian army was disbanded as an independent formation. It became again the 3rd army corps as before, and was placed under the command of the Epirus army.[1]

In the meantime, the King and Government had decided on 16 April to leave for Crete the following day. At this point Palairet took an important step. In an audience with the King he asked him 'if he did not think the moment had come to form a real national Government which would represent the whole of Greece in the eyes of [the] Greeks who would be under German domination'. The King said that 'he must take the present Cabinet to Crete but would take the opportunity later to make changes'.[2] The proposed measure would have been a decisive break with the dictatorship established four-and-a-half years before and a positive step towards a return to legality. Similar action would still have been possible, if the King had possessed the nerve to take the daring step in this direction: and subsequent Greek trials might have been avoided. A national government would have crowned the national unity which had been forged in the war, and which would soon disappear. At this moment the King's lack of nerve, or unwillingness, was, to say the least, deplorable.

For the Greek Orthodox, 18 April was Good Friday. The day started with a conference at Tatoi Palace. Those present were the King, Papagos, Wilson, Palairet, and members of the British Military Mission. After a review of the situation, Wilson assured the King that there could be no threat to his personal safety or that of his Government for at least a week. As a result, the King decided to postpone departure for Crete for the present and agreed to issue a statement to that effect. But news of the intention to evacuate the Government had

---

[1] Tsolakoglou, op. cit., pp. 87–8; *End of an Epic*, p. 180.
[2] Athens Tel. No. 735, 16 Apr. 1941, F.O. 371/29818.

already had a serious effect on the morale of the army.[1] About the same time, 9.00 a.m., Pitsikas pressed Koryzis on the telephone for a decision and secured his promise that he would have official permission for an armistice by noon. Soon afterwards, Pitsikas asked Panaghiotis Kanellopoulos, who was serving as a corporal in the 13th division (3rd army corps), to draft an armistice agreement.[2] At the same time he dispatched a cable addressed to both the Commander-in-Chief and the President of the Council: 'Situation seriously deteriorated. Units of 17th [division] are abandoning their positions. 1st army corps reports disintegration of 8th division. 11th division disintegrating. In the name of God, save the army from the Italians.'[3]

Meanwhile, the three corps commanders were taking matters into their own hands. While Pitsikas beseeched Papagos and the Government to take a decision at the earliest possible moment, Demestichas, Bakos, and Tsolakoglou, as well as the Metropolitan of Jannina, Spyridon, decided to take the initiative for an armistice. Late on 17 April Spyridon visited Bakos at his H.Q. and early next morning went to Demestichas's H.Q., where it was decided that the commanders should hold a meeting later the same day. The meeting was held at 10.15 p.m. on 18 April. It was decided to send a telegram to the Government, presenting it with a 12-hour ultimatum to reach a decision; otherwise, they would form a government at Jannina under the Metropolitan and the three corps commanders. Demestichas was empowered to dispatch the telegram after making an effort to secure the approval of Pitsikas and the divisional commanders. The telegram reads: 'Our repeated appeals have been left without reply. In order to prevent the dishonouring of the victorious army by allowing it to disintegrate and surrender to the defeated enemy . . . it is imperative to sign an armistice with the Germans. This is the demand of the entire Epirus army.' If the Government refused to act on the demands of the commanders, they would take the initiative themselves to prevent the catastrophe.[4]

[1] Athens Tel. No. 745, 18 Apr. 1941, F.O. 371/29819.
[2] Tsolakoglou, op. cit., p. 94; *End of an Epic*, p. 213.
[3] Epirus army to G.H.Q. and President of the Council, No. 9373/1365, 18 Apr. 1941, General Staff, F634.
[4] *End of an Epic*, pp. 214–15.

In Athens the crisis had already come to a head. Early in the afternoon of that Good Friday the King summoned a Cabinet meeting at which he presided himself. The rapidly deteriorating situation in Epirus and signs of treachery or defeatism, as well as the unauthorized orders for leave and partial demobilization, impelled the King, according to one source, to call this meeting.[1] At the meeting, which was stormy, certain Ministers were said to have 'severely attacked the policy which had been followed'.[2] Papadimas, it seems, read a number of telegrams from the field commanders imploring the Government to allow them to sign an armistice with the Germans.[3] Koryzis had already received a telegram from Bakos, in which he reported many cases of mass desertion and insubordination, despite the shooting of deserters, and begged him to end the hostilities by treating with the Germans.[4] Papadimas also expressed the view that, even if the British could hold the Thermopylae position for several days as they had stated to the King earlier that day, such resistance was, from the Greek point of view, futile, and better dispensed with in view of the tragic situation in Epirus. The issue, it seems, was whether, or not, to tell the British to re-embark their forces as soon as possible in order to leave the commanders free to start *pourparlers* with the Germans. Some members were also in favour of the Government immediately departing for Crete with the same end in mind, while others pressed for immediate action by the Government to end the war. Naturally, the King ruled out the last alternative as it would have meant the end of the Anglo-Greek alliance and co-operation. The meeting was inconclusive. Koryzis is said to have proposed at the end that a military government should be formed to take charge of the situation, and that the King promised to give it some thought.[5] According to a member of the Cabinet present, two alternatives were discussed at the meeting: (*a*) appointment of a military government, or (*b*) the King taking over the Government personally, with Koryzis as Vice-President of the Council. According to the same account, at 2.30 p.m., the King, Koryzis, Maniadakis, and Papadimas met again in

[1] Lee, op. cit., p. 85.   [2] Pipinelis, *George II*, p. 106.
[3] Sakellariou, op. cit., p. 214.   [4] Kotzias, op. cit., p. 371.
[5] *End of an Epic*, p. 177.

another room of the Grande Bretagne. After this meeting Koryzis went home alone.[1] Pipinelis says that at the end of the second meeting Koryzis implored the King to relieve him of his duties, but the request was turned down; resignations at a critical time like that served no purpose at all, the King said. Everyone had to stay at his post.[2] Koryzis then kissed the King's hand and proceeded home to shoot himself.[3] At 5.35 p.m. Palairet telegraphed London: 'President of the Council has just committed suicide after telling the King that he had failed him in the task entrusted to him.'[4]

After Koryzis's suicide, King George decided to take over the Government personally. The King was prey to fears of possible disturbances in Athens, but relied on British troops to help maintain order. In his audience with the King a couple of hours later, Palairet raised again the issue of a national government. 'I urged him to form a Government of national concentration [co-operation?] and to broadcast to the nation himself to explain the situation and the reason which [the] President of the Council gave [the] King for [his] suicide.' But as we shall see, very few, if any, were prepared at this point to assume the responsibilities of government. Palairet feared that Koryzis's suicide could be exploited by enemy propaganda, and suggested that it would be wise to emphasize that Koryzis's policy had been laid down by Metaxas, not by the British. It could also be pointed out that the suicide had not been due to any immediate deterioration in the military situation: Koryzis had always suffered from bad health, and the strain had been more than he could bear.[5]

Meanwhile, reports of defeatism, insubordination, desertion, and acts of sabotage were reaching the King and Palairet with alarming frequency. Palairet feared the pro-German elements in Athens and particularly the pro-German army and police officers, who constituted in Palairet's view a threat to public security.[6] At midnight the King summoned the British Minister

---

[1] Kotzias, op. cit., pp. 402–4.   [2] Pipinelis, *George II*, p. 106.
[3] Lee, op. cit., p. 85; Archer, op. cit., pp. 182–3; Kotzias, op. cit., p. 404.
[4] Athens Tel. No. 747, Most Immediate, Most Secret, 18 Apr. 1941, 5.35 p.m., F.O. 371/29819.
[5] Athens Tel. No. 748, Most Immediate, 18 Apr. 1941, 8.00 p.m., F.O. 371/29819.
[6] Athens Tel. No. 752, 19 Apr. 1941, F.O. 371/29819.

to announce that he proposed to make Kotzias Vice-President of the Council 'for the time that the Government would remain in Athens'. He needed an 'energetic demagogue' to revive declining morale, and Kotzias suited that purpose: he was the only person near the King who had not advised him to leave for Crete at once. Palairet was horrified at the suggestion of appointing someone with a pro-German reputation, and pointed out the unfortunate effects of such an appointment. Kotzias's pro-German reputation was, of course, no news to the King, who tried to reassure the Minister, saying that he was 'absolutely certain of Kotzias doing exactly what he wished while under his control'. Palairet, evidently not completely satisfied with the King's assurance, next saw Kotzias and, after talking with him for a while, got the impression that he 'sincerely meant to work for the Anglo-Greek cause'. All the same, Palairet considered the appointment inappropriate and only hoped that the King had made the right decision. Other candidates had either declined the offer or were ruled out for one reason or another. A likely candidate was Gen. Pangalos, the dictator of old, but his candidacy was ruled out by the King, because, contrary to what many people believed, Pangalos's influence with the army was negligible.[1]

Kotzias's appointment did not come off, despite his frantic efforts to find enough people to complete his list of Ministers:[2] many found collaboration with him distasteful, because of his pro-German reputation and close association with Metaxas.[3] The spacious rooms and corridors of the Grande Bretagne now became congested as the King summoned various political and military leaders. Sophoulis, the leader of the Liberal Party, was among them, and so were Admiral Sakellariou, Commander of the Fleet, and retired generals Alexandros Mazarakis, Pangalos, and Manetas. But the King's efforts to find someone with the necessary prestige and courage to assume the responsibilities of government remained fruitless, and he was the only one who took political decisions. The Fleet was torn apart by mutiny; the field commanders on the front manœuvred for an armistice disregarding the Commander-in-Chief and the Government;

[1] Athens Tel. No. 754, 19 Apr. 1941, 12.35 a.m., F.O. 371/29819.
[2] Kotzias, op. cit., pp. 406–8.
[3] A. Michalopoulos, *Greek Fire*, London, 1943, pp. 16–18.

the Service Ministries did not function; Papagos wavered and was losing what little control he had over the armed forces. For three days, until Emmanouil Tsouderos was sworn in as Premier and formed a Cabinet, the King stood alone acting as President of the Council, War Minister, and Foreign Minister, working through day and night, without a moment's relief from the burden of practically running the state at a most critical time.[1]

In the afternoon of 19 April Palairet and the American Minister had an audience with the King, and urged him to appoint a strong military government at once, which he was in fact preparing to do. His efforts to restore confidence by appointing Kotzias had had the opposite effect. The King was doing his utmost to achieve the formation of a military government before meeting Wavell later in the afternoon. Palairet was convinced that this measure was the only way of dealing with defeatism and disorganization in the army, and took care to impress his fears on the King. The spread of defeatism and disorganization would imperil the British forces in Greece, a danger to which the King was fully alive.[2]

When Wavell and Palairet arrived at Tatoi in the afternoon they found that Gen. Mazarakis, a retired Venizelist officer, had been practically appointed Vice-President of the Council; but the King had not yet been able to complete the Government. Palairet urged him again to include Pangalos, for whom there was a 'general demand', but without success. Mazarakis, although a good choice in terms of prestige, did not strike Palairet as a leader; but the King was sorry to admit that there was 'none'. At the conference Wavell reviewed the military situation, and stated that the British forces could hold the Thermopylae position, if they could count on the support of the Greek forces. But Papagos gave a gloomy picture of the situation in Epirus, and recommended the evacuation of the British forces at the earliest possible moment, since an attempt to hold the Thermopylae position would only prolong the devastation of the country. This was a serious statement to make, and even more serious to accept. The King was put in

[1] Lee, op. cit., p. 85; Pipinelis, *George II*, pp. 106–7; Sakellariou, op. cit., pp. 216–18; Michalopoulos, op. cit., pp. 16–18.
[2] Athens Tel. No. 757, 19 Apr. 1941, 2.25 p.m., F.O. 371/29840.

a difficult position, for devastation, which was not really the case, was hardly a reason to ask an ally to depart before engaging the enemy from a strong position; while the real reason, the disintegration of the army, was terribly hard to admit. The King finally expressed the wish to send up a general to investigate whether the situation was 'really as bad in Epirus as General Papagos described [it]'. Obviously, Papagos was losing the confidence of the King. Palairet's telegram describing this meeting ends:

> General Wavell made it clear that unless [the] Greek Govern-ment wished us to depart he was prepared to hold on for a very considerable time providing the Greek Army in Epirus can do the same. [The] King made it equally clear that Greece would con-tinue fighting till victorious even if she could only do so in Crete and the islands. [The] King after the meeting spoke to me with tears in his eyes about the dilemma in which he and we were involved.[1]

Events in Epirus were running their own course. In the evening of 19 April Demestichas asked for Pitsikas's orders. The reply was to hold on until the 21st. He had just talked on the telephone with a senior officer at G.H.Q., who told him on behalf of the Commander-in-Chief and in the presence of several senior officers, that after the 21st he would be free to act as he thought best, even to sign an armistice. Pitsikas had asked for a written order on exactly the same lines, or he would invite the corps commanders for a conference the next day to decide about the next step. On hearing this Demestichas issued an order to his divisional commanders to put up a stiff resistance. But Bakos was of a different mind. He entreated Demestichas in a letter of the same date (19 April) to replace Pitsikas in the command of the Epirus army, adding that the formation of a government would immediately follow suit and a message to the Greek people would be drafted. In a second letter to Demestichas, dated 20 April, Bakos informed him that Tsola-koglou had already assumed command of the Epirus army and undertaken to form a government with the Metropolitan of Jannina as President of the Council and the three corps commanders as members.[2]

---

[1] Athens Tel. No. 760, Most Immediate, 19 Apr. 1941, 10.20 p.m., F.O. 371/29840. See also Playfair, op. cit., vol. ii, p. 94; Connell, op. cit., pp. 416–17.

[2] *End of an Epic*, pp. 217–19.

Tsolakoglou had stolen a march on the other commanders by a trick. He had sent a trusted officer, Col. Chrysochoou, to Athens, where he arrived in the afternoon of 18 April. While trying to meet Papagos, Chrysochoou saw a number of senior officers at G.H.Q., all of whom were critical of Papagos's indecisive attitude. According to Chrysochoou, these officers informed him that they had tried to persuade Papagos to heed the appeals from the field commanders for an armistice, but to no avail. When pressed hard, Papagos is reported to have said: 'Why don't the generals there do it themselves?' This hint was telegraphed to Pitsikas by the same officers, who urged him to act on it at once, giving him their word that he would have the full support of the entire G.H.Q. Chrysochoou met Papagos late in the afternoon of 18 April, and pressed on him the known views of the commanders, only to receive the usual reply: he could not possibly authorize a ceasefire so long as the British were fighting on Greek soil. At 6.00 p.m. Chrysochoou, after trying without success to reach Tsolakoglou on the telephone, sent off a signal, in which he described the situation he found in Athens as 'confused', and concluded by saying that the only solution was a ceasefire signed by the field commanders. According to the official History, which is based on Chrysochoou's version of the affair, he sent off a second signal to Tsolakoglou on the 19th, which reads: 'Secret. Personal for the General. Initiative rests with the Army. If you assume responsibility, consent of the other corps commanders is necessary, authorizing you to take action, as you have established contact with the Germans. Chrysochoou.' The cable has G.H.Q. as place of origin, but as we shall see this was intentionally misleading. It was received by Tsolakoglou around 2.00 a.m. on 20 April, and it is said that it was this signal that made him decide to proceed immediately to send officers to make contact with the Germans.[1]

In a report to the General Staff after the war Papagos maintains that he had never seen, let alone approved of, the two cables sent by Chrysochoou. In fact, the cables in question were not transmitted from G.H.Q. (Grande Bretagne Hotel), but from the nearby Foreign Ministry building. A soldier, who served in the cipher department of the Ministry, asked to

[1] *End of an Epic*, pp. 220–2; Tsolakoglou, op. cit., p. 130.

be received by Papagos on 21 April, when Tsolakoglou's *pronunciamento* of the previous day became known, and reported that he had transmitted two cables to Epirus and submitted the coded text of the second, which Papagos includes in his report. Also included is the first cable, which is deciphered and reads: 'Following today's telegrams from Bakos and Pitsikas, Koryzis committed suicide. Koryzis's suicide and rumours about King's departure created a confused situation. Commander-in-Chief refuses to take the initiative. I think that the proposal of the Metropolitan of Jannina must be considered. Whatever the decision, it must be taken fast.'[1]

At 5.45 a.m. on 20 April Tsolakoglou telephoned Pitsikas to announce that he had been authorized by G.H.Q. to sign a ceasefire the same morning; and he sent him a copy of the second cable from Chrysochoou, making it appear, however, that this was from Papagos. At 6.00 a.m. he sent off the emissaries to negotiate a ceasefire with the Germans.[2] At the same time that Tsolakoglou sent off his emissaries, Pitsikas received a cable from Papagos announcing the departure of an officer, Gen. Gialistras, sent by the prospective President of the Council (Mazarakis) to inspect the military situation and report to him. By the same signal, the corps commanders were ordered to attend a noon conference at Jannina in order to meet the Government representative and report on the situation. It is said that Tsolakoglou promised Pitsikas to suspend action for a ceasefire until he met the emissary from Athens.[3]

In Athens the governmental crisis had not yet been solved. Mazarakis, who had undertaken to form a Government on the previous day, now declined the mandate,[4] 'chiefly from defeatism and partly from reluctance to work with Maniadakis', according to Palairet.[5] Early on 20 April, Easter Sunday, Admiral Sakellariou was summoned by the King who asked him: 'What would you say if I were to ask you to become Vice-President with myself as President of the Council?' To which the admiral replied: 'Is this what we have come to, Your

---

[1] Report by Gen. Papagos, 'Some Remarks on the Capitulation of the Epirus Army' (in Greek), 23 Apr. 1943, General Staff, F634.

[2] *End of an Epic*, p. 222; Tsolakoglou, op. cit., p. 138. Tsolakoglou gives 8.10 a.m. as the time the emissaries were sent off.

[3] *End of an Epic*, p. 223.   [4] Mazarakis, op. cit., pp. 608–10.

[5] Athens Tel. No. 769, 20 Apr. 1941, 11.00 p.m., F.O. 371/29819.

Majesty?' At midday Sakellariou was sworn in as Vice-President and Minister of the Marine in a Government headed by the King.[1] Many candidates had failed the King, as none was willing to assume responsibility at that critical hour. 'It has not been a creditable day for Greece', commented the British Minister. When he saw the King in the evening, he put the awkward question whether it was true that many of his Ministers had advised him to sign a separate peace with the Germans. The King replied that only Papadimas had done so. Before his audience with the King, Palairet had seen Tsouderos, who made a good impression on him. Tsouderos had made the first step to power.[2]

Tsouderos's candidacy, in fact, had been under consideration since 19 April. The Foreign Office was very well disposed towards him, and this proved decisive. He was Venizelist, opposed to the dictatorship, and a Cretan. 'If the Government is to establish itself comfortably in Crete, a Venizelist Vice-President of the Council is highly desirable, since Crete, as the birth place of Venizelos is strongly anti-Monarchist', minuted Pierson Dixon of the Foreign Office. Generally, it was felt that it was advisable to include as many Venizelists and Cretans in the Government as possible in order to ease its establishment in Crete.[3] Interestingly enough, Tsouderos felt that the British did not particularly favour his appointment. Writing to Simopoulos a few months later, he said: '. . . Unfortunately, *and contrary to all expectations*, when I first took office certain English, Palairet included, were not really satisfied with my appointment. Fortunately, the King, with his characteristic foresight, did not allow himself to be influenced by these reservations, and even reacted [against them]. What could be the reason [for these reservations]? I have no idea. The Minister, especially, must have surely known that I have been the greatest victim of the former Government on account of my pro-British sentiments and my friendship with Lord Lloyd.' Moreover, Tsouderos went on to say, but for him, the King would have found it impossible to stay in Crete for a single day.[4] As

[1] Sakellariou, op. cit., pp. 218–19.
[2] Athens Tel. No. 769, 20 Apr. 1941, F.O. 371/29819.
[3] Foreign Office Minutes, 19 Apr. 1941, R4121/11/19, F.O. 371/29819.
[4] Letter to Simopoulos, Johannesburg, 11 July 1941, Simopoulos Papers. Italics in the original.

already seen in a previous chapter Tsouderos's 'suffering' at
the hands of Metaxas and Maniadakis had nothing to do with
his pro-British sentiments. Regarding his appointment, Tsouderos wrote in great seriousness of a rather bizarre affair. One
month before he was called to form a government, he had
'communicated' with the dead Eleutherios Venizelos through
a medium. Venizelos 'had come to announce that very soon,
and after national disasters that were approaching, I would be
called to take office, and advised me not to hesitate in accepting.
He also promised to help me in that difficult task.' He goes on to
say that Venizelos even 'dictated' to him the speech he made
on accepting office.[1]

On the morning of 21 April a meeting was held to discuss the
situation and immediate policy. Those present were the King,
Wavell, Wilson, Palairet, and Tsouderos, the newly sworn
Premier. Papagos, however, was a conspicuous absentee. The
British representatives were mainly concerned about the military situation, and particularly over the fate of the British
forces in Greece. Wavell asked the King whether the Greek
army was in a position effectively to protect the left flank of the
British forces deployed on the Thermopylae position. The King,
although he had no precise information from Epirus, was not
optimistic about the prospects, and admitted that no organized
Greek units could arrive in time to render effective aid before
the Germans attacked. This was a hard statement to make, but
the situation demanded nothing less than the truth, hard as it
was for a head of state to admit it. Wavell then proposed to take
immediate steps for the re-embarkation of his forces, or what
portion of them could be extricated. The King agreed and
promised that the Greeks would do their utmost to stop an
enemy advance from the west. But this promise was based
solely on his sincere wish to be helpful, for, as we shall see
shortly, what portions of the Greek army had not already
laid down their arms, no longer existed as organized units.
Finally it was agreed that the King and Tsouderos must be
the only ones to know of the decision to evacuate the British
forces.[2]

---

[1] E. Venezis, *Emmanouil Tsouderos* (in Greek), Athens, 1966, pp. 180–1.
[2] Athens Tel. No. 772, 21 Apr. 1941, 2.40 p.m., F.O. 371/29819. See also Playfair, op. cit., vol. ii, p. 95.

On the point of early evacuation from Greece Churchill was of a different mind. He felt that if the generals on the spot thought that they could hold on in the Thermopylae position for a fortnight or three weeks and could keep the Greek army fighting, the British Government should support them. In a note for Eden, dated 20 April, he wrote:

I do not believe the difficulties of evacuation will increase, if the enemy suffers heavy losses. On the other hand, every day the German Air Force is detained in Greece enables the Libyan situation to be stabilized, and may enable us to bring in extra tanks. If this is accomplished safely and the T[hermopylae] position holds, we might even feel strong enough to reinforce from Egypt. I am most reluctant to see us quit; and if the troops were British only and the matter could be decided on military grounds alone, I would urge Wilson to fight if he thought it possible . . .[1]

In his Memoirs Churchill wrote about the decision to hold Thermopylae: 'The intervening ages fell away. Why not one more undying feat of arms?'[2]

But the Chiefs of Staff saw the situation from a different angle. Late in the evening on 20 April they held a meeting with Eden in the chair to discuss the situation in Greece in relation to military developments in the Middle East. Eden argued in favour of holding the Thermopylae position, but the Chiefs were divided on the matter and no decision was reached that night. From the purely military point of view, there were strong arguments in favour of early evacuation, besides the new dangers caused by the apparent collapse of Greek resistance. Among other things, a large number of troops and some equipment would be saved for Egypt, while the chances of successful evacuation would be greater because there would be less danger of the Greek Government and army disintegrating. Moreover, prolonged resistance at Thermopylae would require additional forces, while the chances of evacuating the bulk of the forces would diminish.[3] Wavell's reason for considering the Thermopylae position untenable, namely that the Greeks could not protect the left of his forces, did not, in the event, prove to be accurate. No threat to the British forces

---

[1] Churchill note for Eden, 20 Apr. 1941, R4180/11/19, F.O. 371/29819.
[2] Churchill, *Grand Alliance*, p. 228.
[3] J. Kennedy, *The Business of War*, edit. B. Fergusson, London, 1957, pp. 98–9.

developed from that direction, but rather from the right.[1] Moreover, before meeting the Greek leaders on the morning of 21 April, when evacuation was decided, Wavell had been briefed by his commanders, whose view was that the Thermopylae position could not be held for very long and that the only sound course was evacuation.[2]

In Epirus the first protocol of armistice was a day old. At 6.00 p.m. on 20 April Tsolakoglou had signed the accord ending hostilities between Germany and Greece. The terms given by the German commander on the spot, Gen. Dietrich of S.S. Adolf Hitler division, were surprisingly generous. But Marshal List, commander of the Twelfth army, compelled Tsolakoglou to sign the next day a second and less generous protocol. Tsolakoglou had surrendered to the Germans on the explicit understanding that he was not surrendering to the Italians, who had been defeated by the Greeks;[3] but, as we shall see, the Germans did not eventually honour their word on that point, which was so important to the Greek military.

Was Tsolakoglou a traitor, or a sacrificial lamb? In his Memoirs he has maintained that 'both the Government and the Commander-in-Chief, although they shared the common conviction that everything was lost, that the disaster was unprecedented, and that the once victorious army was about to be taken prisoner, did not want to assume responsibility for the armistice, because they were bound by the obligations of the alliance'.[4] The tragic situation in Epirus argued in favour of the action he took from the purely military point of view; but the fact that he accepted a German proposal to form a government cast doubts on his intentions. He has maintained, of course, that he never really intended to form a government until it was forced on him by circumstances;[5] but as we have already seen, the formation of a government had been considered at least as early as 19 April, and definitely before the first protocol of armistice was signed. It seems that Tsolakoglou was less reluctant to take power under the Germans than he has maintained. In a conversation with Ioannis Politis in May 1941, Tsolakoglou, after trying to enlist the services of the

---

[1] G. Long, *Greece, Crete and Syria*, Canberra, 1953, p. 195.

[2] Playfair, op. cit., vol. ii, p. 95.   [3] Tsolakoglou, op. cit., pp. 140–3.

[4] Ibid., p. 115.   [5] Ibid., p. 159.

Greek diplomat, is said to have expressed the conviction that Germany would certainly win the war and that Greece should ally herself with Germany and make some concessions to Bulgaria. 'He expressed the opinion', Politis noted, 'that it is to our interest to propitiate the Germans, pointing out that even in terms of the society we must work in that direction.'[1]

To resume the narrative, on 20 April at midday Pitsikas called Tsolakoglou to ask why he had not arrived at Jannina for the conference as he had been ordered and had promised to do. That was unnecessary, replied the rebellious general, as he and the other two commanders had decided to initiate negotiations with the Germans. Pitsikas next signalled the President of the Council and the Commander-in-Chief, informing them of the step taken by his commanders and imploring them to deal with the matter themselves to avoid a division in the army. When the Government emissary arrived at Jannina early in the afternoon, he was told by Pitsikas that he had come 'too late'. Pitsikas then asked for permission to depart for Athens, as he had no further business at Jannina. Later on in the day he heard of the signing of the armistice. He set off for Athens in the early hours of 21 April, after informing Tsolakoglou that he considered himself as having resigned his command of the Epirus army.[2] The unfortunate commander fell ill on the way and was prevented from reaching Athens the same day, but he ordered Panaghiotis Kanellopoulos who was riding with him to proceed and report to the King. Kanellopoulos reached the Grande Bretagne in the late evening after a small Odyssey, and duly reported to the King and Papagos, who were eager to have a first-hand account of the capitulation.[3]

Earlier in the evening of 21 April the King had summoned Palairet, and in the presence of Tsouderos stated that the Greek forces in Epirus would hold on for four to five days. This assurance came as a result of a discussion he and Tsouderos had just had with Papagos, who obviously knew nothing about developments in Epirus; or, he probably knew and refused to believe. This statement was, to say the least, strange, because

[1] Notes of a meeting with Tsolakoglou, May 1941, Private Papers of Ioannis Politis, separate folio in Venizelos Papers, Benaki Museum.

[2] *End of an Epic*, pp. 224-7.

[3] P. Kanellopoulos, *The Years of the Great War, 1939-1944* (in Greek), 2nd edn., Athens, 1964, pp. 28-9 n.

the King had already received a cable from the general sent
to Jannina to report, saying that Tsolakoglou had initiated
negotiations with the Germans for an armistice. Moreover,
Pitsikas, as already seen, had also informed the Government
and Papagos at midday that Tsolakoglou had decided to send
emissaries to the Germans. Most probably, both the King and
Papagos knew of the commanders' *pronunciamento*, but felt that
they could check developments by just taking strong measures:
the reaction to this news was an order to arrest Tsolakoglou.
It is interesting that neither the King nor Tsouderos believed
that the rebellious general was a traitor, and thought that he
had been 'infected by the disease of defeatism'.[1] The same day
Tsouderos handed Palairet a note which released the British
from any obligation to fight in Greece. Britain was asked to
evacuate her forces to prevent further and useless bloodshed
and the 'collapse' of the Greek army.[2]

On 22 April the King and Government prepared to abandon
the Greek mainland in order to continue the struggle in Crete.
They left the following morning. A motley crew of retired
officers, Venizelists, and some Metaxists—soon to be removed—
formed the last Government of free Greece. Wilson was asked
to agree to Papagos's resignation and the liquidation of G.H.Q.
'in order to leave no one in a high position who might make
terms with the Germans'.[3] In his application to the War
Ministry, dated 23 April 1941, Papagos requested that he should
be relieved of his command and put on the retired list. It was
granted by a royal decree of the same date.[4] In the Foreign
Office it was felt that Papagos's resignation and the dissolution
of G.H.Q. meant that the Greek Government was no longer
sure of the general.[5] Early on 23 April Tsolakoglou was compelled to sign yet a third protocol, in which the Italian commander was also a signatory party. This was an indignity at
which the unfortunate general protested, and which he later
disowned.[6] The same day in Epirus a Greek artillery major

---

[1] Athens Tel. No. 774, 21 Apr. 1941, 7.00 p.m., F.O. 371/29819.
[2] Athens Tel. No. 777, 21 Apr. 1941, 7.00 p.m., F.O. 371/29819.
[3] Athens Tel., Personal from Wilson to Wavell, 23 Apr. 1941, R4615/11/19,
F.O. 371/29820.   [4] Papagos's report to the General Staff, op. cit., F634.
[5] Minute by E. Warner, 24 Apr. 1941, seen by Dixon, Nichols, Sargent, Cadogan, and Eden, R4615/11/19, F.O. 371/29820.
[6] Tsolakoglou, op. cit., p. 140.

shot himself when a German unit ordered him to surrender his battery. The brief cable reads: 'Artillery Major Versis, when ordered by the Germans to surrender his battery, assembled the guns, and after saluting them, shot himself, while his gunners were singing the National Anthem.'[1] The deed measured up with the tragedy of the country.

A British Ministry of Information propaganda directive oᴌ 2 May 1941 gave the line to be followed with regard to occupied Greece. The aim was to foster and increase anti-German feeling in Greece by 'attaching to Germany' Greek hatred of Italy and Bulgaria, and by 'continually giving news of German selfishness, plunder, maladministration and Gestapo activities in other occupied countries, particularly Poland'; but it was necessary to 'avoid suggesting that exactly the same thing will happen in Greece or challenging comparison with the more repressive side of the Metaxas regime'. Another directive of the same period reads: 'References to the Metaxas regime are better avoided.'[2]

[1] The signal is included in Gen. Demestichas's war report to the General Staff, F641, p. 22.

[2] Ministry of Information, 'Propaganda Directives, Greece', 2 May and 26 June 1941, communicated to the Foreign Office, F.O. 371/29852.

Conclusion

Anglo-Greek relations in the second half of the thirties revolved round an ill-defined and rather general appreciation of common interests, and were conducted by a limited and close network of men on a more or less personal basis. A notable characteristic of relations between Greece and Britain was their unequal nature, the natural concomitant of relations between a small country and a great power. The imbalance in this case was made more striking by a host of internal and external factors that put Greece at a disadvantage *vis-à-vis* Britain. The traditional Anglo-Greek friendship was revitalized during the Abyssinian crisis of 1935–6, at a time when Britain was looking for friends in the Mediterranean to counter the growing threat represented by Italy, and Greece was seeking support against the same threat. However, Greece's relations with Britain were also viewed from another angle. The Greek Government of the time, set on the restoration of the monarchy, saw in Britain an obvious patron of the King's cause; and while there is little doubt that the British Government tried to steer clear of internal Greek affairs, the Abyssinian crisis and the consequent need for Greek support in the Mediterranean obliged the British to set aside their misgivings and associate with Greece and tolerate her anomalous constitutional and political developments. The restoration of the monarchy in the person of King George II, who was conveniently pro-British, was felt to be desirable, since the King could reasonably be expected to secure for Britain a friendly and dependable Greece, though the manner in which the restoration was effected left much to be desired. But by the time Britain became involved in Greek affairs, the Greek Republic had almost run its course and the restoration of the monarchy had become virtually inevitable.

The change of regime in Greece in 1935 must be seen as a Greek affair, a characteristic by-product of the Greek political scene and the typical recourse after a political deadlock or crisis of an unusual intensity. The dictatorship of August 1936

that followed the restoration conformed to some extent to
the logic of this Greek political pattern. Metaxas, though unsuccessful in politics, was very much the product of the Greek
political scene, as much as Venizelos, Tsaldaris, Papanastasiou,
Kondylis, and the rest; only he played the game of the political
world more roughly than the rules normally allowed. The
'Fourth of August' dictatorship, though objectionable in every
sense and though it created far more problems than it solved,
was essentially the outcome of a general disregard for constitutional principles and practice, and the end result of the
deterioration of political life since World War I. Metaxas and
King George share responsibility for the dictatorship: Metaxas
for imposing it in the first place, and the King for not bringing
himself to prevent its establishment, or to call an end to it.
Both the King and the dictator infringed the constitution of the
country in a way that must diminish any argument in their
favour; but it is only just to see their role and responsibilities
within the context of the Greek political scene and practices
and in the climate of the time.

As far as Britain's role in its connection with the Metaxas
dictatorship is concerned, the principal conclusion is that the
British, although they did nothing to install the dictatorship,
found it very difficult not to exploit a situation which they
found increasingly profitable and convenient. Yet for most of
the period of the dictatorship the British Government had little
use for the dictator himself, and instead had their attention
focused on the King, whom they considered the only stable and
dependable element in the country. But, in time, they came to
see and appreciate the merits of the dictator as well. The
British were in a position to discern the very essence of the
Greek situation: a vulnerable dictator, dependent on the King,
who in the first two years might have discarded him without
much difficulty when he felt his usefulness had passed. When,
however, in the course of the dictatorship Metaxas became too
powerful *vis-à-vis* the King, who by then had compromised his
position by his long and intimate association with the dictator,
the British began to have second thoughts about the regime.
By this time, however—the end of 1938—the downfall of the
dictatorship was expected to carry away the monarchy as well.
Moreover, from the point of view of their national interests,

the British Government had every reason to be satisfied with Metaxas's conduct of affairs.

Metaxas gave the impression that he was doing his utmost to disprove the pro-German reputation which his role in the Great War had earned him. This was, certainly, one source of his weakness *vis-à-vis* the British. He was a man still attached sentimentally and ideologically to Germany, while realities, both internal and external, drew him inexorably towards Britain. The pro-German reputation, which he might have used to threaten Britain into promising more positive support, frightened no one more than himself. His profuse confidences and declarations of devotion to Britain were to a considerable extent the result of uneasiness and insecurity. Metaxas was entangled in a net much of which was not of his own making. The King, on whose favour he had depended for the most crucial part of his years in office, and behind whom he knew stood the British; the military, who were largely out of his immediate control; and finally, what was left of Venizelism, and of Venizelos's past associates whom he had reason to suspect of conspiring with the British and the French to provide a possible alternative to his rule, were all elements which from time to time seemed to him potentially dangerous to his position. When all is said, Metaxas was a limited dictator with a limited freedom of action. Yet it was left to Metaxas, despite all his limitations, both inherent and imposed, to play a vital role at a most critical hour in Greek history and the war; and what is more, he rose to the demands of the occasion, heroic and at the same time tragic as that occasion proved to be.

There was another aspect of Anglo-Greek relations in the period 1935–41, which had to do with a quite different perception of Mediterranean realities by the two countries, as well as with the unequal balance of power between Britain and Greece. From 1935 the British were able to press on the Greeks the form of bilateral relation which suited them best; that is, a close but essentially informal collaboration both in time of peace and war. The British needed a friendly, not an allied Greece; and it was in this specification that the difficulties of the Greeks lay. Metaxas never fully grasped this cardinal desideratum and its significance, or he would not have pursued the British in the way that he did, making repeated proposals for an Anglo-Greek alliance. The only result of his strenuous efforts was to make such an alliance more and more unlikely. The British became convinced that they would eventually enjoy all the benefits of an alliance without entering into any formal commitment to support Greece militarily in time of war. It is true, of course, that Metaxas's desire to formalize Anglo-Greek relations had much to do with developments in the Mediterranean, and with the situation in the Balkans and Europe in general; yet, it is precisely these realities and developments which, as far as the British were concerned, ruled out an alliance with Greece. The Greek appraisal of Mediterranean developments suffered from the serious shortcoming that Greek leaders tended to over-estimate Greece's real value to Britain, a value moreover which constantly diminished as British power and potential in the Mediterranean *vis-à-vis* Italian power visibly diminished. Greece's strategic value as an air and naval base, from which attacks could be launched against Italy and communications in the Aegean controlled, depended on the ability of Britain to secure her communications in the Eastern Mediterranean; and of this there was simply little prospect, as long as Britain's strength in the Mediterranean did not appreciably improve and Italy remained entrenched in the Dodecanese. Moreover, and this was the decisive factor in British strategic thinking about Greece, the intrinsic value of Greece was negligible and did not appreciably increase with time, since the Greek General Staff had organized their military and economic resources for a defensive static war, and a Balkan war at that. What the British Chiefs of Staff feared most in a war against Italy was any form of Anglo-Greek co-operation which would place at risk a British expeditionary force in the eminently indefensible territory of Greece within striking distance of Italy, while the Greeks themselves would be mainly preoccupied with the defence of their long and vulnerable frontiers. The British were convinced that the Greek emphasis on preparations for a static war against Bulgaria was woefully misguided and out of date, and from the point of view of British strategy simply beside the point.

The Italian occupation of Albania caught the Greeks off balance and facing the wrong enemy. In April 1939 the Greek

General Staff saw with awe a gaping hole in their defences on the Albanian frontier which they had practically no means, not even a plan, to block. One way might have been a mobile reserve force, but there had been very little done on these lines. Money and energy had been lavishly spent on building a formidable wall to seal off Bulgaria; and neither new plans nor last-minute improvisations could make good years of mis-placed emphasis. On Anglo-Greek strategic considerations after April 1939, and consultations for co-operation in time of war, a point can be made about the mutual expectations and promises of the two countries. By their solemn assurance of April 1939, the British had pledged themselves to assist the Greeks if they became the victims of aggression and chose to resist that aggression. But the British assurance amounted to little more than a moral obligation, and was very far from a substantive commitment. This, indeed, was the distance separating the British attitude towards Greece and Greek expectations of Britain. Greek expectations were based on past experience and Greek appreciation of current developments. Present in Greek minds was a deep-rooted belief, almost amounting to conviction, that in the event of war in the Mediterranean Britain would be forced by the course of events to take Greece under her wing; Greece's geographical position, it was felt, would make this protection almost inevitable. Metaxas's failing in this respect had to do with a tendency to see Mediterranean realities in the light of World War I experiences and strategic considerations, an attitude, of course, which was shared by the majority of the Greeks, who thought along similar lines.

Britain's policy towards Greece after the outbreak of war, and until the Italian attack against Greece, was essentially a continuation of her policy in the sanctions period. Britain regarded Greece mainly in relation to British policy towards Italy. Greece was always part of that futile game of the British Government to win over Italy, mainly by empty words which lacked both force and conviction. In September 1939 Greece was advised not to put her relations with Italy on a more definite basis than hitherto, so that she would be available, and at Britain's disposal, in the event of an Anglo-Italian war in the Mediterranean. The Italian factor influenced British policy towards Greece in another way: it strengthened the decision of the British Government to avoid an Anglo-Greek alliance, for it was believed that such an alliance would offend the Italians, and particularly Mussolini. When the courtship of Mussolini came to an end in June 1940, after the Italian attack on France, the British reconsidered policy towards Greece, but it still provided little satisfaction for the Greeks: for, now, the British simply concentrated their attention on Crete. With Italy an enemy and seriously threatening Britain's position in Egypt, the British Government ruled out such distractions as the commitment of forces, in particular land forces, for the effective defence of mainland Greece; and the Italian attack on Greece left this policy virtually unaltered.

The great surprise for the British—and a most welcome one— was the unexpectedly stiff resistance of the Greeks, a resistance moreover which could reasonably be expected to pin down, and wear down, considerable enemy forces. The Greeks proceeded to take the edge off the Italians' ardour for offensive operations and, indeed, inflicted on them a humiliating defeat. There was some prospect that their wild country might become both a grave for the Duce's soldiers and a dumping ground for his military equipment. But this had to be done mainly by the Greeks alone. Britain could spare little, and that mainly in the form of aircraft, adequate only for limited operations, not to knock out the forward Italian bases in Albania. The moral obligation to help Greece and the common fight until final victory were of course amply aired, but the Greeks had to content themselves with limited British material assistance. The British Chiefs of Staff and the commanders in the Middle East felt that very little could be spared for the Greek theatre of operations, admittedly still not a vital theatre as far as general British strategy was concerned. As it was, the Greco-Italian war was already fulfilling a most useful function, draining away Italian reserves in men and materials. In December 1940 when the Germans advertised their intention to mediate in the Greco-Italian war, the British felt fully justified in undermining every attempt to negotiate a separate peace between Greece and Italy, and Metaxas proved once more obliging and ready to conform.

Germany's intention to invade the Balkans was responsible

for a complete reversal of British policy not to commit land forces in mainland Greece. Greece now became the key to British policy in the Balkans. If she could be persuaded to accept British forces, there were some grounds for hoping that Yugoslavia and Turkey could be induced to join Britain and Greece in a common front against the Axis. The trouble now was that Metaxas was dead; and his successors, although resolved to resist the Germans, were undecided on the proper way to meet the German threat. Anglo-Greek relations in the last stage of the Greek war were subject to a fundamental divergence of views, which various factors tended to obscure or disguise. What counted more in the last analysis was, not what was explicitly stated, but what was left unsaid. The British decision to help Greece in resisting the Germans was based on both political and strategic considerations, particularly the need to placate world opinion and to induce Yugoslavia and Turkey to form a common front against Germany. Greece was the last card Britain had in the Balkans, and she was determined to play it with some show of courage. Greece, on the other hand, though not oblivious to the long-term allied interests, had more limited objectives. Already the victim of aggression by one partner of the Axis, she tried to avoid provoking or precipitating an attack from the other partner; but if Greece had to fight Germany, her Government was resolved to fight for a quick and honourable defeat. This attitude, although unrealistic and contrary to allied interests and strategy, can be justified to some extent by arguing that British help fell far short of the forces required to hold the Germans with a fair chance of success. By this time it is very doubtful whether the Greeks wanted British help at all; and the attitude of Yugoslavia and Turkey was anything but promising. But the British had decided to fight for a lost cause; to fight and share in a disaster was felt to be preferable to doing nothing at all for a country whose independence they had solemnly assured.

Bibliography

I. UNPUBLISHED SOURCES

1. *British*

British State Papers (at the Public Record Office, London). Foreign Office Papers, vols. F.O. 371/19504, 19505, 19506, 19507, 19508, 19509, 19510, 19513, 19514, 19515, 20381, 20382, 20383, 20384, 20389, 20390, 21143, 21144, 21145, 21146, 21147, 21148, 21149, 21150, 22354, 22355, 22360, 22362, 22363, 22368, 22370, 22371, 23760, 23761, 23762, 23765, 23766, 23769, 23770, 23776, 23779, 23780, 23782, 24866, 24867, 24868, 24886, 24887, 24890, 24904, 24905, 24909, 24910, 24911, 24912, 24915, 24917, 24919, 24920, 24921, 24922, 24924, 24942, 24944, 29798, 29813, 29818, 29819, 29820, 29825, 29839, 29840, 29843, 29852, 29855, 29862, 33145, F.O. 434/6.
Cabinet Papers, vols. Cab. 24/259, 262, Cab. 27/623, 624, 627, Cab. 65/2, 13, 16, 17, 21, 22, Cab. 66/1, 15, Cab. 79/1, 3, 7, Cab. 80/3, 9, 10, 11, 16, 17, 21, 24, Cab. 105/2.
Premier 3/209.

2. *Greek*

The Private Papers of Ioannis Metaxas (in the General State Papers, Athens).
The Private Papers of Charalambos Simopoulos (in St. Antony's College, Oxford).
The Private Papers of Eleutherios Venizelos, collections of letters of the period 1935–6 (in the Benaki Museum, Athens).
The Private Papers of Alexandros Zannas (in the possession of Mrs. Virginia Zannas, Athens).
General Staff Papers, vols. F623, 627, 628, 631, 634, 641, 643 (at the Greek General Staff, Army Historical Section, Athens).

II. PUBLISHED SOURCES

1. *Collections of Documents*

Diplomatika engrapha. I italiki epithesis enantion tis Ellados (Diplomatic Papers, The Italian Attack against Greece), Athens, Royal Ministry for Foreign Affairs, 1940. English edition, *The Greek White Book*, London, 1942.

Documents on British Foreign Policy, 1919–1939, 3rd Series, vols. iv, v, vi, London, H.M.S.O.

Documents on German Foreign Policy, 1918–1945, Series C, vols. iv, v, Series D, vols. v, viii, x, xi, xii, London, H.M.S.O.

I Documenti Diplomatici Italiani, Ottava serie (1936–9), vols. xii, xiii, Nova serie (1939–43), vols. i, ii, Rome, Ministero degli Affari Esteri, Libreria dello Stato.

K.K.E., Episima Keimena (Greek Communist Party, Official Documents), vol. iv (1934–40), Athens, 1974.

2. *General*

Amery, Julian, *Sons of the Eagle*, London, 1948.

—— *Approach March, A Venture in Autobiography*, London, 1973.

Archer, Laird, *Balkan Journal*, New York, 1944.

Argyropoulos, Pericles, *Apomnimonevmata* (Memoirs), 2 vols., Athens, 1970–1.

Armellini, Quirino, *Diario di guerra, Nove mesi al Commando Supremo*, Rome, 1946.

Avon, Earl of, *Memoirs, Facing the Dictators*, London, 1962.

—— *Memoirs, The Reckoning*, London, 1965.

Badoglio, Pietro, *Italy in the Second World War*, Transl. Muriel Currey, London, 1948.

Birtles, Bert, *Exiles in the Aegean*, London, 1938.

Buckley, Christopher, *Greece and Crete, 1941*, London, H.M.S.O., 1952.

Cadogan, Sir Alexander, *Diaries, 1938–1945*, ed. D. Dilks, London, 1971.

Campbell, John, and Sherrard, Philip, *Modern Greece*, London, 1968.

Casson, Stanley, *Greece against the Axis*, London, 1941.

—— *Greece and Britain*, London, 1943.

Cervi, Mario, *Storia della guerra di Grecia*, Milan, 1965. Engl. transl. Eric Mosbacher, *The Hollow Legions, Mussolini's Blunder in Greece, 1940–1941*, London, 1972.

Churchill, W. S., *The Second World War*, vols. i–iii, London, 1948–50.

Ciano, Count, *Diary, 1939–1943*, ed. Malcolm Muggeridge, London, 1947.

—— *Diplomatic Papers*, ed. Malcolm Muggeridge, London, 1948.

Colvin, Ian, *The Chamberlain Cabinet*, London, 1971.

Connell, John, *Wavell, Scholar and Soldier*, London, 1964.

Creveld, Martin van, *Hitler's Strategy, 1940–1941, The Balkan Clue*, Cambridge, 1973.

—— '25 October: a historical puzzle', *Journal of Contemporary History*, vol. vi (1971).

—— 'In the Shadow of Barbarossa: Germany and Albania, January–March 1941', *Journal of Contemporary History*, vol. vii (1972).

—— 'Prelude to Disaster: the British Decision to Aid Greece, 1940–1941', *Journal of Contemporary History*, vol. ix (1974).

Cunningham, Viscount, of Hyndhope, *A Sailor's Odyssey*, London, 1951.

Dalton, Lord, *Memoirs, 1931–1945*, London, 1957.

Daphnis, Grigorios, *I Ellas metaxy dyo polemon, 1923–1940* (Greece between Two Wars, 1923–1940), 2 vols., Athens, 1955.

—— *Sophocles E. Venizelos* (in Greek), Athens, 1970.

Davin, D. M., *Crete (Official History of New Zealand in the Second World War)*, Wellington, N.Z., 1953.

De Guingand, Francis, *Operation Victory*, London, 1947.

—— *Generals at War*, London, 1964.

Evelpidis, Chrysos, *Oikonomiki kai koinoniki istoria tis Ellados* (Economic and Social History of Greece), Athens, 1950.

Gonatas, Stylianos, *Apomnimonevmata, 1897–1957* (Memoirs, 1897–1957), Athens, 1958.

Grazzi, Emanuele, *Il principio della fine, l'Impresa di Grecia*, Rome, 1945.

Greek General Staff, *The Greek Army in the Second World War: Aitia kai aphormai tou ellino-italikou polemou, 1940–1941* (Causes of the Greco-Italian War, 1940–1941), Athens, 1959; *I italiki eisvoli, 28 Oktovriou–13 Noemvriou 1940* (The Italian Invasion, 28 October–13 November 1940), Athens, 1960; *I elliniki antepithesis, 14 Noemvriou 1940–6 Ianouariou 1941* (The Greek Counter-Attack, 14 November 1940–6 January 1941), Athens, 1966; *Cheimerinai epicheiriseis, 7 Ianouariou–26 Martiou 1941* (Winter Campaigns, 7 January–26 March 1941), Athens, 1966; *Agones eis tin Anatolikin Makedonian kai Dytikin Thrakin, 1941* (Struggles in Eastern Macedonia and Western Thrace, 1941), Athens, 1956; *To telos mias epopoiias, Aprilios 1941* (The End of an Epic, April 1941), Athens, 1959; *I machi tis Kritis* (The Battle of Crete), Athens, 1967.

Halder, Franz, *Diaries*, vols. iii–vi, Washington D.C., 1950.

Halifax, Earl of, *Fullness of Days*, London, 1957.

Harvey, Oliver, *Diplomatic Diaries, 1937–1940*, ed. John Harvey, London, 1970.

Heckstall-Smith, Anthony, and Baillie-Grohman, H. T., *Greek Tragedy '41*, London, 1961.

Howard, Michael, *The Mediterranean Strategy in the Second World War*, London, 1968.

Jacomoni, Francesco, *La politica dell'Italia in Albania*, Bologna, 1965.

Kaklamanos, Demetrios, *General Metaxas in Greece, In Peace and War*, London, 1942.

Kanellopoulos, Panaghiotis, *1935–1945, Enas apologismos* (1935–1945, An Account Sheet), Athens, 1945.

—— *Ta chronia tou megalou polemou, 1939–1944* (The Years of the Great War, 1939–1944), Athens, 1966.

Karassos, C. D., *O polemos kata ton Germanon en ti Kentriki Makedonia, 1941* (The War against the Germans in Central Macedonia, 1941), Athens, 1948.

Katheniotis, Dimitrios, *Istorikon polemikon epicheiriseon, 1940–1941* (Account of War Operations, 1940–1941), Athens, 1945.

—— *Ai kyrioterai stratigikai phaseis tou polemou, 1940–1941* (The Main Strategic Phases of the War, 1940–1941), Athens, 1946.

Kavvadias, E. P., *O nautikos polemos tou 1940* (The Naval War of 1940), Athens, 1950.

Kennedy, Sir John, *The Business of War*, ed. Bernard Fergusson, London, 1957.

Kerner, R. J., and Howard, H. N., *The Balkan Conferences and the Balkan Entente, 1930–1935*, Berkeley, 1936.

Kitsikis, Dimitri, *I Ellas tis 4es Avgoustou kai ai megalai dynameis* (Greece of the Fourth of August and the Great Powers), Athens, 1974.

—— 'La Grèce entre l'Angleterre et l'Allemagne de 1936 à 1941', *Revue Historique* (juil.–sept. 1967).

Knatchbull-Hugessen, Sir Hugh, *Diplomat in Peace and War*, London, 1949.

Knéjévitch, R. L., 'Prince Paul, Hitler, and Salonika', *International Affairs*, vol. xxvii (Jan. 1951).

Koronakis, I. G., *I politeia tis 4es Avgoustou, Phos eis mian plastographimenin periodon tis istorias mas* (The Fourth of August Regime, Light on a Forged Period of Our History), Athens, 1950.

Korozis, Athanasios, *Oi polemoi tou 1940–1941, Epitychiai kai euthynai* (The Wars of 1940–1941, Successes and Responsibilities), 2 vols., Athens, 1958.

Kotzias, Kostas, *Ellas, O polemos kai i doxa tis* (Greece, Her War and Glory), 3rd edn., Athens, 1947.

Kousoulas, D. G., *Revolution and Defeat, The Story of the Greek Communist Party*, London, 1965.

—— *The Price of Freedom, Greece in World Affairs, 1939–1953*, Syracuse, N.Y., 1953.

Kyrou, A. A., *Elliniki exoteriki politiki* (Greek Foreign Policy), Athens, 1955.

Lee, A. S. G., *The Royal House of Greece*, London, 1948.

Linardatos, Spyros, *Pos ephtasame stin 4e Avgoustou* (How We Reached the Fourth of August), Athens, 1965.

—— *I 4e Avgoustou* (The Fourth of August), Athens, 1966.

—— *I exoteriki politiki tis 4es Avgoustou* (The Foreign Policy of the Fourth of August), Athens, 1975.

Long, Gavin, *Greece, Crete and Syria*, Canberra, 1953.

Malainos, Miltiades, *I 4e Avgoustou, Pos kai diati epevlithi i diktatoria tou I. Metaxa* (The Fourth of August, how and why the dictatorship of I. Metaxas was imposed), Athens, 1947.

Mantzoufas, G. A., and Koumaros, N. D., 'Ai themeliodeis syntagmatikai archai tou neou kratous' (The Fundamental Constitutional Principles of the New State), *To Neon Kratos*, vol. xi (1938).

Mazarakis-Ainian, Alexandros, *Apomnimonevmata* (Memoirs), Athens, 1949.

Merkouris, S. S., *Georghios Kondylis* (in Greek), Athens, 1954.

Metaxas, Ioannis, *To prosopiko tou imerologio* (His Personal Diary), ed. C. Christidis (vols. i–ii, 1896–1920), P. M. Siphnaios (vol. iii, 1921–1932), P. Vranas (vol. iv, 1933–1941), Athens, 1951–64.

—— *Logoi tis protis trietias, 1936–1939* (Speeches of the First Three Years, 1936–1939), Athens, Ethniki Etairia (1939).

—— *To politevma tou Ioannou Metaxa* (The Political System of Ioannis Metaxas), ed. Loukia I. Metaxas, Athens, 1945.

Mondini, Luigi, *Prologo del conflitto italo-greco*, Rome, 1945.

Nepheloudis, B. A., *Achtina Theta, Anamniseis, 1934–1940* (Section Theta, Memories, 1934–1940), Athens, 1974.

Nepheloudis, Pavlos, *Stis pighes tis kakodaimonias, Ta vathytera aitia tis diaspasis tou K.K.E., 1918–1968* (To the Sources of the Misfortune, The Deeper Causes of the Split of the Greek Communist Party, 1918–1968), Athens, 1974.

Nikoloudis, Theologos, *Ioannis Metaxas* (in Greek), Athens, 1941.

—— *I elliniki krisis* (The Greek Crisis), Cairo, 1945.

Papadakis, B. P., *I chthesini kai i avriani Ellas* (Greece, Yesterday and Tomorrow), Athens, 1946.

—— *Diplomatiki istoria tou ellinikou polemou, 1940–1945* (Diplomatic History of the Greek War, 1940–1945), Athens, 1956.

—— *Histoire diplomatique de la question nord-epirote*, Athens, 1958.

Papagos, Alexandros, *O polemos tis Ellados, 1940–1941*, Athens, 1945. Engl. transl. *The Battle of Greece, 1940–1941*, Athens, 1949.

—— *O ellinikos stratos kai i pros polemon proparaskevi tou, 1923–1940* (The Greek Army and its war preparedness, 1923–1940), Athens, 1945.

Papanastasiou, Alexandros, *Meletes, logoi, arthra* (Studies, Speeches, Articles), ed. X. Leukoparidis, Athens, 1957.

Papavasileiou, Ippocrates, *To nautikon mas kata tin propolemikin kai tin polemikin periodon, 1936–1941* (Our Navy in the Pre-War and War Period, 1936–1941), Athens, 1945.

Papen, Franz von, *Memoirs*, London, 1952.

Peponis, I. A., *Nikolaos Plastiras* (in Greek), vol. ii, Athens, 1948.

Pesmatzoglou, Georghios, *Gyro apo tin palinorthosin tou 1935* (On the Restoration of 1935), Athens, 1950.

Petropoulos, N. D., *Anamniseis kai skepseis enos palaiou nautikou, 1923–1941* (Memories and Thoughts of an Old Sailor, 1923–1941), 2 vols., Athens, 1966–70.

Pezas, Mikia, *The Price of Liberty*, New York, 1945.

Pipinelis, P. N., *Istoria tis exoterikis politikis tis Ellados, 1923–1941* (History of Greek Foreign Policy, 1923–1941), Athens, 1948.

—— *Georghios B'* (George II), Athens, 1951.

Playfair, I. S. O., *The Mediterranean and the Middle East*, vols. i–ii, London, H.M.S.O., 1954–6.

Psiroukis, Nikos, *O fasismos kai i 4e Avgoustou* (Fascism and the Fourth of August), Athens, 1974.

Pyromaglou, Komninos, 'I 4e Avgoustou kai o polemos tis Ellados, 1940–1941' (The Fourth of August and the Greek War, 1940–1941), *Istoriki Epitheorisis*, vol. i (1963).

—— *O Georghios Kartalis kai i epochi tou, 1934–1957* (George Kartalis and His Times, 1934–1957), vol. i, Athens, 1965.

Raditsa, Bogdan, 'Venizelos and the Struggle around the Balkan Pact', *Balkan Studies*, vol. vi, No. 1 (1965).

Rendel, Sir George, *The Sword and the Olive, Recollections of Diplomacy and the Foreign Service, 1913–1954*, London, 1957.

Ribbentrop, Joachim von, *Memoirs*, London, 1954.

Richter, Heinz, *Griechenland, Zwischen Revolution und Konterrevolution, 1936–1946*, Frankfurt am Main, 1973.

Ryan, Sir Andrew, *The Last of the Dragomans*, London, 1951.

Sakellariou, A. E., *I thesis tis Ellados kata ton Deuteron Pankosmion Polemon* (Greece's Position in the Second World War), New York, 1944.

Sarafis, Stephanos, *Istorikai anamniseis* (Historical Memories), Athens, 1952.

Schramm von Thadden, Ehrengard, *Griechenland und die Grossmächte im Zweiten Weltkrieg*, Wiesbaden, 1955.

Seferis, George, *Cheirographo, Sept. '41* (Manuscript, Sept. '41), Athens, 1972.

Stewart, I. McD. G., *The Struggle for Crete, 20 May–1 June 1941, A Story of Lost Opportunity*, London, 1966.

Svolopoulos, Konstantinos, *To Valkanikon Symphonon kai i elliniki exoteriki politiki, 1928–1934* (The Balkan Pact and Greek Foreign Policy, 1928–1934), Athens, 1974.

Sweet-Escott, Bickham, *Greece, A Political and Economic Survey, 1939–1953*, London, 1954.

—— *Baker Street Irregular*, London, 1965.

Tabakopoulos, A. P., *O mythos tis diktatorias* (The Myth of the Dictatorship), Athens, 1945.

Templewood, Viscount, *Nine Troubled Years*, London, 1954.

Tessara chronia diakyverniseos I. Metaxa, 1936–1940 (Four Years of Government by I. Metaxas), 4 vols., Athens, Ministry for Press and Tourism, 1940.

Toscano, Mario, *The Origins of the Pact of Steel*, Baltimore, 1968.

Tsolakoglou, Georghios, *Apomnimonevmata* (Memoirs), Athens, 1959.

Tsouderos, E. I., *Diplomatika paraskinia, 1941–1944* (Diplomacy Behind the Scenes, 1941–1944), Athens, 1950.

Tsvetkovitch, Dragisha, 'Prince Paul, Hitler, and Salonika', *International Affairs*, vol. xxvi (Oct. 1951).

Vansittart, Lord, *The Mist Procession*, London, 1958.

Venezis, Ilias, *Emmanouil Tsouderos* (in Greek), Athens, 1966.

Veremis, Thanos, 'The Greek Army in Politics, 1922–1935' (Doctoral dissertation, Trinity College, Oxford, 1974).

Vouros, Georghios, *Panaghis Tsaldaris* (in Greek), Athens, 1955.

Waller, R. P., 'With the 1st Armoured Brigade in Greece', *The Journal of the Royal Artillery*, vol. lxxii, No. 3 (July 1945).

Waterlow, Sir Sydney, 'The Decline and Fall of Greek Democracy, 1933–1936', *Political Quarterly*, vol. xviii, Nos. 2 and 3 (1947).

Wavell, Earl, 'The British Expedition to Greece, 1941', *The Army Quarterly*, vol. lix, No. 2 (Jan. 1950).

Weizsäcker, Ernst von, *Memoirs*, London, 1951.

Wilson, Sir Maitland, *Eight Years Overseas, 1939–1947*, London, 1950.

Windsor, Duke of, *A King's Story, The Memoirs of H.R.H. the Duke of Windsor*, London, 1951.

Wiskemann, Elizabeth, *The Rome–Berlin Axis*, rev. edn., London, 1966.

Woodward, Sir Llewellyn, *British Foreign Policy in the Second World War*, vol. i, London, H.M.S.O., 1970.

INDEX